SOURCES IN EUROPEAN POLITICAL HISTORY
Volume 1: THE EUROPEAN LEFT

SOURCES IN EUROPEAN POLITICAL HISTORY

Volume 1
The European Left

Chris Cook
*Head of Department of History, Philosophy and
European Studies, Polytechnic of North London*

and

Geoff Pugh
Former Research Assistant, Polytechnic of North London

MACMILLAN
PRESS

First published 1987

Published by
THE MACMILLAN PRESS LTD
Houndmills, Basingstoke, Hampshire RG21 2XS
and London
Companies and representatives
throughout the world

Typeset by Latimer Trend & Company Ltd, Plymouth

Printed in Hong Kong

British Library Cataloguing in Publication Data
Sources in European political history.
Vol. 1: The European Left
1. Archives—Europe   2. Europe—
Politics and government—19th century
—Sources—Catalogs—3. Europe—
Politics and government—20th century
—Sources—Catalogs
I. Cook, Chris   II. Pugh, Geoff
016.9402′8   CD1002
ISBN 0–333–23996–2

CONTENTS

Preface and Acknowledgements   vii

Introduction   ix

List of Abbreviations   xi

Note on Sources Cited   xv

Personal Papers of the European Left   1

Appendix I   A Note on the Archives of the Paris Commune   235

Appendix II   A Note on the Archives of the Norwegian Labour Movement   236

Appendix III   Select Bibliographical Note   237

PREFACE AND ACKNOWLEDGEMENTS

A very large number of people helped in the preparation of this volume. Whilst it would be impossible to thank all by name, we must make certain special acknowledgements. An extremely deep debt of gratitude is due to the following staff at the International Institute of Social History, Amsterdam – Ms Mies Campfens; Ms Daisy Devreese; Mr Tristan Haan; Ms Pauline Huizenga and Dr Elly Koen. In Copenhagen, Mr Gerd Callesen gave generously of his time, giving particular help with translation. Likewise in Stockholm our thanks are due to the Director Stefan Anderson, and his colleagues, Klaus Misgeld, Martin Gras and Maria Bosdotter at the Archive and Library of the Swedish Labour Movement. In Turin, our thanks are due to Aldo Agosti, Archive Director of the Gramsci Institute.

At the Bundesarchiv, Koblenz, the project's thanks are due to the Director and his staff, in particular to Dr Kreikamp and Ms Marianne Loenartz. At the Archiv der sozialen Demokratie (AdsD), Bonn, Dr Werner Krause gave most generously of his time and made available unpublished material on the holdings of the archive. Among individuals who have also given their time and expertise, particular thanks are due to Markus Bergi (Switzerland) and Marie Bittlestone (for Belgium).

A wide variety of sources, published and unpublished, have been used in the compilation of this volume. A more detailed listing is given in the Select Bibliographical Note (see p. 237). A very special mention must be made, however, of the absolutely invaluable guide for Germany produced by Professor Mommsen. No words of praise can do justice to the value of this monumental work. Although this volume includes known additions and changes to that of Professor Mommsen, its debt to that pioneering volume remains very high. Similarly, the works of Jean Maitron for France and Mies Campfens for Holland have provided enormous help (see p. xv). The survey conducted by the International Association of Labour History Institutions (IALHI) appeared during the compilation of this volume. It is an extremely useful reference tool.* The paucity of existing published guides to European archives only serves to re-emphasize the debt owed to the scores of archivists who so readily co-operated in the production of this volume.

The compilation of this guide would not have been possible without the help of Dr Pugh. This assistance was made available by the allocation of funds by the Polytechnic of North London to provide a research assistant. We must record our grateful thanks to the Polytechnic for this support. Also at the Polytechnic we must thank Jane Clark, Ben Fowkes, Tim Kirk, Val Lintner, Bob Moore and Mike Newman. Elsewhere, we are indebted to Richard Storey at the Modern Records Centre, University of Warwick and Angela Raspin at the British Library of Political and Economic Science. At Macmillan, our thanks are due to Tim Farmiloe and Keith Povey for their help and indeed patience with this book.

Of all the debts owed by the compilers, however, there is one that can never be adequately repaid. It is to the Director and his staff at the International Institute of Social History in

---

*Directory, International Association of Labour History Institutions (IALHI), compiled and printed, 1981, by the Bibliothek des Archivs der sozialen Demokratie, Bonn Bad-Godesberg. This volume should be consulted for the addresses of the major labour history institutions cited in this volume.

Amsterdam. The original idea for this book was born whilst we were working in Amsterdam. The compilation of this volume has required frequent visits to that city. This book is dedicated to our friends and colleagues in that beautiful city.

Polytechnic of North London
1 November 1986

CHRIS COOK
GEOFF PUGH

INTRODUCTION

This is the first volume in the planned series of *Sources in European Political History*. It aims to provide an outline guide to the surviving personal papers of over 1000 individuals active in the socialist, labour, radical and revolutionary movements in Europe. The period covered is broadly from the revolutions of 1848 through to the end of the Second World War in 1945. In a few cases, where relevant information is available, individuals active both before and after this period have been included.

Within this constraint, it is hoped that nearly all the major themes in the history of the European Left have been covered. However, there are enormous problems in trying to assemble such information. By the very nature of the history of the European socialist and revolutionary movement, papers have either not been kept or have been lost. This is particularly the case of movements deemed illegal or subversive, where police raids, prosecution, exile and banishment were commonplace. Similarly, successive European governments of the far right have ensured that there are enormous gaps in the information available in Portugal, Spain and Italy, for example. It is hoped that subsequent volumes in this series will supplement the information given here and fill these, and other, gaps in this volume.

This volume deliberately does not include within its scope any personal papers of the British or Irish Left. These are to be found in the parallel series *Sources in British Political History 1900–1951* (ed. Chris Cook, Macmillan, 6 vols, 1975–1985). Nor does this volume include those collections of personal papers in Eastern Europe which are not normally available for access by Western scholars.

This gap is partly compensated for by the rich holdings of Russian and Eastern European material in archive centres both in Western Europe and North America. Particular mention must be made of the holdings of the International Institute of Social History in Amsterdam, the Scandinavian centres such as Stockholm, and above all the holdings in North America at both the Hoover Institution on War, Revolution and Peace at Stanford University, California, and also at Columbia University Library.

The migration of archives relating to the European Left has posed one of the greatest problems in compiling this volume. Thus, the historian of the Spanish Civil War (or the historian of anarchism) will need to use the archives in Amsterdam. And, by a curious irony, the papers of such diverse figures in the Russian revolution as Kerensky and Leon Trotsky are to be found in America.

It is hoped that this volume will help reduce the difficulties facing the historian and research student in tracing the vital archive material for their research. But, none the less, the compilers of this volume are only too aware of the limitations of producing a guide such as this. Most entries were compiled from questionnaires sent to record offices. The entries in this volume in no way imply that the papers cited are necessarily available. In all cases, research students should *write* to the institution concerned to check availability and access.

Finally, the compilers would ask that any known additions and changes to the information cited here be given to them for use in future editions. Correspondence should be addressed to Dr Chris Cook, c/o International Archives Survey, Polytechnic of North London, Prince of Wales Road, Kentish Town, London NW5.

LIST OF ABBREVIATIONS

ABA	Arbejderbevaegelsens Bibliotek og Arkiv (The Labour Movement Library and Archive, Copenhagen)
ADAV	Allgemeiner Deutscher Arbeiterverein
ADGB	Allgemeiner Deutscher Gewerkschaftsbund
AdsD	Archiv der sozialen Demokratie (Friedrich-Ebert-Stiftung, Bonn)
ALÖS	Auslands Organisation der Österreichisch Sozialisten
AMSAB	Archief en Museum van de Socialistische Arbeidersbeweging (Ghent)
ARAB	Arbetarrörelsens arkiv och bibliotek (Archive and Library of the Swedish Labour Movement, Stockholm)
AVA	Allgemeines Verwaltungsarchiv (General Administration Archive)
BRD	Bundesrepublik Deutschland
CAP	Commission administrative permanente (organisme dirigeant, entre deux congrès du Parti Socialiste SFIO)
CDU	Christlich-Demokratische Union
CEDIAS	Centre D'Etudes, De Documentation et D'Action Sociale
CFDT	Confédération Française Démocratique du Travail
CFTC	Confédération Française des Travailleurs Chrétiens
CGT	Confédération Générale du Travail
CGTU	Confédération Générale du Travail Unitaire
CHS	Centre d'histoire du syndicalisme de l'Universitaire de Paris
CNT	Confederación Nacional del Trabajo
CPSU	Communist Party of the Soviet Union
CRC	Comité Révolutionnaire Central
CRHMSS	Centre de Recherches d'Histoire des Mouvements Sociaux et du Syndicalisme (Paris)
DAG	Deutsche Angestelltengewerkschaft
DDP	Deutsche Demokratische Partei
DDR	Deutsche Demokratische Republik
DFU	Deutsche Freiheitsunion
DGB	Deutscher Gewerkschaftsbund (Düsseldorf)
DKP	Danmarks Kommunistiske Parti
DÖW	Dokumentationsarchiv des Österreichischen Widerstandes (Documentation archive of the Austrian Resistance) (Vienna)
DSF	Danish Federation of Trade Unions
ECCI	Executive Committee of the Communist International
ECSC	European Coal and Steel Community
FAI	Federación Anarquista Ibérica
FO	Force Ouvrière (abbreviations for CGT FO)
FTSF	Fédération des Travailleurs Socialistes de France
GVP	Gesamtdeutsche Volkspartei

HHStA/	
HHSA	Haus-, Hof- und Staatsarchiv (Vienna)
IALHI	International Association of Labour History Institutions
ICFTU	International Confederation of Free Trade Unions
IFHS	Institut Français d'Histoire Sociale
IG	Industriegewerkschaft
IISH	International Institute of Social History (Amsterdam)
IKD	Internationale Kommunisten Deutschlands
ILO	International Labour Organisation
ISK	Internationaler Sozialistischer Kampfbund
IWMA	International Working Men's Association
IWW	Industrial Workers of the World
KAG	Kommunistische Arbeitsgemeinschaft
KAPD	Kommunistische Arbeiterpartei Deutschlands
KPD	Kommunistische Partei Deutschlands
KPDO	Kommunistische Partei Deutschlands (Opposition)
KPS	Kommunistische Partei der Schweiz (Swiss Communist Party)
LO	Landsorganisationen (Swedish TUC)
NAS	National Arbeids Secretariaat (National Labour Secretariat – Holland)
NSDAP	Nationalsozialistische Deutsche Arbeiterpartei
OURS	Office Universitaire de Recherche Socialiste
PCB	Parti Communiste Belge
PCF	Parti Communiste Français
PCI	Partito Comunista Italiano
PO	Parti ouvrier (correctly, Parti des travailleurs socialistes de France)
POB	Parti ouvrier Belge
POF	Parti ouvrier Français
POSR	Parti ouvrier socialiste révolutionnaire (the party of Jean Allemane)
POUM	Partido Obrero de Unificación Marxista
PSA	Parti Socialiste Autonome (forerunner of PSU)
PSB	Parti Socialiste Belge
PSdeF	Parti socialiste de France (fusion of POF and PSR)
PSDI	Partito Socialista Democratico Italiano
PSF	Parti socialiste français (the regrouping of those who supported Millerand under Jaurès)
PSI	Partito Socialista Italiano (Italian Socialist Party)
PSOP	Parti socialiste ouvrière et paysan
PSR	Parti socialiste révolutionnaire
PSU	Parti Socialiste Unifié
PvdA	Partij van de Arbeid
RSDLP	Russian Social Democratic Labour Party
RSFSR	Russian Soviet Federal Socialist Republic
SA	Sturmabteilung
SAJ	Sozialistische Arbeiterjugend
SAK	Suomen Ammattiliittojen Keskosjäjestö (Finnish TUC)
SAP	Sveriges socialdemokratiska arbtareparti (Swedish Social Democratic Labour Party); also Sozialistische Arbeiterpartei (German)
SD	Socialdemokratiet Parti (Social Democratic Party), of Denmark
SDAP	Sozialdemokratische Arbeiterpartei Deutschlands
SDS	Sozialistische Deutsche Studentenbund
SED	Sozialistische Einheitspartei Deutschlands
SKP	Sveriges kommunistiska parti (Swedish Communist Party)
SOPADE	SPD in exile (see next entry)

SPD	Sozialdemokratische Partei Deutschlands
SPÖ	Sozialdemokratische Partei Österreichs
SPS	Socialistische Partei der Schweiz
SR	Social Revolutionary
TA	Työväen Arkisto (Finnish Labour Archives)
USPD	Unabhängige Sozialdemokratische Partei Deutschlands
USR	Union socialiste révolutionnaire
VGA	Verein für Geschichte der Arbeiterbewegung (Association for the History of the Labour Movement)
WSLA	Wiener Stadt- und Landesarchiv (Vienna City and Provincial Archive)
WSLB	Wiener Stadt- und Landesbibliothek (Vienna City and Provincial Library)

NOTE ON SOURCES CITED

As mentioned in the Preface and Acknowledgements, certain existing published guides have been of invaluable help in the compilation of this volume. These are constantly referred to in the text. They are:

Campfens, Mies — *De Nederlandse archieven van het Internationaal Instituut voor Sociale Geschiedenis te Amsterdam* (Amsterdam, 1984)

Maitron, Jean — *Dictionnaire biographique du mouvement ouvrier français*
1ᵉ partie: 1789–1864, 3 vols, Paris (1964–68)
2ᵉ partie: 1864–71, 6 vols, Paris (1967–71)
3ᵉ partie: 1871–1914, 6 vols, Paris (1971–82)

Mommsen, Wolfgang A. — *Die Nachlässe in den deutschen Archiven (mit Ergänzungen aus anderen Beständen)* Teil I (Boppard am Rhein, 1971)
Die Nachlässe in den deutschen Archiven (mit Ergänzungen aus anderen Beständen) Teil II (Boppard am Rhein, 1983)

ABATE, Erasmo (1895–1977)

Italian anarchist.

Abate's papers have been placed in the IISH, Amsterdam. The collection is listed alphabetically by correspondent and covers the period 1917–75.

ABICHT, Fritz (b. 1912)

German social democratic exile from Nazi persecution. White-collar employee. Member of the SAJ, SPD, and of the Reichsbanner. Exile in Czechoslovakia in 1933, in France in 1938, and finally, in Sweden. Member of the SOPADE and the German trade union group. Worked as an engineering worker. Remained in Sweden.

Abicht's papers are in the ARAB, Stockholm.

ABRAMOVIČ, Rafail (1879–1963)

Russian socialist.

The IISH, Amsterdam, has some of Abramovič's correspondence for the 1930s.

ACKER, Achille van (b. 1895)

Belgian socialist and trade unionist. Entered parliament 1927. During the Second World War was the leader of the underground socialist party in Belgium and one of the organisers of the resistance. He became Minister of Labour and Social Security from September 1944 to February 1945, was Prime Minister and Minister of Coal, February 1945 to January 1946 and March to July 1946; Minister of Transport from March 1947 to June 1948, and Prime Minister again from 1954 to 1958.

The Archives Générales du Royaume, Brussels, has Van Acker's archive but this has not yet been classified and is for this reason inaccessible. The AMSAB, Ghent, possesses a Fonds Achiel van Acker, consisting of 24 boxes of papers including correspondence, notes and reports, covering van Acker's career 1944–58. Permission is needed for consultation. The Archief en Museum voor het Vlaamse Cultuurleven, Antwerp, has a collection (ref. A.1835) which includes documents, letters and manuscripts. The extent of the collection is unknown. Permission is needed for access.

ADLER, Emma (1858–1935)

See under ADLER, Victor

ADLER, Friedrich Wolfgang (1879–1960)

Austrian and international socialist leader. Secretary of the Austrian Social Democratic Party (SPÖ) 1911–16. Leader of the SPÖ Left and opponent of the First World War. Assassinated the Austrian Premier in 1916 and imprisoned. Freed by the 1918 Revolution. Leader of the Workers' Councils. Co-founder, with Otto Bauer, of the International Union of Socialist Parties (the 'Two-and-a-half International') which he led back into the Second International in 1923, becoming Secretary of the amalgamated Labour and Socialist International.

A large part of Friedrich Adler's papers are combined with those of his father, Victor Adler (q.v.), in an extensive collection held by the Archiv des Vereins für Geschichte der Arbeiterbewegung (VGA), Vienna. A further large and rich collection of Friedrich Adler's papers, for the years 1890–1921 and 1940–57, is in the IISH, Amsterdam. This includes mainly political correspondence for the years 1911–19 and 1940–47, notebooks, manuscripts, and a collection of material on his trial in 1917. This collection is particularly important for the history of the Socialist International, Austrian and German social democracy, German emigration, the Austrian Labour Committee and anti-Nazism. The Vienna City Library has fifteen letters from Adler to J. L. Stern dating from 1941 to 1954.

ADLER, Kathia (1897–1969)

Russian anarchist.

There is a little of Kathia Adler's correspondence in the IISH, Amsterdam and also in the Schweizerisches Sozialarchiv, Zürich.

ADLER, Max (1879–1960)

Austrian social democrat. Sociologist and leading Austro-Marxist theorist.

Adler's papers were given to the staff of Vienna University's Institute of Philosophy (Social Philosophy) by his daughter Lore Sutton. They have been copied and constitute a separate Max Adler Archive comprising 150 files. The papers contain much unedited material in Adler's own handwriting, which is difficult to read. The material includes, *inter alia*: Adler's own published works in manuscript form; unedited manuscripts and typescripts; manuscripts of lectures; notes in preparation for lectures at Vienna University and at the Workers' High School; and secondary literature relating to Adler's work.

ADLER, Victor (1852–1918)

Pioneer Austrian socialist. Doctor. Founder of the Austrian Social Democratic Party (SPÖ). Founder of the *Arbeiterzeitung* in 1891. Led the successful struggle for universal suffrage from 1903 to 1906. Deputy in the Reichsrat from 1905. Supporter of the First World War.

In addition to Victor Adler's papers in the Archiv des Vereins für Geschichte der Arbeiterbewegung (VGA) in Vienna (see Friedrich Adler) there is also a small but important collection in the IISH, Amsterdam. This contains important correspondence relating to German and Austrian social democracy (and, in particular, to Bernstein's 'Revisionism'), an unpublished biography of Victor Adler by Emma Adler, and circulars, pamphlets and reports of the International Socialist Bureau during the 1914–18 war. A large part of this correspondence was published by Friedrich Adler: Victor Adler, *Briefwechsel mit August Bebel und Karl Kautsky, sowie Briefe von und an I. Auer, E. Bernstein, A. Braun, M. Dietz, F. Ebert, W. Liebknecht, H. Müller und P. Singer* (Wien: 1954). In addition, the Vienna City Library has thirteen letters from Adler to Marie von Ebner-Eschenbach and Auguste Fickert.

ADLER-KARLSSON, Gunnar

Swedish 'constructive socialist'. Economist (pupil of Gunnar Myrdal, q.v.). Professor in Denmark.

Twenty boxes of Adler-Karlsson's papers are in the ARAB, Stockholm. Special permission must be obtained before consulting these papers.

AGARTZ, Viktor (1897–1964)

German socialist economist. Co-director of the Trade Union Institute for Economic Science in Cologne since 1948. Member of the North Rhine-Westphalian Landtag (for the SPD from 1947 and the DFU from 1960).

The most extensive collection of Agartz's papers is in the Humboldt University in the DDR. This comprises lectures and articles relating to his professional and political activity, and particularly to his role as a theoretician of the Trade Unions and Co-operatives. A second collection in the Bundesarchiv, Koblenz, includes manuscripts of works on the development of the trade unions and co-determination in Germany. In addition there is a collection of material and correspondence arising out of his activity in the *Zentralamt*, the *Zweizonen-Wirtschaftsamt*, and as Director of the Trade Union Institute for Economic Science. Thirdly, the DGB archive in Düsseldorf has a small collection of press items, correspondence and declarations of solidarity concerning the dispute between Agartz and the DGB in 1955, and the legal proceedings against Agartz in 1957. (See Mommsen, *op. cit.*)

AHLERS, Conrad (1922–80)

German social democratic politician. Journalist. Member of the SPD 1968. Member of the Bundestag 1972–80.

Ahler's papers for the years 1968 and 1972–80 are in the AdsD, Bonn. This is a fragmentary collection, comprising manuscripts of speeches, articles and radio talks, as well as a collection of material concerning events in Czechoslovakia in 1968.

AHLSTRÖM, Axel (1891–1934)

Finnish social democratic politician. Journalist 1917–34, and Editor-in-Chief of *Arbetarbladet* 1921–34. Executive member of the Social Democratic Party (SDP) 1926–34. Chairman of the Union of Swedish Speaking Members of the SDP 1924–34. Member of Helsinki City Council 1929–30. Member of Parliament 1929–34. Member of the Administrative Council of the biggest co-operative firm in Finland 1932–4.

Ahlström's papers from the years 1908–34 are in the Finnish Labour Archives, Helsinki. This collection is concerned with, in particular, Ahlström's journalistic activity, the Swedish–Finnish Social Democratic movement and co-operation between the labour movements of Scandinavia. Among the papers in this collection is correspondence (with prominent figures in the Finnish labour movement, writers and artists, Scandinavian and other Western journalists), diaries, manuscripts (writings and speeches), newspaper cuttings, and photographs. An outline inventory is available.

AKIMOV-MACHNOVEC, Vladimir Petrovič (1872–1921)

Russian revolutionary and historian of the Social Democratic movement. Active in St Petersburg among the 'Group of Narodovol'tsy'. Banished to Siberia in 1897 but escaped to Switzerland. Participated in the exiled RSDLP. Returned illegally to Russia in 1905. Formed Social Democratic circles. Elected to the Secretariat of the Central Bureau of Professional Unions. Member of the St Petersburg Soviet. Delegate, in 1906, to the Stockholm Congress of the RSDLP (where he rejected the armed uprising and supported participation in the Duma). Ceased revolutionary activity and became involved in Co-operatives.

Akimov-Machnoveč's notes, 1905–14, are in the IISH, Amsterdam.

AKSEL'ROD, Pavel Borisovič (1842–1928)

Russian Menshevik leader. Exiled in Switzerland in 1874 after the police crackdown on the 'Go-to-the-People' movement. At first a Narodnik of the 'Black Partition' tendency but embraced Marxism in the early 1880s. Worked to establish an independent working-class party. Co-founder of *Iskra* in 1900. One of the main opponents of Lenin at the Second Congress of the RSDLP in 1903 – thereafter, the outstanding ideologist of Menshevism. During the 1914–18 war spokesman for the 'Internationalist' group of Mensheviks. Returned to Russia in May 1917 and supported the Provisional Government. In August 1917 left for Stockholm as Menshevik delegate to the planned International Socialist Peace Conference and never returned. Became the outstanding Marxist critic of Bolshevism.

Aksel'rod's papers from *c.* 1880 until his death are in the IISH, Amsterdam. Apart from articles and other texts by him, the main part of this collection is made up of correspondence (his many correspondents include Abramovič (q.v.), Fedor Il'ič Dan (q.v.), Karl Kautsky (q.v.), Martov (q.v.), Potresov (q.v.), Radek and Zetkin (q.v.)). An inventory is available.

ALADIN, A. F. (fl. 1890s–1910s)

Russian socialist. Active in Britain.

A collection of Aladin's papers is in Manchester University Library.

ALBARDA, Johan W. (1877–1957)

Dutch SDAP member in second chamber, 1913–39. Member of Dutch government in exile 1940–45.

Some of Albarda's notes, memoranda and articles (1925–52), together with a few letters, are in the IISH, Amsterdam. An inventory is available. (See M. Campfens, *op. cit.*)

ALBERS, Jan W. (1895–1973)

Member of Nederlands Verbond van Vakvereeniging and Dutch Transport Workers' Union.

A small amount of Albers's material, mainly press-cuttings, 1927–40 is in the IISH, Amsterdam. An inventory is available. (See M. Campfens, *op. cit.*)

ALBRECHT, August (b. 1890)

German social democrat. Husband of Lisa Albrecht (q.v.). Transport worker. Secretary of the Association of German Young Workers' Clubs (later Verband der Sozialistischen Arbeiterjugend) and co-founder of the Socialist Youth International. Manager of the socialist book club, 'Der Bücherkreis' 1929–33. Member of the SPD Executive in Hanover 1946. From 1951 employed by the DGB.

Albrecht's papers are in the AdsD, Bonn.

ALBRECHT, Elisabeth (Lisa) (1896–1958)

German social democratic politician. Secretary for women in the SPD district of Branden-burg 1928–33; several times arrested after 1933. Chairman in 1946 and Vice-Chairman in 1947 of the SPD's Bavarian organisation; member of the Central Party Committee for Womens' Questions. Member of the Bundestag 1949–58.

The AdsD, Bonn, has Lisa Albrecht's papers from the years 1945–54 concerning the International Women's Movement, the SPD, and the Advisory Committee on Artistic Matters to the Deutsche Bundespost. In addition, there is publisher's correspondence concerning the journal *Das Volk* 1947–51. (See Mommsen, *op. cit.*)

ALEKSINSKII, Grigorii Alekseevič (1879–1967)

Russian politician. Bolshevik spokesman in the second Duma. Later left Lenin and joined Bogdanov and Lunacharskii in the *Vperëd* group. Emigrated to France after the revolution.

A collection of Aleksinskii's papers is held by the Bakhmeteff Archive at Columbia University, New York. The collection comprises about 2400 items in fifteen boxes, and includes photocopies of his memoirs for 1905–14. There is also substantial material on the RSDLP between 1907–14, including correspondence, documents, petitions and pamphlets, relating above all to the socialist movement during the First World War; German influence and propaganda in Russia; the execution of Nicolas II; Russian soldiers and prisoners in Germany and France during the First World War; the London Congress; the *Vperëd* group; the Social Democratic Capri school; and the *Okhrana* penetration of the Social Democratic party. Aleksinskii's correspondents include Maksim Gorkii, G. Plekhanov, V. I. Lenin, Iu. Martov, D. Z. Manuilskii and A. Lunacharskii.

ALLEMANE, Jean (1843–1935)

French socialist leader. Communard. Typographer. Imprisoned in 1862 after participation in a typographers' strike. Combatant for the Commune. Deported. Amnestied in 1880. Active in the Parti ouvrier – supported the 'possibilists' after the schism in 1880. Prominent militant in the FTSF and in the struggle against Boulanger. Leader of the tendency in the FTSF opposed to the purely electoral and compromise politics of Brousse. Eponymous leader of the POSR (le parti 'allemaniste'). Anti-authoritarian and free-thinker. Proponent of the General Strike. Founding member of the SFIO. Unsuccessfully attempted to form an opposition tendency in 1911. Deputy for the Seine 1901–2 and 1906–10.

Two letters from Allemane are in the IFHS. The text of his defence of his conduct during the Commune – *Ma défence, mes témoins* – is in the Archives Nationales, Paris.

AMEDUNE*

* Pseudonym of DUNOIS, Amédée Gabriel

ANDERS, Karl (b. 1907)

German communist and then social democrat. Manual worker. Secretary of the KPD in Berlin-Brandenburg 1931–32. Illegal Party work 1933. Exile in Czechoslovakia (member of the KPD until 1937) and England in 1934. With the Central Election Organisation of the SPD in Bonn 1960–61. From 1961 advisor of the IG Bau-Steine-Erden.

Anders's papers for the years 1960–69 are in the AdsD, Bonn. These comprise material concerning elections and SPD election planning and organisation. A further deposit of Anders's papers is to be expected.

ANDERSEN, Alsing (1893–1962)

Danish social democratic leader and politician. Secretary of the SD. Chairman of the Parliamentary Group of the SD. Minister of Defence 1935–40.

Three listed folders of Andersen's private papers for the years 1930 to 1945 are to be found amongst the SD archive in the ABA, Copenhagen.

ANDERSEN, Harild (1906–80)

Danish communist of the interwar period. Lecturer.

Fifteen boxes of Andersen's papers for the years 1914–80 are in the ABA, Copenhagen. These include correspondence with, amongst others, Arnold Petersen of the American Socialist Labour Party, Hermann Gorter, Iwan Katz and Karl Korsch (q.v.). An inventory is available.

ANDERSEN, Ole Christian (1830–99)

Danish pioneer of international socialism. Travelling representative of the IWMA. Attempted to establish a socialist party in Denmark.

One box of Andersen's papers, comprising mainly letters received by him, is in the ABA, Copenhagen.

ANDERSEN-NEXØ, Martin (1869–1954)

Prominent intellectual in the Danish Communist Party (DKP). Writer.

Two boxes of Andersen-Nexø's papers, including correspondence and manuscripts, are in the ABA, Copenhagen. In addition, there is a large collection of his papers in the Royal Danish Library, Copenhagen.

ANDERSSON, Gunnar (1890–1946)

Swedish trade union leader. Elected President of the LO in 1946.

A small collection of Andersson's papers is in the ARAB, Stockholm.

ANGRAND, Charles (1854–1926)

French painter and libertarian. Financial supporter and collaborator of *Temps Nouveaux*.

See under GRAVE, Jean.

ANKERSMIT, Johan F. (1871–1942)

Editor-in-Chief, Dutch socialist daily newspaper, *Het Volk*, 1920–37.

The IISH, Amsterdam has a small amount of correspondence. (See M. Campfens, *op. cit.*)

ANSEELE, Eduard (1856–1938)

Belgian socialist pioneer and politician. At first printer. Active in the IWMA. Founder and leader of the Flemish Socialist Party. One of the founders, and from 1884 director, of the co-operative society Vooruit. Imprisoned in 1886 for an article attempting to persuade soldiers not to fire on strikers. Member of the General Council and one of the most influential early leaders of the Belgian Workers' Party. Member of Parliament from the 1890s. After the 1914–18 war prominent socialist cabinet minister.

Anseele's archive is held by his family. No access has been granted to date. The Archief en Museum voor het Vlaamse Cultuurleven, Antwerp has some papers (ref. A.354) including letters, documents, manuscripts and cuttings. The extent of the collection is not known. Permission is needed for consultation.

ANTRICK, Otto Friedrich Wilhelm (1858–1924)

German social democratic politician. Minister of State in Braunschweig. Member of the Reichstag.

There is a little of Antrick's correspondence, 1892–1915, in the IISH, Amsterdam.

ANZI, Felice (fl. 1920s)

Italian socialist.

The papers are in the Feltrinelli Institute, Milan. The collection, covering the period 1901–27 comprises letters, articles, essays and press cuttings. Of particular interest is the correspondence with Costantino Lazzari (forty-six letters 1900–27), which shed further light on this important Socialist Party member and friend of Anzi. Other correspondence includes letters to E. Ferri, A. Costa, O. Morgari, C. Prampolini, G. Menotti, F. Turati, A. Graziadei, E. Malatesta, G. Zirardini, M. Todeschini, D. Rondani, A. Cabrini, G. Braga and B. Maglione.

ARMAND, E. (1872–1962)

French anarchist. Founded, 1901, the journal '*L'Ère nouvelle*', an organ of the Christian anarchists. Subsequently he became an anarchist-individualist. Devoted himself to the relationship of the individual to society and sexual relations.

Papers are reported in the IFHS, Paris.

ARNAUD, Frédéric (1819–78)

French 'social Christian'. At first lawyer. Fervent Catholic but sympathetic to Fourier and his followers. Defended the right to work but repudiated class struggle. Leading proponent of democratic and social catholicism. Member of the Constituent Assembly in 1848, and of the Legislative Assembly in 1848–69. Mayor of the Seventh arrondissement in Paris, November 1870 (moderate republican). Republican Senator for l'Ariège, 1876.

Recently, numerous unpublished manuscripts of Arnaud's were reported still in private hands in Castillon-en-Couserans (Ariège). His diaries, however, have been lost.

ARNDT, Adolf (1904–74)

German social democratic politician and legal specialist. Member of the Bundestag 1949–69. Leading legal authority and secretary of the parliamentary group. Member of the Party Executive (Parteivorstand) and Legal Policy Committee (Rechtspolitischer Ausschuss) of the SPD 1956–65.

The AdsD, Bonn, has an extensive collection of Adolf Arndt's papers for the period 1945–65, concerning the Bundestag Legal Committee (Rechtsausschuss), the Saar Agreement, the debate over the statutory period of limitation for murder in relation to Nazi crimes, and criminal proceedings against individuals and the press over slander.

ARNDT, Claus (b. 1927)

German social democratic politician. Lawyer. Deputy Chairman of the League of German Socialist Students (SDS) 1950–55. Member of the Bundestag 1968–72 and 1974–76. Prolific writer.

Arndt's papers for the years 1970–6 are in the AdsD, Bonn. These comprise material concerning the Federal and Land Commission of Enquiry on Constitutional Reform, the work of the Bundestag Committee of Investigation into the Guillaume Affair, and various Bundestag committees.

ARNOLD, Felix*

* Pseudonym of RAPPOPORT, Charles

ARQUER, Jordi (fl. 1930s)

Catalonian trade union militant and revolutionary socialist. At first founder and main leader of the Partit Comunista Català, and then, in turn of the Bloc Obrer i Camperol and the POUM. Combatant in the Civil War. Active in the Republican exile. Died in exile.

Arquer's papers are in the Centre D'Estudis Historics Internacionals at the University of Barcelona.

ASCHBERG, Olof (1877–1960)

Swedish banker. Supporter and financier of the labour movement. Born of Jewish Russian *émigrés*. Sympathiser of the Russian Revolution. First westerner to establish financial and business links with the Soviet Republic. Aided refugees from Republican Spain. Bequeathed property to the Swedish labour movement.

Some thirty-one boxes of Aschberg's papers are in the ARAB, Stockholm. Special permission must be obtained before consulting this collection.

ATABEKIAN, Alexander A. (fl. 1870–1935)

Georgian anarchist. Friend of Peter Kropotkin (q.v.). In the 1890s one of the founders of the anarchist movement in Southern Russia. Active propagandist during the period of the Russian Revolution and Civil War.

A collection of Atabekian's papers constitutes part of the Nettlau (q.v.) collection in the IISH, Amsterdam. The main part of this collection is made up of letters from various anarchists in the 1890s (including Kropotkin, q.v.).

AUERBACH, Walter (1905–75)*

German trade unionist. Writer on social policy. In the General Secretariat of the International Transport Workers' Federation in Amsterdam and then London 1933–6. Vice-President of the Central Labour Office of the British Occupation Zone 1946–8 and Permanent Under-Secretary of State in the Lower Saxony Ministry of Labour, 1948.

Auerbach's extensive papers for the years 1933–48 are in the AdsD, Bonn. They comprise correspondence, manuscripts and printed material. (See Mommsen, *op. cit.*)

  * Known by the pseudonym Dirksen.

AUFHÄUSER, Siegfried (1884–1969)

German trade unionist. Social democratic politician. Founder of the Arbeitsgemeinschaft Freie Angestelltenverbände (Association of Free White-Collar Workers' Unions) 1915. Chairman of the Allgemeinen Freien Angestelltenbundes (AFA) (General Free White-Collar Workers' Union) 1917–33. Member of the Reichstag 1921–33. Exiled in 1933.

Collections of Aufhäuser's papers are held in both the Archive of the DAG Berlin and at the Historische Kommission der Freien Universität, Berlin. They relate to his work for these organisations. (See Mommsen, *op. cit.*)

AULAS, Jean (fl. 1920s–30s)

French educational trade unionist.

Aulas's papers are in the IFHS, Paris. These concern the Fédération unitaire de l'Enseignement about 1925–30.

AURIOL, Vincent (1884–1966)

French socialist politician. First President of the Fourth Republic. Lawyer. Member of the SFIO 1905. Editor of *Midi Socialiste* and founder of the first union of journalists in this area. Deputy from Haute-Garonne, 1914–42. General Secretary of the Socialist Group, 1928. Minister of Finance, 1936–7, and of Justice, 1937–8. Co-ordinating role in Blum's second Government 1938. Imprisoned in 1940 for six months. Went underground in 1942. In London in 1943. Deputy from Haute-Garonne in the two National Constituent Assemblies (1945 and 1946) and in the National Assembly, 1946–7. Minister of State 1946–7. Delegate to the first session of the UN. President of the Republic 1947–54. Supported de Gaulle and resigned from the SFIO in 1958.

About 150 boxes of papers relating to the whole of Auriol's life and political career have been deposited by his widow and son in the Fondation Nationale des Sciences Politiques, Paris.

AUSTERLITZ, Friedrich (1862–1931)

Austrian social democrat. Editor-in-Chief of the *Arbeiterzeitung*, 1895–1931. Deputy, 1919–31.

Vienna City Library has four letters to Moritz Necker from 1898.

BAADE, Fritz (1893–1974)

German social democratic politician and economist. Member of the Reichstag 1930–33. Advisor in the Turkish Ministry of Economics 1934–46. Professor of Economics 1948. Member of the Bundestag 1949–65.

The Bundesarchiv, Koblenz, has extensive correspondence from Baade's emigration period in Turkey, as well as from the above-mentioned occupations generally and, in particular, on political and academic matters since 1945. (See Mommsen, *op. cit.*)

BABEUF, Gracchus (1760–97)

French communist, theorist and insurrectionist. At first clerk. Known by the name of his journal *Tribun du Peuple*. Demanded that 'common happiness' become the reality of the Republic. Formed a seven-man committee in March 1796 to direct propaganda and organise amongst the soldiers and workers of Paris a communist insurrection. Arrested after the plot was betrayed and condemned to death.

There are numerous manuscripts of Babeuf in French archives, as well as in the Institute for Marxism-Leninism, Moscow, and the Feltrinelli Foundation, Milan (mainly photocopies). Much, but by no means all, of his correspondence has been published. The Moscow collection is particularly rich in relation to Babeuf's activity up to the period of the Thermidor, while the period after the fall of the Revolutionary Government and the 'conspiracy of equals' is well documented by the holdings in French archives (particularly the Archives Nationales in Paris). Fortunately there is an exhaustive published bibliography and inventory of Babeuf's papers: V. Daline *et al.*, *Inventaire des Manuscrits et imprimés de Babeuf* (Paris: 1966).

BACKERT, E. (fl. 1930s–40s)

German brewery-workers' trade unionist.

Backert's memoirs are in the DGB Archive, Düsseldorf. (See Mommsen, *op. cit.*)

BÄCKSTRÖM, Knut (b. 1903)

Swedish social democrat and later communist. Editor and historian of the Swedish labour movement.

One box of Bäckström's papers is in the ARAB, Stockholm.

BÄHLER, Louis A. (1867–1941)

Dutch Christian – anarchist pastor.

The IISH, Amsterdam, has a little of Bähler's correspondence for 1915. An inventory is available. (See M. Campfens, *op. cit.*)

BAIDALAKOV, Viktor M. (fl. 1930s–50s)

Russian public servant. Head of the Popular Labour Union (*Narodno-Trudovoi Soiuz*) 1933–55.

The Bakhmeteff Archive of Columbia University, New York, has a collection of his papers containing his history of the foundation and organisation of the NTS. There are restrictions on access.

BAIKALOV, Anatolii Vasilevič (fl. 1920s)

Russian socialist. Member of the RSDLP before 1917 and active in the Siberian cooperative movement. Sent to England in 1919 to study cooperatives and decided to stay in the West.

The Bakhmeteff Archive, Columbia University, New York, has a collection of his papers comprising twenty-five boxes (about 6200 items). The holding includes Baikalov's manuscripts, correspondence with A. I. Guchkov, the Duchess of Atholl, Bernard Pares, the Labour Party, Malcolm Muggeridge, the American Slavic Colonisation Trust, W. M. Citrine and the Trades Union Congress General Council, Russian émigrés, Boris Nicolaevsky, Sidney Webb and other British authors and politicians. Access is restricted.

BAKELS, Antonius C. (1898–1964)

Dutch anarchist.

The IISH, Amsterdam, has some of Bakels's correspondence (1914–62). (See M. Campfens, *op. cit.*)

BAKKER, Willem de (1907–82)

Dutch syndicalist.

The IISH, Amsterdam, has some of Bakker's correspondence and circulars (1923–36). An inventory is available. (See M. Campfens, *op. cit.*)

BAKUNIN, Michael Aleksandrovič (1814–76)

Russian revolutionary. Pioneer and theoretician of anarchism. Aristocratic origin. Officer in the Russian army 1833–5. Became a friend of A. I. Herzen (q.v.). Left Russia 1840. Militant opponent of the Imperial regime. Russian delegate to the Slav Congress in Prague in 1848. Participated in the unsuccessful Prague uprising against the Austrian army in June 1848; involved in the German Revolution in Dresden in 1849. Arrested. Death sentence commuted in 1850, and extradited to Russia in 1851. Imprisoned in 1851–7 and then exiled in Siberia. Escaped in 1861. In London contributed to *Kolokol* (*Bell*), and established contacts with the Land and Liberty underground organisation in Russia. Participated in the Polish Revolution in 1863. After the overthrow of Napoleon III went to Lyons in 1871 and advocated the destruction of the state. Unsuccessful attempt to participate in a libertarian rising in Bologna in 1874. Leading anarchist theoretician and publicist from the 1860s (proponent of a stateless federation of autonomous communities). Founded secret societies as the instrument of revolutionary risings. Joined the IWMA. Bitter conflict with Marx (q.v.). Founded the International Alliance of Socialist Democracy in 1868. Expelled from the IWMA in 1872, but by then had substantial bodies of supporters – especially in Spain, Italy, and the Jura part of Switzerland, and among Russian students in Switzerland (who increased Bakunin's influence over Russian populism and contributed to the 1874 decision to 'Go-to-the-People').

There are two main collections of Bakunin's papers. The first, consisting mainly of manuscripts, is in the IISH, Amsterdam. The second, including correspondence, is in the Feltrinelli Institute, Milan. A third collection, which in 1927 was in the Hauptstaatsarchiv, Dresden, and consisted mainly of confiscated political papers from the 1840s, cannot now be traced. Bakunin's papers, moreover, have been subject to a major publishing enterprise. (See A. Lehning, A. J. C. Rüter and P. Scheibert (eds) *Archives Bakounine*, vols 1–7 (Leiden: IISH, Amsterdam, 1961–8)).

BALABANOFF, Angelica (1878–1965)

Ukrainian-born international socialist activist. Studied at the University of Rome where she fell under the influence of Antonio Labriola. Joined the PSI about 1900. Launched a journal for women *Su Compagne*. Central Committee member of the PSI and Co-Editor of *Avanti* in 1912. Secretary of the Zimmerwald Executive. Returned to Russia in June 1917 and joined the Bolsheviks on the basis of their opposition to the war. Foreign Minister of the Soviet Ukraine. Secretary of the Comintern under Zinoviev. Moved into opposition after the Kronstadt rebellion. In 1921 emigrated to, in turn, Vienna, Paris and, during the Second World War, the United States. After the war returned to Italy and took up organisational work among women for the Democratic Socialist Party of Italy.

Balabanoff's papers for the years 1914–62 are in the IISH, Amsterdam. This extensive collection is especially complete for the post-1945 period, and contains a great deal of material relating to the Italian Social Democratic Party. Apart from various manuscripts, this collection also includes extensive correspondence (mainly letters to Balabanoff in the years 1914–15, 1920, 1927–8 and 1936–62 from, in particular, Italian social democrats). An inventory is available. The Bakhmeteff Archive, Columbia University, New York, has tape recordings of interviews with her, in which she discusses V. I. Lenin, the Communist International, Mussolini (q.v.), G. Zinoviev, Giacinto Serrati and John Reed (13 reels).

BANG, Gustav (1871–1915)

Danish Marxist historian. Theorist of Danish social democracy.

Four boxes of Gustav Bang's papers for the years 1899–1915, including a few letters and manuscripts, are in the ABA, Copenhagen.

BANG, Nina (1866–1928)

Danish social democratic politician. Minister of Education in the first social democratic government.

Three boxes of Nina Bang's papers for the years 1899–1928 are in the ABA, Copenhagen. As well as manuscripts, these contain a small quantity of correspondence (including letters written to Karl Kautsky, q.v.). An inventory is available.

BARBÉ, Henri (fl. 1920s)

French communist. Leading official, French Communist Party, 1920–34, and on the Executive Committee, Communist International, 1927–31.

One volume of Barbé's memoirs (n.d.) is in the Hoover Institution, Stanford University, California.

BARBUSSE, Henri (1873–1935)

French communist leader.

Barbusse's papers, at present closed, are in the Institut Maurice Thorez, Paris.

BARENTS, Jan (1916–61)

Dutch newspaper editor and member of the Dutch Labour Party (PvdA).

The IISH, Amsterdam, has Barents's correspondence (1933–61). Access is restricted. (See M. Campfens, *op. cit.*)

BARTH, Emil (1897–1941)

German engineering worker. As a leading member of the Revolutionary Shop Stewards (Obleute) became a member of the Council of People's Commissars for the USPD (10 November–29 December 1918). After the withdrawal of the USPD from the Council, remained active in the labour movement (becoming a Party Secretary for the SPD) but without his former prominence.

The major part of Barth's papers are in the Friedrich-Ebert-Stiftung, Bonn. These almost all stem from the time of the Council, and are informative on relations between the Central Government and the Workers' and Soldiers' Councils (especially the Berlin Executive Council), and antagonisms between the SPD and USPD, as well as questions of economic and social policy, nutrition, justice, the armistice and peace matters. In addition, the DGB Archive in Düsseldorf has correspondence and documents for the years 1917–20 and 1926. (See Mommsen, *op. cit.*)

BATTISTI, Luigi (fl. 1939–45)

Italian resistance leader.

Some of Battisti's papers are in the Istituto Nazionale per la Storia del Movimento di Liberazione in Italia in Milan. There is correspondence, 1946–8, concerning the activity carried on in the 'Constituente' and letters on the problem of 'Alto Adige'.

BAUER, Otto (1881–1938)

Austrian social democratic leader and foremost representative of 'Austro-Marxism'. Editor of the *Arbeiterzeitung* in 1907, and co-founder of the theoretical journal *Der Kampf*. Deputy in the Reichsrat and Secretary of the Social Democratic Group. Prisoner of war in Russia 1914–17. Secretary of State for Foreign Affairs November 1918–July 1919. Opponent of Bolshevism following their method of revolution in Austria. Became the main leader and theorist of Austrian social democracy. Co-founder, with Friedrich Adler, of the International Union of Socialist Parties (the 'Two-and-a-half International') and from 1923 an Executive Member of the Labour and Socialist International. Member of Parliament 1923–34. Exiled in 1934.

The Haus-, Hof- und Staatsarchiv, Vienna, has a collection of papers relating to Bauer's time as Foreign Minister. The collection includes material relating to St Germain and the Anschluss question. In addition, a few letters from 1924, but, most importantly, a collection of Bauer's papers from the exile years, 1934–8, are in the IISH, Amsterdam. This collection is comprised of correspondence (mainly letters to Bauer from, amongst others, leaders of the Labour and Socialist International), but also includes manuscripts, notes and other material concerning, in particular, the underground activity of Austrian social democracy and the anti-fascist resistance.

BAUR, Valentin (1891–c. 1974)

German trade unionist and social democratic politician. Member of the Bavarian Landtag 1946–7, of the Frankfurt Economic Council (Wirtschaftsrat) 1947–9, and of the Bundestag 1949–61.

The DGB Archive in Düsseldorf has a little of Baur's documentation from the period of exile in Switzerland 1933–45. (See Mommsen, *op. cit.*)

BAUZIN, Lucien (1880–1970)

French President of the Seine Federation of the Radical–Socialist Party.

Bauzin's papers are in the Archives Nationales, Paris.

BAZIN, Gustave Pierre (fl. 1842–1906)

French socialist and Communard. Jeweller. Member of the International. Combatant for the Commune. In exile 1871–3 in Geneva, and then 1873–9 in Brussels and London. Continued to be active in the International and its congresses. Co-founder in 1875 of the Chambre du Travail, Fédération des Sociétés ouvrières bruxelloise. Later an active Guesdist.

Bazin's letters to Vickery H. Jung and César de Paepe (q.v.) are in the IISH, Amsterdam.

BEBEL, August (1840–1913)

German socialist pioneer and publicist. Leader of German social democracy. Turner by trade. From 1865 active, with his life-long friend Wilhelm Liebknecht (q.v.), in turning the originally liberal German Workers' Associations towards socialism to form the Social Democratic Labour Party (SDAP) in 1869. Although an opponent of Lassalle (q.v.), participated in the Unity Conference with the ADAV at Gotha in 1875 and became, until his death, Chairman, but more than that the authoritative spokesman and tribune of German social democracy. A member of the First International (IWMA) in 1866, Bebel was close to Friedrich Engels (q.v.) and a major source of Marxist influence within the German labour movement. Several periods of imprisonment. Member of the North German Reichstag and then of the Reichstag from 1867.

Bebel's extensive and rich correspondence, together with collections of printed material, manuscripts, notes and excerpts, is held by the IISH, Amsterdam (a detailed list of contents is available).

BECHER, Johannes R. (1891–1958)

German communist and writer. Exiled in 1933. Editor-in-Chief of the Moscow journal *Internationale Literatur – Deutsche Blätter*. Minister for Culture in the DDR in 1945, founder and President of the Cultural League for the Democratic Renewal of Germany. Member of the Volkskammer.

The Archiv der Deutschen Akademie der Künste in East Berlin, has personal records, manuscripts, correspondence, first editions of Becher's works and photographs, together with a collection of material concerned with Becher. (See Mommsen, *op. cit.*)

BECHERT, Karl (1901–81)

German social democratic politician. Physicist. Member of the Bundestag 1957–72. Member of the Science Committee of the SPD Executive 1958–65.

Bechert's extensive papers for the years 1934–81 are in the AdsD, Bonn. As well as personal documents, memoirs, general correspondence and manuscripts of political interest (especially in relation to the German and European peace movement, energy policy and environmental protection), there are also documents from the Nazi period and Bundestag committees.

BECKER, Johann Philipp (1809–86)

Pioneer German socialist. Revolutionary of 1848. Leading organiser and publicist for the International from exile in Switzerland. Publisher of the journal *Der Vorbote*.

Becker's papers are in the IISH, Amsterdam. These comprise several hundred letters to Becker from the period of the IWMA (mainly relating to *Der Vorbote*), and also 120 letters written by Becker about the republican movement in 1848–9. An inventory is available. (See Mommsen, *op. cit.*)

BECKER, Karl Heinrich (1896–1961)

German communist and trade unionist. Local Councillor in Dittersbach 1929. Member of the Reichstag 1930–33. Exile in Czechoslovakia 1933. In England 1939. After 1945 Secretary in the mineworkers union (IG Bergbau).

The DGB Archive in Düsseldorf has a small holding of Becker's papers, mainly of copies.

BEERMANN, Hermann (1903–73)

German trade unionist. Active in the Woodworkers' Union. Member of the ISK. Imprisoned for resistance activity 1938. Chairman of the DGB in Lower Saxony and Bremen 1947. Full-time Executive member 1956 and Vice-Chairman of the DGB 1962.

Beermann's papers for the years 1959–68 are in the AdsD, Bonn. These comprise circular letters and correspondence with, amongst others, Walter Auerbach (q.v.), Ludwig Preller (q.v.), Helmut Rohde and Ernst Schellenberg, concerning trade union and social policy matters.

BEHR, Werner (b. 1922)

German civil service trade unionist. Editor of the journal *Der Deutsche Beamte*.

Behr's papers for the years 1951–80 are in the AdsD, Bonn. These comprise correspondence and manuscripts concerning the journals *Der Deutsche Beamte* and *Gewerkschaftliche Monatschefte*, as well as material concerning the DGB and individual unions.

BÉLUZE, Jean-Pierre (1821–1908)

Icarian communist. Pioneer of the French co-operative movement. Organiser of the first Co-operative Conference in Paris.

Part of Béluze's papers are reported to be in the IISH, Amsterdam.

BENGSTON, Bernhard (1889–1947)

Swedish social democratic politician. Journalist and editor. Eventually a Landshövding (County Governor).

Nine boxes of Bengston's papers are in the ARAB, Stockholm. A provisional inventory is available.

BENOIT, Joseph (1812–80)

French neo-Babeuvian communist. Founder of a secret propaganda society in 1835. After the setback to the Parisian movement in 1839, repudiated conspiracy and violent revolution in favour of propaganda. Collaborated on *La Fraternité de 1845*. 'Communiste babouviste' Deputy for the Rhône in the Constituent and then Legislative Assembly. Proponent of compulsory, free primary education and of decentralisation. Arrested and exiled in December 1851. Returned to France in 1865. Municipal Councillor in Lyons, September 1870.

The Municipal Library of Lyons has three important manuscripts, including Benoit's autobiography – *Les Confessions d'un proletaire*.

BERGCRANTZ, Knut (1909–78)

Swedish trade unionist. Secretary of the Wood Industry Workers' Union.

One box of Bergcrantz's papers is in the ARAB, Stockholm.

BERGEGREN, Hinke (1861–1936)

Swedish revolutionary. Agitator and publicist. Leading figure in the anarchist tendency of the early Swedish labour movement. Expelled from the SAP in 1908. Active in the socialist (then anarchist) youth movement. Editor of the anarchist paper *Brand* 1904–11, 1912–16. Member of the SKP until 1929 and then of the Independent Communist Party.

A large collection of Bergegren's papers is in the ARAB, Stockholm. This comprises personal documents, manuscripts, notebooks (including accounts for looking after refugees in 1906), correspondence (including letters from Russians and a copy of his letter to Kollontai (q.v.) in 1933), extracts from minutes and other material relating to his political activity. With the exception of the notebooks, his papers are inventorised and freely accessible.

BERGLUND, Johan Emil (1861–1952)

Early Swedish trade unionist. Official in several trade unions (notably the Railwayworkers').

One box of Berglund's papers is in the ARAB, Stockholm. An inventory is available.

BERGMEIJER, Jan A. (1854–1941)

Teacher, editor and Dutch SDAP member.

The IISH, Amsterdam, has one file of Bergmeijer's correspondence, 1884–1900. (See M. Campfens, *op. cit.*)

BERKMAN, Alexander (1870–1936)

Russian–American anarchist. Influenced by Populism in his youth. Emigrated to the USA in 1888. In New York joined the German *Freiheit* group led by Johann Most. Active supporter of the Homestead steel strike 1892. Imprisoned 1892–1906 for an attempted assassination of Henry Frick (manager of the Carnegie works). Became one of the two leading organisers, publicists and agitators of the American anarchist movement. Edited *Mother Earth* in 1906–18. Deported with Emma Goldman (q.v.) to Russia in December 1919. Worked for the

Bolshevik regime on cultural matters. Emigrated to Europe in 1921, after the Kronstadt uprising. Continued as an anarchist militant in France, concentrating on relief work for fellow anarchists and anarchist prisoners in Russia. Took his own life in June 1936.

Berkman's papers are in the IISH, Amsterdam. This extensive collection includes, in particular, correspondence and manuscripts. A list of the collection, which covers the period 1892–1936 is available.

BERNASCHEK, Richard (1888–1945)

Austrian social democrat. Leader of the Upper Austrian *Schutzbund* (SDAP paramilitary organisation); played a decisive role in the Austrian civil war of 1934.

His papers are at the Ludwig Boltzmann Institut für Geschichte der Arbeiterbewegung, Linz.

BERNER, Rudolf (fl. 1930s)

Swedish syndicalist. Participant in the Spanish Civil War.

Thirteen boxes of Berner's papers are in the ARAB, Stockholm. A preliminary inventory is available.

BERNHARD, Otte (b. 1883)

German Christian trade unionist. Chairman of the Gesamtverband der christlichen Gewerkschaften Deutschlands (The General Association of German Christian Trade Unions). Chairman of the Internationaler Bunder Christlicher Gewerkschaften (International Federation of Christian Trade Unions).

A small collection of Bernhard's papers for the years 1922–33 is in the Bundesarchiv, Koblenz. This comprises correspondence, reference files and circulars from his trade union activity.

BERNSTEIN, Eduard (1850–1932)

German socialist theoretician (revisionist) and publicist. Active in the SDAP from 1871 (1875 delegate to the Gotha Unity Congress). Visited Marx (q.v.) and Friedrich Engels (q.v.) with August Bebel (q.v.) in London in 1880. Became one of their most important supporters within German social democracy. Edited the illegal Party organ *Der Sozialdemokrat* in exile 1881–90 (first in Switzerland and then in London). Forced to remain in England until 1901 (when the threat of prosecution for his illegal activities under the Sozialistengesetz was lifted). Bernstein came under the influence of Fabian socialism. From this arose his book *Die Voraussetzungen des Sozialismus und die Aufgaben der Sozialdemokratie* (1899: published in English as *Evolutionary Socialism*) in which the main tenets of Marxist socialism were criticised and correspondingly revised. Subsequently acknowledged as the main representative of Revisionism within German social democracy. Member of the Reichstag 1902–6, 1912–18 and 1920–28. Voted against war credits in 1915. Left the SPD for the USPD but returned to the SPD in 1919. Member of Party Commission to draft a new programme in 1920. Ensuing Görlitzer Programme fundamentally influenced by Bernstein.

The IISH in Amsterdam has an extensive collection of Bernstein's papers including correspondence as well as manuscripts, notes and drafts for articles, lectures and speeches, excerpts and printed material (newspaper and journal cuttings and proofs). In addition, the documents and records include a dossier on the 'Görlitzer Programme'. The archive covers largely the period 1890–1930 and especially the 1914–18 war: a detailed list of contents is available (see also KAMPFFMEYER, Paul). (See Mommsen *op. cit.*)

BERTAS, Pierre (1864–1950)

French socialist militant. Proudhonist (q.v.). Teacher and publicist. Municipal Councillor in Marseilles 1895–1902. Later devoted himself to journalism and historical studies.

Bertas's papers are in the Municipal Archives of Marseilles. These include a large number of manuscripts, index cards and journals, as well as letters from Paul Margueritte, Maurras, Millerand (q.v.), Mistral, Rodin and others. (See Maitron *op. cit.*)

BERTHELSEN, Einar (1913–78)

Leader of the Danish Trade Union for Ships' Stokers in the post-war period.

Seven boxes of Berthelsen's papers for the years 1942–78, including personal papers, correspondence and manuscripts, are in the ABA, Copenhagen.

BERTHET, Arthur (fl. 1970s)

Belgian socialist. Secretary of the Thuin Federation of the Belgian Socialist Party.

Berthet's correspondence for the years 1970–80 is in the archive of the Thuin Federation of the Belgian Socialist Party.

BERTONI, Luigi (1872–1947)

Swiss anarcho-syndicalist.

Six files of Bertoni's papers are in the IISH, Amsterdam. The collection includes correspondence with Enrico Malatesta and others, newspaper cuttings and material on the Spanish Civil War.

BERTRAND, Louis (1856–1943)

Pioneer Belgian socialist. Founder and influential early leader of the Belgian Workers' Party. Proponent of a pragmatic reformism. Member of Parliament for Brussels. Historian of socialism.

Bertrand's papers are in the Institut Emile Vandervelde, Brussels. Of particular importance is his correspondence, continuing from the late 1870s, with numerous Belgian and international socialists. This has been itemised by Robert Abs in Catalogue I (1969) and Catalogue II (1972) – together with a small quantity of other documents in Catalogue IV (1974) – of the Emile Vandervelde Institut.

BEUZEMAKER, Nicolaas (1902–44)

Chairman of the Dutch Communist Party.

The IISH, Amsterdam, has Beuzemaker's diary and other manuscripts, 1940–43. An inventory is available. (See M. Campfens, *op. cit.*)

BEYREIS, Max (1900–73)

German social democratic politician. Trade union secretary and town councillor in Flensburg.

Beyreis's papers are in the Stadtarchiv, Flensburg. These comprise writings and other material on SPD municipal policy, border policy and trade union work. (See Mommsen, *op. cit.*)

BIERNATH, Hubert (1907–67)

German social democratic politician. Minister of the Interior of North Rhine-Westphalia 1956–8. Member of the North Rhine-Westphalian Landtag 1946–50 and 1958–67.

Biernath's papers are in the Hauptstaatsarchiv, Düsseldorf. These concern the Zonal Advisory Council (1947–9), and the Provincial Landschaftsverband of Westphalia (1950–56), as well as the Federal Executive, the Bundestag and Landtag Groups (for North Rhine-Westphalia) and the sub-district Hamm of the SPD (1951–8). (See Mommsen, *op. cit.*)

BILL, Friedrich (1894–1976)

Austrian–Czechoslovakian social democrat. Lawyer and journalist.

Bill's papers are in the Leo Baeck Institute, New York.

BILT, Christiaan W. J. van de (1886–1968)

Chairman of the Dutch Mineworkers' Union (Algemeene Nederlandsche Mijnwerkersbond) in the inter-war period.

The IISH, Amsterdam, has Bilt's correspondence and documents. The collection covers the period 1912–45, and an inventory is available. (See M. Campfens *op. cit.*)

BJÖRK, Kaj (b. 1918)

Swedish social democratic official, politician and diplomat. International Secretary of the SAP 1947–56. From 1956 Editor of the SAP's *Ny Tid*. Member of Parliament. Ambassador to Peking and then Ottawa.

Björk's papers are in the ARAB, Stockholm. These relate mainly to his work as International Secretary of the SAP, and include manuscripts and drafts written for the Prime Minister.

BJÖRKLUND, Carl Johan (1884–1971)

Swedish anarchist. Journalist and publicist. Worked for some years in Berlin, Prague and Vienna. Active in the syndicalist and anarchist movement. Editor of the anarchist paper *Brand* 1916–17 and 1918–48. Co-founder and activist in the Swedish Pensioners' Organisation 1941.

A large collection of Björklund's papers from the years 1908–70 is in the ARAB, Stockholm. This comprises personal documents, correspondence, manuscripts, transcripts, leaflets, pamphlets, posters, newspaper cuttings and other material concerning his political and journalistic activity. An inventory is available.

BLACHSTEIN, Peter (1911–77)

German social democratic politician. Journalist. Member of the SPD 1928 and of the SAP from 1931. Under political arrest then exile in Scandinavia 1933–4. Fought with the International Brigade in Spain. Member of the SPD Land Executive in Hamburg 1948–76. Member of the Bundestag 1949–68. First ambassador of the BRD to Yugoslavia 1968–9.

The main part of Blachstein's papers, for the years 1936–76, is in the AdsD, Bonn. They include personal documents, correspondence (with, amongst others, Willy Brandt (q.v.), Helmut Schmidt (q.v.) and Herbert Wehner), manuscripts and other material concerning SPD conferences, the SPD Land Organisation for Hamburg, Bundestag elections, SPD factory organisation, cultural policy and the exile. Other Blachstein papers, comprising correspondence and manuscripts for the years 1936–45, are in the Archives and Library of the Swedish Labour Movement, Stockholm. An inventory is available for this collection.

BLAGOEV, Dimitŭr (1856–1924)

Co-founder of the Bulgarian Communist Party.

There are typescript translations of two unpublished books by Blagoev – *Contributions to the History of Socialism in Bulgaria* (1906) and *Memoirs* – in the Hoover Institution, Stanford University, California.

BLANC, Jean Joseph Louis (1813–82)

French journalist, historian, socialist theoretician and politician. Author of *Organisation du Travail* (1840). President of the Commission on Labour under the 1848 Provisional Government. Subsequently in exile in England. Returned to France, 1871. Leading figure, and member of the National Assembly, in the Radical Party.

Various archives have material relating to Blanc. These include the Feltrinelli Institute, Milan, and the Schweizerisches Sozialarchiv in Zürich (see Maitron *op. cit.*). There is also material among the Emile Digeon (q.v.) papers in the Archives Nationales in Paris. The Hoover Institution, Stanford University, California has a microfilm (1 reel) of letters from Garibaldi (q.v.), A. Herzen, W. Mickiewicz and others, 1859–73.

BLANQUI, Louis-Auguste (1805–81)

French communist insurrectionist and theorist. Imprisoned as a leading member of the republican Societé des Amis du Peuple 1832. Came under the influence of Babeuvian communism. One of the two leaders of the Societé des Familles imprisoned for making explosives 1836–7. Helped form the Societé des Saisons 1837. Judged the situation in Paris favourable for insurrection 1839. Defeated after two days fighting. Sentenced to life-imprisonment. In Paris 1848. Founded the Societé republicaine centrale. Sentenced to 10 years imprisonment in 1849. Imprisoned for organising a secret society. His influence resulted in the formation of a Blanquist 'Party'. Launched a daily paper in September 1870 (jailed in December) and continued his attempts at insurrection. Arrested at Bordeaux in March 1871. Elected to the Paris commune while imprisoned. Pardonned in 1879 after a campaign in *L'Égalité*, and his election as Deputy for Bordeaux.

Some 21 bundles (in eight cartons) of Blanqui's philosophical manuscripts are in the Bibliothèque Nationale, Paris. These represent the part of Blanqui's papers that he bequeathed to Ernest Granger (q.v.): unfortunately, the worth of these has been questioned because of possible changes made by Granger. Some of Blanqui's manuscripts are also in the municipal library of Bordeaux, and in private hands.

BLIND, Karl (1826–1907)

German writer and political refugee.

There is some correspondence of Blind's, including letters from Blanc (q.v.), Mazzini (q.v.), etc. in the British Library, London.

BLOS, Wilhelm (1849–1927)

German social democratic politician. Member of the Reichstag 1877–1918. State President of Württemburg, Foreign Minister and member of the Landesversammlung 1918–19. Member of the Reichstag 1921.

Blos's papers were divided after confiscation by the Gestapo in 1934. The first part was returned to the Institut für Sozialforschung, Frankfurt, in 1954, but lately could no longer be located there. The second part, covering the period 1876–1927, was returned to the Deutsches Zentralarchiv, Potsdam, in 1959. (See Mommsen, *op. cit.*)

BLUM, Léon (1872–1950)

French socialist leader and writer. At first lawyer. Activist and delegate to socialist congresses from 1899. Leader of the SFIO after the schism at the Tours Congress (1920). Formed two Popular Front Governments 1936–8. Arrested by the Vichy Government and imprisoned by the Germans. Prime Minister December 1946–January 1947.

Some 145 files of Blum's papers have been deposited by his widow and son in the Fondation Nationale des Sciences Politiques. These concern, in particular, his literary and journalistic activity, the formation of the Popular Front Government, and the Riom trial. An inventory is available.

BLUME, Isabelle (1892–1975)

Belgian socialist politician. Prominent communist in her later years. At first teacher. Active in the Centrale d'Education Ouvrière. In charge of the Belgian Workers' Party's activities amongst women (especially on the suffrage question). Elected Deputy from Brussels in 1936. During the Second World War in London. Expelled from the Socialist Party in 1951 for her differences over international policy. Remained in Parliament as an independent. Stood for Parliament as a candidate of the Belgian Communist Party (PCB) in 1961. Central Committee member of the PCB in 1966.

Blume's extensive papers for the years 1945–51 are in the Institut Emile Vandervelde, Brussels. This important collection is rich in correspondence and other documentation concerning, in particular, the Belgian Socialist Party (PSB), the women's movement, her numerous international contacts, and Belgian society generally during the post-1945 reconstruction years. An exhaustive *Inventaire d'Archives de Fonds Isabelle Blume* has been published by Linda and Robert Flagothier (Brussels, 1980). (This collection does not include material on Blume's expulsion from the PSB in 1951. Material on this question, however, is to be found among the papers of Max Buset (q.v.) also in the Institute.)

BODE, August (b. 1895)

German social democrat. After 1945 Chairman of the SPD's committee on land reform.

The Hauptstaatsarchiv in Düsseldorf has a small holding of Bode's papers for the years 1947–55 concerning land reform. (See Mommsen, *op. cit.*)

BOEKE, Cornelis (Kees) (1884–1966)

Dutch Quaker. Activist in the peace movement.

The IISH, Amsterdam, has Boeke's personal archive and correspondence. An inventory is in preparation. (See M. Campfens, *op. cit.*)

BOEKMAN, Emanuel (1889–1940)

Dutch SDAP activist.

The IISH, Amsterdam, has some of Boekman's files and correspondence (1920–36). An inventory is available. (See M. Campfens, *op. cit.*)

BÖGLER, Franz (1903–76)

German social democratic politician. Member of the Bavarian Landtag 1929–33. Exile. District Chairman of the SPD in Pfalz 1945. Member of the Rhineland-Palatinate Landtag 1947 (after 1962 as an independent). Regional President in Neustadt until 1962.

Bögler's papers for the post-1945 period are in the Landesarchiv, Speyer. These comprise documentation concerning his position in the SPD, as Group-Chairman in the Rhineland-Palatinate Landtag, as a Regional President and as Chairman of the District Conference of the SPD in Neustadt. (See Mommsen, *op. cit.*)

BOHM, Hans (1890–1957)

German trade unionist and social democratic politician. Secretary of the Gesamtverband Deutscher Gewerkschaften 1928–33. Member of the Executive Committee of the DGB in the British Occupation Zone 1949, and in the BRD 1949–56. Member of the Bundestag 1949.

The DGB Archive in Düsseldorf has a number of reference files arising from Bohm's activity on the DGB Executive in the years 1953–4. (See Mommsen, *op. cit.*)

BÖHM, Vilmos (1880–1949)

Hungarian socialist. Leader of the Hungarian Social Democratic Party 1917–18. Minister of Defence in Bela Kun's Soviet Government. Emigré under Horthy. After 1945 Hungarian ambassador to Austria, Czechoslovakia and then Sweden. After 1948 exiled. Died in Sweden.

Seven boxes of Böhm's papers, including letters and annotated books, are in the ARAB, Stockholm. Permission from Böhm's family must be obtained in order to consult this collection.

BOLGANN, Georg (1880–1959)

Danish co-operator. Chairman of the Danish–Russian Association.

One box of Bolgann's papers for the years 1903–50, including letters from Nicholai Petersen and Gerson Trier (q.v.), is in the ABA, Copenhagen.

BÖLL, Winfried (b. 1925)

German social democrat. Active in various official and semi-official organisations concerned with Third World Development.

Böll's papers for the years 1961–79 are in the AdsD, Bonn. These mainly concern Third World Development Agencies and official aid schemes.

BOMHOLT, Julius (1896–1969)

Danish social democratic politician. Minister of Culture.

A large collection of Bomholt's papers is in the State Archive at Esbjerg. A detailed inventory is available. In addition, three boxes of his papers for the years 1950–69 are in the ABA, Copenhagen.

BONGER, Willem A. (1876–1940)

Dutch socialist. Editor, *De Socialistische Gids.*

The IISH, Amsterdam, has a small amount of Bonger's correspondence, 1906–24. (See M. Campfens, *op. cit.*)

BORGBJERG, Frederik (fl. 1920s)

Danish social democratic politician. Editor of *The Social Democrat*. Minister of State for Education.

Borgbjerg's archive consists mainly of state papers in the Rigsarkivet, Copenhagen.

BÖRTH, Friedrich (b. 1914)

German social democrat. Imprisoned 1935–8 for resistance activity, and concentration camp victim 1938–45. Deputy District Mayor of Neuhaus/Elbe in the Soviet Occupation Zone 1945. Party Secretary in different North German SPD organisations 1947–63. District Secretary 1964–78.

Börth's papers for the years 1931–63 are in the AdsD, Bonn. These comprise pamphlets, leaflets, newspapers and 'Tarnschriften' from the anti-Nazi resistance (KPD, SPD and others).

BOSBACH, Wilhelm (1887–1945)

German Christian trade unionist. Trade Union Secretary for the Christlicher Metallarbei-terverband in Bavaria.

Bosbach's papers – comprising his correspondence with, and about, Erzberger in the years 1920–29 – are in the Deutsches Zentralarchiv, Potsdam. (See Mommsen, *op. cit.*)

BOSMAN, Fokke (1893–1971)

Secretary of the Dutch Revolutionary Socialist Party, 1933–5. Chairman of the Plaatselijk Arbeids Secretariaat, Zaanstreek 1934–6 and secretary 1936–40. Previously connected with the Dutch Communist Party.

The IISH, Amsterdam has Bosman's personal and political correspondence, 1935–62, together with a manuscript autobiography, articles (mainly post-1945), leaflets, and newspaper cuttings (1918–53). An inventory is in preparation. (See M. Campfens, *op. cit.*)

BOUCHARDY, Marcel (fl. 1960s–70s)

French trade unionist.

Bouchardy's papers for the years 1967–75 – arising from his position in the departmental organisation of the FO in Savoie – are in the Savoie Departmental Archives.

BOUET, Gabrielle (b. 1885)

Wife of Louis Bouet. Teacher and trade union activist both in association with her husband and in her own right. Signatory of the *Manifeste des instituteurs syndicalistes* 1905 and drew up with Louis Bouet the *Manifeste des instituteurs syndiqués* 1912.

See under BOUET, Louis.

BOUET, Louis (1880–1969)

French revolutionary syndicalist in the Fédération Nationale des Instituteurs (National Federation of Teachers). National Secretary 1919–21. Several times victimised for his activity. Joined the SFIO 1906. During the war opposed the 'union sacrée' in both Party and Union. Elected to the leading body of the PCF in 1921 but resigned in 1922. Expelled from the PCF 1930. Briefly associated with a group of 'democratic communists'.

The archive of Louis and Gabrielle Bouet in the IFHS, Paris, is particularly important for educational trade unionism in the inter-war period.

BOUHEY-ALLEX, Jean-Baptiste (1855–1913)

French militant republican and then pioneer socialist in the Côte-d'Or. Poor peasant. Municipal Councillor 1881 and Mayor in Villers-la-Faye 1884–1904. From 1889 member of the General Council of the Côte-d'Or. Became a socialist. Deputy for Dijon 1902–6 and 1906–13. Especially active on agrarian questions.

The letters and personal papers of Bouhey-Allex are reported to be in the possession of the families of his children. (See Maitron, *op. cit.*)

BOURSON

See under ZÉVAÈS, Alexandre

BOUWMAN, Engelbertus (1882–1955)

Dutch left-wing activist connected with Communist and Revolutionary Socialist Party.

The IISH, Amsterdam, has some of Bouwman's manuscript material. Access is restricted. (See M. Campfens *op. cit.*)

BRACKE-DESROUSSEAUX, Alexandre (1861–1955)

French socialist politician. Classical scholar. Influenced by Marx's *Capital* towards socialism and membership of the POF 1886. Member of the National Council of the POF 1900 and leading figure in the movement towards socialist unity. Member of the CAP and International Secretary of the SFIO. Prominent member of the Second International. Supported the 'union sacrée' 1920. Member of the minority at the Tours Congress 1920. Executive Member of the Labour and Socialist International 1923. Deputy for Paris 1912–24 and for Lille 1928–36.

A collection of Bracke-Desrousseaux's papers was deposited at the IISH, Amsterdam, shortly after his death.

BRANDT, Willy (b. 1913)*

German social democratic politician. Publicist. Member of the SAP 1931. Exiled in Scandinavia from 1933. Clandestine activity in Berlin 1936. Established links between German socialist exile groups. Representative of the SPD Executive in Berlin 1948–9. Berlin representative in the Bundestag 1949–57. Mayor of Berlin 1957–66. SPD Chairman 1963. Vice-Chancellor and Foreign Minister 1966–9. Federal Chancellor 1969–74. President of the Socialist International and of the North-South Commission.

Brandt's papers from 1932 on have been deposited in the AdsD, Bonn. As well as personal papers, these comprise correspondence, notes, manuscripts and collections of material concerning his journalistic activity, exile (1933–46; including the SAP), Berlin (1947–66), the SPD Executive, SPD organisation at every level and Bundestag elections, as well as his activity as Foreign Minister and Chancellor. These papers may be consulted only with Brandt's personal permission.

* Original name, Herbert Frahm.

BRANTING, Anna

Wife of Hjalmar Branting (q.v.). Swedish journalist and writer.

Anna Branting's papers are in the ARAB, Stockholm. An inventory is available.

BRANTING, Georg (1887–1965)

Swedish social democratic politician. Lawyer. Member of Parliament 1931–61. Stood on the left of the SAP. Participated in many political trials both in Sweden and abroad (including the trial of Sacco and Vanzetti in the USA, 1921). Prominent in the international struggle against fascism and for aid to Republican Spain. Son of Hjalmar Branting (q.v.).

A large collection of Georg Branting's papers from the end of the 1890s to 1963 is in the ARAB, Stockholm. This comprises personal documents, correspondence, manuscripts, pamphlets, newspaper cuttings and other printed material, together with other material concerning his political and legal activity. An inventory is available.

BRANTING, Hjalmar (1860–1925)

Pioneer Swedish socialist. Astronomer and journalist. Chairman of the SAP until 1925. Editor-in-Chief of the SAP central organ *Social-Demokraten* (1886–92, 1896–1908 and 1911–17). Member of Parliament 1896–1925. Chairman of the SAP Group 1906–20, 1921 and 1924. Minister of Finance 1917–18. Prime Minister 1920, 1921–3 (also Foreign Minister) and 1924–5. Active in the Second International and the League of Nations. Nobel Peace Prize 1921.

A large collection of Hjalmar Branting's papers for the years 1868–1925 is in the ARAB, Stockholm. This comprises his extensive correspondence (including letters from Bark, Elpidin, Lavrov, Lenin, Vecheslov and Weüdel), as well as notebooks, manuscripts, newspaper cuttings, pamphlets, books and other material concerning his political and journalistic activity. Other papers are in the Riksarchivet, Stockholm.

BRANTING, Lars Gabriel (fl. 1850s–70s)

Father of Hjalmar Branting (q.v.).

Lars Branting's papers, which are mainly of personal interest, are in the ARAB, Stockholm. An inventory is available.

BRANTING-WESTERSTAHL, Sonja (1890–1981)

Swedish social democratic politician. Lawyer. Executive member of the Social Democratic Women's Organisation 1936–52. On the editorial board of *Morgonbris*. Member of Parliament 1948. Active in the international struggle against fascism and for aid to Republican Spain. Daughter of Hjalmar Branting (q.v.).

A large collection of Branting-Westerstahl's papers is in the ARAB, Stockholm. These comprise correspondence, notebooks, manuscripts and printed matter, as well as other material concerning legal and anti-fascist activity. An inventory is available.

BRAUER, Max (1887–1973)

German social democratic politician. Lord Mayor of Altona, member of the Prussian Staatsrat and the German Städtetag 1924–33. After 1933 Professor at Columbia University, New York. Mayor of Hamburg 1946–53 and 1957–60. Member of the Bundestag and the Bundesrat 1961.

The Staatsarchiv in Hamburg has an extensive holding of Brauer's papers, including correspondence 1946–72, speeches and publications 1934–67, together with papers relating to the World Council of Churches and the German Labour Delegation during his exile 1934–46, and his activity in the SPD Executive 1948 and 1953–6, the Deutsche Bühnenverein 1950–72, Bilderberg Conferences 1954–64, the Bundestag 1961–4, and the Study Group Kampf dem Atomtod 1956–65. (See Mommsen, *op. cit.*)

BRAUN, Adolf (1862–1929)

German social democratic politician. At first journalist, writer and editor for socialist newspapers and journals. Functionary in the Nuremberg labour movement 1898. From 1919 to 1920, member of the Weimar National Assembly and from 1920 to 1928 of the Reichstag. Secretary of the SPD Executive.

Adolf Braun's correspondence and papers concerning the Committee on Austrian Party Comrades (1908), and the Workers' and Soldiers' Council in Nuremberg together with material on Austrian tobacco workers and other manuscripts (*Lage der Arbeiterklasse in Deutschland* and *Gewerkschaften*) were returned to the Institute for Social Research in Frankfurt in 1954, but recently could no longer be located. (See Mommsen, *op. cit.*)

BRAUN, Heinrich (1854–1927)

German social scientist. Social democratic politician. From 1888 founder (and, until 1903, editor) of the *Archiv für Soziale Gesetzgebung und Statistik*. Member of the Reichstag 1903–4.

Remnants of Heinrich Braun's papers are in the Leo Baeck Institute, New York, in the holding of Julie Braun-Vogelstein (q.v.), his second wife. In addition, the manuscript *Das Geld bleibt im Lande* (1917) was formerly in the Institute for Social Research, Frankfurt. (See Mommsen, *op. cit.*)

BRAUN, Lily (1865–1916)*

German socialist novelist. Played a leading role in the German women's movement. First wife of Heinrich Braun (q.v.).

Lily Braun's papers are in the Leo Baeck Institute, New York, in the holding of Julie Braun-Vogelstein (q.v.), Heinrich Braun's second wife.

   * née Kretschmann, the widow of Gizycky

BRAUN, Otto (1872–1955)

German social democratic politician. Leader of the agricultural workers' movement. Member of the Prussian Chamber of Deputies 1913. Member of the Weimar National Assembly and then of the Reichstag 1918. Prussian Minister of Agriculture 1918–20. Prussian Ministerpräsident 1920–33. Exile in Switzerland 1933.

There are several important collections of Otto Braun's papers. The Staatsarchiv Preussischer Kulturbesitz, Berlin, has diaries 1914–16; manuscripts of his book *Von Weimar zu Hitler* (1940); minutes of meetings of the Prussian Staatsministerium (Ministry of State) 1912–25; correspondence 1918–55 with, amongst others, Karl Heinrich Becker (q.v.), Otto Boelitz, Bill Drews, Adolf Grimm, Albert Grzesinski (q.v.), Gerhart Hauptmann, Theodor Heuss, Paul von Hindenburg, Wilhelm Hoegner (q.v.), Robert Kempner, Käthe Kollwitz, Heinrich Ritzel (q.v.), Louise Schroeder, Henri Spaak, Gustav Stresemann, Hermann Sudermann, Otto Suhr (q.v.), Hildegard Wegscheider, Herbert Weichmann, Josef Wirth and Theodor Wolff and newspaper cuttings, photographs and honours 1918–53. This holding also has files of the lawyer (and SPD leader) Hugo Maase arising from legal proceedings against Braun and his Königsberg comrades in 1904–5. The IISH, Amsterdam, has the next largest collection. It contains scarcely any personal papers and little from the period 1903 to the November Revolution (25 items) or from the years of exile (18 items). The main part of the material arises from his function as Prussian Minister for Agriculture and Ministerpräsident and includes collections of documents on the Kapp Putsch (March 1920) and on Papen's Staatsstreich in Prussia (July 1932) and ensuing political developments in Prussia and Germany as a whole. There are also a few items concerning his activity as a Reichstag member and as a member of the SPD and Reichsbanner in the Weimar period. In addition, this holding includes some correspondence with other SPD leaders in connection with his official position in Prussia. The AdsD at the Friedrich-Ebert-Stiftung, Bonn, has two smaller collections. First, 50 documents from 1923–7 concerning the illegal activities of Reichswehr groups, self-defence organisations and Major Waldemar Pabst. Secondly (as copies), minutes of meetings of the Kronrat 1906–17 and of the Prussian Staatsministerium 1913–18; notes by Theobald von Bethmann Hollweg on suffrage 1917; domestic politics 1918–33 – dissolution of the Prussian Abgeordnetenhaus (Chamber of Deputies), property of the former monarch, plans of Erich Ludendorff, Reichskonkordat, Help-for-the-East ('Ostilfe'), the Reichsbanner, parties; relations between Prussia and the Reich 1932–3; notes from Braun on 1933; speeches and lectures by Braun; correspondence 1919–32 and 1940–50 together with transcripts of diaries 1916–18. The Deutsches Zentralarchiv, Potsdam has four files concerning personal matters, administrative and constitutional reform, Church agreements and the question of 'greater-Hamburg'. The DGB Archive in Düsseldorf has correspondence concerning reparations and Braun's testament 1953–6. Finally, there is a memorandum and a letter (1943–4) concerning the prospects for post-Second World War reconstruction in Germany in the Hoover Institution, Stanford University, California. (See Mommsen, *op. cit.*)

BRAUN-VOGELSTEIN, Julie (1883–1971)

German writer. Second wife of Heinrich Braun (q.v.).

Braun-Vogelstein's papers are in the Leo Baeck Institute, New York. These comprise not only her own papers (including correspondence, manuscripts and notes), but are supplemented by papers of her husband, Heinrich Braun (q.v.), as well as of his first wife, Lily Braun (q.v.) and their son Otto Braun (q.v.). (See Mommsen, *op. cit.*)

BRAUNTHAL, Julius (1891–1972)

Austrian social democratic leader. Socialist youth leader. Editor of the Warnsdorf *Volksstimme* 1912. Assistant to Julius Deutsch the Secretary of State for Defence 1918–20. Executive member of the Austrian Social Democratic Party. Exile in Belgium 1934, and from 1936 in England. Editor-in-Chief of the monthly *International Socialist Forum* 1914–48. Worked in the Secretariat 1938 and as General Secretary of the Labour and Socialist International 1951–6. Noted historian of the International.

Braunthal's extensive papers are in the IISH, Amsterdam. These include correspondence for the years 1891–1972 as well as manuscripts and other documents. A detailed printed inventory is available.

BREITNER, Hugo (1873–1946)

Austrian socialist. Vienna city senator responsible for finances, 1919–32, the period known as 'Red Vienna'.

His papers were deposited at the WSLA, Vienna, in 1969. The material includes correspondence with Max Adler (q.v.), Dollfuss, Miklas, and Julius Tandler (q.v.) and a collection of (mostly anonymous) protest letters from the years 1921–31. The WSLB, Vienna, has a collection of nineteen letters from the years 1905–46.

BREITSCHEID, Rudolph (1874–1944)

German social democratic politician. Prussian Minister of the Interior. Chairman of the SPD Reichstag group.

Some of Breitscheid's correspondence, notes, financial documents and other material are in the IISH, Amsterdam.

BRESHKO-BRESHKOVSKAÎA, Ekaterina Konstantinovna (1844–1934)

Prominent Russian populist and leader of the Social Revolutionary (SR) Party. At first a supporter of reform, and by 1873 a supporter of Bakunin and the political use of terror. Active in the 'Go-to-the-People' campaign 1874. Arrested and exiled in Siberia (where she served several years hard labour). Permitted to return to European Russia 1896. Resumed revolutionary activity and in 1898 went underground. One of the builders and, in 1901, one of the main leaders in Russia of the SR Party. Helped found the Peasant Union in Saratov 1902. Recruited widely for the Party and its 'terror' organisation. Active in the 1905 Revolution. Arrested and again exiled 1907. Became close friends with Kerensky (q.v.). Leader of the SR Party right wing and uncritical supporter of Kerensky 1917. Worked underground against the Bolsheviks 1918. Left for the USA and eventually went into exile in Czechoslovakia.

Breshko-Breshkovskaîa's papers for the years 1919–31 are in the Hoover Institution, Stanford University, California. In both Russian and English, these include correspondence, biographical data, photographs, and drafts of her book *The Hidden Springs of the Russian Revolution* (1931). In addition, this collection includes a manuscript by Kerensky (with an English translation) about her. A preliminary inventory is available.

BRILL, Louis Hermann (1895–1959)

German social democratic politician. Member of the Thuringian Landtag (USPD; from 1922 SPD) 1919–33. Member of the Reichstag 1932. Thuringian Ministerpräsident and Minister of the Interior 1945 (until Thuringia was given over to the Soviet Occupation Zone). Flight to the West. Secretary of State and head of the Hessian State Chancellory 1946–9. Professor of Law, University of Frankfurt. Member of the Bundestag from 1949 to 1953.

There are two collections of Brill's papers. The considerably larger collection is in the Bundesarchiv, Koblenz. This comprises personal documents; memoranda, reports, preparatory notes, files and correspondence arising out of both his scientific and political activity – especially on the situation in Thuringia, the Conference of Prime Ministers of the Western occupation zones, the establishing of the BRD, the working out of a constitution and administrative reform in Hesse, and activity in the SPD and in the German Council of the European Movement. The smaller collection at the Archiv der sozialen Demokratie at the Friedrich-Ebert-Stiftung, Bonn, stems from the post-1945 period and concerns, amongst other matters, the dispute with the Soviet occupation authorities, the Central Committee (Zentralausschuss) of the SPD in Berlin, the SPD in Thuringia and Hesse, electoral law, land reform, school reform in Hesse, European questions and Brill's activities as a publicist. (See Mommsen, *op. cit.*)

BRINGOLF, Walther (fl. 1930s)

Swiss communist. Attempted to form a Soldiers' Council in the Swiss army. Member of the KPS until the early 1930s. Led a section of the KPS into the Brandlerite KPS (opposition).

Bringolf's papers are in the Staatsarchiv at Schaffhausen Switzerland.

BRION, Hélène (1882–1962)

French militant feminist. Socialist and revolutionary syndicalist. Secretary of the National Federation of Teachers 1914–17. At first supported the war effort, and then a militant pacifist opponent. Arrested in November 1917. Henceforth dedicated to feminism.

Brion's index cards relating to an *Encyclopédie Féministe* are in the IFHS, Paris.

BRIPON

See under ROBIN, Paul.

BRIZON, Pierre (1878–1923)

French socialist politician. At first a teacher but in continual conflict with the authorities over his militant socialist activity. Councillor for the District of Bourbon l'Archambault 1907–13. Mayor of the Commune Franchesse from 1908. Deputy for Moulins (Alliers) 1910. Stood on the left of the SFIO. Prominent anti-militarist. During the war opposed the SFIO's policy of the 'union sacrée' and denounced the war. Participated in the Second International Conference at Kienthal. Collaborated on the organ of the minority, *Le Populaire*. Member of the Committee for the Defence of International Socialism. Launched *La Vague* in January 1918. Beaten at the elections of 1919. Joined the PCF but was expelled in 1922. Worked for socialist-communist unity.

Photocopies of Brizon's papers have been deposited by Mme Rebérioux at the CRHMSS, Paris. These comprise, in particular, Brizon's correspondence before 1914, letters received by him in 1916, and the text of a declaration made in 1916.

BRONSTEIN, Lev Davidovič

This is the original name of Leon Trotsky. See full description under TROTSKY, Leon.

BROUSSE, Paul (1843–1912)

Prominent French anarchist and then leader of reformist socialism in France. At first a doctor. Member of the International 1872. In exile 1872–80. Sided with the anarchists 1873. Prominent in the Fédération Jurassienne. Part of the extreme anarchist tendency at the Conference of the International in 1877. Several times imprisoned and eventually banished from Switzerland. Moved away from anarchism as the Fédération Jurassienne began to crumble. Returned to Paris in 1880. Active in the Parti Ouvrier. Remained with the 'possibilists' 1882. Eponymous leader and theorist of the FTSF (especially after the 'allemanist' schism in 1890). Supported Millerand's (q.v.) entry into Ministerial office. Took his Party into the PSF and into the SFIO in 1905. Proponent of an evolutionary, reformist socialism based on electoral work (especially at municipal level). Consistent opponent of Marxism. Deputy for the Seine 1906–10.

Virtually no letters addressed to Brousse survive. His own letters are widely scattered in Parisian and Italian archives, but notable holdings are in the Nettlau Archive in the IISH, Amsterdam, and the James Guillaume collection in the State Archive, Neuchâtel, as well as in a private collection in Neuchâtel. In addition, private papers of Brousse are still in the possession of his family.

BRÜMMER, Johannes (1886–1966)

German social democratic politician (SPD/USPD). Until 1956 one of the three chairmen of the IG-Metall.

The Stadtarchiv, Mannheim has a small collection of personal papers and others concerning Brümmer's trade union and political activity. (See Mommsen, *op. cit.*)

BRUNELLIÈRE, Charles (1847–1917)

French socialist organiser and propagandist. Member, POF National Council. Active in creation of first peasant unions. Founder of Socialist Federation of Brittany, 1900. General Secretary, 1905. Supported 'union sacrée' during the First World War.

An extensive and important collection of Brunellière's papers is in the IFHS, Paris. The 80 volumes of correspondence, covering the period 1880 to 1917, are particularly valuable for the emergence of peasant unionism in Brittany (See C. L. Willard, *La Correspondence de Charles Brunellière, socialiste nantais, 1880–1917* (Paris: 1968).)

BRÜNEN, Eberhard (1906–80)

German social democratic politician. Turner. Member of the SPD 1928 and of the SAP 1931. Clandestine activity. Imprisoned 1935–45. Secretary of the SPD in Duisburg 1945. Member of the Landtag in North Rhine-Westphalia (eight years) and of the Bundestag 1949–54 and 1961–72. Town Councillor in Duisburg 1946–69.

Brünen's papers for the years 1945–80 are in the AdsD, Bonn. These are mainly comprised of speeches and articles concerning, in particular, reparations, municipal policy in Duisburg, the SPD and Jusos, the relationship between the SPD and KPD, Germany under fascism, rearmament, SPD factory groups, Bundestag and Landtag elections, the Working Group 'Persecuted Social Democrats', factory council elections and right wing extremism. There are only a few documents from the period before 1945.

BRUPBACHER, Fritz (1874–1945)

Swiss anarchist. Doctor. Collaborator on various revolutionary and anarcho-syndicalist papers. Internationalist 1914–18. Joined, but later expelled from, both the SPS and the KPS. Active in the movement to legalise abortion (1920s).

There are two collections of Brupbacher's papers. The first, in the IISH, Amsterdam, comprises a mass of correspondence with his political friends throughout the world, as well as detailed diaries. These are particularly interesting for the period of the First World War and for the years 1922–4 when Brupbacher was in Moscow. The second collection of Brupbacher's papers is in the Schweizerisches Sozialarchiv, Zurich. This is particularly extensive and comprises about 120 volumes of his diary (1896–1944), letters sent (in chronological order, 1893–1944) letters received (alphabetically ordered according to the sender), manuscripts, newspaper articles, biographical material, letters and newspaper articles concerned with sexual questions and abortion, notes on psychology, and files concerning the early history of the KPS.

BRUSEWITZ, Per Emil (1887–1974)

Swedish social democrat. Lawyer. In the Commission for Industrial Democracy 1920–23. Diplomatic service in Petrograd and Moscow 1917–18. From 1936 Chairman of the Social Democratic Association of White Collar Employees.

Seventy boxes of Brusewitz's papers for the years 1917–72 are in the ARAB, Stockholm. These include personal documents, correspondence, manuscripts, transcripts and reports, together with printed and other material concerning his political activity.

BRUSILOV, Aleksei A.

Russian revolutionary.

Some papers (twenty-five items) are held at the Bakhmeteff Archive, Columbia University, New York. They consist of handwritten and carbon copies of Brusilov's memoirs about the Russian revolution and the early years of the Soviet system; letters to his wife from the First World War; and his wife's papers. There are restrictions on the use of the collection.

BUONARROTI, Filippo-Michele (1761–1837)

French communist conspirator and theorist. Took part in the French Revolution. Close to Robespierre. Imprisoned 1795. Met Babeuf (q.v.). Participated in the Babeuvist conspiracy 1796. Arrested and deported. Began to form secret societies dedicated to republican and egalitarian revolution in Europe and aiming at communism, 1802. Inspired the renewal of Babeuvism and influenced many European revolutionaries.

Various papers of Buonarroti from the years 1791–1835 are in the Bibliothèque Nationale, Paris. These comprise correspondence, notes and other items (including some relating to the conspiracy of Babeuf).

BÜRKLI, Karl

Pioneer of the Swiss labour movement. Follower of Fourier (q.v.). Active in promoting the co-operative movement. Member of the IWMA and prominent in the Second International.

Bürkli's papers are understood to have been lost.

BURTSEV, Vladimir L'vovič (1862–1942)

Russian revolutionary. Member of the People's Will Party in 1880s, then associated with the Social Revolutionary Party. Imprisoned in 1885 for his political activity. Went into exile 1886. In Geneva co-editor of the newspaper *Svobodnaia Rossiia* (*Free Russia*). Advocated terrorism. In London in 1891 edited the journal *Narodnovolets* (*Member of the People's Will*). From 1900 Editor of *Byloe* (*Things of the Past*). Noted in this period for his unmasking of Tsarist secret police agents in the Russian revolutionary parties. In Paris in 1911–14 published the newspaper *L'Avenir*. After the October Revolution published an anti-Bolshevik newspaper *Obshchee Delo* (Common Cause), first in Southern Russia and then in exile in Paris. Co-founder of the anti-Bolshevik émigré 'National Committee' in 1921.

There is a collection of Burtsev's papers for the years 1906–35 in the Hoover Institution, Stanford University, California. This comprises one box of correspondence, memoirs, essays, and printed matter, relating to the Menshevik and Social Revolutionary movements before 1917, Evno Azev and other Okhrana agents, and counter-revolutionary movements during the Russian Revolution. There are letters from Burtsev to Leo Bernstein and some letters from General Wrangel.

BUSCH, John (1908–74)

German social democrat. SAJ member in 1924 and SPD member in 1929. From 1945 member of the DAG, Town Councillor in Celle, and official positions in the SPD in Hanover.

Busch's papers for the years 1929–62 are in the AdsD, Bonn. These comprise correspondence concerning the SPD and municipal politics in Celle.

BUSET, Max (1896–1959)

Belgian socialist politician. Enabled by a scholarship from the Centrale d'Éducation Ouvrière (CEO) to study first at the Free University of Brussels and then in 1921 at Ruskin College, Oxford. Teacher at the École Ouvrière Supérieure. Secretary of the CEO 1929. Founded the theoretical journals *Vie Ouvrière* and *Opgang* 1932–59. Member of Parliament for Thuin. Edited the journal *Plan* in the campaign for the Plan du Travail in 1933. Active in support of Republican Spain. As editor of *La Revue Socialiste*, opposed de Man's (q.v.) campaign for Belgian neutrality. Escaped to England in 1940. Broadcast for the Resistance on the BBC. President of the Belgian Workers' Party (BWP) (henceforth the Belgian Socialist Party – BSP) in 1945. Minister of State in 1948.

Buset's papers for the years 1945–59 are in the Institut Emile Vandervelde, Brussels. This collection contains extensive material on all the areas in which he was involved as President of the BWP/BSP and as a politician; not only the internal life and decision-making of the Party but also Belgian and international politics generally. Examples of where the papers offer a particularly rich source include the Belgian socialist trade union and co-operative movement, the dissolution and reconstruction of the international socialist movement, post-war reconstruction in Belgium, international relations and the movement towards European co-operation and unity. A detailed *Inventaire d'Archives du Fonds Max Buset* has been published by Linda and Robert Flagothier (Brussels: 1982).

BUTTINGER, Josef (b. 1906)*

Austrian social democrat. Active for the Exile Organisation of the SPÖ in Paris. Writer. Emigrated to the USA in 1939. Active for the International Rescue Committee. Extensive contacts with German and Austrian exiles.

Buttinger's papers for the years 1933–48 are in the AdsD, Bonn. These comprise correspondence and other material concerning the German-speaking exile. The VGA, Vienna, has a collection of ten folders of his papers, including protocols, material on his conflict with Julius Deutsch (q.v.), 1939–40; material on exile organisations in New York, 1939–42; correspondence with Friedrich Adler (q.v.) 1937–51; correspondence with Hugo Breitner (q.v.), Oskar Pollak (q.v.), and others. There is also a small collection of correspondence at the DÖW, Vienna, which includes an exchange of letters with Julius Deutsch (q.v.).

* Known by the pseudonym Gustav Richter.

CABET, Étienne (1788–1856)

French theorist of Icarian communism. Launched *Le Populaire*, 1833. Published *Voyage en Icarie* (1840) and *Vrai Christianisme suivant Jésus-Christ* (1846). In 1848, founded an Icarian communist colony in Illinois.

There is material on Cabet reported in the Bibliothèque Nationale, the Bibliothèque Historique de la Ville de Paris (BHVP) and IISH, Amsterdam.

CACHIN, Marcel (1869–1958)

Leading French socialist and then communist. At first teacher of philosophy. Active in the POF. Municipal Councillor and Deputy Mayor of Bordeaux (Gironde) 1900–4. Full-time propagandist for the Socialist Party SFIO 1906. Specialist on colonial questions. Editor of the *Populaire du Centre* (socialist daily paper in Limoges) 1908–12. From 1912 Secretary to the Commission administrative permanente (leading body of the SFIO) between Congresses. Editor of *L'Humanité* 1913. Elected Municipal Councillor 1912 and Deputy in Paris 1914–32. Active on behalf of the French war effort. Founding member of the PCF 1920, after the Tours Congress. Member of the Central Committee and Politburo until his death. Member of ECCI 1924. Senator from 1936 until his expulsion in 1940. Imprisoned in 1941, under the Nazi occupation. Member of the Consultative Assembly 1944. Deputy in the First and Second National Constituent Assemblies 1945–6. Deputy in the National Assembly 1946–58. Active until his death.

Cachin's papers are in the Institut Maurice Thorez, Paris.

CALACE, Vincenzo (fl. 1940s)

Italian resistance leader.

Some papers are in the Istituto Nazionale per la Storia del Movimento di Liberazione in Italia in Milan. The papers, 1944–9, include minutes of the 'Giunta esecutiva permanente dell'Italia liberata' and correspondence with politicians from Southern Italy.

CAMET, Camille (fl. 1870s–90s)

French revolutionary. At first weaver. Member of the International 1869. Soldier. Deserted in April 1871 but returned to Lyons during the revolution of April 30–May 1. Renewed exile in Switzerland. Represented the French sections at the Congress of the 'anti-authoritarian' International in September 1872. Returned to lead the International in Lyons. Imprisoned in 1874–9. Later a leading Guesdist in Lyons.

There are three letters written by Camet amongst the papers of Albert Richard, in the Municipal Archive of Lyons.

CAMPOLONGHI, Luigi (fl. 1940s)

Italian socialist and anti-fascist.

Four boxes of Campolonghi's papers are in the Istituto Nazionale per la Storia del Movimento di Liberazione in Italia in Milan. The papers, 1927–58, consist of correspondence with Italian and foreign politicians and documents on the 'Lega italiana dei diritti dell'uomo'.

CANNE MEIJER, Henk (1890–1962)

Dutch communist. Activist in international communist organisations.

A small amount of Canne Meijer's material on various communist organisations, 1917–35, is in the IISH, Amsterdam. An inventory is available. (See M. Campfens, *op. cit.*)

CARLESON, Carl N. (b. 1865)

Swedish socialist and trade unionist. Agitator. Journalist for the social democratic press. Member of the Zimmerwald Commission. Secretary of the Left-Socialist Party 1918–19. Joined the SKP but left in 1923.

One box of Carleson's papers is in the ARAB, Stockholm. An inventory is available.

CARNOT, Lazare (1801–88)

French Saint-Simonist. Publicist and propagandist for Saint-Simonism from *c*. 1827. Sided with Bazard during the schism with Enfantin (q.v.). Thereafter remained interested in socialism but turned towards a political career as a radical republican.

Carnot's papers are in the Archives Nationales, Paris. They include letters received by him, the manuscript of a *Mémorial* on the 1848 Revolution (which he witnessed as Minister of Public Education under the Provisional Government), as well as papers stemming from his later official positions during and after the siege of Paris. In order to consult these papers, written permission is necessary from Mme Ardré Carnot. An inventory is available.

CASATI, Alfredo (fl. 1882–1920)

Italian militant socialist.

The papers covering the period 1882 to 1920 are in the Feltrinelli Institute, Milan. Part of this archive has been published in L. Briguglio, *Il Partito Operaio Italiano e gli anarchici* (Rome: 1969).

CASPARSSON, Ragnar (1893–1978)

Swedish syndicalist and later social democratic trade unionist. At first worker in a rolling mill. Collaborator on the anarchist paper *Brand* and on the *Syndikalisten* 1911–21. Editorial Secretary of the syndicalist paper *Arbetaren* 1922–8. Trade union Editor of the social democratic central organ *Social-Demokraten* 1929–33. Press Officer of the LO 1935–51. President of Västmanland 1952–60.

More than 50 boxes of Casparsson's papers for the years 1917–76 are in the ARAB, Stockholm. These comprise personal documents, correspondence, notebooks, manuscripts and other material arising out of his activity as a publicist. An inventory is available.

CAVALLOTTI, Felice (fl. 1870s)

Italian socialist. Entered Parliament 1873. Soldier under Garibaldi.

A large collection of papers is in the Feltrinelli Institute, Milan. The collection consists of a mass of documentation collected and classified by Cavallotti himself. The first part contains letters by the Cavallotti family, including Gian Domenico, Giacomo and Francesco. Then there are documents relating to Giuseppe and Felice, tracing them from their school days, through the Risorgimento to the death of Giuseppe at Dijon, and the activity of Felice in the Crispi period and beyond. Finally there is a wealth of correspondence with literary and theatrical figures including Guerrazzi, Lodi, Cameroni, Bizzoni and Pareto.

CAZE, Robert (1853–86)

French. During the Commune, private secretary to Paschal Grousset (q.v.) – delegate for external relations. Exile in Switzerland 1872–80. Collaborated on the radical journal *Le Progrès*.

A letter from Caze to Gabriel Deville (q.v.) and V. Marouck survives in the private collection of Maurice Dommanget (q.v.) now in the IFHS, Paris.

CHAMPSEIX, Léodile (1832–1900)*

French revolutionary socialist. Publicist. From *c.* 1868 agitator for women's rights. Activist for the Paris Commune. Exile in Switzerland. Partisan of Bakuninism against Marxism. Lived with Benoît Malon (q.v.) 1872–8.

See under Lucien Descaves.

* Known by the pseudonym André Léo.

CHARLOT, Jean (b. 1901)

French socialist politician. Freemason. Secretary of the Federal Committee of the SFIO in Var 1933. Supporter of *La Bataille Socialiste*. Active in promoting the Popular Front. Member of the Directorate and Political Bureau of the Mouvement de Libération Nationale. Imprisoned in 1944. Deputy in both Constituent Assemblies 1945 and 1946. Deputy for Var 1946–58. Opponent of the EDC 1954. French representative in the Assembly of the ECSC in 1956 of the European Communities. Member of the Directorate of the SFIO Federation in Var 1956–8, for electoral agreements with the PCF and for negotiations with the FLN. Critic of the Government of Guy Mollet (q.v.). Prominent in the SFIO minority who opposed the investiture of de Gaulle. Resigned from the SFIO and joined the Parti Socialiste Autonome, and the PSU in 1960.

Charlot's papers cover only the post-war period. None the less, they provide an extensive documentation of the political life of the SFIO at both national and local levels throughout the period of the Fourth Republic, as well as that of the PSA and PSU in the period 1958–68. In addition to correspondence, private papers and extensive collections of material arising from all aspects of his political activity, this private archive deposited by Charlot in the CRHMSS, Paris, also includes a large quantity of printed documentation. An inventory has been published in the CRHMSS *Bulletin*, no. 5 (1980–81).

CHAUSSE, Emile (1850–1941)

French 'municipal socialist'. Trade unionist from 1868. Founded a section of the International in Saint-Antoine 1870. Active in the rebirth of the labour movement after the Commune. Imprisoned in 1879 for one year, for his activity as director of *Le Prolétaire*. Member of the PO. Followed Allemane into the POSR. Municipal Councillor in Paris 1893–1935.

Chausse did not leave any papers. (See Maitron, *op. cit.*)

CHAUVIN, Georges (1885–1953)

French radical-socialist politician. Eventually Vice-President of the Radical Socialist Party. Local politician in Evreux from 1913. Deputy for Eure 1924–8 and 1932–6. Under Secretary of State for the liberated regions 1925–6. Mayor of Evreux 1936–40 and 1945–7. Suspended for hostility to the Vichy Government 1940. Taken hostage and deported to a concentration camp in Germany 1944. Deputy in the first National Constituent Assembly 1945. Councillor of the Republic 1946–8. Member of the Left Republican group.

A collection of Chauvin's papers for the years 1918–53 has been deposited by his widow in the Departmental Archives of Eure. These concern his activity as Mayor of Evreux, as Deputy for Eure and as Councillor of the Republic. They comprise mainly press cuttings and printed material concerning elections, proceedings of the Assembly and Senate, and the Radical Party.

CHERNOV, Viktor Mikhailoviĉ (1873–1952)

Russian leader and theoretician of the Social Revolutionary (SR) Party. While at Moscow University joined a student group of the People's Will Party in 1892. Arrested in 1894 and in administrative exile in 1895–9. In Western Europe in 1899 promoting his project for the national political organisation of the peasantry. In Paris in 1900 – founder of the Agrarian-Socialist League. Instrumental in 1901–2 in bringing the disparate *émigré* groups into membership of the new SR Party of which he became a leading member. Co-editor of *Revoliutsionnaia Rossiia* (*Revolutionary Russia*) in 1902–5. Leading theorist and representative of the SR party at international congresses. Active in Russia in 1905–7, before being forced back into exile. Associated himself with the 'Internationalist' minority of the SR Party in 1914. Delegate to the Zimmerwald Conference in September 1915. Returned to Russia in April 1917. Vice-President of the Petrograd Soviet. Minister of Agriculture in the Provisional Government in May 1917. Elected President of the Constituent Assembly in January 1918, which, after its dissolution by the Bolsheviks, he attempted to establish as the basis of a 'third force' government in the Volga before its destruction by Admiral Kolchak. Emigrated first to Czechoslovakia in 1920 and then to the USA.

Some of Chernov's material, relating to the activities of the SR Party during the Russian Revolution, is in the Hoover Institution, Stanford University, California. There is also some correspondence, manuscripts and printed material, 1879–1939, at the IISH, Amsterdam.

CHRISTENSEN, Christian (1882–1960)

Danish syndicalist leader. Editor of *Solidaritet* 1910–20.

A small collection of Christensen's papers, including the manuscript of his published memoirs, is to be found in the ABA, Copenhagen.

CHRISTENSEN, Mikkel (1879–1971)

Danish social democrat. Editor. Before 1914 active on the left of the SD youth movement. Later active in Friendly Societies.

Eleven boxes of Christensen's papers for the years 1905–71, including manuscripts on the youth movement, and of his memoirs, are in the ABA, Copenhagen.

CLARIS, Aristide Jean (1843–1916)

French Communard. Republican under the Empire. Collaborated on Blanqui's *Patrie en Danger*. Director of the Office of the Parisian Press under the Commune. Exile in Switzerland 1871–9. Member of the International. Hostile to Marx's influence. Correspondent for the Bulletin of the Bakuninist Fédération Jurassienne. Founding member of the Association Syndicale Professionnelle des Journalistes Républicains in 1881.

Claris's papers are in the IFHS, Paris. These include notes, printed material, pictures and family papers, as well as a biography written by his son. (See Maitron, *op. cit.*)

CLÉMENCE, Adolphe (1838–89)*

French Communard. Book-binder and co-operator. Founding member of the International in France. Elected member of the Commune. Member of the Justice Commission. Voted with the minority against the Committee of Public Safety. From 1871 to 1885 exiled in Switzerland.

Clémence's notebook/diary was confiscated during a search of his previous home in August 1871, and is now in the Archives de la Préfecture de Police, Paris. This important personal record runs continuously from 14 July 1870 to 18 March 1871 (with the exception of 1 January and 1 March for which the pages have been lost).

* Used the pseudonym, Roussel, during his Swiss exile

CLÉMENDOT, Gaston (1868–1952)

French socialist and trade unionist. Secretary of the Federation of Socialist Workers of Yonne 1897–1905. Delegate to the SFIO's National Commission on agrarian questions. Executive member of the National Union of Teachers in the inter-war period.

The unpublished manuscript of Clémendot's *La Fédération des Travailleurs socialistes de l'Yonne* passed into the hands of Maurice Dommanget (q.v.) and is now in the archive of the latter in the IFHS, Paris. In addition, material on educational trade unionism in the years 1860–1955, and socialism in Yonne, is to be found amongst Clémendot's papers in the CRHMSS, Paris. There is a published inventory in the CRHMSS *Bulletin*, no. 3.

* Known by the pseudonyms Dusillon, Duvillage and Fergan

CLÉMENT, Léopold Emile (1826–81)

French Communard. At first shoemaker. Imprisoned 1856–9 and 1862 (briefly) for activity in a secret society and a clandestine print works. Possibly a member of the International. Member of the Paris Commune. Arrested in May 1871 for collaboration with the police under the Empire, then released. In exile in England in 1872. Condemned to death in his absence.

Clément's papers were seized under the Commune and are now in the Archives de la Préfecture de Police, Paris. These include two letters which raised suspicions about the reasons for his release from prison in 1862 (see also Appendix I).

COHEN, Alexander (1864–1961)

Dutch anarchist.

The IISH, Amsterdam has some correspondence and articles (1897–1952). (See M. Campfens *op. cit.*)

COMBAULT, Amédée (1837–84)

French founding member of the International in France. Communard. Jeweller. Freemason. Member of the General Council of the International in London 1866–7. Imprisoned in 1866 and 1879. Member of the Commune. In exile in London 1871–9.

A printed compilation of items confiscated during a search of Combault's home in 1870 is to be found in the Musée Social, Paris. This is under the title of *Association Internationale des Travailleurs* (without date or place) (see also Appendix I).

COMORERA, Joan (fl. 1930s)

Spanish socialist militant. Founder and main leader of the Partit Socialista Unificat de Catalunya (member of the Third International). During the Civil War, minister in the Catalonian Government. Died in prison under Franco.

Joan Comorera's papers are in the Centre D'Estudis Historics Internacionales at the University of Barcelona.

COMPÈRE-MOREL, Constant (1872–1941)

French socialist politician. At first horticulturalist. Member of the POF from 1893. Strict Guesdist. Municipal Councillor 1902 and Mayor of Breteuil-sur-Noye (Oise) 1904. Elected deputy for the d'Uzès Division of Gard by a largely peasant electorate 1909–36. Specialist on peasant matters for the SFIO. Author of theoretical and programmatic works on agrarian problems. Member of the CAP Commission 1914–33. Supported the war effort. Initially opposed participation in Government, but accepted an official post as Commissioner for Agriculture in 1917 (which he held until 1919). Remained with the minority after the Tours Congress (1920). Continued to oppose socialists taking ministerial positions 1924–33, but then supported the group wanting close collaboration with the Radical Party. One of the deputies leaving the SFIO for the Parti socialiste de France (the so-called parti néo-socialiste) in November 1933.

Four boxes of Compère-Morel's papers for the years 1898–1938 are in the CRHMSS, Paris. These include correspondence (1898–1938) as well as files on *L'Encyclopédie Socialiste* (1912), *Raison socialiste* and *Populaire*, and the manuscript of *De ma vie* (27 pages).

CONSIDÉRANT, Prosper Victor (1808–93)

French Fourierist (q.v.) leader and theorist. At first Officer. Editor of *Le Phalanstère* 1832. Popularised but went beyond Fourier's doctrine politically by proposing that the École Sociétaire be complemented with a 'social party'. Launched *Démocratie pacifique* in 1843 as the daily organ of a wider, more militant socialist Fourierism. Member of the Constituent and then Legislative Assembly in 1848. Abjured class struggle and violence. Disappointed by the Assembly's refusal to create a 'Minister of Progress and Experiment' or sponsor the Phalanstère and Proudhon's 'People's Bank'. Exiled in 1849 after the 'July Days'. Experimented 1854–69 with a communitarian agricultural colony in Texas. Returned to Paris in 1869. Joined the International. Supported the Commune.

Various papers of Considérant's are in the Archives Nationales, Paris. These include correspondence, and documents on the École Sociétaire (1792–1899).

CORNELISSEN, Christiaan (1864–1942)

Dutch syndicalist and social scientist. Co-worker with Domela Nieuwenhuis (q.v.) and theorist of the syndicalist Nationaal Arbeids-Secretariaat from its formation in 1893. Founded the *Bulletin international du mouvement syndicaliste* in 1907 but lost influence in the European anarchist movement after he supported the allies in the 1914–18 war.

There is a small collection of Cornelissen's papers in the IISH, Amsterdam. These include a photocopy of the manuscript of his autobiography, and the manuscript of his *Introduction à une Sociologie Générale* (which was completed in 1944 by Mrs Reclus-Cornelissen).

COSTA, Andrea (d. 1910)

Italian socialist and internationalist. Elected to Parliament 1882.

An extensive archive is in the Feltrinelli Institute, Milan, and constitutes an important source for the beginnings of the Italian workers and socialist movement. The collection covers the period 1870–1910, and includes the whole of his political activity. It can be divided into two parts. Part one (1870–82) includes papers from his university days. Of principal interest are police documents on his activities including his arrest, interrogation and trial. It also contains some correspondence with members of the International including Malatesta, Pezzi and Cerretti, and a letter from Garibaldi (1872).

The second part (1882–1910) is notable for about 200 letters, including correspondence with Anna Kuliscioff, F. Turati, C. Prampolini, A. Negri, G. Zirardini, A. Labriola, as well as communications with French Socialist groups. This part also contains many copies of socialist newspapers of the time, documents on Costa's life and a vast collection of photographs.

COSTA, Baptiste Amédée (1828–99)

French socialist and Communard. Teacher and accountant in turn. Corresponded with, and influenced by, Louis Blanc (q.v.). Served in the National Guard and in the Ministry of Education under the Commune. Narrowly avoided execution in 1871. Sent back to Corsica. Became Mayor of Cognocoli. Supporter of Guesde (q.v.) and the POF towards the end of his life.

Several of Baptiste Costa's unpublished manuscripts – including a study of Louis Blanc and his unfinished memoirs from the Commune – remain in the family archive. Of these, *Souvenirs de la Commune* has been deposited at the IFHS in Paris by his grandson.

COSTA, Louis Étienne (1863–1943)

French pioneer of socialism and communism in Corsica. Freemason. Founded a socialist group in Pila Canale in 1898. General Secretary of the Socialist Federation of Corsica 1903. Sympathetic to anarchism. Municipal Councillor and then Mayor of Cognocoli (1919). Secretary of the Communist Party in Corsica 1920–36.

Louis Costa's papers, including a considerable quantity of correspondence, are in the Costa family archive.

COUDON, Henri

See under MÉRIC, Victor

COURMEAUX, Théodor Eugène (1817–1902)

French socialist. From *c.* 1845 follower of Fourier (q.v.) and propagandist of his doctrines in Rheims. Democratic socialist. In exile 1851–60. Elected as a 'socialist' in the municipal elections in Rheims in April 1871. Deputy for the Marne 1881–5. Re-elected as a 'radical-socialist' in 1893. Helped bring about an alliance of socialists and radicals in Rheims in 1900–1.

Personal notes revealing the political thought of Courmeaux are in the municipal library of Rheims.

COURNET, Frédéric (1839–85)

French Communard. Journalist. Elected Deputy for the Seine to the National Assembly in February 1871. Elected to the Commune. Member of the Commission for General Security.

Voted for the Committee of Public Safety. Exiled in London 1871–80. Member of the General Council of the International. Disagreed with the transfer of the General Council to New York. Blanquist (q.v.) from *c.* 1872. Founder member of the Comité révolutionnaire central in 1881.

A file in the Archives de la Préfecture de Police, Paris, contains photographs and a photocopy of one of Cournet's letters (see also Appendix I).

CRAMER, Charles G. (1879–1976)

Dutch SDAP member and Christian Socialist. Active for the party in Indonesia and involved in fund-raising. Member of the States General 1923–37.

The IISH, Amsterdam, has Cramer's manuscript memoirs together with other documentation, newspaper cuttings and reports from Indonesian Social Democrats to the SDAP (1904–52). (See M. Campfens, *op. cit.*)

CRISPIEN, Artur (1875–1946)

German social democratic politician. Member of the USPD from 1917. One of the Chairmen of the 'reunited' SPD 1922–33. Member of the Reichstag and on the Executive of the SPD group. From 1933 exiled in Switzerland.

The AdsD at the Friedrich-Ebert-Stiftung, Bonn, has the manuscript of Crispien's memoirs (written after 1933): *Ein Proletarierleben für das Proletariat.* (See Mommsen, *op. cit.*)

CRONER, Nelly (1894–1978)

German anti-Nazi émigré. Participated in founding the first school pupils' organisation in Germany. Chairwoman of the Freie Studentenschaft (a revolutionary-pacifist student organisation) during the 1914–18 war. From November 1918 in the Press Commission of the Bavarian Provisional Government. From 1933 exiled in Spain, Prague and, finally, Sweden.

A small collection of Croner's papers for the years up to 1965, including personal documents, manuscripts (including a dissertation) and newspaper cuttings, is in the ARAB, Stockholm. An inventory is available.

DAKRENDORF, Gustav (1901–54)

German co-operative leader and social democratic politician. Chairman of the *Grosseinkaufgesellschaft deutscher Konsumgesellschaften* and of the *Zentralverband deutscher Konsumgesellschaften.* Member of the Hamburg Bürgerschaft and of the Reichstag.

Gustav Dakrendorf's papers are still reported to be with the family. (See Mommsen, *op. cit.*)

DALADIER, Edouard (1884–1970)

Leading French radical politician. Radical deputy for Vaucluse 1919–40 and 1946–58. Held Cabinet rank from 1924 onwards. Prime Minister in 1934. Proponent of co-operation with socialists. Decisive role in the formation of the Popular Front. Support in the Radical Party confirmed by his election as head of its Executive Committee in January 1936. Minister of War under Léon Blum. Prime Minister after the final fall of Blum's Popular Front Government (April 1938). Resigned March 1940 (but remained Minister of Defence at the insistence of the radicals until May 1940, and Foreign Minister from May/June 1940). After the Armistice placed under surveillance and then imprisoned. Deported to Germany in 1943. Member of the Second Constituent Assembly in May 1946. Opposed 1946 Constitution but failed to persuade the Radical Party to abstain from government office. President of the Radical Party in the National Assembly in 1956, but lost his seat in the elections of November 1958.

There are two holdings of Daladier's papers. The first is in 82 boxes deposited by his widow and son at the Fondation Nationale des Sciences Politiques, Paris. These papers concern the activities of Daladier in the years 1919–58 and, in particular, problems of preparing for war and the responsibility of defeat in the years 1938–40. An inventory is available. The second comprises five boxes of photocopied papers recovered from Germany after the Second World War and now in the Archives du Ministère des Affaires Étrangères, Paris. These concern political and military problems in relation to the origins of the Second World War and the war itself (July 1936–June 1940). An inventory is available.

DALSTRÖM, Kata (1858–1923)

Swedish socialist pioneer. First great female socialist agitator. From 1894 member of the SAP and member of the Committee for Agitation amongst Women 1897–1902. Member of the Party Executive 1900–5. Collaborator from 1908 on the paper of the youth organisation and of the party opposition *Stormklockan*. Member from 1917 of the Left-Socialist Party and then of the SKP. Active in educational work.

Sixteen boxes of Dalström's papers are in the ARAB, Stockholm. These comprise personal documents, correspondence, manuscripts, pamphlets, newspaper cuttings, printed and other material concerned with her political activity. An inventory is available.

DAMME, Bernard (1864–1953)

Member of the Dutch Independent Socialist Party.

The IISH, Amsterdam, has a small manuscript. (See M. Campfens, *op. cit.*)

DAN, Fedor Il'ič (1871–1947)*

Russian Menshevik leader. Doctor. Helped form the Union of Struggle for the Liberation of the Working Class in 1895. Arrested and exiled to Vyatka Province in 1896. Emigrated abroad in 1900. Joined the Menshevik faction in 1903. Returned to Russia in 1905. Co-editor of *Nachalo* and leading Menshevik. Exiled in Western Europe 1907–14. Co-editor and political inspirator of the Paris Menshevik journal *Golos Sotsial demokrata*. Menshevik leader and Presidium member of the Petrograd Soviet 1917. Supporter of the socialist alliance with the Constitutional Democrats and of offensive military action in June 1917. After the Kornilov revolt critic of the Kerensky (q.v.) Government. Opponent of the October Revolution, but refused to support those who advocated armed struggle against the Soviet regime. Worked as a doctor in 1919. Exiled from the RSFSR in 1922. Member of the 'Two-and-a-half International'. Editor of the Menshevik émigré journal *Sotsialisticheskii Vestnik* (*Socialist Herald*); helped organise the reunited Labour and Socialist International. Continued to accept that the Soviet regime represented a force for socialism; propagated a synthesis between Socialism and Communism.

A collection of Dan's papers, including correspondence and a number of manuscripts of his publications is in the IISH, Amsterdam. In addition, this collection includes papers from his wife, Lidiia Dan. An inventory is available.

  * Known by the pseudonym Gurvich

DAN, Lidiia Osipovna (1878–1963)

Russian Menshevik. Wife of Fedor Il'ič Dan (q.v.). Arrested in 1899. Exiled in 1901. Worked for the Editorial Board of *Iskra*. Returned to Moscow for Party work in 1901. Arrested in 1902, but escaped in 1904 and returned to exile. Returned to Russia in 1905. In Paris 1907–11 with her husband, then returned to St Petersburg. Followed her husband into renewed exile in Siberia in 1914. Lived in Moscow and St Petersburg 1917. Exiled from the RSFSR in 1921. In Berlin 1922–33, in Paris 1933–40 and from 1940 in New York. Representative of the Russian Social Democratic Party at the Socialist Women's International.

See above, under DAN, Fedor

DANIELSSON, Axel (1863–99)

Pioneer Swedish socialist. Journalist. Member of the first leadership of the SAP. Leader of the Labour movement in the south. Founder and editor 1887 of the Party paper in Malmö *Arbetet*. Author, 1897, of the first programme of the SAP.

A small collection of Danielsson's papers for the years 1862–1915 is in the ARAB, Stockholm. This includes correspondence, manuscripts, notebooks and newspaper cuttings. An inventory is available.

DANNEBERG, Robert (1885–1942)

Austrian social democratic leader. Died in concentration camp during the Nazi occupation.

A small collection of Danneberg's papers is in the IISH, Amsterdam. This comprises mainly his prison correspondence from both 1934–8 and the period after 1938, as well as material concerning the Youth Section of the Social Democratic Party of Austria before 1914. In addition, the WSLB, Vienna, has a collection of correspondence from 1925 and 1933.

DARNAUD, Emile (1826–1914)

French anarchist sympathiser. Soldier. Mayor of Roquefixade 1881–6 and 1896–1912.

There are 11 letters in the Grave (q.v.) papers in the IFHS, Paris.

DASS, Herbert (fl. 1920s–40s)

German social democrat. Glassblower. Executive member of the Arbeiter-Turn-und-Sportbund (ATUS) and President of the Sozialistische Arbeitersportinternationale (SASI) 1925–33. Contact with the SOPADE during the Nazi period. Active in the reconstruction of the SPD in Leipzig, 1945–6. Flight to West Berlin, 1948.

Dass's collection of material concerning the ATUS is in the AdsD, Bonn.

DAUMAL, Léon (d. 1941)

French socialist militant. Active in the Ardennes. Teacher.

Two manuscripts of Daumal's – a *Livret d'éducation pacifique* and a novel *La Vengeance du Père Béchu* – are in the Archives of the Socialist Federation of the Ardennes. (See Maitron, *op. cit.*)

DAVID, Eduard Heinrich (1863–1930)

German social democratic politician. Leading opponent in 1890 of the SPD's agrarian policy (important 'revisionist' attack on Kautsky (q.v.), its 'orthodox' proponent). President of the Weimar National Assembly. Minister of the Interior. Member of the Hessian Landtag and of the Reichstag.

David's papers were lost during the Second World War, with the exception of his diaries March 1914–March 1919 and 1922 in the Bundesarchiv, Koblenz. (See Mommsen, *op. cit.*)

DE ANDRES, Jesus Louzara (1883–1973)*

Spanish anarchist.

The IISH, Amsterdam, has a small collection containing De Andres's personal documents and printed material, mainly from the period 1912–33, but also from 1952.

* Known by the pseudonym R. Lone.

DEBOCK, Louis (b. 1822)

One of the first members of the International in France. French Communard. Member of the first Parisian Bureau of the International January 1865–October 1866. Editor of *Tribune ouvrière* (June–July 1865). Took over the direction of the Imprimerie nationale in March 1871 in the name of the Central Committee of the Paris Commune (helped prevent the destruction of this as well as the Archives Nationales). Exiled in Brussels 1871–9.

Numerous letters addressed to Debock in his capacity as Director of the Imprimerie nationale are in the Bibliothèque Historique de la Ville de Paris (BHVP).

DEBUCHY, Desiré Pierre François (b. 1826)

French pioneer trade unionist. At first apprentice-butcher. Self-educated. Socialist and active republican. President of the first trade union organisation in Roubaix October 1848. Several times arrested. Went into exile in London 1851 and finally settled in New York.

Two of Debuchy's letters are in the Departmental Archive Nord – to the Prefect, 8 January 1849, and to the Mayor of Croix, 20 September 1849.

DECOOPMAN, Jules (1866–1935)

French Catholic trade unionist (active in Tourcoing).

Notes made by Decoopman are in the possession of his son, Canon Decoopman. (See Maitron, *op. cit.*)

DECOSTÈRE, Léon (1871–1950)

French militant trade unionist. From 1908, Secretary of the Metal Workers' Federation of the CGT in Tourcoing. Secretary, 1928–35, of the CGT in the Department Nord. Active in the strikes of 1912 and 1920–21. Member of the SFIO from 1919.

Decostère's papers are in the possession of his daughter Mme Lagache-Decostère in Tourcoing. (See Maitron, *op. cit.*)

DEFUISSEAUX, Alfred (1843–1901)

Pioneer Belgian socialist. Lawyer (active in workers' compensation cases). Founder of the first socialist party organisation in Wallonia. One of the leaders of the suffrage movement. Influential among the miners of the Walloon Province of Hainaut. In 1887 instrumental in promoting a general strike amongst miners for universal suffrage. Arrested 1894 but released upon his election to Parliament. Expelled by the General Council of the Belgian Workers' Party. Replied by founding the Republican Socialist Party.

Defuisseaux's papers are in the archive of the University of Brussels.

DEHNKAMP, Willy (b. 1903)

German social democratic politician. Engineering worker. SPD Secretary 1928–33 in the Bremen sub-district Vegesack-Blumenthal-Osterholz. Municipal councillor and active in the Reichsbanner. Three years in concentration camp for resistance activities. Prisoner of war in Russia (until 1948). Senator for Education in Bremen 1951–65. President of the Senate and Mayor of Bremen 1965–7. Publications on cultural, school and education policy.

A small collection of Dehnkamp's papers for the years 1919–54 are in the AdsD, Bonn. This includes pamphlets for social democratic voters in the Weimar period, Young Socialist circular letters in Hannover-Bonn (1949–50), and leaflets (1919–54).

DEIST, Heinrich (1902–64)

German social democratic politician. From 1953 member of the Bundestag. Vice-Chairman of the SPD group. After 1958 member of the European Parliament. From 1958 member of the SPD Präsidium. An economics expert with decisive influence on the economic policy of the Godesberg Programme (1959).

The AdsD at the Friedrich-Ebert-Stiftung, Bonn has an extensive collection of Deist's papers. The material includes reference files 1953–64 – speeches on economic policy, articles, interviews and correspondence, especially on the SPD's basic programme, energy and property policy, as well as co-determination, European unity, Bundestag elections, and matters relating to the Volkswagen works. In addition there are records and material concerning the talks on reorganising the Iron and Steel industry (decartelisation), 1946–7. (See Mommsen, *op. cit.*)

DEKANOZICHUILI, Georgei (1867–1910)

Georgian socialist.

Two cartons of Dekanozichuili's papers, including his diary and correspondence after 1888, are in the Archives Nationales, Paris.

DELAW, George (1871–1938)

French contributor to *Les Temps Nouveaux*.

There are 11 letters written by him in the Grave papers (q.v.)

DELERY

French educational trade unionist.

Delery's papers are in the CRHMSS, Paris, and constitute an especially complete collection of material on the Syndicat national confédéré des Professeurs adjoints-répétiteurs et répétitrices in the years 1934–5. There is a published inventory in the CRHMSS *Bulletin*, no. 3.

DELESALLE, Paul (1870–1948)

French anarchist and revolutionary syndicalist. After 1877, assistant to Jean Grave (q.v.). Deputy Secretary, CGT. Active propagandist through *Temps Nouveaux* and *Voix du Peuple*. After 1908, pursued his propaganda through publishing.

The IFHS has letters and correspondence, particularly covering the period 1904 to 1916. The material is particularly relevant to syndicalism and anarcho-syndicalism in this period (see also Jean Maitron, *Le Syndicalisme révolutionnaire, Paul Delesalle* (Paris: 1952)).

DELESCLUZE, Charles

See DELESCLUZE, Henri

DELESCLUZE, Henri (1819–79)

French. Took part in the Revolution of 1848. Involved 1850 in a conspiracy of the Nouvelle Montagne. Arrested, imprisoned, and then banished. From 1854 in America. Later a member of the International. Returned to Paris to die.

Delescluze's papers are in the Archives Nationales, Paris. These comprise letters received by Delescluze in the years 1841–79, letters written to his elder brother (Charles Delescluze, one of the most important leaders of the Paris Commune), as well as his note-books from prison and exile.

DELHAAS, Stephanus H. (b. 1891)

Member of the Dutch Independent Socialist Party and the Revolutionary Socialist Party.

The IISH, Amsterdam, has a small collection of Delhaas's papers which includes letters and newspaper cuttings and covers the period 1917 to 1934. (See M. Campfens, *op. cit.*)

DENIS, Hector Achille (1842–1913)

Pioneer Belgian socialist. Professor of Sociology and Statistics at the University of Brussels. Socialist theoretician – influenced by Proudhon (q.v.). One of the first group of socialist Members of Parliament. Active in promoting the reform of family law and the extension of public services.

There is some of Denis's correspondence in the IISH, Amsterdam. This comprises letters from prominent Belgian and international socialists, artists and scholars. In addition there are miscellaneous letters (1845–1919) probably forming part of a collection of letters from 'well-known' Belgian and French persons.

DESCAVES, Lucien (1861–1949)

French libertarian socialist and writer. Author of works on the Paris Commune, anarchist colonies and Russian nihilism. Wrote for *Temps Nouveaux*.

Along with Descaves's papers, the IISH, Amsterdam, has his important collection of material on the Paris Commune. His papers include letters from Charles Daudet, James Guillaume (q.v.), Peter Kropotkin (q.v.), Maxime Lisbonne (q.v.), Elisée Reclus (q.v.), Paul Reclus, and others, as well as a collection of newspaper cuttings.

DESCHAMPS, Charles Frédéric (1809–75)

French democratic socialist. Property owner and lawyer. Commissioner of the Provisional Government in Rouen 1848. Popular amongst the workers whose interests he defended. In April 1848 his defeat at the Constituent Assembly elections caused widespread rioting which marked the end of his political career.

Deschamps's papers are in the Departmental Archive of Seine-Maritime. These comprise a file of 121 items (under the heading of Fabrique, Ouvriers) and include copies of his political and social platform with thousands of signatures collected by workers organising support for him.

DESLINIÈRES, Lucien (1857–1937)

French socialist and publicist. At first a republican anti-socialist, but *c.* 1891 joined the PO. Prominent in the POF. Founded *Le Socialiste des Pyrénées-Orientales* in 1902 and from 1910 Secretary of the SFIO in this Department. Proponent of experimental communist colonies supported by the state. Although an anti-Marxist and critic of Bolshevism, his enthusiasm for socialist construction took him to Soviet Russia where he occupied a minor post (1920).

A collection of *c.* 65 letters written to Deslinières is in the IISH, Amsterdam.

DESTRÉE, Jules (1863–1936)

Belgian socialist. Member of Parliament and Cabinet Minister.

The Archives Générales du Royaume, Brussels, has some of Destrée's private papers concerning his period as Minister of Education, 1919–24. Permission is needed for certain dossiers. The Archief en Museum voor het Vlaamse Cultuurleven, Antwerp, has a collection (D.358) which includes letters and documents. The extent of the collection is not known. Permission is needed for consultation.

DEUTSCH, Julius (1884–1968)

Austrian social democrat. War Minister, 1918–20; leader of the *Republikanischer Schutzbund*; General in the Spanish Civil War; member of the Austrian parliament, 1919–34; co-founder of ALÖS with Otto Bauer.

The Institute of Contemporary History, Vienna, has three files of papers from the years 1942 to 1945, including press cuttings, manuscripts of speeches, press releases and copies of correspondence. The DÖW, Vienna, has a collection of correspondence, including letters relating to ALÖS. The War Archive, Vienna, has two boxes of material relating to Deutsch.

DEUTSCHER, Isaac (1907–67)

Polish communist. Historian and journalist. From 1926 member of the Polish Communist Party. Leader and spokesman of the anti-Stalinists. Expelled in 1932. Leading member of the Polish Left Opposition. From 1939 exiled in London. On the staff of *The Economist* and *The Observer*. Leading Marxist historian (especially noted for his biographies of Stalin and Trotsky).

Deutscher's papers are in the IISH, Amsterdam. The collection includes extensive correspondence with many socialist leaders and academics – including Heinrich Brandler, E. H. Carr, Pierre Frank, Daniel Guérin (q.v.), Bertrand Russell and Natalya Sedova-Trotsky (q.v.). There are also numerous manuscripts of Deutscher's works. The collection was acquired in 1977 from his widow.

DEVILLE, Gabriel (1854–1940)

French socialist. Pioneer populariser of Marxist theory in France. Lawyer. Joined the Marxist wing of the International in 1872. Collaborator on *L'Égalité*. Strict Guesdist. Prominent in the POF. Author of a celebrated abridgement of *Das Capital* in 1883. Moved away from the Guesdist interpretation of Marxism. Joined the PSdeF in 1902. Deputy for Paris 1896–8 and 1903–06. Resigned from the Parliamentary group after the formation of the SFIO in 1905. Departed from political life and pursued a diplomatic career in 1907.

Some of Deville's records are in the possession of his family – in particular, Dr Emile Carrère, the nephew, and George Carrère, the great-nephew of Deville. In addition, several interesting but undated letters from Guesde (q.v.), as well as from Friedrich Engels (q.v.) and Dormoy, to Deville, now form part of the Maurice Dommanget (q.v.) archive in the IFHS, Paris.

DEVILLE, Jean-Marie Joseph (1787–1853)

French democratic socialist. Fought under Napoleon. Lawyer. From April 1848 member of the Constituent Assembly and from May 1849 of the Legislative Assembly for the Department Hautes-Pyrénées. Sat with the Montagne and voted consistently with the extreme-left. Participated in the 'June days' 1849. Deported November 1849.

In 1965 Deville's papers were still in the hands of his family in Tarbes. (See Maitron, *op. cit.*)

DIEDERICH, Franz (1865–1921)

Austrian social democrat. Poet. Active in workers' education and social democratic cultural policy.

There is a large collection of Diederich's papers for the years 1885–1921 (and including family papers up to *c.* 1950) in the IISH, Amsterdam. This collection includes letters from personal and literary friends (editors, etc.), personal documents, notebooks, manuscripts of poetic and journalistic work, a collection of his own publications and reviews, etc., collections of material for his publications, and photographs, relating to his work as poet, journalist, lecturer in workers' education on cultural, historical and scientific subjects, and to social democratic cultural policy. An inventory is available. In addition, another part of Diederich's papers – mainly his political correspondence – is still in the possession of his family.

DIEPENHORST, Cornelis A. M. (1895–1969)

Activist in Dutch Labour Party (PvdA), based in The Hague.

His notes and reports, 1947–68, are in the IISH, Amsterdam. (See M. Campfens, *op. cit.*)

DIETZ, Johann (1843–1922)

German pioneer social democrat. Printer and socialist publisher. Member of the Reichstag, 1881–1918.

Some relevant material is in the IISH, Amsterdam.

DIGEON, Emile (1822–94)

French revolutionary socialist. Journalist. Republican. In 1851, deported after the coup d'état. Upon his return collaborated on *La Fraternité* (organ of democratic opinion in Aude). Leader of the insurrectionary 'commune' in Narbonne (Aude) 24–31 March 1871. Arrested but acquitted by a jury. Active social revolutionary until his death.

Digeon's papers (1 carton, 1860–94) are in the Archives Nationales, Paris. They include his correspondence as well as manuscripts of Louis Blanc.

DIJK, Abraham D. van (1901–82)

Dutch. Secretary of the Dutch SDAP in Zuid-Holland.

The IISH, Amsterdam has a small collection of various documents, 1921–77. (See M. Campfens, *op. cit.*)

DIMITROV, Georgi M. (1903–72)

Bulgarian émigré politician. Secretary-General of the International Peasant Union. President of the Bulgarian National Committee.

One box of Dimitrov's papers is in the Hoover Institution, Stanford University, California. These include his memoirs relating to Bulgaria and the Bulgarian Agrarian Union in the inter-war period, world agriculture, and agriculture in the USSR. They may not be quoted, however, without the written permission of their donor, Charles A. Moser. An inventory is available.

DIOUF, Galandou (1875–1941)

Deputy from Senegal to the French Assembly 1934–41. Member of the Independent Left group. Farmer. Mayor of Rufisque, Senegal.

There are three boxes of Diouf's papers for the years 1914–39 in the Archives Nationales, Paris. These comprise files concerning his business as a Deputy, correspondence with the Minister for Colonies and the President of the Council (1934–6), documentation on his Party (known as the 'parti dioufiste'), transcripts of the proceedings of the Conseil Superieur des Colonies (October 1934–May 1935) and the card index of his interventions. An inventory is available.

DIRKSEN*

* Pseudonym of AUERBACH, Walter.

DITTMANN, Wilhelm (1874–1954)

German social democratic politician. At first joiner. From 1899 editor of the *Norddeutsche Volksstimme*. Party Secretary 1904–9. Member of the Reichstag 1912. USPD member of the Council of Peoples' Commissars 1918. After the split in the USPD in 1920 one of the Chairmen of the Socialist minority and pioneer of reunification with the SPD. From 1920 senior member of the SPD Executive and member of the Reichstag. Exile in Switzerland in 1933.

After his return from Switzerland in 1951, Dittman worked in the SPD Archive in Bonn and deposited a part of his papers there. Now at the Friedrich-Ebert-Stiftung, Bonn, this collection comprises: personal papers, notes, speeches and manuscripts; notes from meetings of the SPD Reichstag group during the First World War; reports and photographs from the visit to Moscow of USPD representatives in 1920; numerous documents and letters (including photocopies) 1899–1931 and in the period of exile; printed material 1905–33. There are also papers in the IISH, Amsterdam (correspondence, 1939–47), and the Institute for Marxism-Leninism, Moscow.

DITTMER, Henry (b. 1905)

German social democrat. Printer. Member of the SOPADE Group in Sweden and executive member of the Swedish Group of German Trade Unionists. Honorary Secretary of the Internationale Sozialistischer Alkoholgegner (ISA) 1933–52. Friend of Erich Ollenhauer (q.v.). Remained in Sweden.

Dittmer gave his extensive correspondence with Ollenhauer to the AdsD, Bonn. His own papers from the period since 1933 are in the same place. These comprise correspondence, articles, notes, conference reports and periodicals concerning German exiles in Sweden, the ISA, the Socialist Youth International and the international labour movement generally. In addition, a collection of his newspapers, pamphlets and other printed material for the years 1937–48 is in the Archives and Library of the Swedish Labour Movement, Stockholm. (See Mommsen, *op. cit.*)

DMITRENKO, Petr Petrovič

Russian engineer.

A collection of his papers is at the Bakhmeteff Archive, Columbia University, New York. They include material on elections to the first duma; the mood of railwaymen and the political activities of engineers in 1905 and 1917; international conferences attended by Dmitrenko; and the early history of the Kadet party.

DOBBERT, Alfred (b. 1897)

German trade unionist and social democratic politician and journalist. Member of the Saxon Landtag 1926–30. Member of the Reichstag 1930–33. Jail and concentration camp 1933. Member of the North Rhine-Westphalian Landtag 1946–66. Chief Editor of the *Rhein-Echo* 1946–51.

The AdsD at the Friedrich-Ebert-Stiftung, Bonn, has a small quantity of material (mainly single editions of periodicals) relating to the SPD in Wuppertal in the period after 1946. (See Mommsen, *op. cit.*)

DOBROGEANU-GHEREA, Alexsandru (1879–1937)

Romanian communist leader. Engineer. Joined the Socialist Party of Romania in 1910, and became a leader of the left wing when it changed its name to the Romanian Social Democratic Party in 1918. Delegate to the Second Comintern Congress 1920. Deputy in the Romanian Parliament 1920. Founder member of the Romanian Communist Party 1921, and Central Committee member 1924. Sent to the USSR 1925, and represented the Romanian Party on the ECCI. Member of the CPSU 1927. Returned to Romania for Party work in 1929. Several times imprisoned. Returned to the USSR 1932. Member of the Auditing Commission of the First International Congress of International Organisations to Aid Revolutionary Fighters. Executed in 1937 during the purges. Posthumously rehabilitated.

Dobrogeanu-Gherea's papers are in the IISH, Amsterdam. This collection is, however, closed.

DOEL, Johannes van den (b. 1937)

Member, Dutch Labour Party (PvdA).

The IISH, Amsterdam, has some correspondence and other documents, 1962–76. Access is restricted. (See M. Campfens, *op. cit.*)

DOLLÉANS, Edouard (fl. 1930s)

French historian of the labour movement.

The IFHS, Paris, has his letters from Delesalle (q.v.), Monatte (q.v.) and others (*c.* 1937–8) concerning the *Histoire du mouvement ouvrier*.

DOMELA NIEUWENHUIS, Adriaan J. (1850–1935)

Dutch anarchist. Brother of Ferdinand Domela Nieuwenhuis (q.v.).

The IISH, Amsterdam, has some of Adriaan Domela Nieuwenhuis's articles (1870–1907). (See M. Campfens, *op. cit.*). The Algemeen Rijksarchief, The Hague, has an extensive collection of Domela Nieuwenhuis family papers which cover the eighteenth to the twentieth century. Other family papers can be found in the Rijksarchief in Noord-Brabant, 's Hertogenbosch.

DOMELA NIEUWENHUIS, Ferdinand (1846–1919)

Dutch anarchist and campaigner against militarism.

The IISH, Amsterdam, has a collection of correspondence. An inventory is available (see also the archive of E. Douwes Dekker, also in the Institute). The Algemeen Rijksarchief, The Hague, also has an extensive collection of Domela Nieuwenhuis family papers which cover the eighteenth to the twentieth century. Other family papers can be found in the Rijksarchief in Noord-Brabant, 's Hertogenbosch.

DOMMANGET, Maurice (b. 1888)*

French socialist, trade unionist and free-thinker. At first teacher. Contributor to the socialist press. Historian of socialism and the labour movement. General Secretary of the Fédération unitaire de l'Enseignement 1926–8.

Dommanget donated his enormous archive to the IFHS, Paris. As well as his own papers relating, in particular, to educational trade unionism, Dommanget's archive comprises several collections of personal papers which he collected from other militants.

  * Known by the pseudonyms Jean Prole and Jean Social.

DOPF, Karl (1883–1968)

Austrian social democrat and then anarchist. Functionary of the Social Democratic Party and trade unions in Salzkammergut 1910. After 1912, an anarchist. In Hamburg 1913–47. At first anarchist publicist and then (non-political) writer of popular science. From 1947 once again in Austria.

A large collection of Dopf's manuscripts, diaries 1912–20, correspondence (with, amongst others, social democrats, anarchists, syndicalists and religious-sectarian circles) and a collection of mainly anarchist newspapers, journals, pamphlets, books and leaflets is held by the Ludwig Boltzmann Institut für Geschichte der Arbeiterbewegung at the Hochschule für Sozial- u. Wirtschaftswissenschaften in Linz, Austria.

DRAKE, Heinrich (1881–1970)

German social democratic local politician. Until 1933 Land President of Lippe in Detmold. After 1945 District President of the Government District Detmold. Director of the Landesverband Lippe in Detmold.

The Staatsarchiv, Detmold has a large collection of Drake's papers and other material concerning the Workers' and Soldiers' Council in Detmold 1918, the Landespräsidium of Lippe 1919–33 and 1945–54, his participation in the Zonal Advisory Board 1945–6, negotiations over the incorporation of the Land Lippe into the Land North Rhine-Westphalia or the Land Lower Saxony, and his activity as District President of Detmold 1947–52 as well as on the Landesverband Lippe 1949–53 and 1956–66. (See Mommsen, *op. cit.*)

DRIESTEN, Hendrick Th. van (1911–42)

Dutch revolutionary socialist involved in aid to German and Spanish refugees in the 1930s. Chairman, Dutch Revolutionary Socialist Workers' Party (RSAP).

The IISH, Amsterdam, has a small collection of correspondence, circulars, leaflets and material on various aid committees and youth organisations (1931–9). (See M. Campfens, *op. cit.*)

DRÖSCHER, Wilhelm (1920–77)

German communist and then social democratic politician. From 1946–8 KPD member, then SPD in 1949. Mayor of Kirn-Land 1949–67. From 1956 Chairman of the SPD sub-district Nake-Hunsrück and from 1967 of the SPD district Rhein-Hessen-Nassau. Member of the Landtag in Rhineland-Palatinate 1955–7 and of the Bundestag 1957–71. Treasurer of the SPD 1975. From 1974 President of the Social Democratic Group of parties in the EEC.

A small collection of Dröscher's papers for the years 1971–3 is in the AdsD, Bonn. This comprises correspondence and circular letters of, and concerning, the Hambacher Kreis (an Evangelical Church association) and other church matters. A further deposit of Dröscher's papers is expected.

DROTT, Karl (b. 1906)

German social democratic politician. From 1930 to 1933 Youth and Education Secretary of the SPD in Hesse. From 1946 member of the Landtag in Hesse.

Drott's papers for the years 1946–54 are in the AdsD, Bonn. These comprise correspondence and manuscripts concerning the Bollwerk-Verlag, the Socialist Writers' and Publishers' Group, and political education.

DRUCKER, Wilhelmina E. (1847–1925)

Dutch feminist.

One file of correspondence (1889–90) is in the IISH, Amsterdam. (See M. Campfens, *op. cit.*)

DUBOIS, Daniel (fl. 1950s–70s)

French trade unionist.

His papers concerning trade unionism amongst post, telephone and telegraphic workers in the 1970s are to be found in the IFHS, Paris.

DUBUISSON, Jules (1836–*c.* 1905)

French militant free-thinker and socialist sympathiser in Yonne. Engineer and writer.

Dubuisson's papers are in the Municipal Library of Auxerre. These comprise three large manuscripts drafted in 1881 and reworked in 1902, together with letters, personal notes and comments of a semi-philosophical nature.

DUCLOS, Jean (b. 1850)

French Communard.

See Appendix I.

DUDEVANT, Baroness*

* See under George Sand.

DUGAST-MANTIFEUX, Charles (1812–94)

French historian and philanthropist. Concerned with the development of popular education. In 1848 attempted to create a butchers' co-operative. Opposed the coup d'état.

Dugast-Mantifeux's papers have been placed in Nantes Municipal Library. Apart from a large quantity of historical notes, there is correspondence with such figures as B. Fillon and A. Guépin. A printed inventory is available. (See Maitron, *op. cit.*)

DUMAY, Jean-Baptiste (1841–1926)

French socialist. Organiser of Creusot strike of miners and metalworkers, 1870. In exile, 1871–9. Later active in the FTSF, then in POSR after 1890. Deputy for Belleville, 1889–93. Mayor of Chelles, 1914.

Dumay's unpublished *Mémoires* are cited by Maitron, *op. cit.* (vol. 5).

DUNCKER, Hermann (1874–1960)

German specialist in political education, at first as a functionary of the SPD and then (from its formation) for the KPD. Social scientist.

The Hochschule der Deutschen Gewerkschaften 'Fritz Heckert', Bernau bei Berlin, has Duncker's letters, manuscripts, collections of material, personal papers, family papers, documents, tape-recordings and transcripts of lectures and talks, photographs and library.

DUNE, E.

Russian Red Guard.

The Bakhmeteff Archive has a typescript entitled *Zapiski krasnogvardeitsa*, about his experiences in the Red Guard, 1917–19.

DUNOIS, Amédée Gabriel (1878–1945)*

French socialist (at times a communist), writer and historian. A collaborator on *Les Temps Nouveaux* (1905–6) and later on *La Bataille syndicaliste* (1908–12). Joined SFIO in 1912, collaborating on *L'Humanité*. Founder of PCF after the 1920 Tours Conference of the SFIO. Rejoined SFIO in 1930. Director of its Office of Documentation and Propaganda. Co-director, *Nouvelle Revue Socialiste*. Arrested by Gestapo, 1943. Died in a concentration camp.

Dunois's papers, particularly concerning his work on *La Bataille syndicaliste* are in the IFHS, Paris.

 * Born Cantonné. His pseudonym was Amedune.

DUSILLON*

 * Pseudonym of CLÉMENDOT, Gaston.

DUVILLAGE*

 * Pseudonym of CLÉMENDOT, Gaston.

DUX, Rudolf (1908–79)

German social democrat. Before 1933 SPD District Secretary in Magdeburg and leading member of the Reichsbanner. From 1933 to 1945 active in the clandestine Socialist Front in Hannover-Magdeburg. Imprisoned 1934 and 1937–40 and condemned to service in a penal battalion 1944. SPD Secretary in Magdeburg 1945. From February 1946 in the 'Büro Schumacher'. From 1949 Economics Editor in the Social Democratic Press Service.

Dux's papers are in the AdsD, Bonn. These comprise a small quantity of correspondence, together with a large quantity of notes, statistics, pamphlets and newspaper cuttings concerning reparations, the recovery of the German economy, the Saar question, the Montan-Union, the EEC, and matters associated with his work for the DGB.

DVINOV, Boris L. (1886–1968)

Russian Menshevik. Comrade of Fedor Il'ič Dan (q.v.) in exile.

A small collection of Dvinov's papers for the years 1946–59 is in the IISH, Amsterdam. This includes, in particular, correspondence and minutes of the Russian Social Democratic Party. A provisional inventory is available.

EBE, Einar (b. 1897)

Swedish social democrat. Chief Editor of the FIB (Labour Movement Publishing Organisation). Important figure in the social democratic cultural movement.

Six boxes of Ebe's papers are in the ARAB, Stockholm. A provisional inventory is available.

EBERHARD, Fritz*

* Pseudonym of RAUSCHENPLAT, Helmut von.

EBERT, Friedrich (1871–1925)

President of the Weimar Republic.

His Nachlass, in private hands, was lost during the Second World War. Other papers (two cases) were reported to be in the hands of collector Max Stein (1933), but there was no trace of them in 1952. (See Mommsen, *op. cit.*)

ECKERT, Georg (1912–74)

German social democrat. Contact with Greek anti-fascists while a Wehrmacht officer stationed in Greece. Influence on the cultural policy of the SPD and on the Godesberg Programme. Main activity directed towards the revision of schoolbooks and history teaching (Director of the International Schulbuchinstitut at Braunschweig).

Eckert's papers are in the AdsD, Bonn.

EHMKE, Horst (b. 1927)

German social democratic politician. From 1969 member of the SPD Executive and of the Bundestag. Federal Minister for Research and Technology 1972–4.

Ehmke's extensive papers for the years 1969–79 are in the AdsD, Bonn. These comprise correspondence as well as lectures, speeches and interviews concerning his political and ministerial activity as well as particular questions such as the Ostverträge and the 'Orientierungsrahmen '85'.

EICHLER, Willi (1896–1971)*

German social democratic politician and publicist. Joined SPD in 1923. Organiser (until its dissolution) of the ISK. Exiled in 1933. Publisher and editor of the *Sozialistischer Warte* and of the *Reinhart-Briefe* (for illegal distribution in Germany). In London, Executive member of the Union deutscher sozialistischer Organisationen in Grossbritannien. Returned to Germany in 1945. Subsequently Chief Editor of the *Rheinischer Zeitung* (Cologne). Member of the North Rhine-Westphalian Landtag 1947–9, of the Economic Council in Frankfurt 1948–9 and of the Bundestag 1949–53. Member of the SPD Executive and Chairman of the Party's Cultural Committee 1946–68. Leading influence in the formulation of the Godesberg Programme (Chairman of the drafting committee). Author of numerous works and publisher of the journal *Geist und Tat*.

The AdsD at the Friedrich-Ebert-Stiftung, Bonn, has a large collection of correspondence, material arising out of his activity as a publicist, notes, and collections of material dating from the mid-1950s. The latter concern Church and social questions, international politics (development aid and the EEC), property, co-determination, legal questions, education and university organisation, student organisations, social theories, Marxism, communism, German history, history of social democracy (and its programme)). In addition there is general correspondence, manuscripts, etc. from 1967, relating to *Geist und Tat*. (See Mommsen, *op. cit.*)

* Known by the pseudonym Martin Hart.

EILERS, Elfriede (b. 1921)

German social democratic politician. Social worker. From 1966 Executive member of the SPD. Chairwoman of the SPD Working Group for Women 1973–7. Member of the Bundestag 1957–80.

Eilers's correspondence arising from her political work in the years 1969–78 is in the AdsD, Bonn.

EISLER, Elfried (1895–1961)*

Austrian communist. In Germany from 1921. Member of Politburo of KPD and Presidium of Communist International 1924. Member of the Reichstag. Expelled from the KPD in 1927. Exiled in France 1933 and in the USA 1941.

Her papers before 1940 were lost in the course of repeated exile. Those from 1941 are in Harvard University Library, Cambridge, Massachusetts, USA. (See Mommsen, *op. cit.*)

* Known by the pseudonym Ruth Fischer.

EISNER, Kurt (1867–1919)

German social democrat and revolutionary leader. From 1890 editor of various SPD newspapers. After 1917 member of the small Bavarian USPD. In 1918 Chairman of the Workers' and Soldiers' Council in Munich. From 7 November 1918 to his assassination (5 January 1919) Ministerpräsident and Foreign Minister of the independent Bavarian People's State.

There are several collections of Eisner's papers and other material. In 1948 the Hauptstaatsarchiv Munich returned 30 boxes and 3 crates of his literary works to private hands. Relevant official files are also to be found in the holding Staatsministerium des Äusseren of the Bavarian Hauptstaatsarchiv, Munich. The Institut für Sozialforschung, Frankfurt, also has a small collection of newspaper cuttings. Finally, it is thought that the Institut für Marxismus und Leninismus in East Berlin has an important collection of papers (perhaps those returned to private keeping in 1948). (See Mommsen, *op. cit.*)

EJVES, Bror Werner (1897–1962)

Swedish social democrat. Journalist, editor and publisher.

Six boxes of Ejves's papers are in the ARAB, Stockholm. An inventory is available.

EK, Viktor (b. 1890)

Swedish social democrat. Official in the Transport Workers' Union. Secretary of the SAP in Stockholm.

One box of Ek's papers is in the ARAB, Stockholm.

EKENDAL, Sigrid (b. 1904)

Swedish social democrat. Trade unionist and politician. First woman trade union official. After 1945 a leading official in the LO. Especially important in relation to women's questions in the trade union movement. Member of Parliament.

Two boxes of Ekendal's papers are in the ARAB, Stockholm.

ELFVING, Gösta (b. 1908)

Swedish social democrat. Executive member of the SAP. Active in the social democratic Christian and Temperance groups. Landshövding (County Governor).

Elfving's papers are in the ARAB, Stockholm.

ELIASBERG, Georg (1906–72)

Russian-born activist in the German resistance. Imprisoned and then expelled from Germany 1935–40. Close to the Neu Beginnen Group.

Eliasberg's papers from the years 1940–50 are in the AdsD, Bonn. These contain material concerning the German exile in the USA.

ELLENBOGEN, Wilhelm (1863–1951)

Leading Austrian social democrat on the Renner wing of the party. Reichsrat deputy, 1901; entered government as Under Secretary of State for Commerce, 1919–20.

The VGA, Vienna, has twenty files, including manuscripts, memorial speeches, notebooks, printed material, documents relating to the emigration, including the Austrian Labor Committee, based in the United States; and correspondence between 1940 and 1950. Ellenbogen's correspondents included Leichter (q.v.), Pollak (q.v.), Schärf (q.v.) and Renner (q.v.). A further collection of correspondence is at the Vienna City and Province Library (WSLB). In addition, the Arbetarrörelsens Arkiv, Stockholm, has two volumes of letters and two volumes of book registers. The material is not classified.

ELSNER, Willi (1895–1967)

German member of the Hamburg SPD Executive.

The Forschungsstelle für die Geschichte des Nationalsozialismus in Hamburg has papers concerning the SPD (especially the Land organisations in Hamburg and Schleswig-Holstein) 1945–7, the KPD 1943–5, relations between the SPD and KPD and the Sozialistischen Einheitspartei (especially in Hamburg) 1945–8 and the trade unions 1945–7. (See Mommsen, *op. cit.*)

ELTZBACHER, Paul (1868–1928)

German historian and theorist of anarchism.

Part of Eltzbacher's papers are scattered in private possession. However, the IISH, Amsterdam, has his collection of letters from, amongst others, Jean Grave (q.v.), Peter Kropotkin (q.v.), Gustav Landauer (q.v.), Henry Mackay, Max Nettlau (q.v.) and Rudolf Rocker (q.v.). (See Mommsen, *op. cit.*)

ENFANTIN, Prosper (1796–1864)

French follower of Saint-Simon and socialist economist. Transformed Saint-Simonism into a religious sect. Finally businessman and anti-socialist.

Enfantin left his extensive papers to the Bibliothèque de l'Arsenal, Paris, where they form the Saint-Simonist archives. These include correspondence, manuscripts, documents, pamphlets and books. A catalogue is available.

ENGBERG, Arthur (1888–1944)

Swedish social democratic politician. Editor, writer and publicist in the SAP. Minister for Religion. Later Minister of Education.

Three boxes of Engberg's papers, with a provisional inventory, are in the ARAB, Stockholm.

ENGELS, Friedrich (Frederick) (1820–95)

German co-founder of scientific socialism. Life-long friend and comrade of Karl Marx (q.v.).

Freidrich Engels's papers form part of a single collection with those of Marx (q.v.) in the IISH, Amsterdam. There are also a considerable number of letters from Engels amongst the papers of August Bebel (q.v.) at the IISH, Amsterdam. There are copies of letters from Engels to his brother Hermann in the Stadtarchiv, Wuppertal. (See Mommsen, *op. cit.*)

ENGELS, Jacq (1896–1982)

Dutch socialist. Active in SDAP, and later PvdA.

The IISH, Amsterdam, has Jacq Engels's autobiography and some organisational archives (1926–55). An inventory is available. (See M. Campfens, *op. cit.*)

ENGSTRÖMS, Elin (1860–1957)

Swedish pioneer of the social democratic women's and trade union movements in the early twentieth century.

Two boxes of Engströms's papers, with an inventory, are in the ARAB, Stockholm.

ERHART, Franz (1853–1908)

German pioneer socialist and social democratic politician. Secretary of the Communist Workers' Association in London 1878–9. Founder of the Palatinate SPD. Member of the Ludwigshafen City Council 1890, of the Bavarian Landtag 1893–1908, and of the Reichstag 1898–1908.

The Stadtarchiv, Ludwigshafen, has a substantial holding of papers supplemented by collections of printed material and party files. It covers the origin and development of social democracy in the Palatinate 1878–1908 and comprises court records, manuscripts of speeches, accounts, administrative reports of the Palatinate SPD Executive and postal services, membership books of social democratic and workers' groups in Ludwigshafen, newspaper cuttings, books and pamphlets.

ERIKSSON, Bernhard (1878–1952)

Swedish social democratic politician. Leading figure in the SAP (especially in the Palarna local organisation). Naval Minister.

Four boxes of Eriksson's papers are in the ARAB, Stockholm.

ERKELENZ, Anton (1878–1945)

German. Working Secretary of the Hirsch-Duncker Trade Associations 1921–9. First Chairman of the DDP Executive. Member of the National Assembly 1919 and of the Reichstag 1920–30. From 1930 member of the SPD.

The Bundesarchiv, Koblenz, has a collection for the years 1902–35 of Erkelenz's manu-scripts, files, and correspondence concerning his activity as Working Secretary and the politics of the DDP. (See Mommsen, *op. cit.*)

ERLER, Fritz (1913–67)

German social democratic politician. SAJ 1928. SPD 1931. After 1933 illegal activity as a member of the 'Neu-Beginnen' group. Arrested in 1938 and sentenced to concentration camp (escaped April 1945). District President in Bieberach (Württemberg) and then Tuttlingen May 1945–9. Member of the Constituent Assembly of Württemberg. Member of the first Landtag 1947. Member of the Bundestag 1949. Expert on foreign and defence policy. Founder member of the German Council of the European Movement 1949. Member of the Advisory Assembly of the European Council 1950. Voted on to SPD Executive 1956. Vice-Chairman of Bundestag group 1957. Vice-Chairman of SPD 1964, and – as successor to Erich Ollenhauer (q.v.) – Chairman of the Bundestag group. Important influence in bringing the SPD around to a revision of its Heidelberg Basic Programme of 1925 after the second Bundestag election (1953). Supporter of the Grand Coalition.

The AdsD at the Friedrich-Ebert-Stiftung, Bonn, has an extensive collection (including one volume from before 1945) of Erler's personal papers, correspondence and publications, as well as files concerning the SPD's Bundestag group and its Executive, the SPD Executive and Presidium, organisational and electoral matters, as well as his main areas of political interest (including foreign, defence and security policy). (See Mommsen, *op. cit.*)

ESSER, Gerard (1908–83)

Dutch anarchist.

A few documents are in the IISH, Amsterdam. An inventory is available. (See M. Campfens, *op. cit.*)

ESSER, Thomas (1870–1948)

German co-operator and Centre Party (Zentrum) politician. Chairman of the Rhineland Co-operative Association. Member of the Prussian Landtag and of the Reichstag.

The main part of Esser's papers was destroyed in 1944. Those that survive, mainly comprising various political correspondence (including letters from Stegerwald (q.v.)) for the years 1919–32, are in the Bundesarchiv, Koblenz. (See Mommsen, *op. cit.*)

EUDES, Emile (1843–88)

French Blanquist leader. Communard. Collaborator on *La Patrie en danger*. Commander, 20th Legion, National Guard. A leader of the 18 March insurrection. Member of the Executive Commission and Military Commission of the Commune. In exile, 1871 to 1879.

The surviving archive (one large carton) was deposited by his son in the IFHS, Paris. The deposit includes draft copies of his out-letters (see J. Maitron, 'En dépouillant les archives du Général Eudes' in *L'Actualité de l'Histoire*, no. 6 (January 1954)).

FABBRI, Luigi (1877–1935)

Italian anarchist.

A small collection of Fabbri material is in the IISH, Amsterdam. These papers, 1901–28, include correspondence from Malatesta (q.v.) and others. A list is available.

FABRIZI, Nicola (1804–85)

Italian revolutionary and member of parliament.

The Archivio Centrale dello Stato, Rome, has seven boxes of papers covering the period 1847 to Fabrizi's death, supplemented by documents from the years 1885–1910. The collection comprises correspondence relating to his political activity during the risorgimento.

FAGERHOLM, Karl-August (b. 1902)

Finnish social democratic leader. Chairman of the Finnish Hairdressers' Union. Chairman of the Finnish Union of Commercial Workers 1920–23. Editor 1923–34 and Editor-in-Chief 1934–42 of *Arbetarbladet*. Chairman of the Swedish section of the Finnish Social Democratic Party 1934–56. Executive member of the Finnish Social Democratic Party 1944–6 and

1963–9. Member of Parliament 1930–66. Spokesman 1945–7, 1950–6, 1957–8 and 1965–6. Minister of Social Affairs 1937–47 and 1954. Prime Minister 1948–50, 1956–7 and 1958.

Fagerholm has deposited his papers for the years 1917–78 in the Finnish Labour Archives, Helsinki. These comprise correspondence, speeches, lectures and statements, notes from the last period of the war (autumn 1944) and, in particular, material concerning the Ministry of Social Affairs, Fagerholm's governments, and inter-governmental agreements and co-operation between the Nordic countries. This collection is fully catalogued, but may be consulted only with Fagerholm's personal permission.

FAHRENBRACH, Heinrich (1878–1950)

German Christian trade unionist and Zentrum politician. After 1920, Chairman of the Textile Workers' Union. Member of the Reichstag 1928–33.

The DGB Archive, Düsseldorf, has Fahrenbrach's correspondence with Christian trade unionists concerning compensation through the German Labour Front for the years 1933–41. (See Mommsen, *op. cit.*)

FAIVRE, Benoît (1798–1869)

French Saint-Simonist. Early 1830s organiser of the Saint-Simonists in Metz. Later a Christian Socialist.

Faivre's manuscripts are in the archives of the Academy of Metz and in the Departmental Archives of the Moselle. (See Maitron, *op. cit.*, vol. 2)

FAURE, Paul (1878–1960)

French socialist politician. Active in the POF from 1901. Municipal councillor 1903. Mayor of Grignols 1904. During the First World War stood for peace and renewal of relations between the parties of the International, and later for the 'reconstruction' of a new International including the Bolsheviks. Opponent of affiliation to the Third International. After the Tours Conference (1920) General Secretary of the SFIO (until 1949). Together with Léon Blum (q.v.) defended the SFIO's 'neo-guesdism' against opposition from both right and left. Mayor of Le Creusot 1924. Deputy for Saône-et-Loire 1924–32 and 1938–42. Active for disarmament. In spite of misgivings, one of the SFIO representatives on the committee negotiating the Popular Front. Minister of State under Blum and Chautemps June 1936–January 1938 and March–April 1938 (responsible for liaison between the Government and the SFIO and the nationalisation of the war industries). Stood for relaunching the Popular Front on a programme of structural reform and extensive nationalisation. Differences with Blum over foreign policy (recommended negotiations with Hitler and caution in relation to Franco-Russian alliance) and opposed Blum's policy of a National Government. Defeated at the SFIO Congress December 1938, but arrived at a compromise with Blum at the May 1939 Congress.

A part of Faure's private papers are to be found in the OURS, Paris. This comprises, in particular, his correspondence in the years 1929–35 and 1940–44.

FECHENBACH, Felix (1894–1933)

German social democratic activist and journalist. As member of the USPD, personal secretary to Kurt Eisner (q.v.). Sentenced to 10 years' imprisonment in 1922 (later reduced to three and a half years) for high treason. Active as writer in Berlin and Editor of SPD organ in Detmold from 1930. Arrested and murdered by the SA in 1933.

Fechenbach's papers survive at the AdsD at the Friedrich-Ebert-Stiftung, Bonn. They include letters from the period before 1933 (including some written after arrest and whilst imprisoned), personal papers, material arising from his activity in the Youth Section of the Munich SPD 1914–16, documentation for his work *Der Revolutionär Kurt Eisner*, handwritten manuscripts of his book *Im Haus der Freudlosen* together with a number of anecdotes, children's stories and political pieces.

FEDELI, Ugo*

 * Pseudonym of TRENI, Ugo.

FELDER, Josef (b. 1900)

German social democratic politician and journalist. Editor of the *Schwäbische Volkszeitung* (Augsburg) 1924–33. City Councillor in Augsburg 1930–33. Member of the Reichstag 1932–3. Concentration camp Dachau 1933–6. Chief Editor of the *Südostkurier* (Bad Reichenhall) 1946–54 (when it ceased publication). Chief Editor of *Vorwärts*. Member of the Bundestag 1957–69.

A small collection of Felder's papers for the years 1932–68 is in the AdsD, Bonn. These include material concerning the reorganisation of *Vorwärts* (1954–5), and material arising from his activity as a Bundestag Deputy.

FERGAN*

 * Pseudonym of CLÉMENDOT, Gaston.

FERRER, Francisco (1859–1909)

Spanish anarchist who repudiated violence. Educational reformer and founder of the Free School Movement. Involved in a republican rising in 1886. In exile in Paris 1886–1901. Returned to establish a 'Modern School' in Barcelona 1901. Became well known for his ideas on education. Arrested in 1906 and acquitted after a year's imprisonment. Judicially framed and murdered in 1909.

Six letters written by Ferrer are in the IISH, Amsterdam.

FIMMEN, Edo (1881–1942)

German international trade union leader. Secretary of the International Federation of Trade Unions. General Secretary of the International Transport Workers' Federation.

Fimmen's papers for the years 1923–37 are in the Bundesarchiv, Koblenz. These include notes and correspondence relating to the International Transport Workers' Federation.

FISCHER, Edmund (1864–1925)

German writer and social democratic politician. Director of the Saxon Land Agency for Public Utilities in Dresden. Member of the Reichstag.

Papers for the years 1907–22 are held at the Deutsches Zentralarchiv in Potsdam. (See Mommsen, *op. cit.*)

FISCHER, Ernst (fl. 1940s)

Austrian communist.

Thirty-six files containing his papers are at the Institute of Contemporary History, Vienna. The collection includes personal documents; manuscripts; reports and correspondence of the KPÖ; a file of material from Moscow, 1943–5; and speeches and essays, 1945–53.

FISCHER, Hermann (1895–1967)

German social democratic exile. Instrument worker. Before 1933 trade union and Reichs-banner official in Coburg. Exile in Czechoslovakia, Norway (1939) and Sweden (1940). Leader of the SPD group in Lottefors.

Fischer's papers for the years 1940–7 are in the AdsD, Bonn. These comprise mainly correspondence with German exiles (SOPADE and trade union) and concern the political and personal problems of exile, as well as wider questions such as the reconstruction of a socialist party in Germany.

FISCHER, Ruth*

* Pseudonym of EISLER, Elfried.

FLAISSIÈRES, Siméon (1851–1931)

French municipal socialist. Doctor. A radical 1885 and a socialist Municipal Councillor 1888. First socialist Mayor of Marseilles 1892–1906 and 1914–29. Favourable to co-operation with the radicals. Remained an independent socialist outside the SFIO 1905.

In the Municipal Archive of Marseilles there are letters written by Flaissières to Chanot (especially in 1905), as well as correspondence between Flaissières and Bertas (q.v.) during the election campaign of 1898 (in the Bertas Archive).

FLAX*

* Pseudonym of MÉRIC, Victor.

FLECHINE, Senya (1894–1981)

Russian-American anarchist. During the First World War worked in the offices of Emma Goldman's (q.v.) *Mother Earth*. Returned to Russia in 1917, settling in Kharkov. Member of the Nabat (Tocsin) Confederation of Anarchist Organisations based in the Ukraine in 1918. Arrested by the Cheka in Kharkov in 1920 and then allowed to leave Russia. Active in the movement to free political prisoners in Russia.

There is a large collection of Flechine's papers from about 1920 in the IISH, Amsterdam. These are of particular importance for the Russian Relief Fund, and form a single collection with the papers of Mollie Steimer (q.v.).

FLOOD, Hulda (1886–1968)

Swedish pioneer of the social democratic women's movement. Dressmaker. From 1928 Executive member of the Women's Association, and from 1928 member of the Party Secretariat responsible for women's questions. Member of Parliament 1948–9.

Flood's papers (c. 24 boxes) are in the ARAB, Stockholm. These comprise personal documents, correspondence, manuscripts, transcripts, pamphlets, newspaper cuttings, photographs, printed and other material concerning her political activity. A provisional inventory is available.

FÖCHER, Matthias (1886–1967)

German Christian trade unionist. Vice-Chairman of the DGB in the British Zone 1947 and for the BRD 1949–56.

The DGB Archive in Düsseldorf has files of the DGB Executive 1947–50 containing Föcher's business correspondence. (See Mommsen, *op. cit.*)

FORSSLUND, Karl Erik (b. 1872)

Swedish pioneer of popular education. Poet and novelist. Founded the Brunnsviks Folkhögshola.

One box of Forsslund's papers is in the ARAB, Stockholm.

FOUET, Louis (b. 1833)

French Communard.

See Appendix I.

FOURIER, (François Marie) Charles (1772–1837)

Pioneer French social reformer and proponent of the co-operative system. Founder of the École sociétaire (or Phalanstérienne). Author of numerous books and journals. Identified poverty as the main cause of social disorder.

Reference should be made to the Fourier archive in the Archives Nationales, Paris. An inventory of Fourier's unpublished manuscripts has been published in Emile Poulat, *Les Cahiers manuscrits de Fourier* (Paris: 1957). In addition, in 1938 Duke University, North Carolina, USA, acquired a collection of relevant material (284 items, 5 vols). This consists mainly of a MS copy of 4 volumes of E. Silberling's *Dictionnaire de sociologie phalanstérienne* (Paris: 1911) with material on Fourier's followers etc.

FOURNIÈRE, Joseph (1857–1914)

French socialist and trade unionist. A follower of Guesde and collaborator on *L'Égalité* (1879–81). Supported Millerand's (q.v.) entry into Waldeck-Rousseau cabinet, 1902. Joined PSF, 1902, then joined SFIO, 1905. Deputy for L'Aisne, 1898–1902.

The Fournière archive at the IFHS, Paris, comprises Fournière's library, copies of his writings, together with his unpublished memoirs and other manuscript material. There is also correspondence of Brousse (q.v.) and de Paepe (q.v.).

FRAHM, Herbert

See under BRANDT, Willy.

FRANK, Karl Boromäus (1893–1969)

Austrian social democrat and pacifist. Leader of the German socialist émigré group 'Neu Beginnen'.

Frank's papers for the years 1937–61 are in the Hoover Institution, Stanford University, California. These include correspondence, manuscripts and documents, and concern mainly the years 1940–58 and his time in the United States. A microfilm copy of this collection is in the IISH, Amsterdam.

FRANK, Ludwig (1874–1914)

German social democratic politician. At first lawyer. Founder of the Sozialistischen Arbeiterjugend in Baden. Leader of the SPD in Baden. From 1907 member of the Reichstag. On the right and, from the outbreak of the First World War, pro-war wing of the SPD (although earlier supporting Rosa Luxemburg (q.v.) on the use of mass strike tactics over the Prussian suffrage). Died as war volunteer in 1914.

The AdsD at the Friedrich-Ebert-Stiftung, Bonn, has 38 letters to Ludwig Frank's friend Anny Kessler (1909–14).

FRERICHS, Elisabeth (1883–1967)*

German social democratic local and Land politician. Councillor in Rüstringen (now Wilhelmshavn) and Alderman in Oldenburg (Niedersachsen). Before 1933 member of the Oldenburg and, after 1945, of the Lower Saxon Landtag. Wife of Friedrich Frerichs (q.v.).

The Staatsarchiv, Oldenburg, has a small collection of Elisabeth Frerichs's correspondence for the years 1928–56 concerning her activity in the SPD, Industrial Welfare and the Lower Saxon Landtag. (See Mommsen, *op. cit.*)

* Née Seifert.

FRERICHS, Friedrich (Fritz) (1881–1945)

German social democratic local functionary and Land politician. Councillor in Rüstringen (now Wilhelmshavn). Member of the Oldenburg (Niedersachsen) Landtag.

The Staatsarchiv, Oldenburg, has a very small collection of Friedrich Frerichs's personal papers and correspondence concerning his activity in the SDP and Landtag. (See Mommsen, *op. cit.*)

FRIED, Alfred (1864–1921)

Austrian jurist and pacifist.

Relevant material can be found in the Suttner-Fried papers in the United Nations Library, Geneva. This extensive collection consists of correspondence and literary manuscripts of Fried and his fellow pacifist, Baroness Bertha von Suttner (q.v.). The Fried papers contain correspondence (1883–1921), literary manuscripts, photographs, medals, etc. For a certain period, the correspondence is in-coming letters only. There is also a microfilm of Fried's letters to Hans Wehberg (the originals are in the Bundesarchiv, Koblenz). The collection is open to research, except for 72 of Fried's letters which are closed until AD 2000. In addition, the Hoover Institution, Stanford University, California, has acquired 18 volumes of his wartime correspondence and diaries (1915–19), relating to the international peace movement (particularly during the 1914–18 war), pacifism, international co-operation, and the question of guilt for the First World War.

FRIEDEBERG, Raphael (1863–1940)

German social democrat and then anarchist. Prominent social democrat in Berlin. Delegate to the 1907 International Anarchist Congress in Amsterdam.

There is a small collection of Friedeberg's papers in the IISH, Amsterdam. This comprises mainly correspondence in the years c. 1903–21 with, amongst others, F. Domela Nieuwenhuis (q.v.) and Peter Kropotkin (q.v.), but also includes some personal documents and newspaper cuttings. A provisional card index is available.

FRIEDLÄNDER, Otto (1897–1954)

German social democratic exile from Nazi persecution. Economics correspondent. Member of the SPD. Chairman of the German Socialist and Republican Student Association 1924–9. Chairman and Secretary of the Socialist Student International 1926–32. Exiled in Czechoslovakia 1933, in Norway 1938 and in Sweden 1940. Member of the SOPADE and the Free German Cultural League. Editor of the *Sozialistische Tribüne*. Employed as an archivist and freelance journalist. Remained in Sweden.

Friedländer's papers for the years 1918–54 are in the ARAB, Stockholm. These comprise personal documents, correspondence, manuscripts and drafts, and other material from his political and journalist activity, as well as leaflets and newspaper cuttings. An inventory is available.

FRISCH, Harting (1893–1950)

Danish social democratic politician in the 1930s and 1940s. Professor. Once leader of the SD parliamentary group. Minister of Education.

Sixty-five boxes of Frisch's papers for the years 1915–49, including extensive correspondence, are in the ABA, Copenhagen. A detailed printed inventory is available.

FRISCHAUER, Paul

Austrian communist.

The Institute of Contemporary History, Vienna, has forty files of his papers. The collection consists mainly of political documents and correspondence on party matters.

FRITZNER, Andreas (1888–1969)

Danish syndicalist.

One box of Fritzner's papers for the years 1925–69 is in the ABA, Copenhagen.

FRÖLICH, Paul (1884–1953)

German communist and communist oppositionist. At first clerk. Before 1914 editor of SPD newspapers in Leipzig, Hamburg and Bremen. As a member of the IKD, founder member KPD (1918). Member of KPD Central Committee. Member of the Reichstag 1921–4 and 1928–30. Member of the 'Right Faction' of the KPD, consequently expelled (1928). Founding and leading member of the 'Brandlerite' KPO. Entered with KPO-minority into the SAP in 1932, and elected to its Executive. Concentration camp 1933. Exile in France where active for the SAP. Interned 1939. Exile in the USA 1941. Returned to BRD 1950. Extensive activity as journalist and publicist and theoretician. Editor of Rosa Luxemburg's (q.v.) works as well as her biographer.

Frölich's papers were lost in the course of repeated exile. Manuscripts arising from his work as a publicist, however, are to be found in the AdsD at the Friedrich-Ebert-Stiftung, Bonn. (See Mommsen, *op. cit.*)

FRUIN, Thomas A. (1890–1964)

Dutch member of the SDAP and PvdA.

The IISH, Amsterdam, has a collection of Fruin's miscellaneous documents covering the years 1945–8. (See M. Campfens, *op. cit.*)

FURNÉMONT, Léon (fl. 1890s)

Pioneer Belgian socialist. Lawyer. Leading member of the Belgian Workers' Party from the 1890s. One of the first group of socialists elected to Parliament 1894. Early influence on Emile Vandervelde (q.v.). General Secretary of the Fédération Internationale de la Libre Pensée.

Furnémont's papers are in the Institut Emile Vandervelde, Brussels.

FURTMÜLLER, Karl (1880–1951)

Austrian socialist and educationalist. Editor, *Zeitschrift für Individualpsychologie*, 1914–16; *Wiener Schule*, 1930–3.

The VGA, Vienna, has six files of papers. The collection includes personal and family documents, correspondence, 1919–49, material relating to AVÖS, and the emigration in France, 1939–40, including reports from Vienna and other parts of Austria, circulars, material relating to the emigration in Spain, including reports on imprisonment, and a draft typescript entitled 'Die politischen Ereignisse in österreich zwischen der Begegnung von Berchtesgaden und dem Anschluss'; essays and lectures from the USA; material on the Austrian Labour Committee from 1942 and 1947; and correspondence, 1943–6 and from 1947 and after.

FURTWÄNGLER, Franz Josef (1894–1965)

German trade unionist. From 1923 Foreign Secretary of the ADGB in Berlin. Director of the Akademie der Arbeit in Frankfurt 1946–9, then independent writer and political journalist. Member of the Hessian Landtag 1950.

The DGB Archive in Düsseldorf has Furtwängler's correspondence, together with manuscripts of his books, articles and speeches for the years 1931–3 and 1946–65.

GALLAND, Alphonse

See under ZO D'AXA.

GARIBALDI, Giuseppe (1807–82)

Italian general and politician.

The Archivio Centrale dello Stato, Rome, has one volume of Garibaldi's memoirs for the years 1871–5.

GARVI, Peter Abramovič (1881–1970)

Russian socialist.

Some of Garvi's typescript manuscripts (in Russian) are in the Hoover Institution, Stanford University, California. These include *Memoirs of a Social Democrat* (relating to the RSDLP, 1906–17), *Trade Unions of Russia in the First Years of the Revolution* and *Workers' Cooperatives in the First Years of the Russian Revolution* (1917–21). There is a little correspondence and other manuscript material in the IISH, Amsterdam.

GAUME (fl. 1960s)

French trade unionist.

Gaume's papers arise from his activity in the CFDT in the Compagnie des Ateliers et Forges de la Loire in the years 1955–78, and are to be found in the Departmental Archives of the Loire.

GAUMONT, Jean (1876–1972)

French leading co-operativist and historian of the co-operative movement in France. Secretary, Municipal Employees' Federation. Member, 1913–35, of the Central Council of the Co-operative Federation.

A variety of Gaumont's unpublished manuscripts have been deposited. These include *La Révolution dans le département de la Côte-d'Or (1789–95)* and *Histoire des idées sociales et du socialisme en Côte-d'Or* in the town hall of Dijon; *Quatre familles consulaires de Saulieu, Côte-d'Or* in the Library at Saulieu; and *Histoire de Précy-sous-Thil* in the Town Hall of Précy. (See Maitron, *op. cit.*)

GAY, Désirée (1810–90)

Pioneer French socialist and feminist. A supporter of Fourier. Co-founder, 1848, of the *Club de l'Émancipation des Femmes.* Founded *La Politique des Femmes.* Briefly President, Women's Section, of the International. Later active in the Belgian Socialist Party.

Désirée Gay's correspondence with Victor Considérant (q.v.) is in the Fonds Fourier et Considérant at the Archives Nationales, Paris.

GAY, Jules Léopold (1807–*c.* 1880)

French Owenite. Theorist of neo-babeuvian democratic communism. Corresponded with Robert Owen.

Some of Jules Gay's correspondence is in the Archives Nationales, Paris (Correspondence fouriériste). His correspondence with Owen is in the Co-operative Union, Manchester.

GECK, Adolf (1854–1942)

German social democratic politician. Editor and publisher in Offenburg. Member of the Baden Landtag 1897–1918. Member of the Reichstag (SPD/USPD) 1898–1924.

The Generallandesarchiv in Karlsruhe has a large collection of Adolf Geck's papers, including personal papers, manuscripts, newspapers and journals and political correspondence for the years 1882–1942. The latter is especially notable for correspondence with leading social democratic politicians such as August Bebel (q.v.), Rosa Luxemburg (q.v) and Klara Zetkin (q.v.). (See Mommsen, *op. cit.*)

GECK, Oskar (1867–1928)

German social democratic politician. Political correspondent for various social democratic newspapers 1894–9. Editor of the Mannheim *Volksstimme* 1901. City Councillor in Mannheim 1905. Member of the Reichstag (SPD) 1914–28.

The Stadtarchiv, Mannheim, has a small collection of Oskar Geck's personal papers. (See Mommsen, *op. cit.*)

GECK, Tell (b. 1894)

German correspondent of social democratic and communist politicians. Artist and music teacher.

Tell Geck's correspondence with, amongst others, Kostja Zetkin and Stephan Heymann is in the Generallandesarchiv, Karlsruhe. (See Mommsen, *op. cit.*)

GEERS, Gerard J. (1893–1965)

Dutch socialist and pacifist.

The IISH, Amsterdam, has a small collection of letters and documents. Correspondents include Juan Andrade. (See M. Campfens, *op. cit.*)

GELEFF, Poul (1842–1928)

Pioneer Danish socialist. Agitator and publicist. Founder with Louis Pio (q.v.) of the SD.

One box of Geleff's papers for the period from the 1880s to 1928 – including correspondence – is in the ABA, Copenhagen.

GERBER, Rudolf*

* Pseudonym of SCHLESINGER, Rudolf.

GERHARD, Hendrik (1829–86)

Dutch socialist. Active in the First International.

The IISH, Amsterdam, has a few of Gerhard's letters and other documents (1870–1929). A list is available. (See M. Campfens, *op. cit.*)

GIEBEL, Carl (1878–1930)

German social democratic politician and trade unionist. Secretary 1904 and Chairman 1906 of the Verband der Büroangestellten Deutschlands. Member of the Reichstag 1912–28 (and Nationalversammlung). Representative of the Revolutionary Government in the High Command of the Reichswehr 1918. Assistant to the State Secretary in the Reichsmarineamt 1919. Expert on social policy.

Giebel's papers are in the AdsD at the Friedrich-Ebert-Stiftung, Bonn. Particularly noteworthy are his notes on Party Committee and Reichstag Group meetings in the period 1914–27. In addition, there is material concerning the split in the Reichstag Group during the war, the Wilhelmine army and the Workers' and Soldiers' Councils, together with a large number of letters, personal papers and correspondence arising from his Reichstag constituency (Cottbus-Spremberg). (See Mommsen, *op. cit.*)

GIOT, Hippolyte (1849–1933)

French socialist. House painter. Member of the Federal Council of the International in Paris. Active in the POF. Municipal Councillor in Ivry-sur-Seine and then Bondy in Paris. Secretary of the SFIO in Viroflay (Seine-et-Marne).

Twelve letters written by Giot to Lucien Roland (q.v.) in the period 1928–33 now form part of the Maurice Dommanget (q.v.) archive in the IFHS, Paris.

GNIFFKE, Erich W. (1895–1964)

German social democratic politician. White-collar trade unionist. District leader of the Reichsbanner Schwarz-Rot-Gold. Politically persecuted after 1933. After the end of the Second World War, Executive member of the Central Committee of the SPD in the East. After the unification of the SPD and KPD in the Soviet Occupation Zone, member of the Central Secretariat of the SED. Chairman of the Deutscher Volksrat. Break with the SED 1948. Flight to West Germany. Renewed membership of the SPD. Thereafter active at local level.

Gniffke's papers are in the AdsD at the Friedrich-Ebert-Stiftung, Bonn. These comprise lecture notes, manuscripts of his memoirs (mainly unpublished), general and business correspondence, and collections of material (mainly newspaper cuttings).

GNOCCHI-VIANI, Osvaldo (d. 1917)

Pioneer Italian socialist. One of the first organisers of the Italian workers' movement.

A collection of Gnocchi-Viani's correspondence and manuscripts is in the Feltrinelli Institute, Milan. The collection, covering the period 1870 to 1917, is in three parts. It does not include material on his period as a soldier with Garibaldi (q.v.) or much on the Socialist Party or his links with the International. The collection can be divided into three parts. The first consists of over 100 items of correspondence between Gnocchi and various workers' organisations from 1870 to 1915. The second contains documents on his trial in 1873 and his experience as a Socialist Party candidate at elections in 1882, 1889 and 1890. The third, covering his Mazzinian period, contains an article and some correspondence with I. Pederzolli.

GOERTZ, Ernst (1869–1960)

German trade unionist. SPD member and member of the Workers' and Soldiers' Council in Lüneberg, 1918–19.

The Stadtarchiv in Lüneberg has a large collection of papers mostly arising from Goertz's local activity. These include poems (1891), his diary for 1892, and workbooks from the years 1916 to 1919. This holding is supplemented by the minutes of the Lüneberg trade union cartel (1910–18), the Lüneberg SPD (1913–22) and of the Lüneberg Arbeiterbildungsaus-schuss (Workers' Education Committee). (See Mommsen, *op. cit.*)

GOES, Frank van der (1859–1939)

Founder member of Dutch SDAP. Newspaper editor, later connected with Independent and Revolutionary Socialists.

The IISH, Amsterdam, has a large collection of correspondence and documentation (1891–1909). An inventory is available. (See M. Campfens, *op. cit.*)

GOES van NATERS, Marinus van der (b. 1900)

Dutch SDAP member and later representative in the *Tweede Kamer* for the PvdA.

A small number of Goes van Naters's dossiers relating to party matters can be found at the IISH, Amsterdam. The papers cover the period 1929–66, and an inventory is available. (See M. Campfens, *op. cit.*). Other papers can be found at the Algemeen Rijksarchief, The Hague. A summary inventory is available (2.21.198: Coll. 334).

GÖHRE, Paul (1864–1928)

German evangelical pastor, then social democratic politician. General Secretary of the Evangelical-Social Congress in Berlin 1891–4. Second Chairman of the National Social Party and co-founder of the National-Social Association 1897–9. From 1900 member of the SPD. In the face of disciplinary proceedings left the Church. Member of the Reichstag 1903, 1910–18. Stood on the right of the SPD and volunteered for military service during the war. Secretary of State in the Prussian Ministry of State 1919–23. Author of important social studies (including *Drei Monate Fabrikarbeiter und Handwerksbursche*, 1891). Extensive publicist activity.

The AdsD at the Friedrich-Ebert-Stiftung, Bonn, has Göhre's war-time diaries (1915–18) together with general correspondence, manuscripts of his publications and newspaper articles.

GOLDENBERG, Boris (b. 1905)

German communist, then socialist. Russian-born. Member of the SPD 1924 and of the KPD 1927. Later member of the KPDO and then of the SAP. Collaborated on the *Sozialistische Arbeiterzeitung*. Arrested in 1933 and then exiled in Paris. Member of the SAP exile leadership. In Cuba 1941–60 (returned as an opponent of Castro).

Goldenberg's papers for the years 1961–8 are in the AdsD, Bonn.

GOLDMAN, Emma (1869–1940)

Russian-American anarchist. From 1886 in the USA. Editor of the leading anarchist journal *Mother Earth*. Pioneer of women's emancipation, birth control, and anti-militarist agitation. With Alexander Berkman (q.v.), and other anarchists, deported to Soviet Russia in December 1919. Worked on cultural matters. Protested to Lenin and other Soviet leaders about the persecution of anarchists and syndicalists, and warned against the violent suppression of the Kronstadt uprising. Disillusioned with the Bolsheviks 1921. Left the USSR for France. Active in aiding refugees and anarchist prisoners in Russia. Remained prominent in the anarchist movement. Eventually settled in Canada.

A large collection of Goldman's papers – mainly from the exile period – is in the IISH, Amsterdam. This includes extensive correspondence, manuscripts on anarchism and literature, notes and documents. A list is available. See also Frank Heiner.

GOLITSIN, Aleksandr Dmitrevič

Russian revolutionary.

His papers are at the Bakhmeteff Archive, Columbia University, New York. They include his memoirs, *Vospominaniia kniazia A. D. Golitsina*, covering the zemstvos and the Revolution, 1880–1917; and handwritten memoirs in two notebooks.

GOLTKE, Marie

See under JUCHACZ, Marie.

GONZALLE, Jean-Louis (1815–79)

French Icarian. Weaver, shoe-maker and poet. President of the Comité électoral de la Démocratie in Rheims 1848. Later supported the Empire.

Gonzalle's papers are in the municipal library at Rheims. These include notes and manuscripts (notably his *Souvenirs de la Révolution à Rheims* in two unpublished volumes).

GÖRLINGER, Robert (1888–1954)

German social democratic politician. Executive member of the SPD's District organisation in Oberrhein 1924–33. After 1933 in exile. After 1945 SPD Executive member. Lord Mayor of Cologne 1948. Member of the North Rhine-Westphalian Landtag. From 1949 member of the Bundestag.

Görlinger's papers concerned with his political activity since 1945 are in the Stadtarchiv, Cologne. A second part of his papers remains in private hands. (See Mommsen, *op. cit.*)

GOTTFURCHT, Hans (b. 1896)

German trade unionist. After 1933 Director of the organisation (Landesgruppe) of German Trade Unionists in Great Britain (Landesgruppe deutscher Gewerkschafter in Grossbritannien). Vice-General Secretary of the International Confederation of Free Trade Unions.

The DGB Archive in Düsseldorf has a large holding of Gottfurcht's papers concerning the construction and history of German trade unions after 1945, and including files of the German Trade Unions in Britain (Landesgruppe deutscher Gewerkschafter in Grossbritannien) from 1941–5. (See Mommsen, *op. cit.*)

GOUBITZ, J. (1875–1939)

Dutch communist.

The IISH, Amsterdam, has some correspondence covering the period 1903–28. A list is available. (See M. Campfens, *op. cit.*)

GOZZOLI, Virgilio (1886–1964)

Italian anarchist. Also playwright and poet.

Some of Gozzoli's papers were acquired by the IISH, Amsterdam, after 1967. The collection is open and a provisional list is available. The material includes letters written during the 1950s and 1960s by, for example, Valerio Isca, Joseph Mascii and Hugo Rolland (q.v.). There are notes, articles and other material concerning his publications.

GRAIZELY, Adrien (1845–1925)

French pioneer trade union organiser. Swiss-born watchmaker and trade unionist. Settled in Besançon 1876. Pioneer of trade unionism in Besançon. Helped create the Workers' Federation of Besançon in 1891, which, in 1894, set up a Bourse du Travail with Graizely as its permanent secretary (until 1924). Reformist.

A manuscript of Graizely's written in 1914, and relevant to the labour movement in Besançon, is to be found in the Bourse du Travail, Besançon.

GRAMSCI, Antonio (1891–1937)

Italian communist leader and theorist. Active in the PSI. Among the leaders of the anti-war insurrection in Turin in 1917. Elected Secretary of the Turin branch of the PSI. Studied Marx (q.v.) and Engels (q.v.) Became a convinced Marxist who rejected reformism and emphasised the struggle for power. A leader of the Factory Councils Movement and founder of the newspaper *Ordine Nuovo* in May 1919. Helped formulate a programme in accordance with the principles of the Third International. Helped lead the break from the PSI at the Livorno Congress in January 1921 and in the formation of the PCI. Elected General Secretary of the PCI, 1924. Founded *Unità*. Elected to Parliament. Arrested 1926. Whilst in prison, outlined his theories in his *Prison Notebooks*. Released in poor health, April 1937. Died a week later.

Gramsci's papers are in the Gramsci Institute, Turin.

GRANGER, Ernest Henri (1844–1914)

Leading French publicist of Blanquism in France. Commanded 159th Battalion of the National Guard during the siege of Paris. In exile in London, 1871–80. Helped establish *La commune révolutionnaire* group. Supported orthodox Blanquism against Vaillant (q.v.). A supporter of Boulanger. Deputy, 1889–93, for 19th arrondissement, Paris.

Four small dossiers of Granger's papers are in the Institut Universitaire de Hautes Études Internationales, Geneva. There is some photocopied material in the IISH, Amsterdam.

GRATZ, Leopold (b. 1920)

Austrian social democrat. SPÖ national secretary, 1963; Bundesrat deputy for Vienna, 1963; Nationalrat deputy for Vienna, 1966; education secretary in Kreisky government, 1970; Mayor of Vienna; Foreign Minister in Sinowatz administration. Resigned 1986 after election of Waldheim as President.

The Vienna City Library (WSLB) has a collection of miscellaneous papers relating to his period of office as Mayor of Vienna, covering the years 1970–80.

GRAVE, Jean (1854–1939)

French militant anarchist and writer. Proponent of violent revolution after 1888, but after 1896 turned towards education and propaganda. Supporter of Allies in the First World War. Prime role in development of anarchist journals *La Révolte* and *Temps Nouveaux*.

A large and important collection of *c*. 1600 letters received by Grave is in the IFHS, Paris. The collection constitutes a major archival source for the anarchist, anarcho-syndicalist and libertarian left, from the 1890s to the 1920s. Among a long list of correspondents are Charles Angrand (q.v.), Emile Darnaud (q.v.), George Delaw (q.v.), Théodor Jean (q.v.), H.-G. Jossot (q.v.), Francis Jourdain (q.v.), Peter Kropotkin (q.v.) (*c*. 108 letters), Charles Laisant (q.v.), Maximilien Luce (q.v.), Charles Malato de Cornet (q.v.), Pierre Martin (q.v.), Joaquin Maurin (q.v.), Régis Meunier (q.v.), Théodule Meunier (q.v.), Camille Pissarro (q.v.), Pierre Quillard (q.v.), Paul Robin (q.v.), Paul Signac (q.v.), Adolphe Tabarant (q.v.) and Félix Vallotton (q.v.). In addition, the Félix Nadar (q.v.) archive at the Bibliothèque Nationale, Paris, contains *c*. 80 letters written by Grave.

GREULICHS, Herman (1842–1925)

One of the founders of the Swiss Social Democratic Party. Originally German. Member of the IWMA in Zürich. Secretary of the Government Labour Secretariat (where he researched labour conditions). Prominent in the Second International. Leader of the SPS right-wing. Opposed the affiliation of the SPS left-wing to the Comintern.

Most of Greulichs's papers are reported to have been destroyed. However, some important documents written by Greulichs are to be found in the Schweizerisches Sozialarchiv, Zürich. A little correspondence, 1893–1925, is in the IISH, Amsterdam.

GRIMLUND, Otto (1893–1969)

Swedish communist leader. From 1911 member of the Social Democratic Youth Organisation. Founder and leading member of both the Left-Socialist Party (1917) and of the SKP (1921–5). Editorial Secretary of the Left-Socialist and then Communist Party paper, *Politiken*, becoming *Folkets Dagblad Politiken*. Joined the SAP in 1929. Active in 1920s and

1930s in Stockholm municipal politics. Chairman of the Tenants' League 1924–36. Farmer 1941–55.

Two boxes of Grimlund's papers for the years 1889–1967 are in the ARAB, Stockholm. These comprise correspondence, manuscripts, transcripts, pamphlets, leaflets, newspaper cuttings, as well as other printed matter and material concerning his political activity. An inventory is available.

GRIMM, Robert (1881–1958)

Swiss social democrat. Prominent in the SPS. One of the leaders of the General Strike. Editor of the *Berne Tagwacht*. One of the organisers of the Zimmerwald Conference and International Secretary of the Zimmerwald Secretariat. Opposed affiliation to the Comintern.

Grimm's papers concerning his activity during the First World War and in the Zimmerwald movement are in the IISH, Amsterdam. Other papers are reported in the possession of Jenny Grimm, Berne.

GRÖNVALL, Johan (1866–1954)

Swedish bakery worker and trade unionist.

One box of Grönvall's papers, containing material about the Bakery Workers' Union, is in the ARAB, Stockholm. An inventory is available.

GROSS, Jacques (1855–1928)

Swiss anarchist.

Some of Gross's papers are in the IISH, Amsterdam. This includes correspondence, 1878–1927. A list is available.

GROSSMANN, Rudolf (d. 1942)*

Austrian anarchist and publicist. Editor of *Erkenntnis und Befreiung*, 1919–27, and of *Der Anarchist* 1927–33. Active anti-militarist.

The IISH, Amsterdam, has a large collection of Grossmann's correspondence, manuscripts, notes, official documents, files, circulars, and printed material covering the period 1892–1936.

  * Known by the pseudonym Pierre Ramus.

GROTE-MISMAHL, Ulrich (fl. 1940s–50s)

German trade union economist. Employed by the DGB, 1947–51.

Grote-Mismahl's papers are in the AdsD, Bonn.

GROTEWOHL, Otto (1894–1964)

German social democratic politician. SED leader. At first printer. Member of the Braunschweig Landtag (SPD) 1920–22. Minister of the Interior and Education in Braunschweig

1921–3 and of Justice 1923–4. Member of the Reichstag 1925–33. President of the Landesversicherungsanstalt for Braunschweig. Chairman of the SPD's Central Committee in the DDR 1945. Entered the SED 1946. President of the Volkskongress 1947. Prime Minister of the DDR 1949–64.

The main part of Grotewohl's papers are at the Zentrales Parteiarchiv at the Institut für Marxismus-Leninismus beim Zentralkomitee der SED in East Berlin.

GROUSSET, Paschal (1844–1909)

French independent socialist. Elected to Paris Commune from XVIII arrondissement. Deported, 1871. After 1893, Deputy for Paris.

Two letters written by Grousset are in the IFHS, Paris.

GROUSSIER, Arthur (1863–1957)

French socialist politician. Secretary, 1890–93, of the Fédération nationale des Métallurgistes. Deputy for Paris, 1893–1902, 1906–24. Established the *Alliance communiste révolutionnaire* in 1897. Founding member of the PSdeF.

Groussier's papers are in the CRHMSS, Paris. These comprise letters received by him in the years 1902–21, as well as material on legislative elections (especially in the Seine) from 1885–1902 and from 1909–28, and material on municipal elections 1886–1925.

GRZESINSKI, Albert (1879–1947)

German social democratic politician. Chairman of the Kassel Workers and Soldiers Council, 1918–19. In charge of the Berlin police, 1924–6 and 1930–32. Prussian Minister of the Interior 1926–30. Member of the Prussian Landtag from 1921 to 1933. Exiled in France after 1933 and then the United States.

Some of Grzesinski's papers are in the IISH, Amsterdam. This extensive holding stems mainly from the years 1918–34 and is organised according to his own categories of 'correspondence' and 'dossiers'. Correspondence includes all letters to and from Grzesinski (the latter being mainly drafts or notes), which were not placed in dossiers according to their content. The dossiers include all letters and documents (both private and official) relating to his official and political activity. A detailed catalogue is available. The greater part of Grzesinski's papers arising from his exile disappeared in the United States. (See Mommsen, *op. cit.*)

GUÉRIN, Daniel (b. 1904)

French socialist.

A collection of correspondence, manuscripts, notes, miscellaneous files and printed matter is in the IISH, Amsterdam. The collection, which is listed, covers the period 1932 to 1959.

GUESDE Jules (1845–1922)

French pioneer socialist. Populariser of Marxism in France. Began his career as a popular journalist. Supported Paris Commune. Sentenced to imprisonment and went into exile. Founded, 1877, *L'Égalité*. Increasingly influenced by Marx (q.v.) and Friedrich Engels (q.v.). Dominant leader of the POF and, after 1902, of the USR. Founded, 1907, *Le Socialisme*. Supported the 'union sacrée'. Entered the Government as Minister of State, 1914–16.

An important collection of Guesde's papers (*c.* 5000 items, 56 dossiers) is in the IISH, Amsterdam. The collection, arranged chronologically, includes not only personal correspondence (particularly rich for the period 1890–1905) but also certain POF archives. In addition, certain private papers, including correspondence with Malon (q.v.), are believed still to be with his grandson (J-M. Guesde).

GUILLAUME, James (1844–1916)

Swiss anarchist. School teacher. Leading anarchist among the workers and artisans in Jura. Supporter of Bakunin (q.v.) in the IWMA.

There is a collection of Guillaume's papers in the IISH, Amsterdam. The collection, covering the period 1862–1915, includes correspondence and printed material. In addition, some 17 of his letters to Jean-Louis Pindy (q.v.) are in the Library of La Chaux-de-Fonds in Switzerland. Reference should also be made to M. Vuilleumier, 'Les archives de J. Guillaume', *Le Mouvement Social*, no. 48 (July–September 1964).

GUILLAUME-SCHACK, Gertrud (1845–1905)

Swiss socialist and campaigner for women's rights.

There is a small collection of Guillaume-Schack's papers from the 1880s in the IISH, Amsterdam. This includes letters, manuscripts, notes, articles, circulars, leaflets, pamphlets and newspaper cuttings, relating to the position of women and women's rights (and related matters such as prostitution). Originally part of the Nettlau (q.v.) collection.

GUILLAUMIN, Emile (1873–1951)

French trade unionist. Member of earliest peasant union. Edited its journal and drafted its manifesto. Later a journalist, specialising in agrarian questions.

Guillaumin's papers are in the IFHS, Paris. The archive is of particular value for peasant unionism in Allier in the first part of the 20th century.

GUIRAUD, Gaston (b. 1881)

French trade union leader. Secretary, 1920, Seine CGT. Resigned when the 'minority' took control. Resumed office, becoming Treasurer in 1936. Resigned again in 1938. Excluded from trade unions after accepting responsibilities under Vichy.

Guiraud's papers, of most value for the *Union des syndicats de la Seine, c.* 1910–50, are in the IFHS, Paris.

GURVICH*

* Pseudonym of DAN, Fedor Il'ič.

GUSTAFSSON, Ruth (1881–1960)

Swedish social democratic agitator and politician. Editor. Active in the Social Democratic Women's Movement. Member of Parliament.

Two boxes of Gustafsson's papers are in the ARAB, Stockholm. An inventory is available.

GUSTAVSSON, Hans (b. 1912)

Swedish trade unionist and social democratic politician. Engineering worker. Prominent in the Metal Workers' Union. Government Minister in the 1960s.

Three boxes of Gustavsson's papers are in the ARAB, Stockholm. A preliminary inventory is available.

GYLLING, Edvard (1881–1942)

Finnish communist. University teacher. Member of the Finnish Social Democratic Party. Member of Parliament. Member of the Finnish People's Commissariat. Communist from 1918.

Gylling's papers are in the National Archives of Finland, Helsinki. Special permission from the Director is needed to consult these papers.

HAASE, Hugo (1863–1919)

German social democratic politician. At first lawyer. Member of the Reichstag 1879–1907 and 1912–18, and of the Weimar National Assembly 1919. Leader of the SPD Reichstag group 1912. Leader of the USPD 1916. Member of the Council of Peoples' Commissars 1918.

According to Mommsen, *op. cit.*, all Haase's papers were destroyed during the Second World War.

HABERMANN, Max (1885–1944)

German trade union official. Member of the temporary Reich Economic Council. Active in the resistance.

Habermann's papers were confiscated by the Gestapo and have not been subsequently located. (See Mommsen, *op. cit.*)

HAEKKERUP, Per (1915–79)

Danish social democratic politician. Chairman of the International Union of Socialist Youth 1946–54. Chairman of the SD Parliamentary Group. Foreign Minister 1962–6 and, in the 1970s, Economy and Budget Minister.

Thirty-two boxes of Haekkerup's papers for the years 1956–79 are in the ABA, Copenhagen. Together with a small collection of letters and a collection of newspaper cuttings, these contain mainly state papers and personal notes. A summary inventory is available.

HAENISCH, Konrad (1876–1925)

German social democratic politician and writer. Member of the Reichstag. Prussian Minister for Science, Art and Education.

The main part of Haenisch's papers, covering 1874–1924, are in the Deutsches Zentralarchiv, Potsdam. In addition, there is a collection of his papers for the years 1907–15 in the Hoover Institution, Stanford University, California. These comprise correspondence and issues of newspapers concerning political conditions, the socialist movement in Germany, and the role of the SPD in the 1914–18 war. (See Mommsen, *op. cit.*)

HAGEN, Georg (1887–1958)

German social democratic politician. First Vice-President of the Bavarian Landtag.

Hagen's papers are in the Stadtarchiv, Kulmbach. These comprise his diaries as well as correspondence with the SPD Group in the Bavarian Landtag and Bundestag and individual deputies. (See Mommsen, *op. cit.*)

HÄGGLUND, Joel

See under HILL, Joe.

HALONEN, George (fl. 1918–22)

Finnish. Karelian Workers' Commune representative in the USA (1918–19).

One box of Halonen's papers for the years 1918–22 is in the Hoover Institution, Stanford University, California. These comprise correspondence, manuscripts, reports and printed matter concerning the activities of the Finnish Information Bureau in the USA in publicising and seeking US recognition of the Soviet government of Finland. In particular, this collection includes writings and correspondence of Santeri Nuoreteva, Head of the Finnish Information Bureau. A preliminary inventory is available.

HAMACHER, Heinrich (1899–1975)

German social democratic politician. City Councillor in Cologne 1946–58. Member of the Bundestag 1957–69.

The Stadtarchiv, Cologne, has papers arising from Hamacher's activities as a freethinker, and on behalf of water sports in the Greater Cologne area from both before 1933 and after 1945. Others concern persecution under the Third Reich and compensation. In addition there is correspondence with the SPD-district Mittelrhein from 1957 to 1969, as well as SPD printed material from 1946 to 1952. (See Mommsen, *op. cit.*)

HAMON, Augustin (1862–1945)

French anarchist and writer. Prominent in the international anarchist movement. Editor of *L'Humanité Nouvelle*. Contributor to *Les Temps Nouveaux*.

There is a collection of Hamon's material in the IISH, Amsterdam. This includes a large quantity of newspaper cuttings on themes such as anarchism, literature, politics, militarism and religion, etc. A provisional inventory is available.

HANSEN, Hans Christian (1906–60)

Danish social democratic politician. Minister of Finance 1947–50. Foreign Minister 1953–5. Prime Minister 1955–60.

Some 26 boxes of Hans Hansen's papers for the years 1922–60 are in the ABA, Copenhagen. These include correspondence and important papers concerning Danish foreign policy. Part of this collection is closed.

HANSEN, Julius (1892–1971)

Danish social democratic Mayor in the post-war period. Previously active in the SD youth movement.

Six boxes of Julius Hansen's papers for the years 1910–*c*. 1961 are in the ABA, Copenhagen. As well as personal papers and manuscripts, these include letters from, amongst others, Gustav Bang (q.v.), Karl-August Fagerholm (q.v.), Thorvald Stauning (q.v.) and Gerson Trier (q.v.).

HANSEN, Paul (Kalundborg) (1913–66)

Danish social democratic politician. Minister of Defence 1956–62. Minister of Finance 1962–5.

One box of Paul Hansen's papers from the years 1932–3 and 1945–52 is in the ABA, Copenhagen. Apart from letters received by Hansen, this collection comprises mainly material about him, together with correspondence and material on the journal *Verdens Gang*.

HANSEN, Werner*

* Pseudonym of HEIDORN, Heinrich.

HANSSON, Per Albin (1885–1946)

Swedish social democratic politician. Commercial employee. Journalist. Co-founder 1903 and Chairman of the Social Democratic Youth Organisation 1908–9. Editor of its paper *Fram* 1905–8. From 1910 employee and Editor-in-Chief 1917–24 of the SAP central organ *Social Demokraten*. Chairman of the SAP 1925–46. Member of Parliament 1918–46. Minister of Defence 1921–3, 1924–6. Prime Minister 1932–46 (with a brief interruption in 1936).

Sixty boxes of Per Albin Hansson's papers for the years 1906–46 are in the ARAB, Stockholm. These comprise diaries, correspondence, manuscripts, transcripts, pamphlets, photographs, newspaper cuttings, printed matter and other material concerning his political activity. An inventory is available and, with the exception of notes from the Foreign Policy Committee during the Second World War, the whole collection is freely accessible.

HANSSON, Sigfrid (1884–1939)

Swedish social democratic politician. At first bricklayer. Employee of the SAP paper in Göteborg *Ny Tid* 1905–8, and of the SAP central organ *Social Demokraten* 1908–16, 1919–20. Member of Parliament 1919–37. Editor of the central trade union paper *Fackförenings-*

rörelsen 1920–37. Author of many works on the trade union movement. Active in workers' education.

A large collection of Sigfrid Hansson's papers covering the years 1902–39 is in the ARAB, Stockholm. This comprises diaries, correspondence, manuscripts, sketches and notes, photographs, newspaper articles, books and other material concerning his political and journalistic activity.

HANUSCH, Ferdinand (1886–1923)

Austrian trade unionist and social democrat. Secretary of State for Social Affairs, 1918–20.

The VGA, Vienna, has a collection of six manuscripts.

HARDEN, Maximilien (1861–1927)*

German writer and publicist. Editor of *Zukunft* 1892–1922. Bitter opponent of Wilhelmine policy. Annexationist and then pacifist in the 1914–18 war. Sympathiser of the socialist left in the Weimar period.

Harden's papers are in the Bundesarchiv, Koblenz. In the main these comprise manuscripts and an extensive correspondence with writers (including Hofmannsthal, Arno Holz, Thomas Mann and Rilke), journalists, politicians (including Erzberger and Rathenau), economists (including Ballin), leading civil servants, and artists. (See Mommsen, *op. cit.*)

   * Originally known as Felix Ernst Witkowski.

HARSMAN, Theo (1905–76)

Dutch anarchist.

The IISH, Amsterdam, has a few of Harsman's manuscripts and correspondence (1939–1970s). An inventory is available. (See M. Campfens, *op. cit.*)

HART, Martin*

   * Pseudonym of EICHLER, Willi.

HART, Pieter P. van't (1910–75)

Dutch socialist and communist.

A large collection of Pieter Hart's books, pamphlets and archives was given to the IISH, Amsterdam, by his widow, Mrs C. M. van't Hart-van Gerdingen. The collection is particularly rich on the revolutionary socialist movement (especially Henk Sneevliet), the Spanish Civil War and Indonesia. (See M. Campfens, *op. cit.*)

HARTTORFF, Johannes P. M. (1869–1955)

Dutch social democrat.

The IISH, Amsterdam, has a few of Harttorff's letters, 1892–9. (See M. Campfens, *op. cit.*)

HATZFELDT, Sophie Gräfin von (1805–81)

German political disciple and intimate friend of Ferdinand Lassalle (q.v.) over 20 years. Financial patron of the General German Workers' Union (ADAV). 'Ultra-Lassallean' – opposed the ascendancy of J. B. von Schweitzer in the ADAV. Fomented, in 1867, the breakaway minority in the ADAV that became the separate and self-styled Lassallean-ADAV (which was of little significance during the two years before it reunified with the ADAV).

The Countess Hatzfeldt's papers form part of the von Hatzfeldt family archive in the Schloss Sommerberg bei Frauenstein bei Weisbaden. However, copies of these papers have been united with material from the ADAV to form the ADAV/Hatzfeldt collection in the IISH, Amsterdam. As well as correspondence between von Hatzfeldt and Lassalle (q.v.), this collection comprises material on the ADAV (correspondence, conference reports, circulars and other printed material, etc.), the events in Geneva (summer 1864) and the dispute over Lassalle's inheritance (correspondence, documents, etc.), and other miscellaneous items. Permission of the von Hatzfeldt family is needed if items are to be published. A summary inventory is available.

HAVE, Johanna N. ten (1898–1982)

Dutch feminist and pacifist.

The IISH, Amsterdam, has a collection of Have's letters and documents on various women's organisations, covering the period 1940–66. (See M. Campfens, *op. cit.*)

HAWKE, Peter (1801–87)

British-born socialist. Active in France. A pioneer of Saint-Simonism in Anjou.

Hawke's correspondence relating to Saint-Simonism and other manuscripts is in the municipal library at Angers. Much of this was published in the *Revue d'Anjou*, 1880. There are also some of his letters in the Fonds Saint-Simon at the Bibliothèque de l'Arsenal.

HEDTOFF-HANSEN, Hans Christian (1903–55)

Danish social democratic politician. Prime Minister 1947–50 and 1953–5.

Some 64 boxes of Hedtoff-Hansen's papers covering the years 1929–55 are in the ABA, Copenhagen. The part of this collection concerning the Nordic Defence Pact and Danish membership of NATO is closed.

HEFFLER, Hugo (d. 1970)

Swedish socialist. Long-standing official in the Labour Education Movement (ABF).

One box of Heffler's papers, together with those of his wife, are in the ARAB, Stockholm.

HEIDORN, Heinrich (1905–72)*

German trade unionist and social democratic politician. Member of ISK. Chairman of DGB in North Rhine-Westphalia, 1947–56. Executive member of the DGB. SPD member of the Bundestag, 1953–7. Contributor to socialist papers and journals.

There are two major collections of Heidorn's papers. The first holding, at the North Rhine-Westphalian Hauptstaatsarchiv, Düsseldorf, comprises papers on trade union reconstruction after 1945, the relationship between trade unions and political parties, youth work, white-collar workers, emergency laws, and co-determination 1951–62. The collection, which also contains some correspondence, covers the period 1944–72, and comprises 205 archive volumes. The second and even larger holding is at the DGB archive in Düsseldorf. This concerns the reconstruction and history of the trade unions, especially in the British Occupation Zone. Finally a few items are to be found in the AdsD, Bonn.

* Known by the pseudonym Werner Hansen.

HEIJENOORT, Christian Gras van (fl. 1920s–30s)

Secretary of Trotsky (q.v.) 1929–39.

Heijenoort's papers from his period as Trotsky's secretary form part of the Trotsky Archive at the Houghton Library, Harvard University, USA.

HEILAND, Rudolf (1910–65)

German social democratic politician. Mayor of Marl 1946. SPD member of the Landtag 1947–9. Member of the Parliamentary Council 1948–9. Member of the Bundestag, 1949–65. Vice-President of the German Gemeindetag.

The North Rhine-Westphalian Hauptstaatsarchiv, Düsseldorf, has 107 archive volumes of Heiland's papers. The material concerns mainly parliamentary, municipal and SPD politics.

HEILMANN, Ernst (1881–1940)

German social democratic politician and journalist. Co-founder of the Reichsbund der Kriegsbeschädigten. Member of the Prussian Landesversammlung and Landtag (Chairman of the SPD group). Member of the Reichstag. Murdered after seven years in Buchenwald concentration camp.

Heilmann's papers have been much divided. Those for the period before 1933 were confiscated and either destroyed or lost during and shortly after the Second World War. In 1962 his letters to his family and photographs from Buchenwald were still in private hands. However, there is a microfilm copy in the Bundesarchiv, Koblenz, and some photocopies are to be found in the Wiener Library, London. Finally, 17 of Heilmann's letters from the concentration camp are in the AdsD at the Friedrich-Ebert-Stiftung, Bonn. (See Mommsen, *op. cit.*)

HEIMERICH, Hermann (1885–1963)

German social democratic local and provincial politician. At first lawyer. Nuremberg City Councillor 1919–25. Mayor of Kiel 1925–8. Lord Mayor of Mannheim 1928–33. Provincial President of Mittelrhein-Saar 1945. Again Lord Mayor of Mannheim 1949–55.

The Stadtarchiv, Mannheim, has a very large collection of Heimerich's papers for the years 1919–63. These include papers concerning his professional, political and official activity, as well as personal matters, together with speeches, lectures and articles, etc. There is correspondence with, amongst others, Albert Bassermann, Fritz Cahn-Garnier, Theodor Eschenburg, Theodor Heuss, Hans Luther, Reinhold Maier, Gustav Radbruch (q.v.), Hans Reschke, Carlo Schmidt (q.v.), Franz Schnabel and Hermann Veit (q.v.). In addition, this holding is enriched by the papers of his wife Annaluise Heimerich, and photocopies from official files of the Mittelrhein-Saar Oberregierungspräsidium. (See Mommsen, *op. cit.*)

HEINE, Fritz (b. 1904)

German social democratic functionary. From 1924 employee of the SPD Central Committee in Berlin. Exiled in Prague 1933–8, in France 1938–40 and in England 1940–46. Several months in Africa in 1943 to establish contact with social democrats amongst the prisoners of war. Full time member of the SPD Executive responsible for press, propaganda and election campaigns 1946–58. Co-editor of the *Hannoversche Presse, Neuer Vorwärts* and *Sopade-Informationsdienst*.

Fritz Heine's papers covering the years 1947–57 are in the AdsD, Bonn. These comprise general correspondence concerning, apart from personal matters, reparations, trials, the press, elections and propaganda, SPD organisation and press, and overseas visits of social democratic politicians.

HEINE, Wolfgang (1861–1944)

German social democratic politician and jurist. Lawyer by profession. Defence work in a number of political trials against social democrats. Member of the Reichstag 1898–1918 and then of the National Assembly. 'Revisionist'. Representative of the SPD–right wing. Prussian Minister of Justice 1918–19 and Minister of the Interior 1919–20. Resigned office shortly after the Kapp Putsch. No major political role thereafter. Exiled in Switzerland 1933.

There are three holdings of Wolfgang Heine's papers. First, papers arising from his work as a lawyer and member of the Reichstag in the period 1892–1930 are in the Deutsches Zentralarchiv, Potsdam. Secondly, a small collection of his political memoirs and a few items from the years of exile are to be found at the Bundesarchiv, Koblenz (covering 1938–44). Finally, the IISH, Amsterdam, has a large collection concerning German politics from *c.* 1890 to *c.* 1933 arising from his professional and political activity. (It contains scarcely any personal papers or private correspondence.) This holding is particularly rich in relation to politically-motivated prosecutions of social democrats, freedom of association, the 'Budget question' in the years 1908–16, revolutionary uprisings in January/February 1919 and the Kapp Putsch. A printed inventory is available. (See Mommsen, *op. cit.*)

HEINEMANN, Gustav (1899–1976)

German politician. CDU member and Lord Mayor of Essen 1946. Minister of Justice, North Rhine-Westphalia 1947–8. Minister of the Interior in the first Adenauer administration 1949–50. Resignation from government over defence and rearmament and domestic policies 1950. Founder of the Notgemeinschaft für den Frieden Europas (Emergency Association for European Peace). Resignation from the CDU 1951. Co-founder of the Gesamtdeutsche Volkspartei (for a unified and neutral Germany) 1952. Membership of the SPD on the dissolution of the GVP in 1957. SPD member of the Bundestag and executive member of the SPD from 1957. SPD Justice Minister in the Grand Coalition, 1966. Federal President, 1969–74.

Most of Heinemann's papers, which cover the years 1919–69, are in the AdsD, Bonn. These comprise correspondence, notes, personal papers and collections of material, especially from the period after 1945. They concern, *inter alia*, Heinemann's disagreements with Adenauer; the Notgemeinschaft für den Frieden Europas; the GVP and its journal, the

Gesamtdeutsche Rundschau; his activity as a Bundestag deputy, as Federal Justice Minister, and as President; atomic weapons; the CDU and SPD; church matters, and political and journalistic activity. Heinemann's papers are supplemented by papers of his father, Otto Heinemann, on the Factory Council Law in the Weimar National Assembly, and on the organisation of health insurance before the Second World War. Finally, the Landeskirchliches Archive of the Protestant Church of Westphalia in Bielefeld has a collection of material on the church struggle in the Third Reich, among other matters, in the holding of the Archiv des Kirchenkampfes im Dritten Reich. (See Mommsen, *op. cit.*)

HEINER, Frank

Chicago radical and sociologist. Emma Goldman's (q.v.) lover.

There is a collection of Heiner's papers in the IISH, Amsterdam, comprising mainly correspondence with, and material concerning, Emma Goldman (q.v.). This is – in effect – an annexe to the Goldman collection (to which access is restricted).

HEINIG, Kurt (1886–1956)

German social democratic politician. Journalist and budgetary expert. Member of the Reichstag (SPD). Exiled in Denmark and then Sweden.

The first part of Heinig's papers is in the ARAB, Stockholm. Permission of his family is needed to consult these papers. The second part, including his diaries and personal letters, was in private possession in Sweden. (See also Siegfried Ortloff and Mommsen, *op. cit.*)

HELD, Jakob (1894–1970)

German Christian trade unionist.

Some papers arising from Held's activity in the Christian trade unions from 1924–34 are in the DGB Archive, Düsseldorf.

HELGORSKI, Stanislas

French Communard.

See Appendix I.

HELLENBROCK, Josef (b. 1900)

German social democratic politician. At first turner. City Councillor in Krefeld 1933 and again after 1945. Mayor 1956 and First Lord Mayor of Krefeld 1962. Landtag member in Düsseldorf 1946–50. Member of the Bundestag 1953–69.

Hellenbrock's papers are in the AdsD at the Friedrich-Ebert-Stiftung, Bonn. This quite extensive holding is particularly revealing on co-operation between the SPD Executive, the Bundestag group (and study groups) and the Federal Committee on Regional Planning, as well as city and housing construction during the fifth Bundestag (1965–9).

HELMER, Oskar (1887–1963)

Austrian social democrat on the right of the party. Interior Minister, 1945–59.

The AVA, Vienna, has four boxes of papers relating to his period of office in the Lower Austrian provincial government. The VGA, Vienna, has twenty-six files and thirty-seven photograph albums. The collection includes personal documents, speeches, articles, and correspondence with Julius Deutsch (q.v.), Karl Renner (q.v.), Theodor Körner (q.v.), and Adolf Schärf (q.v.). There is also material relating to the Austrian parliamentary elections in 1959; the Austrian presidential election in 1957; the party publishing houses *Vorwärts* and *Gutenberg*; negotiations between the political parties in 1953, 1954 and 1957; the formation of the government in 1956; the SPÖ in Lower Austria; and the Soviet occupation. The Vienna City Library (WSLB) has a collection of correspondence from the years 1951–61.

HELO, Johan (1889–1966)

Finnish social democratic politician. Diplomat. Municipal politician for the Finnish Social Democratic Party. Cabinet Minister 1920–27. Member of the Finnish People's Democratic League (SKDL) from 1944. Diplomatic post, 1945–54. Ambassador in Paris 1954–6.

Helo's papers are in the National Archives of Finland, Helsinki. Special permission from the Director is necessary to consult these papers.

HELPHAND, Alexander Israel (1867–1924)*

Russian socialist writer and theorist. Left Russia at the age of 19. Active as a radical in the SPD from 1891. Editor of several social democratic papers. Member of the Petrograd Soviet of 1905. Important influence on both German and Russian Marxists before 1910. Left Germany in 1910 for Vienna, and then Constantinople (Istanbul), and there made a personal fortune through trading. Worked for the victory of the Central Powers during the First World War (adviser to the German Foreign Ministry) – its representative in connection with the revolutionary movement in Russia. After 1918 publisher in Berlin and confidant of leading social democrats.

Helphand destroyed most of his personal papers shortly before his death. However, a small collection survives at the Staatsarchiv, Berlin. This includes a diary, notes and other documents arising from his activity in Turkey and the editing of his journal *Die Glocke*, together with business correspondence 1915–19 (with, amongst others, Sklarz in 1916). This collection has also been enriched by letters from 'Parvus' (his pseudonym) (from Turkey, 1910) and by letters from Victor Naumann to Hertling. In addition, there is a photocopy of a receipt for funds from the German government for furtherance of revolutionary activities in Russia (1915), in the Hoover Institution, Stanford University, California. Finally, the bibliography of Z. Zeman and W. Scharlau, *The Merchant of Revolution: The Life of Alexander Israel Helphand (Parvus)* (London: 1965) refers to letters of Helphand in the private collection of Bruno Schönlank (jr), Zürich.

* Known by the pseudonym Parvus.

HEMSATH, Heinrich (b. 1902)

German social democrat. Municipal and Land politician.

The Staatsarchiv, Düsseldorf, has a collection of papers relating to municipal politics, labour questions, and social and health matters. The AdsD, Bonn, has a further collection which includes personal papers, correspondence, speeches and articles. (See Mommsen, *op. cit.*)

HENKE, Alfred (1868–1946)

German social democratic politician. At first cigar maker. Political editor of the *Bremer Bürgerzeitung* from 1901. Member of the Bremen Council 1906–22. Member of the Reichstag (SPD and, from 1917–*c*. 1922, USPD) 1912–32. Prominent role during the revolution in Bremen 1918–19. Close to the 'left radicals' Johann Knief, Franz Mehring (q.v.), Antonie Pannekoek (q.v.), Karl Radek and others. City Councillor in Berlin 1922–33.

Henke's papers covering the years 1907–19 are in the AdsD, Friedrich-Ebert-Stiftung, Bonn. These include letters from the above-mentioned leaders, as well as, amongst others, Philipp Scheidemann (q.v.), Karl Kautsky (q.v.), Heinrich Laufenberg, Klara Zetkin (q.v.), Paul Frölich (q.v.), Erich Rossmann (q.v.) and Heinrich Schulz. In addition, there are manuscripts, notes and collections of material concerning the 'Radek case', the Party schism in the First World War and the revolution in Bremen, 1918–19.

HENRIKSSON-HOLMBERG, Gustaf (1864–1929)

Swedish syndicalist. Agriculturalist. Journalist and publicist. Leading proponent of syndicalism in Sweden. Pioneer agitator amongst agricultural workers. Studied in Germany where he was in contact with Eugen Dühring. Collaborator and editor of several papers in Northern Sweden 1891–1905. From 1906 independent writer.

A small collection of Henriksson-Holmberg's papers for the years 1881–1929 is in the ARAB, Stockholm. These comprise correspondence, manuscripts, leaflets and newspaper cuttings. An inventory is available.

HENSSLER, Fritz (1886–1953)

German social democratic politician. Editor of the social democratic *Dortmunder Presse* 1912–33. City Council Director 1925–33. Member of the Reichstag 1930–33. Many years in prison and concentration camp under the Nazi regime. Chairman of the SPD district Western Westphalia. Member of the SPD Executive. Member of the Agricultural Committee of the Zonenbeirat (Zonal Advisory Board) set up by the British occupation authority. Lord Mayor of Dortmund. Licensee of the *Westfälische Rundschau*. Member of the Landtag (Chairman of the SPD group). Member of the Bundestag.

Henssler's papers are in the AdsD at the Friedrich-Ebert-Stiftung, Bonn. They include only a few fortuitously surviving documents from the Weimar period and the year 1945. From 1946, however, they contain considerable documentation on local and regional politics (to do with its foundation and the policy on coalition), projected agrarian reforms and socialisation in North Rhine-Westphalia, press matters, inner-Party disputes (and personalities), policy on officials and employees, and the trade union movement.

HERDAL, Harald (b. 1900)

Danish communist writer.

Six boxes of Herdal's papers for the years since 1930, including correspondence and manuscripts, are in the ABA, Copenhagen.

HERMANS, Louis M. (1861–1943)

Dutch social democrat. SDAP member.

The IISH, Amsterdam, has a small collection of Hermans's correspondence for the years 1896–1937. (See M. Campfens, *op. cit.*)

HERNANDEZ, Sinesio Garcia (1897–1983)*

Spanish anarcho-syndicalist. Historian. Lived in Argentina 1918–31. Leading role in building the anarcho-syndicalist movement (FORA) in Argentina. Returned to Spain 1931. Member of the FAI. Leading economist of Spanish anarcho-syndicalism. Minister for the Economy in the Catalan Regional Government December 1936. Exile in France. Finally returned to Argentina where he was active mainly as a historian.

There is a large collection of Hernandez's papers in the IISH, Amsterdam. This includes correspondence, manuscripts, documents, and collections of material (some on the history of anarcho-syndicalism).

* Known by the pseudonym Diego Abad de Santillàn.

HERR, Lucien (1864–1926)

French socialist and philosopher. A great influence on Jean Jaurès (q.v.) and Léon Blum (q.v.).

According to Maitron, *op. cit.*, the papers still remained with the family in 1975. These included some draft manuscripts and correspondence (notably his letters to Charles Andler).

HERRMANN, Karl (1882–1951)

German social democratic local politician. At first metal worker. District Secretary of the SPD, at first in Leipzig, and then in Kassel 1919–33. Concentration camp victim under the Nazi regime. After 1945 District President of the Landkreis Kassel.

The AdsD at the Friedrich-Ebert-Stiftung, Bonn, has a small collection of Hermann's papers for the years 1932–49. These concern SPD organisation, the 1946 SPD Conference in Hannover and local politics in Kassel.

HERTZ, Frederik Adolf (fl. 1880s)

Pioneer Danish socialist. Agitator and song writer.

A small collection of Hertz's papers from the late 19th century is in the ABA, Copenhagen.

HERTZ, Paul (1888–1961)

German social democratic politician. Economics expert. SPD member from 1905. War service 1914–17. Joined USPD and was political editor of its central organ *Die Freiheit* 1918–22. Member of the Berlin City Parliament 1919–25. Member of the Reichstag 1920–33 (at first for the USPD and then for the SPD). From 1922 Secretary of the SPD Reichstag group and specialist on taxation and financial policy. Exiled in Prague and Paris 1933–8. Directed the journal *Sozialistische Aktion* and the illegal edition of *Neuer Vorwärts*. Practically withdrew from the SPD Executive in Exile in 1938 because of differences, amongst others, over the attitude towards the communists. In the USA 1939–44. Returned to Berlin upon the request of Ernst Reuter. Senator for Credit 1951–3 and for Economics and Credit in West Berlin 1955–61.

Hertz's extensive papers for the years 1920–61 are in the IISH, Amsterdam. These include his personal (1950–61) and political (1937–50) correspondence concerning questions of Party organisation, the USPD and, in particular, the exiled SPD and KPD in London 1933–45. His correspondents include, amongst others, Otto Bauer (q.v.), August Bebel (q.v.), Léon Blum (q.v.), Karl Kautsky (q.v.), Paul Löbe (q.v.), Ernst Reuter (q.v.), Kurt Schumacher (q.v.), Rudolf Wissel (q.v.) and Klara Zetkin (q.v.). In addition, his papers contain manuscripts (from, amongst others, Karl Kautsky, Paul Sering and Otto Strasser); memoranda, circulars and leaflets; and items connected with his activity as a Senator in Berlin. Finally, copies from the above are to be found in the AdsD at the Friedrich-Ebert-Stiftung, Bonn (46 microfilms mainly concerning the emigration), and at the Ernst-Reuter Archiv, Berlin (64 microfilms). These are also in the Hoover Institution, Stanford University, California, USA. (See Mommsen, *op. cit.*)

HERWEGH, Georg (1817–75)

German revolutionary and political poet. Friend of Marx (q.v.). Leader with Bornstedt of the ill-fated German Legion raised in France in 1848.

Herwegh's papers, covering the period 1848–70, and including correspondence with Alexander Herzen (q.v.), are in the British Library (Add Mss 47664–8). According to Mommsen, *op. cit.*, there are other papers in the Musée Georg Herwegh at Liestal, Switzerland, and in the Schiller-Nationalmuseum, Marbach, West Germany.

HERZ, Carl (1879–1951)

German social democratic politician. At first lawyer. City Councillor in Altona 1910. Opposed the support of war credits 1914. Soldier 1915–18. From *c.* 1917 member of the USPD but resigned in 1919. Active with Dr Laufenberg in Hamburg during the revolution. City Councillor and Deputy Mayor for the Spandau District in Berlin 1921–6. Participated in working out and formulating the SPD's new ('Heidelberg') Programme in 1925. Elected Mayor of the Kreuzberg District of Berlin 1926. Ejected from office by the Nazis as a Jew and a social democrat in 1933. Exiled in London 1939. Settled in Israel 1946.

Herz's papers are in the IISH, Amsterdam. These comprise general correspondence and files arising from his personal, literary and political activity. The latter concern, amongst other subjects: his work as a city councillor in Altona; the Revolution, USPD and other matters in Hamburg; the Spandau and Kreuzberg Districts of Berlin during his periods of office and his exile in Britain. A printed inventory is available.

HERZEN, Alexander Ivanovič (1812–70)

Pioneer Russian socialist and writer. Critic of the Tsarist order. Influenced by Saint-Simon. Imprisoned and then exiled to the Russian Provinces 1834–9. Again exiled 1840. Now rejected the Tsarist order in its entirety. Found in Hegel 'the algebra of revolution' and the way to atheism. Influenced by George Sand (q.v.) towards equality and freedom for women. Permitted to return to Russia in 1842. At the centre of a circle of 'Westernisers'. Became a socialist – influenced by, amongst others, Louis Blanc (q.v.), Fourier (q.v.) and Proudhon (q.v.). Left Russia in 1847 for Paris and then Italy. Worked out his theory of the development of socialism in Russia on the basis of the ancient self-governing peasant commune (which was to be the most influential socialist perspective in Russia up to the turn of the century) 1849–53. In England in 1852–65 where he wrote his memoirs. Founded, in 1853, the influential Free Russian Press which spread Herzen's ideas – and fame – throughout Europe and Russia.

There are two collections of Herzen's papers. The first, in the IISH, Amsterdam, includes correspondence (notably with his son, and with Western European politicians) and part of the manuscript *Byloe i dumy*. A provisional inventory is available. A second collection – comprising mainly correspondence – is in the Feltrinelli Institute, Milan.

HESS, Moses (1812–75)

Pioneer German socialist and Zionist. Publicist. Collaborator on many socialist journals from 1842–3. Early connection with Marx (q.v.) and Friedrich Engels (q.v.). Representative of 'true' or Utopian socialism. Member of the Communist League. From 1848 in exile. At first a supporter of the Lassallean (q.v.) tendency in the re-emergent German labour movement. After participating in Congresses of the International, supporter of the Eisenacher tendency. From the 1850s greatly concerned with problems of Jewish emancipation.

Hess's papers are divided between two collections. The first is in the IISH, Amsterdam, and the second is in the Central Zionist Archives, Jerusalem. There is a detailed published inventory: see Edmund Silberner, *The Works of Moses Hess: An inventory of his signed and anonymous publications, manuscripts and correspondence* (Leiden: 1958).

HESSELS, Abraham (b. 1910)

Dutch conscientious objector.

The IISH, Amsterdam, has a small collection of Hessels's correspondence for the years 1930–36. (See M. Campfens, *op. cit.*)

HIITONEN, Ensio (1900–70)

Finnish politician. Successively a member of the National Progress Party, the Finnish Social Democratic Party and the Finnish People's Democratic League (SKDL). Editor-in-Chief of the bulletin *Vapaa Pohjola* (The Free North). Municipal politician.

Hiitonen's papers are in the National Archives of Finland, Helsinki. Special permission from the Director is necessary to consult these papers.

HILFERDING, Rudolf (1877–1941)

German social democratic theorist and politician. Prominent Austro-Marxist theoretician. USPD member and editor of *Freiheit* (1918–22). Leader and spokesman of the USPD right. Proponent of reunification with the SPD, and executive member of the reunited party. Reich Minister of Finance 1923 and 1928–9. Active in the socialist emigration after 1933. Died at the hands of the Gestapo in France, 1941.

All that remains of Hilferding's papers is the manuscript of one of his last essays, '*Das historische Problem*', and other material relating to the same essay. This was last reported in private hands.

HILGENGA, J. (1883–1968)

Dutch socialist and trade unionist.

The IISH, Amsterdam, has a small collection of Hilgenga's correspondence and other documents. (See M. Campfens, *op. cit.*)

HILL, Joe (d. 1915)*

Swedish emigrant to the USA. Prominent IWW agitator. Victim of judicial assassination 1915. Immortalised as a folk hero and as Labour's poet.

Some of Hill's papers are in the ARAB, Stockholm.

* Swedish name, Joel Hägglund.

HIRCHE, Kurt (b. 1904)

German trade union official. Journalist. From 1953 Director of the Economic Policy Department and from 1955 of the Parliamentary Lobby of the DGB in Bonn.

A small collection of Hirche's papers concerning his trade union activity in the years 1950–55 is in the DGB Archive, Düsseldorf. (See Mommsen, *op. cit.*)

HIRDMAN, Gunnar (1888–1963)

Swedish. Leading activist in the Labour Education Movement (ABF). Teacher.

Seven boxes of Hirdman's papers are in the ARAB, Stockholm. An inventory is available.

HIRSCH, Karl (1841–1900)

German social democrat. Correspondent of the German social democratic press in Paris.

Hirsch's papers are in private hands. (See Mommsen, *op. cit.*)

HIRSCH, Martin (b. 1913)

German social democratic politician and legal expert. Member of the Bundestag 1961–71. Federal Constitutional Judge in Karlsruhe 1971.

The AdsD, Bonn, has a number of items belonging to Martin Hirsch concerning the Bundesgerichtshof (Federal Supreme Court) and the Bundesverfassungsgericht (Federal Constitutional Court) in the years 1961–5. (See Mommsen, *op. cit.*)

HIRSCH, Max (1832–1905)

German anti-socialist (class collaborationist) trade union leader and politician. Economist. Co-founder of the Hirsch-Dunckersche Gewerkvereine (Trade Associations). Member of the Prussian Parliament and of the Reichstag (Fortschrittspartei).

Hirsch's political-economic correspondence is in the Deutsches Zentralarchiv, Potsdam. (See Mommsen, *op. cit.*)

HJERPE, Karl Gösta (b. 1913)

Swedish member of the International Brigade. Bricklayer.

Some of Hjerpe's papers are in the ARAB, Stockholm.

HOCH, Fritz (b. 1896)

German social democrat. Member of the Commission to prepare the Hessian constitution 1946. Member of the Parliamentary Council 1948–9. District President in Kassel until 1961.

Hoch's papers for the years 1948–9 are in the AdsD, Bonn. These include correspondence and notes and concern, in particular, the Parliamentary Council.

HOCH, Gustav (1862–1942)

German social democratic politician. Journalist. Member of the Reichstag 1898–1903 and 1907–28 (SPD).

A large collection of Hoch's papers is in the AdsD at the Friedrich-Ebert-Stiftung, Bonn. These are mainly collections of material comprising manuscripts and articles on historical and contemporary political questions (including the 1848 Revolution, economic questions, social policy and insurance. (See Mommsen, *op. cit.*)

HOCQUARD, Auguste (fl. 1830s–70s)

French Communard.

See Appendix I.

HODANN, Max (1884–1946)

German socialist exile from Nazi persecution. Doctor. Worked for the Institut für Sexualforschung and founded the first Advisory Centre for Mothers in Berlin. Executive member of the Socialist Doctors' Association. Imprisoned 1933. Exile in Switzerland, in Norway 1934–40, and from 1940 in Sweden. Militia Doctor in Spain 1937–8. Member of the Free German Cultural League. Remained in Sweden.

Hodann's papers for the years 1916–46 are in the ARAB, Stockholm. These comprise personal documents, correspondence, manuscripts and drafts, newspaper cuttings and other printed material arising from his political and other activities.

HOEGNER, Wilhelm (b. 1887)

German social democratic politician. Member of the Bavarian Landtag 1924–32 and again since 1962. Member of the Reichstag 1930–33. Exile in Austria and then Switzerland 1933–45. Active for the SPD-in-exile and the group Das Demokratische Deutschland. Prime Minister 1945–6, Minister of Justice 1946–7 and Minister of the Interior in Bavaria 1950.

The Institut für Zeitgeschichte, Munich, has a very large collection of Hoegner's papers. These concern the fate of exiles; US occupation policy after the war; bizonal administration; political and economic reconstruction in Bavaria; the making of the Bavarian constitution; denazification and the construction of the SPD in Bavaria 1945–71. In addition, there is correspondence from his period of exile, together with speeches and articles, political, legal and journalistic works and printed manuscripts. (See Mommsen, *op. cit.*)

HOFF, Hans von (1899–1969)

German trade unionist. Until 1933 Chairman of the Angestelltengewerkschaft (White-Collar Employees' Trade Union) in Lübeck. In the Bizonengewerkschaftsrat (Bizonal Trade

Union Council) in Frankfurt 1947. Executive member of the DGB 1949. Director of the ECSC High Authority in Luxembourg and personal adviser to Jean Monnet 1952.

The DGB Archive in Düsseldorf contains files of the Federal Executive for the years 1951–5 concerning the expulsion of Hoff from his union and subsequent rehabilitation.

HOFLIN, Per (b. 1899)

Swedish trade unionist. Official in the Textile Workers' Union.

Two boxes of Hoflin's papers are in the ARAB, Stockholm. A preliminary inventory is available.

HÖGBERG, Georg (1895–1956)

Swedish anarchist. Railway worker, and gas worker in Stockholm in 1915. Member of the anarchist movement in Stockholm. Temporarily responsible for publishing its paper *Brand*.

Four boxes of Högberg's papers for the years 1912–16 are in the ARAB, Stockholm. These comprise personal documents, correspondence, sketches and notes, membership books, photographs and newspapers. An inventory is available.

HÖGLUND, Zeth (1884–1956)

Swedish communist leader. Editor. Chairman of the Social Democratic youth movement 1909. Executive member of the SAP 1908–11. Leading figure in the SAP Opposition. Editor of its paper *Stormklockan* 1908–18. Co-founder of the Left-Socialist Party 1917. Until 1924 Chairman of the SKP, and Editor-in-Chief of the paper *Folkets Dagblad Politiken* 1919–24. Founded an Independent Communist Party 1924. Rejoined the SAP 1926. Again on the SAP Executive 1928–44. Member of Parliament 1915–17 and 1928–40. Editor-in-Chief of the *Social Demokraten* 1936–40. Important role in Stockholm municipal politics. City Treasurer 1940–50.

A small part of Höglund's papers, for the years 1921–39 is in the ARAB, Stockholm. This comprises circulars, information service material, newspapers and cuttings, pamphlets and other printed matter. An inventory is available.

HOHOFF, Wilhelm (1848–1923)

German Christian Socialist. Catholic priest whose name and anti-capitalist views were used to convince Catholics to join the free trade unions and the SPD (although he was not a member of the SPD).

Hohoff corresponded widely with socialists and economists. Most of his correspondence has not survived, but the AdsD at the Friedrich-Ebert-Stiftung, Bonn, has 13 letters from August Bebel (q.v.), Eduard Bernstein (q.v.), Wilhelm Liebknecht (q.v.), and, above all, Karl Kautsky (q.v.). In addition, there is a microfilm of further correspondence.

HÖLTERMANN, Karl (1894–1955)

German social democratic politician. Editor-in-Chief of the Magdeburg *Volksstimme*. Co-founder of the Reichsbanner Schwarz-Rot-Gold 1924. Directed its central organ *Das Reichsbanner* and succeeded Otto Hörsing (q.v.) as its Chairman in 1930. Member of the

Reichstag 1932–3. Exiled in the Saarland 1933 and later in England (where he remained). During exile he took up a controversial stance in relation to the official policy of the SOPADE.

The AdsD at the Friedrich-Ebert-Stiftung, Bonn has a collection of Höltermann's papers. Apart from correspondence concerning Alfred Ziehm, these comprise notes, manuscripts and collections of material from his period of exile, and later, concerning language problems, political terminology, border questions, military strategy, the November Revolution 1918, the Reichsbanner and disputes between the social democrats and communists. (See Mommsen, *op. cit.*)

HONORÉ, Johannes (b. 1895)

Founding member of the Danish Communist Party. Later rejoined the SD. Printer.

Two boxes of Honoré's papers for the years 1916–25 are in the ABA, Copenhagen. As well as letters to Honoré and manuscripts, these contain papers concerning the early history of the DKP.

HØRDUM, Christen Iver (1846–1911)

Danish social democratic politician. In 1884 one of the first social democrats to enter Parliament.

There is a small collection of Hørdum's letters and manuscripts in the ABA, Copenhagen.

HÖRSING, Otto (1874–1937)

German social democratic functionary and politician. Chairman of the Central Workers' and Soldiers' Council in Upper Silesia in 1919, as well as Reichskommissar for Upper Silesia and Westposen. Member of the Weimar National Assembly and of the Reichstag 1919–22. Member of the Prussian Landtag 1925. Oberpräsident of the province Saxony. Founder 1924, and until 1931 National Chairman of the Reichsbanner Schwarz-Rot-Gold. Expelled from the SPD and Reichsbanner 1931. Founder of the Sozialrepublikanische Partei 1931.

The Historische Kommission zu Berlin has a small collection of Hörsing's papers. These concern the Polish Socialist Party in Prussia and the SPD 1909–13, his activity in the Central Workers' and Soldiers' Council and scattered papers from the later years. (See Mommsen, *op. cit.*)

HOTZ, Charles (1874–1937)

Swiss anarchist.

A collection of Hotz's papers is in the IISH, Amsterdam.

HOUPILLARD, Paul (b. 1852)

French Communard.

See Appendix I.

HUBALEK, Felix (1908–58)

Austrian social democrat. Co-editor-in-chief, *Arbeiterzeitung*. Writer.

The VGA, Vienna, has eight files, containing mainly literary material and correspondence from 1955 and 1957.

HUG, René (fl. 1940s)

French. Secretary of the SFIO.

Hug's correspondence from June to August 1940 is in the OURS, Paris.

HUGHES, Clouis (1851–1907)

French poet and journalist. Independent socialist politician. Deputy for Marseilles, 1881–9 and for Paris, 1893–1906.

Seven letters written by Hughes from prison (1872–5) to his friend Jouvent are in the Inguimbertine Library (Carpentras). A number of items, including a further seven letters – for the years 1877–1907 – are to be found in the Musée Arbaud (Aix). In addition, numerous letters received by Hughes (notably from Victor Hugo), as well as his paintings, are in the possession of his daughter Mme Andrieu. (See Maitron, *op. cit.*)

HUHLE, Robert (fl. 1950s)

Danish social democratic journalist.

Huhle's papers consist of a small collection of letters from Harald Bergstedt (1952) and Hans Hedtoff-Hanson (q.v.) (1951–2) in the ABA, Copenhagen.

HUHN, Willy (1909–70)

German left-wing socialist.

Huhn's extensive papers for the years 1928–70 are in the IISH, Amsterdam. These comprise manuscripts of his theoretical studies and a voluminous correspondence with left-wing socialists of all tendencies in Germany and abroad (1945–70), as well as collections of printed material and informal sources on the SAP (1931–3), the re-establishment of popular education in Berlin and the Eastern Zone of Germany (1945–6), the SPD in Berlin in the 1950s, left-wing socialist groups and periodicals in West Berlin and the BRD in the same period, as well as the campaign for nuclear disarmament. A provisional card index of the collection is available.

HULT, Carl Alrik (1867–1964)

Swedish social democrat. US correspondent for *Social Demokraten*. Engineer and inventor.

Three boxes of Hult's papers are in the ARAB, Stockholm.

HUMBERT-DROZ, Jules (1891–1971)

Swiss communist. Started life as a Protestant minister. Secretary of the ECCI.

The papers of Humbert-Droz are in the City Library of La Chaux-de-Fonds, Switzerland. Photocopies and a microfilm copy of this collection are held, respectively, in the IISH, Amsterdam and the Hoover Institution, Stanford University, California. These papers cover the years 1913–33 and constitute a prime source for the history of the Comintern and its European sections. Although part of this collection is closed, the documents for the years 1919–32 concerning the Comintern have been edited by Siegfried Bahne and published in two volumes (with a third in preparation): *Archives de Jules Humbert-Droz*, vols I and II (Dordrecht: 1970 and 1982).

HUROP, Ferdinand (1853–1934)

Pioneer Danish trade unionist. Founder of the Blacksmiths' Union 1883. Strike leader in 1885. Later emigrated to the USA.

One box of Hurop's papers for the years 1885–1934 is in the ABA, Copenhagen. Most of these, however, stem from the years 1909–34 when Hurop wrote many letters to leaders of the Danish Labour movement concerning problems in the USA.

HUYSMANS, Camille (1871–1968)

Belgian socialist politician. Executive member of the Belgian Socialist Party. Secretary of the International Socialist Bureau of the Second International 1904–19. Influential figure as diplomat and administrator in the international socialist movement. Later prominent in Belgian political life.

There is a large collection (mainly copies) of Huysmans's papers in the Feltrinelli Institute, Milan. This includes extensive correspondence with leading figures in the international socialist movement as well as other documentation of great importance to the history of the Second International and its member parties in the first two decades of the twentieth century.

ÎAREMENKO, A. (fl. 1914–18)

Russian communist.

There is a typescript translation of a memoir by Îaremenko in the Hoover Institution, Stanford University, California. Entitled *Diary of a Communist* (one vol., n.d.), this relates to the Russian Civil War in Siberia, 1918–20.

ICKLER, Gustav (b. 1870)

German National Liberal trade unionist and politician. Chairman of the Kartell Deutscher Reichs- und Staatsarbeiter (Federation of German State Employees) from about 1910 and then of the Association of German Railway Mechanics and Labourers. Member of the Reichstag (National Liberal) 1912–18.

Ickler is reported to have destroyed his papers. (See Mommsen, *op. cit.*)

IDE-BOTTENHEIM, Henriette R. (1889–1981)

Dutch SDAP member.

The IISH, Amsterdam, has one file of Ide-Bottenheim's correspondence (1912–29).

IJZERMAN, Arie W. (1879–1956)

Dutch SDAP member.

The IISH, Amsterdam, has a small collection of Ijzerman's manuscripts and correspondence for three volumes of memoirs, of which two volumes have been published. The holding also contains lecture notes and other correspondence, and covers the period 1915–51.

IMBUSCH, Heinrich (1878–1945)

German Christian trade unionist. At first miner. Chairman of the Deutsche Gewerkschafts-bund 1929. Member of the National Assembly 1919. Member of the Reichstag 1920. Exiled in 1933.

The DGB Archive at Düsseldorf has a collection of Imbusch's correspondence, together with newspaper cuttings concerning Imbusch and his activity in the Christian trade union movement (mostly from the years 1905–33). (See Mommsen, *op. cit.*)

IOFFE, Abram Evseevič (1865–1910)

Russian Narodnik.

The IISH has a small collection of correspondence.

IVANOV, Ivan R. (d. 1975)

Russian anarchist.

The IISH, Amsterdam, has a small collection of Ivanov's manuscripts.

JACOB, Mathilde

Personal secretary of Rosa Luxemburg.

See under LUXEMBURG, Rosa.

JACOBI, Werner (1907–70)

German social democratic politician. Founding member of the Deutsch-Republikanischer Studentenbund 1927. Member of the North Rhine-Westphalian Landtag. Editor of the *Westfälische Rundschau*. State Commissioner responsible for rooting out mismanagement and corruption in North Rhine-Westphalia 1947–50. Member of the Bundestag from 1949. Deputy of the Deutscher Städtetag (City Federation) 1950–56. Managing Director of the Verband Kommunaler Unternehmen (Association of Municipal Enterprises) from 1956.

Jacobi's papers are in the AdsD at the Friedrich-Ebert-Stiftung, Bonn. These include only a few items from before 1956. For the years since then, however, this large collection includes extensive correspondence and documentation arising from his work in municipal policy, regional planning, urban construction, housing and energy.

JACOBS-VEBER, Sara (1900–76)

Russian Trotskyist (for some time secretary of Trotsky).

The IISH has a collection of correspondence covering the period 1935–61.

JACOBY, Johann (1805–77)

German revolutionary of 1848. Doctor. Democratic, and later social democratic, member of the National Assembly. Member of the Prussian Chamber of Deputies.

A rich collection of Jacoby's papers concerning the history of the German labour movement is in the Jewish National and University Library, Jerusalem. In addition, there are copies from this collection in the Bundesarchiv, Koblenz. (See Mommsen, *op. cit.*)

JAENGER, Pierre Paul (1803–67)

French Fourierist, having initially been influenced by Saint-Simon. Leader of the Fourierists in Haut-Rhin. Elected General Councillor for Wintzenheim, 1848. Member, editorial board, *Volksrepublic*.

His correspondence with followers of Fourier for the years 1833–45 is in the Bibliothèque Nationale, Paris. This includes letters from J. Blanc (q.v.), Cantagrel, Victor Considérant (q.v.), Dr Dularry, Laverdant, Just Muiron and C. Pellarin.

JÄNDEL, Ragner (1895–1939)

Swedish author of working-class origins, who wrote about working-class life.

Three boxes of Jändel's papers are in the ARAB, Stockholm. A preliminary inventory is available.

JANITSCHEK, Hans (b. 1934)

Austrian social democrat. Media adviser to the President of the Socialist Party of Austria 1965. From 1967 Assistant General Secretary, and from 1969 General Secretary of the Socialist International in London.

There is a collection of Janitschek's papers in the IISH, Amsterdam.

JANSONIUS, J. G. (1870–1957)

Dutch SDAP activist.

The IISH, Amsterdam has Jansonius's memoirs on microfilm.

JANSSON, Axel (1916–68)

Swedish communist. Member of Parliament for the SKP, and then for the Left-Communist Party (VPK).

Forty boxes of Axel Jansson's papers are in the ARAB, Stockholm. An inventory is available.

JANSSON, Ewald (1910–80)

Swedish trade union leader. Chairman of the Agricultural Workers' Union in the LO.

One box of Ewald Jansson's papers is in the ARAB, Stockholm.

JASPER, Heinrich (1875–1945)

German social democratic politician. From 1909 member, later President, of the Braunschweig Landtag. Member of the Weimar National Assembly (SPD) 1919. Several times Prime Minister of Braunschweig.

Until 1967 Jasper's papers were still in private hands. Since then, apparently, they have been lost. (See Mommsen, *op. cit.*)

JAURÈS, Jean (1859–1914)

French socialist leader. Republican Deputy for Albi, 1884–9. Socialist Deputy for Carmaux, 1893–8. After 1896, leading member of the International. Active supporter of Dreyfus. Helped launch *L'Humanité*. Most prominent leader of SFIO. Assassinated in 1914.

The relatively small number of Jaurès's unpublished papers are divided among numerous institutions. The Musée Jaurès (at Castres) has 80 of his letters. The IFHS, Paris, has 3 letters, written in 1904, concerning the founding of *L'Humanité*. There are 50 letters to or from Jaurès in the Bibliothèque Nationale, Paris. The Musée de l'Histoire, at Montreuil, has his library and some unpublished manuscript material. The IISH, Amsterdam, has relevant material (for example, an important letter from Jaurès in the Bernstein (q.v.) collection).

JEAN, Théodor (1863–1949)

Militant French Libertarian. Active in the *Fédération des groupes socialistes révolutionnaires indépendants* in Marseilles.

A collection of Jean's papers is in the CIRA archive in Marseilles. There is also some correspondence in the Grave (q.v.) papers.

JEANNERET, Gustave (1847–1927)

Swiss socialist. Secretary, 1872, of the Neuchâtel section of the Fédération Jurassienne.

Correspondence has been preserved by the family (see 'La correspondence du peintre Gustave Jeanneret' in *Le Mouvement Social* (vol. 51, April–June, 1965).

JENSEN, Albert (1879–1957)

Swedish syndicalist leader. Watchmaker. Journalist. Extensive activity as a publicist. Co-founder of the syndicalist trade union organisation Sveriges Arbetares Centralorganisation (SAC) 1910, and of the Syndicalist International (IAA) 1920. Editor of the anarchist paper *Brand* 1902–4, of the journal *Syndikalismen* 1925–9 and 1939–50, and of the SAC central organ *Arbetaren* 1922–5 and 1928–51. Extensive contacts with German syndicalists (including Rudolf Rocker (q.v.)) in the 1920s, and with Spanish syndicalists in the 1930s. Leading Swedish representative of syndicalism in the 1930s and 1940s.

A large collection of Albert Jensen's papers for the years 1908–69 is in the ARAB, Stockholm. These include correspondence, manuscripts, transcripts, newspaper articles and other printed material.

JENSEN, Eiler (1894–1969)

Danish trade union leader. President of the Danish Federation of Trade Unions (DSF).

Twenty boxes of Eiler Jensen's papers for the years 1908–67 are in the ABA, Copenhagen. Together with manuscripts of speeches, etc., these comprise mainly organisational papers arising from his Presidency of the DSF.

JENSEN, Georg (1893–1979)

Danish militant syndicalist.

Nine boxes of Georg Jensen's papers for the years 1913–77 are in the ABA, Copenhagen. These are particularly important for the history of the syndicalist movement in the years 1913–20, and include a number of letters from Christian Christensen (q.v.). A printed inventory is available.

JENSEN, Jens (1859–1928)

Pioneer Danish and international trade unionist. Founder of the Danish Federation of Trade Unions (DSF) in Copenhagen. First Chairman of the DSF. In 1888 participated in an international meeting of trade union leaders in London.

Ten boxes of Jens Jensen's papers for the years 1886–1927 are in the ABA, Copenhagen. A printed inventory is available. There is also a collection of his papers in the archive of the Danish Trade Union movement.

JEZIERSKA, Fanny (1887–1945)

Polish socialist.

The IISH has a small collection of correspondence covering the period 1915–38.

JOHNSEN, Niels (1893–1931)

Danish communist. Coppersmith and journalist.

One box of Johnsen's papers for the years 1916–29 is in the ABA, Copenhagen. The papers include the manuscript of his published memoirs as Danish delegate to early Comintern and Profintern Congresses as well as to the ECCI (1920 and 1921).

JOLA*

* Pseudonym of LANG, Josef.

JONGE, Willem C. de (1886–1925)

Dutch trade unionist and SDAP member.

The IISH, Amsterdam, has a collection of Jonge's documents and correspondence covering the period 1898–1919. (See M. Campfens, *op. cit.*)

JORDENS, Gerrit D. (1877–1957)

Dutch social democrat and later communist.

The IISH, Amsterdam, has a small collection of correspondence and documents covering the years 1907–33.

JØRGENSEN, Aage (1896–1960)

Danish communist. Editor of the DKP's central organ 1920–35.

Four boxes of Jørgensen's papers for the years 1906–59 are in the ABA, Copenhagen. These are particularly important for the history of the DKP in the years 1920–35 and include manuscripts as well as letters from, amongst others, Julius Bomholt (q.v.) and Harting Frisch (q.v.).

JOSSOT, H.-G. (1866–1951)

French artist. Collaborator on *Les Temps Nouveaux*, 1905–8.

See under GRAVE, Jean.

JOUHAUX, Léon (1879–1954)

French trade union leader. Secretary (then General Secretary), 1909–47, of the CGT. Supported the war effort, 1914–18, but declined ministerial office. Opponent of revolutionary syndicalism and communism. Interned 1941, deported to Germany 1943. President, CGT-FO, 1948–54. International trade unionist. Vice-President, International Trade Union Federation, 1919–45; Vice-President, World Federation of Trade Unions, 1945–8, etc. Nobel Peace Prize, 1951.

Jouhaux's papers constitute the archive Léon Jouhaux. (See Maitron, *op. cit.*)

JOURDAIN, Francis (1876–1958)

French militant anarchist, later communist. Artist and writer.

See under GRAVE, Jean.

JUCHACZ, Marie (1879–1956)*

German social democratic politician. Leader of the social democratic women's movement. At first factory worker and then tailoress. Active in the social democratic women's movement. Member of the SPD Executive (director of the Women's Office) 1917. One of the founders of the Arbeiterwohlfahrt (Industrial Welfare Organisation). Member of the Weimar Nationalversammlung 1919. Member of the Reichstag 1920–33. After 1933 exile in the Saarland, France and the USA. After her return to Germany in 1949 advisor on the SPD's work amongst women and participated in the activities of the Arbeiterwohlfahrt.

Juchacz's papers are in the AdsD at the Friedrich-Ebert-Stiftung, Bonn. They contain correspondence and a collection of material concerning the social democratic and general women's movement. In addition, there is documentation for women's biographies going beyond what appeared in her book *Sie lebten für eine bessere Welt* (Berlin/Hannover; 1955).

* Née Goltke.

JUNG, Hermann (1830–1901)

Swiss member of the General Council of the International. Watchmaker. Collector of material on the history of the International.

Jung's papers are in the IISH, Amsterdam. These comprise some 650 items of correspondence between members of the International (1865–85). Only a small number date from the time after the collapse of the International. They include reports, circulars, and statements of the General Council from the Conferences of the International (1865–78), documents concerning the various national sections (1865–72), and material concerning the finances of the International.

JÜRGENS, Ludwig (1886–1964)

German social democratic local politician. Senator for Stade 1930–33 and from 1952. Mayor of Stade 1946–52.

A large collection of Jürgens' papers are in the Staatsarchiv, Stade (in the holding Stadtarchiv, Stade). These include minutes, leaflets and correspondence in connection with his position as SPD Chairman in Stade from 1929–33 and 1945–55. (See Mommsen, *op. cit.*)

KAISEN, Wilhelm (1887–1979)

German social democratic politician. At first stucco worker. Editor of the Bremen *Volkszeitung* 1919. Member of the Bremen Bürgerschaft 1921. Senator for Welfare in Bremen 1927–33. Arrested 1933. President of the Senate and Mayor of Bremen 1945–65. Member of the Bundesrat 1949.

The Staatsarchiv, Bremen, has a large collection of Kaisen's papers for the period since 1945. These include his political correspondence, speeches and publications. These concern, in particular, municipal elections, coalition negotiations, the formation of the Senate and SPD politics in Bremen. In addition, there is a small collection of Kaisen's papers for the years 1907–69 in the AdsD, Bonn. Apart from an original letter of August Bebel (q.v. – 1911), this includes correspondence, duplicated material and newspaper articles on European politics (generally and with reference to the SPD).

KÄMPE, Alfred (1877–1936)

Swedish trade union editor. Editor of the paper of the Agricultural Workers' Union.

One box of Kämpe's papers is in the ARAB, Stockholm. This collection includes material from the suffrage movement of the late 1890s.

KAMPFFMEYER, Paul (1864–1945)

German social democratic publicist. From *c.* 1890 one of the 'Jungen'. Later Revisionist. SPD editor in Frankfurt and Munich. Director of the Central Party Archives of the SPD, 1921–33.

The Kampffmeyer collection does not contain his papers but only a small collection of letters to Eduard Bernstein (q.v.) from, amongst others, Wilhelm Liebknecht (q.v.) concerning *Der Sozialdemokrat* (Zürich). The collection is at the AdsD, Bonn.

KAPER, S. (b. 1905)

Dutch pacifist.

The IISH, Amsterdam, has a small collection of Kaper's documents relating to peace organisations covering the period 1945–52. (See M. Campfens *op. cit.*)

KAPP, Arno (1882–1960)

German anti-fascist. Active in Leipzig during the Second World War.

Kapp's papers are in the AdsD, Bonn. As well as his diary for the years 1943–5, these comprise manuscripts and material concerning Bebel (q.v.), Liebknecht (q.v.), and the labour movement and social democracy in Leipzig (1871–1945).

KARLBOM, Torvald (b. 1901)

Swedish trade union official. Until the early 1960s Head of the Education Department of the LO.

Fifteen boxes of Karlbom's papers are in the ARAB, Stockholm. As yet no inventory is available, but much of the material included in this collection is known to concern union organisations outside the LO in the timber industry.

KARPELES, Benno (1868–1938)

German social democratic journalist.

The IISH has a small collection of correspondence covering the period 1892–1905.

KAUTSKY, Benedikt (1894–1960)

Austrian social democrat. Son of Karl Kautsky (q.v.). In the Secretariat of the Social Democratic Party of Austria 1919–20. Secretary of the Vienna Chamber of Labour 1921–38. From 1945 writer. Director of the Economics School of the Chamber of Labour in Vienna 1951–7. Deputy General Director of the Credit-Anstalt Bank in Vienna. Noted anti-communist.

Benedikt Kautsky's papers are held by the Verein für Geschichte der Arbeiterbewegung, Vienna, whilst other material is in the ARAB, Stockholm.

KAUTSKY, Karl (1854–1938)

Austrian social democratic theorist and publicist; active in Germany. Born in Vienna. University education. Wrote for the socialist press from 1875. In the years of the Anti-Socialist Laws edited émigré publications in Switzerland and England. During these years educated himself in Marxism. In direct contact with Marx (q.v.) and Friedrich Engels (q.v.). Founder and editor of *Die Neue Zeit* in 1883. In the 1890s became the foremost interpreter and populariser of Marxism within the Second International before 1914, as well as the ideologue and guardian of Marxist orthodoxy with the SPD (dubbed the 'Pope of Socialism'). Immense political influence. Largely responsible for the SPD's 1891 ('Erfurt') Programme and its interpretation. Semi-official defender of the pre-1914 social democratic orthodoxy against first, Bernstein's (q.v.) revisionism and the SPD-right, and then Rosa Luxemburg (q.v.) and the SPD's 'left-radicals'. But loss of influence, as both were in large part a reaction against the orthodoxy he helped to construct. Further loss of influence as the SPD divided during the First World War. Lost his platform when dismissed from *Die Neue Zeit* in 1917. Reluctantly went into the USPD. Close to Haase (q.v.) 1915–18 but isolated from both the SPD-right and, partly because of his extreme hostility to the Bolsheviks, within the leftward moving USPD. Under the Provisional Government, Under Secretary in the Foreign Office (with special responsibility for publishing documents on the outbreak of war) and Chairman of the Socialisation Commission. After the Leipzig Conference of the USPD in December 1919 virtually withdrew from party activity. Spent the latter half of 1920 in Menshevik Georgia. Resumed activity in the rump USPD to promote reunification with the SPD. Place of honour in the reunified SPD but no official position. Contributed to the new SPD ('Heidelberg') Programme of 1925 but subsequently moved to Vienna and thereafter played no direct role in the SPD.

The bulk of Karl Kautsky's considerable papers are in the IISH, Amsterdam. These include memoirs, manuscripts, articles, and considerable correspondence (notably letters to Kautsky during his years of editing *Die Neue Zeit*, as well as his exchange of letters with Friedrich Engels and members of the Second International). There are also 18 files on subjects including the causes of the war, the work of the Socialisation Commission, Soviet Russia and Georgia. A printed inventory (together with a separate one covering Kautsky's family archive) is available. In addition, the typescript of an article entitled 'Der Demokratische Marxismus: Zum Vierzigsten Geburtstag der Russischen Sozialdemokratie' and concerning the history and future prospects of socialism in Russia, is in the Hoover Institution, Stanford University, California (see also KAUTSKY, Louise).

KAUTSKY, Louise

German social democrat. Wife of Karl Kautsky (q.v.).

There is a collection of manuscripts and other material collected by Louise Kautsky in the ABA, Copenhagen. These include her biographical notes and newspaper cuttings on Karl Kautsky, additional material added to his manuscript entitled 'Die Gemeinsamkeit des sozialdemokratischen und des kommunistischen Endziels' (1933), as well as material on Marx (q.v.) and Marx in the judgement of contemporaries. The main part of this collection, however, is made up of the following manuscript works by Karl Kautsky: *Einige Stunden bei Karl Marx* (typescript); *Theorie und Praxis* (handwritten); *Kommunismus und Sozialdemokratie* (typescript) and *Die Lehren des russischen Oktoberexperiments* (typescript).

KEESING, Isidore (1876–1943)

Dutch trade unionist and SDAP member.

The IISH, Amsterdam, has a small collection of Keesing's correspondence and documents covering the period 1893–1925. (See M. Campfens, *op. cit.*)

KEIL, Wilhelm (1870–1968)

German social democratic politician. Chief Editor of the *Schwäbische Tagwacht*, Stuttgart, 1896–1933. Member of the Württemberg Landtag 1919–20. President of the Württemberg Constitutional Landesversammlung (Land Assembly). Württemberg Minister of Labour and Nutrition 1921–3. Member of the Reichstag 1910–32. After 1945 President of the Provisional Parliament and of the Württemberg-Baden Verfassungsausschuss (Constitutional Committee). Member 1946–52 and President 1947 of the Württemberg-Baden and then Baden-Württemberg Landtag. Also President of the Süddeutscher Länderrat.

The AdsD at the Friedrich-Ebert-Stiftung, Bonn, has the largest collection of Keil's papers for 1893–1966. This comprises memoranda from the First World War, articles and speeches as well as criticisms and remarks on his memoirs. In particular, there is personal correspondence with politicians including Wilhelm Blos (q.v.), Paul Hertz (q.v.), Theodor Leipart (q.v.), Paul Löbe (q.v.), Hermann Müller (q.v.), Louise Schröder, Karl Severing, Friedrich Stampfer (q.v.), Josef Wirth and Rudolf Wissel (q.v.). Secondly, the Haupstaatarchiv, Stuttgart, has a collection of Keil's papers from the period since 1945. Finally, the Stadtarchiv Ludwigsburg (in the holding S 11) has some scattered files including material on the Anti-Nazi Committee and events in Ludwigsburg 1945–6. (See Mommsen, *op. cit.*)

KELLGREN, Nils (b. 1915)

Swedish trade union official and social democratic politician. Official in the LO. Member of Parliament.

A collection of Kellgren's papers, including material concerning the LO, is in the ARAB, Stockholm.

KELLOCK, Harold (b. 1879)

Publicity secretary of the Finnish Information Bureau in the USA (1918).

There is a letter written by Kellock to Lincoln Steffens (1918) in the Hoover Institution, Stanford University, California. This concerns US relations with the revolutionary governments of Finland and Russia.

KERENSKY, Alexander Fedorovič (1881–1970)

Russian moderate socialist and Premier of the Provisional Government. Freemason. Joined the Union of Liberation (a liberal constitutional movement) in 1902. Active in 1905 in providing legal aid to victims of repression. From 1906 noted political defence lawyer. Selected by the Duma in 1912 to investigate the killing of nearly 200 strikers in the Lena River goldfields. Elected to the Duma in 1912 as a member of the moderate socialist Trudovik (Labour) Group. Imprisoned for eight months in 1913. Minister of Justice 1917, then Minister of War and eventually Premier of the Provisional Government, and Vice-Chairman of the Petrograd Soviet (although his commitment to the latter was minimal). Lost his previous popularity with the collapse of the military offensive in June and the gathering economic crisis, and was further weakened with the defeat of Kornilov. Overthrown by the Petrograd Soviet (The October Revolution). Failed in his attempt to organise military resistance to Soviet rule and went underground. Went into exile in Western Europe in May 1918, and from 1940 in the USA.

Kerensky's later papers (in Russian and English) for the years 1945–65 are in the Hoover Institution, Stanford University, California. These include correspondence and writings relating to the Russian Revolution and personal matters (in particular a history by Kerensky entitled *The Genesis of the 'October Revolution' of 1917*, and correspondence with Michael Karpovič and Anatole G. Mazour). A preliminary inventory is available.

KERGER, August (1908–72)

German social democrat. From 1925 member of the SPD. Later active in the Reichsbanner. During 1933 imprisoned for a month. After 1946 Secretary of the SPD in Bonn. Helped reform the Reichsbanner.

A collection of Kerger's papers is in the AdsD, Bonn. As well as personal documents, these comprise papers concerning the Reichsbanner (mainly, but not exclusively, in the years after 1945), the SPD (including conferences) and municipal policy.

KERN, Karl (1902–82)

Danish writer and journalist.

One box of Kern's papers for the years 1923–76 is in the ABA, Copenhagen. This includes correspondence and manuscripts as well as material concerning the Socialist Youth International (1932–45).

KESKUELA, Alexander (1882–1963)

Estonian socialist. Reputed intermediary between Lenin and the German Government during the 1914–18 war.

Keskuela's papers (in German) for the years 1915–63 are in the Hoover Institution, Stanford University, California. This collection comprises personal papers as well as correspondence, memoranda and other writings relating to international socialist and communist movements. A preliminary inventory is available. The papers were purchased from his daughter, Mrs Ingeborg Weidmann, in 1966.

KIEF, Carl Friedrich (Frits) (1908–76)

Dutch journalist and left-wing member of the PvdA.

The IISH, Amsterdam, has Kief's correspondence (1945–75). A list is available. (See M. Campfens, *op. cit.*)

KILBOM, Karl (1885–1961)

Swedish communist leader. Secretary of the Social Democratic youth movement 1915–17. Founding member of the Left-Socialist Party in 1917, and of the SKP in 1921. Leading figure in the Comintern-loyal wing in 1924, after the Party schism. Founder of the Independent Communist Party (later the Socialist Party) in 1929. Rejoined the SAP in 1937. Publishing Director 1917–24 and Editor-in-Chief 1924–36 of *Politiken* (becoming *Folkets Dagblad Politiken*). Member of Parliament 1922–4. Active in Stockholm municipal politics 1929–44.

Sixteen boxes of Kilbom's papers for the years 1908–61 are in the ARAB, Stockholm. These comprise personal documents, correspondence, manuscripts, transcripts, newspaper articles, and other material concerning his political activity. An inventory is available.

KILLY, Leo (1885–1954)

German civil service trade unionist. Federal Chairman of the Allgemeiner Beamtenschutz-bund.

Killy's papers for the years 1945–54 are in the Bundesarchiv, Koblenz. These include files on de-nazification. (See Mommsen, *op. cit.*)

KIRN, Richard (b. 1902)

German social democratic trade unionist and politician. Miner. Secretary of the Saarland Miners' Union 1928–35. Member of the Land Executive of the SPD in the Saar 1927. Secretary of the Miners' Union (CGT) in Lorraine 1936. Founder member of the Coordination Committee of German Trade Unionists in France. Proponent of a united front with the communists. Interned and imprisoned in 1943. Chairman of the Social Democratic Party of the Saar (SPS) 1946–55. Minister for Labour and Welfare in the Saar 1947–51 and 1952–5. Proponent of autonomy for the Saar.

Kirn's papers for the years 1947–59 are in the AdsD, Bonn. These comprise documents concerning the SPS (see above) 1953–4 (in French), and a reply of the SPS to the SPD on the Saarland question (1950), together with articles and pamphlets written by Kirn on policy for the Saar.

KNOERINGEN, Waldemar von (1906–71)

German social democratic politician. SPD member from 1926. Active in workers' welfare and educational organisations. Exile in France and England 1933. Active with the Neu Beginnen group. Member of the Bavarian Landtag 1946–70 (Chairman of the SPD group 1946–62). Chairman of the SPD in Bavaria and simultaneously in the SPD Executive 1947–63. Vice-Chairman of the SPD 1958–62. Member of the Bundestag 1949–51 (resignation due to overwork). Substantial influence on the new ('Godesberg') Programme in 1959. Expert on education and cultural policy.

The AdsD at the Friedrich-Ebert-Stiftung, Bonn, has Knoeringen's extensive papers for the years since 1940. These include correspondence, drafts, manuscripts and speeches (including some from his years of exile) on cultural and educational policy, religious questions and politics in the Landtag and at national level. In addition, there is also a collection of material gathered by him.

KNUDSEN, Peter (fl. 1880s–90s)

Pioneer Danish and international socialist. Chairman of the SDP 1882–1910. Member of Parliament in the 1890s. Prominent in the Second International. Publicist.

There is a small collection of Knudsen's papers, including some correspondence, in the ABA, Copenhagen. There are also, it should be noted, a great many relevant papers in the SDP archive held by the ABA. These include, in particular, his international correspondence with, amongst others, Bebel (q.v.), Huysmans (q.v.) and Vaillant (q.v.).

KNUTTEL, Johannes A. N. (1878–1965)

Dutch socialist and later communist.

The IISH, Amsterdam, has one file of his correspondence (1908–26). (See M. Campfens, *op. cit.*)

KOCK, Johan (1861–1915)

Finnish revolutionary. Army officer. Head of the Red Guards in Helsinki in 1905 during the General Strike. In August 1906 leader of the Red Guards and active among rebellious soldiers during the Viapori uprising. Escaped to the USA and played no further role in the labour movement.

A small collection of Kock's papers for the years 1890–1910 is in the Finnish Labour Archives, Helsinki. This is an especially important collection concerning Finnish politics in the years 1905–6, and comprises diaries (travel records from Russia and Siberia), correspondence, writings concerning his political work in Finland in the years 1905–6 and, in particular, the events of 1906, a cuttings collection of Kock's writing in American papers (1913–14), and a few photographs.

KODICEK, Egon (fl. 1940s–70s)

Austrian communist.

The Institute of Contemporary History, Vienna, has a collection of sixty-two files of his papers, entitled '*Gewerkschaftliche Einheit*' (Trade Union Unity). The collection covers the years 1945 to 1974 and consists mainly of material from and on the KPÖ, relating to the party's trade union activities.

KOEGLER, Theodor (1901–68)

German communist (member of KPD 1920–26). From 1931 member of the SAP.

The Bundesarchiv, Koblenz, has a small collection of Koegler's manuscripts, circulars, and correspondence, mostly on the theme of the re-unification of Germany on a neutral socialist basis. The collection also contains material on the concept of a new ideology to replace Marxism, correspondence with splinter groups, and material concerning the organised spoiling of ballot papers as a form of protest in the 1965 Federal election. The collection covers the period 1946–66.

KOENEN, Willy (1908–80)

German social democratic politician. At first technical salesman. During the Weimar Republic trade unionist and member of the SPD and Reichsbanner Schwarz-Rot-Gold. Soldier 1941–5. After 1945 Manager of the Arbeiterwohlfahrt (Industrial Welfare Organisation) in Düsseldorf. City Councillor in Düsseldorf. Member of the District Executive of the SPD in Niederrhein. Member of the Federal Control Commission of the SPD. Member of the Bundestag from 1953.

A large collection of Koenen's papers for the 1960s and 1970s is in the AdsD, Bonn. This contains very few personal papers, but is made up mainly of an extensive collection of material on welfare and social policy matters.

KOL, Henri H. van (1853–1925)

Dutch social democrat and founder member of the SDAP.

The IISH, Amsterdam, has a collection of correspondence (1875–1924). A list is available. (See M. Campfens, *op. cit.*)

KOL'COV-GINZBURG, B. A. (1865–1920)

Russian Menshevik. Member of the People's Will in St Petersburg in mid-1890s. From 1893 abroad. Secretary of the League of Russian Social Democrats Abroad 1895–8. Left the League in 1900 after its schism. Contributor to *Iskra*. *Iskra* consultative delegate of the RSDLP, thereafter an active Menshevik and contributor to Menshevik organs. Defencist during the 1914–18 war. Member of the Petrograd Soviet in 1917. Opposed the October Revolution. Worked for the Petrograd co-operative system 1918–19.

Kol'cov-Ginzburg's papers for the years 1898–1901 are in the IISH, Amsterdam. Apart from manuscripts this small collection includes correspondence between the League of Russian Social Democrats Abroad and other groups. A provisional inventory is available.

KOLLONTAI, Aleksandra (1872–1952)

Russian communist leader. Aristocratic background. In 1898 left her husband in order to study Marxism in Switzerland. After 1905 worked for the St Petersburg Committee of the RSDLP. Began to devote herself to the problems of women – argued against feminist groups concerned only with suffrage for middle-class women, and for the emancipation of poor and working-class women through social revolution under the leadership of the RSDLP. Also argued against Marxist opponents of special political and organisational efforts to reach working-class women. Organised a club for working women in 1905–8. Exile in 1908 in Finland. Wrote extensively on both the political and psychological dimensions of women's emancipation. Until summer 1915 a Menshevik – joined and became a leading international representative of the Bolsheviks because of their uncompromising position on the 1914–18 war. Returned to Russia in 1917. Central Committee member of the Bolshevik Party. After the October Revolution Commissar for Social Welfare. Resigned in March 1918 in protest over the Treaty of Brest Litovsk. Helped, in 1918, organise a national conference of women workers which was instrumental in persuading the Party to establish a Department for Work Among Women Workers and Peasants (Zhenotdel). Head of the Zhenotdel 1920. Spokeswoman for the Workers' Opposition in 1921. Removed from the Zhenotdel in 1922. From 1923 removed from the political centre and pursued a diplomatic career. Responsible for the peace negotiations between the USSR and Finland in 1944.

The main part of Kollontai's papers is in the Marx-Lenin Institute, Moscow, and is, of course, accessible only to a very small number of Soviet researchers. None the less, small quantities of Kollontai's papers may be found in Scandinavian archives. In particular, letters from Kollontai are to be found amongst the Hjalmar Branting (q.v.) and Ström (q.v.) papers in the ARAB, Stockholm.

KOLTHEK, Harm (1872–1946)

Dutch trade unionist and founder member of Dutch Socialist Party.

The IISH, Amsterdam, has some of Kolthek's manuscript material and correspondence (1926–50). A list is available. (See M. Campfens, *op. cit.*)

KONČALOVSKIJ, Dmitrij Petrovič (1878–1952)

Russian historian and emigrant.

The IISH has a small collection of reports from 1917.

KOOKER, Barend (1906–82)

Dutch free-thinker.

The IISH, Amsterdam, has a collection of minutes and correspondence covering the period 1929–79. (See M. Campfens, *op. cit.*)

KÖRNER, Theodor (1873–1957)

Austrian socialist and Federal President. Officer, First World War; director of Army Office during the First Republic; joined SDAP, 1924; arrested and imprisoned without trial for eleven months, 1934; Mayor of Vienna, 1949–51; Federal President, 1951–7.

There are several separate extant collections of Körner's papers. The first is in the War Archive, Vienna. The Vienna City and Province Archive has three boxes of papers, including biographical notes, personal documents, correspondence, 1911–32; an envelope containing a collection of material towards a history of the year 1848; and a collection of material relating to Vienna during his period of office as Mayor (hospitals, 1946–51; schools, 1946–9; sport, youth activities and leisure, 1947–51; regional planning and construction, 1949–51). The VGA, Vienna, has three files. The first contains miscellaneous notes on military matters, personal documents, speeches, and articles, along with material relating to his visit to London in May 1948. The second contains essays on military subjects, and the third contains material relating to the *Republikanischer Schutzbund*, the socialist paramilitary force of the First Republic, with which he was connected for a number of years. Other papers and books were sold because none of the President's family wanted to take them. There is a collection of correspondence from the years 1943–56 in the Vienna City Library (WSLB). A collection of about 150 books and pamphlets, which were presented to the archive of the *Arbeiterzeitung* in 1957 by Senator Dr Antosch have been integrated into the library of the Association for the History of the Labour Movement in Vienna.

KORSCH, Karl (1886–1961)

German Marxist theorist and communist politician. Professor of Law at Jena University in 1919. Joined the USPD in 1917 and the KPD in 1920. Theorist and participant in the movement for workers' councils and member of the Berlin Socialisation Committee. Member of the Thuringian Landtag (KPD) in 1923 and Thuringian Minister of Justice. Member of the Reichstag 1923–8. Ultra-left oppositionist in the KPD. Dismissed from editorship of *Die Internationale* in 1925. Expelled from the KPD in 1926. Withdrew from organised political activity in 1928. Exile 1933 (from 1936 in the USA). Continued his theoretical research into Marxism. Opponent of mechanistic Marxism (notable critic of the Second International and of Karl Kautsky (q.v.) in particular). Broke with Marxism in the early 1950s. Close friend of Bertolt Brecht.

There are two collections of Korsch's papers. By far the largest is the varied collection in the IISH, Amsterdam. Mainly from the period after 1933, this includes general correspondence (enriched by letters of Korsch to Paul Mattick), and a file of correspondence under the heading 'jobs' (from Korsch's attempts to find work in the USA). In particular, there are a large number of manuscripts (including a work designated 'Work in Progress' at the time of his death). This collection also contains collections of material, translations, printed copies of Korsch's publications and reviews of his work. A printed inventory and detailed guide is available. Finally, Brecht's letters to Korsch are in the Widener Library of Harvard University, Cambridge, Massachusetts.

KÖSTER, Adolf (1883–1930)

German social democratic politician and diplomat. Appointed Prussian State Commissar for the province Schleswig-Holstein 1919. Reich Foreign Minister in 1920. Reich Minister of the Interior 1921–2. Member of the Reichstag 1921–3. Appointed Ambassador to Latvia in 1923 and to Yugoslavia in 1928.

Although part of Köster's papers appear to have been lost, a small collection of his papers covering 1903–30 is in the AdsD at the Friedrich-Ebert-Stiftung, Bonn. These comprise personal papers, manuscripts, correspondence and newspaper cuttings to do with the First World War; material concerning the Schleswig-Holstein question 1919; manuscripts on the Yugoslavian labour movement and correspondence arising from his capacity as Minister and Ambassador. (See Mommsen, *op. cit.*)

KOVARSKII, Il'ia Nikolaevič (fl. 1914–18)

Russian socialist. Member of the Socialist Revolutionary Party.

The Bakhmeteff Archive, Columbia University, New York, has a collection of his papers supplemented by those of M. V. Vishniak. The collection includes correspondence and *Iz perezhitogo*, A. Argunov's memoirs of ideological disputes in the Russian socialist emigration in Europe during the First World War – between internationalists and supporters of the war – and about the situation in Petrograd in 1917 and 1918.

KRAG, Jens Otto (1914–78)

Danish social democratic politician. Several times Prime Minister.

Krag's papers are in the ABA, Copenhagen, and will remain closed until his large archive has been completely catalogued. Even then, it should be noted, certain official papers may remain closed.

KRASIN, Leonid Borisovič (1870–1926)

Russian communist. Electrical engineer. Joined M. I. Brusnev's Social Democratic circle *c.* 1887. Imprisoned 1891. While directing the construction of a power station in the Baku region ran an illegal printing press (printing social democratic and other revolutionary papers, including *Iskra*). Prominent in the agitation leading to the strike in the oil fields in 1903. Supported Lenin 1903 at the Second RSDLP Congress. Co-opted, and 1905 elected, onto the Bolshevik Central Committee. Went underground in 1905 to organise local Party committees and battle squads in Moscow. Found work in St Petersburg and elected to the Soviet. Started an explosives factory and again organised battle squads. Planned the Tiflis bank robbery in 1906. Broke with Lenin in 1908 over the question of legal work and participation in the Duma. Abandoned political activity in 1909. Became a successful engineer and a leading businessman. Member of the War Industries Committee in 1915. In spite of persuasion by Lenin refused to rejoin the Bolshevik Party in 1917. Opposed the October Revolution. Persuaded by Trotsky to join the Russian delegation to Brest Litovsk. Extraordinary Commissar of Supply for the Red Army in November 1918. Sat in the Presidium of the Supreme Council of the National Economy as Commissar for Foreign Trade and for Transport. Responsible for Soviet foreign trade negotiations in 1920. Keen supporter of the New Economic Policy and proponent of gaining the return of foreign investment capital to Russia. First Soviet ambassador to France in 1924 and then to Britain.

A small collection of Krasin's papers for the years 1917–26 is in the IISH, Amsterdam. This comprises some personal, but also a significant number of official, letters and documents relating to the foreign and internal affairs of the Soviet Government. An inventory is available. A further acquisition was made in 1977. The Institute acquired *c.* 80 letters from Krasin to his wife, 1917–25, from his daughter, Mrs L. Mathias-Krasina of London.

KRAVCHINSKY, Sergei Mikhailovič (1851–95)*

Russian populist and writer. After 1873 participated in the 'Go-to-the-People' campaign. Arrested, but escaped, and continued clandestine activity. From 1877 participated in a revolt in Southern Italy. In 1878 returned to Russia and edited *Zemlia i volia* (*Land and Liberty*). Assassinated the Chief of the Third Section as a protest against the treatment of political prisoners. Exile in Geneva, Italy and finally London. Publicised and organised support for the Russian revolutionary cause in Europe and the USA (to which end he founded the paper *Free Russia*).

There is a collection of Kravchinsky's papers (in Russian) in the Hoover Institution, Stanford University, California. This comprises correspondence and manuscripts (1892–1908), as well as printed matter relating to the 19th century Russian revolutionary movements.

* Known by the pseudonym S. Stepniak.

KRETSCHMANN, Lily

See under BRAUN, Lily.

KROL', Moisej Aronovič (1862–1942)

Russian socialist revolutionary.

The IISH has a small collection of correspondence and manuscripts.

KROPOTKIN, Peter (1842–1921)

Russian anarchist. From a Russian princely family. Geographer. Influenced by Proudhon (q.v.) while an army officer. On a visit to Switzerland in 1872 influenced by James Guillaume (q.v.) and the anarchist workers of Jura. Smuggled anarchist literature back to Russia. Resigned from government service and entered into revolutionary activity. Joined the St Petersburg circle around N. V. Tchaikovsky. Advocated the formation of armed peasant groups and rejected piecemeal reform. Imprisoned in 1874. Escaped 1876. Founded the paper *Le Révolté* (which became the main organ of anarchist discussion) in 1879. Proponent of violent action. While in France in 1882 victim of a wave of arrests of French anarchists. Imprisoned 1882–5. In England 1886–1917. Through his books and articles in many languages became the leading theorist of anarcho-communism and mentor to the international anarchist movement. Shocked many of his comrades in 1914 by supporting the war against Germany. Returned to Russia in 1917 after the February Revolution. Refused both the offer of a place in the Provisional Government and, after the October Revolution, the offer of a state subsidy to publish his works. Critic of the Soviet regime for tendencies towards centralism and dictatorship.

There is a considerable quantity of Kropotkin's correspondence, manuscripts and other documents in the IISH, Amsterdam. These papers, however, do not form a single Kropotkin collection, but are scattered throughout many other collections (including those of Atabekian (q.v.), Friedeberg (q.v.), Grave (q.v.), Marsh, Nettlau (q.v.), and Žuk (q.v.). Other letters can be found in the British Library (ref Add Ms 46473).

KRUSE, Alfred (1888–1958)

Danish social democrat and then communist leader. Writer and editor.

Thirty-three boxes of Kruse's papers from 1905 to the 1950s are in the ABA, Copenhagen. This collection concerns mainly the inter-war period and comprises personal papers, correspondence (including many letters to Norwegian and Swedish communists, and letters from, amongst others, Uritsky, Gordon, and Lilly Bengtsson), manuscripts (including the notes made on his second Russian journey), documents (including a 15 000 word copy of his letter to the Danish Communist Party in 1922, and a copy of his letter to Bukharin in 1927) and newspaper cuttings. A summary inventory is available.

KUBEL, Alfred (b. 1909)

German social democratic politician. White-collar employee. Member of the ISK. From 1933 clandestine activity. Imprisoned in 1937. Prime Minister of Braunschweig 1946. Economics Minister, Minister of Labour and Finance Minister, etc. in Lower Saxony 1946–51 and 1957–69. Prime Minister 1970–76.

Kubel's papers for the years 1937–55 are in the AdsD, Bonn. These comprise his diary (1947–52) as well as material concerning the Land Braunschweig, military government, and his trial and imprisonment under the Nazis.

KUDLICH, Hans (1823–1917)

Member of the Austrian National Assembly of 1848–9. Led an initiative for the abolition of rural servitude. Émigré in the United States after 1848.

There is a collection of Kudlich's papers, including correspondence, in the IISH, Amsterdam. These concern mainly his travels and the situation in the Bohemian countries of his homeland.

KUIJKHOF, Johannes G. van (1864–1921)

Dutch socialist. Treasurer, Dutch SDAP.

The IISH, Amsterdam, has a little material related to Kuijkhof's employment (1916–19). (See M. Campfens, *op. cit.*)

KUIPER, Frederick (Frits) (1898–1974)

Dutch pastor and SDAP member.

The IISH, Amsterdam, has a small collection of Kuiper's organisational documents and correspondence covering the years 1919–67. (See M. Campfens *op. cit.*)

KUNKEL, Ernst (b. 1908)

German social democratic politician. District Executive member of the SPD in Dudweiler. Exile in France 1935. Imprisoned 1940. Mayor of Völklingen 1945. District President. Ministerial director in the Saar Ministry of the Interior. Member of the Land Executive of the Social Democratic Party of the Saar (SPS) and of the Landtag 1947–55. Councillor in Dudweiler 1967.

Kunkel's papers for the years 1946–67 are in the AdsD, Bonn. These comprise material concerning the SPS (see above), Land and municipal elections, the Saar plebiscite and the Saar question, the Schuman Plan and reparations. In addition, they include his collection of material on the history of the Saar.

KUNZE, Otto (b. 1904)

German social democratic jurist. Lawyer. Chief legal adviser of the DGB. From 1958 judge in the Constitutional Court of North Rhine-Westphalia. Chairman of the Working Group of Social Democratic Jurists 1959–69.

Kunze's papers concerning his legal work in the DGB and SPD in the years 1951–75 are in the AdsD, Bonn.

KUPERS, Evert (1885–1965)

Dutch trade union leader and SDAP member.

The IISH, Amsterdam, has a collection of Kupers's correspondence and other documents from the years 1931–61. (See M. Campfens, *op. cit.*)

KURANER, Maxim (1901–78)

German communist and then social democratic politician. After 1933 exile in Paris. Courier for the Foreign Division of the KPD. Broke from the KPD over the Hitler–Stalin Pact. Active in the Resistance. Joined the SPD in 1946. Member of the Rhineland-Palatinate Landtag, and Chairman of the SPD District Palatinate 1950–59.

A small collection of Kuraner's papers for the years 1933–73 is in the AdsD at the Friedrich-Ebert-Stiftung, Bonn. These include identity cards from his years of exile (1936–46), newspaper cuttings (concerning mainly politics in the Palatinate, questions to do with socialism, de-Nazification and SPD politics). (See Mommsen, *op. cit.*)

KUTTNER, Erich (1887–1942)

German journalist and politician. SPD member of Reichstag, 1921–33. Editor of *Die Glocke*, 1924–7. Emigration to the Netherlands. Arrest by the Gestapo and imprisonment in Mauthausen concentration camp, 1942.

The IISH, Amsterdam, has a small collection of Kuttner's papers. These include correspondence, personal and official documents, manuscripts, notes, files, and printed material.

KUYPER, Rudolph K. H. (1874–1934)

Dutch SDAP theorist and polemicist.

The IISH, Amsterdam, has some of Kuyper's manuscripts, correspondence and other documents (1919–34). A list is available. (See M. Campfens, *op. cit.*)

KWIATKOWSKI, Antoni Wincenty (1890–1970)

Polish author. Authority on Marxism-Leninism, etc.

A large collection of Kwiatkowski's papers, 1917–69 (in part photocopies) was given to the

Hoover Institution, Stanford University, California, by Annemarie Buschman-Brandes in 1971. The collection, mainly in Polish and Russian, comprises correspondence and memoranda, research notes, literary manuscripts, autobiographical and biographical material, clippings, and other papers, relating to his studies of Marxism–Leninism, dialectical and historical materialism, communism and religion, and the Communist International (1917–69).

LÅÅS, Sigfrid (1886–1970)

Swedish trade union leader. Silversmith. After 1917 member of the Engineering Workers' Union, and from 1929–32 Chairman of various branches (including the Stockholm Goldsmiths' 1929–32). From 1935 Executive member of both the Union and of the LO.

A large collection of Låås's papers for the years 1899–1968 are in the ARAB, Stockholm. These include personal documents and work books, correspondence, manuscripts and photographs, as well as other material arising out of his trade union activity such as piece-rate lists, pamphlets, newspaper cuttings and other printed matter. An inventory is available.

LACAZE-DUTHIERS, Etienne (1876–1958)

Militant French anarchist and pacifist. President, 1933, of the *Union des Intellectuels Pacifistes*. Executive member, *Ligue internationale des combattants de la Paix*.

The papers are in the IFHS, Paris.

LACROIX, Arthur (1906–76)

Belgian socialist politician. President of the Namur Federation of Socialist Friendly Societies (Mutualités Socialistes). Councillor 1935, Deputy Mayor 1938–47, and Mayor of Gembloux 1947–58. Regional Councillor 1946–9. From 1949 Senator for Namur-Dinant-Philippeville.

Lacroix's correspondence for the years 1957–9 is in the archive of the Namur Federation of the Belgian Socialist Party.

LAFARGUE, Paul (1842–1911)

Publicist and populariser of Marxism in France. After 1866, represented Spain on the General Council. Married, 1868, Marx's youngest daughter. Founder member of the POF. Member of the CAP of the SFIO, 1905–11. Committed suicide, 1911.

Lafargue's political correspondence has been published.

LAGER, Fritjof (1905–73)

Swedish communist. Official of the SKP. Editor of *Ny-Dag*. Member of Parliament for the SKP, and for the Left Communist Party (VPK) from the late 1960s.

Some 24 boxes of Lager's papers are in the ARAB, Stockholm. Access is still restricted and special permission must be obtained before consulting this collection.

LAISANT, Charles (1848–1920)

French libertarian, sympathetic to syndicalism. Deputy for Nantes, 1876–93.

There is some of Laisant's correspondence in the Grave (q.v.) papers.

LALOGE, François (1824–72)

French Communard.

See Appendix I (the letters cited in Appendix I have been published in *Le Mouvement Social*, vol. 37, October–December 1961).

LAMAISON, Jacques (b. 1887)

French Guesdist. Teacher. Federal Secretary of the SFIO in the Department Landes, 1907–10, 1911–4.

Lamaison's correspondence with Lucien Roland (q.v.) is now in the archive of Maurice Dommanget (q.v.) in the IFHS, Paris.

LAMBERT, Charles (b. 1828)

French Communard.

See Appendix I.

LAMP'L, Walter (1891–1933)

German social democratic local politician. Chairman of the Workers' and Soldiers' Council for Greater Hamburg. Member of the First Congress of Councils and of the Central Council in Berlin. Member of the Hamburg Bürgerschaft.

The Staatsarchiv Hamburg has a little printed material and files collected by Lamp'l concerning the Workers' and Soldiers' Councils (mainly in Hamburg). (See Mommsen, *op. cit.*)

LANDAUER, Gustav (1870–1919)

German socialist writer. Member of the Council Government in Munich.

The IISH, Amsterdam, has a large collection of material concerning Landauer made after his death. This includes manuscripts, documents and letters (notably from the period of the Council Republic), as well as copies of letters from and to Landauer. (See Mommsen, *op. cit.*)

LANDE, Lev Semenovič (1901–76)

Russian Menshevik.

The IISH has a collection of manuscripts and documents from 1917.

LANDSBERG, Otto (1869–1957)

German social democratic politician. Member of the Council of People's Commissars. Reich Minister of Justice. Later Ambassador in Brussels. Member of the Reichstag and of the National Assembly.

The first part of Landsberg's papers is at the IISH, Amsterdam. It comprises a collection of documents on the labour movement 1890–1920 and on the German Revolution 1918–19. The second part was largely destroyed, but remnants survive at the Bundesarchiv, Koblenz. These comprise political manuscripts 1916–31, together with material on Spartacus (February 1916), legal action of the USPD against the SPD and negotiations with Colonel Conger in 1919. In addition, there is an exchange of letters arising from his position as German chargé d'affaires in Brussels, 1920–22. (See Mommsen, *op. cit.*)

LANG, Josef (1902–73)*

German communist and then social democratic activist. Successively a member of the KAPD, KPD (expelled 1929), KPDO and (1932) the SAPD. Arrested in 1933. Exile in Czechoslovakia in 1934 until 1938, France (until 1940) and the USA (until 1950). Joined the SPD in 1951. Executive member of the SPD sub-district Frankfurt 1957–72.

The AdsD at the Friedrich-Ebert-Stiftung, Bonn, has Lang's papers for the years 1940–71. These comprise his personal papers, manuscripts and newspaper cuttings, material concerning party work in Frankfurt, and correspondence (with, amongst others, SAP members and other exiles). (See Mommsen, *op. cit.*)

* Known by the pseudonym Jola.

LANG, Otto (1863–1936)

Swiss social democrat. Leading theoretician of the SPS. Prominent in the Second International.

There are two collections of Otto Lang's papers. The first (*c.* 1885–1936) is in the IISH, Amsterdam. This concerns Swiss and international social democratic politics, the history of the Swiss labour movement, and Lang's activity in workers' education and legal practice. They include political correspondence with, amongst others, August Bebel (q.v.), Eduard Bernstein (q.v.) and Karl Kautsky (q.v.), personal correspondence with Werner Sombart, manuscripts of publications and lectures (partially in shorthand), printed documents and copies of his own work, and cuttings and notes on various subjects (especially the history of the Swiss labour movement). A provisional inventory is available. The second small collection is in the Schweizerisches Sozialarchiv, Zürich. This includes his diaries (1879–90), letters received (organised alphabetically, according to sender), biographical material and the SPS diary for Zürich membership (1888–92).

LANGE, Eric (1875–1925)

Swedish trade unionist. Treasurer of the Engineering Workers' Union in the LO.

Four boxes of Lange's papers are in the ARAB, Stockholm.

LANGE, Gunnar (1909–80)

Swedish social democratic politician. Minister of Trade and Cabinet Minister in the 1960s.

Some 27 boxes of Lange's papers are in the ARAB, Stockholm. This collection is still closed.

LANGE, Hans (1871–1962)

German professional soldier then convinced republican and social democrat. Regimental commander during the First World War. Participated in the discussions at Spa (1918) which persuaded Ludendorff of the need for an armistice. After the Revolution placed himself at the service of the Republic. Police Colonel in Mecklenburg 1919–24. Forced to resign by a reactionary Cabinet resulting from the 1924 Mecklenburg Landtag election. Co-founder of the Reichsbanner Schwarz-Rot-Gold. SPD member.

Hans Lange's papers for the years 1895–1961 are in the AdsD, Bonn. These comprise a few personal documents, biographical material, articles and correspondence (concerning the First World War, the Kapp Putsch, pensions and reparations). There is also a report concerning the Kapp Putsch.

LANGE, Helene (1848–1930)

Leader of the German women's movement. Co-founder and Chairman of the General Association of German Women Teachers and the General Association of German Women.

Helene Lange's papers were reported destroyed towards the end of the First World War. (See Mommsen, *op. cit.*)

LANGERAAD, Krijn A. van (1865–1943)

Dutch SDAP member and later communist.

The IISH, Amsterdam, has a small collection of Langeraad's manuscripts covering the period 1903–41. The holding also contains correspondence from the same period. (See M. Campfens, *op. cit.*)

LAPIE, Pierre Oliver (b. 1901)

French republican socialist politician. Deputy for Meurthe-et-Moselle, 1936. Under Secretary of State for Foreign Affairs, December 1946–January 1947. Minister of Education, July 1950–July 1951.

Three boxes of Lapie's papers have been deposited by his son in the Archives Nationales, Paris. The collection includes a diary, 1946–58, and notes taken at the Council of Ministers, July 1950–July 1951. A list is available.

LARROQUE, Gustave (b. 1838)

French Communard.

See Appendix I.

LARSSEN, Aksel (fl. 1930s–50s)

Chairman of the Danish Communist Party 1932–58. From 1958 Founder and Chairman of the Danish People's Socialist Party (SF).

Larssen's papers are in the Rigsarkiv, Copenhagen. At present this large collection is closed.

LASSALLE, Ferdinand (1825–64)

Founder and first leader of German social democracy. Revolutionary of 1848–9. Put on trial for treason but acquitted. Close to, and in regular contact with, Marx (q.v.) until their breach in 1862. In 1863 founder, and subsequently President, for life, of the General German Workers' Union (ADAV – usually known as the 'Lassallean Party'). Proponent of German unity under Prussia, universal suffrage, state-backed producers' co-operatives, and a tactical alignment with Bismarck against the liberal Progressive Party.

Since 1945, the whereabouts of the large collection of Lassalle's papers deposited in the Reichsarchiv, Potsdam, in 1927 has been unknown. Lassalle's letter-copy book for the years 1863–4, however, is in the Bundesarchiv, Koblenz (see also Sophie Gräfin von Hatzfeldt).

LAUNAY, Michel

French socialist.

The IISH, Amsterdam, has a collection of manuscripts, reports and printed material. Access is restricted.

LAUSCHER

Austrian communist.

The Institute of Contemporary History, Vienna University, has forty-one boxes of his papers covering the years 1945–74. The collection contains material on Communist Party conferences, the Vienna organisation of the KPÖ, the trade unions, youth, women, labour history, resistance, Austrian domestic politics, elections, the Austrian conservative party (ÖVP) and the Roman Catholic Church; the Communist world movement and the USSR; internal party material on Czechoslovakia; the Czech Communist Party; SED material on the German question; the CPSU and the Yugoslav Communist Party; internal party material on Yugoslavia in 1948; Cuba in 1962; Vietnam; and China.

LAVROV, Peter L. (fl. 1880s)

Russian revolutionary.

The Bakhmeteff Archive, Columbia University, New York, has one box of his papers containing typed copies of forty-eight letters to the revolutionary Aleksandra Vasil'evna Bauler from the years 1876–82 on political theory and the potential for revolution in Russia.

LAZARD, Max (fl. 1910s–20s)

French organiser of international conference against unemployment, 1910. Founder and Assistant General Secretary, *Association internationale pour la lutte contre le chômage*.

Lazard's papers, which include correspondence, card indexes and cuttings, together with personal and family papers for the period 1879–1977, are in the Archives Nationales, Paris. Special permission is necessary to consult the papers.

LEBER, Julius (1891–1945)

German social democratic politician. Editor of the Lübeck *Volksbote*. Member of the Reichstag (SPD). Active in the resistance against the Nazi regime. Concentration camp victim.

Leber's papers were confiscated by the Gestapo and have not been recovered. All that remain are a few photocopies of his letters from the concentration camp in the Bundesarchiv, Koblenz. (See Mommsen, *op. cit.*)

LE BOSSU*

* Pseudonym of MARTIN, Pierre.

LEDEBOUR, Georg (1850–1947)

German social democratic politician. Writer and editor. Prominent on the left of the SPD's Reichstag group. Founding member and co-Chairman of the USPD. Executive member of the Berlin Workers' and Soldiers' Council. Member of the Reichstag (SPD/USPD). After the reunification of the USPD right with the SPD, founder of the Sozialistischer Bund which became part of the SAPD in 1931. Exiled in Switzerland after 1933 (until his death).

The bulk of Ledebour's extensive papers was destroyed during the Second World War. However, a small part of his papers was preserved by his widow and is now in the AdsD, Bonn. These are for the years 1913–47 and, apart from a few sketches, newspaper articles and manuscripts of a more or less unpolitical nature, contain correspondence and other material from exile. In addition there is a collection of letters written to 'Fanny' concerning the socialist movement (1936–9) in the Hoover Institution, Stanford University, California.

LEFRANC, Georges Eugène Auguste (b. 1904)

French trade unionist and social historian.

Lefranc's papers concerning French trade unionism from the mid-1930s to the 1960s are in the CRHMSS, Paris. These include a manuscript (n.d.) on the mass strike movement of 1936, autonomous unions in 1950, biographies of CGT militants (n.d.) and circulars of the CFDT (1965–6). In addition the Hoover Institution, Stanford University, California has purchased nine boxes of papers (*c.* 1895–1973). These include writings, reports, syllabi and printed matter relating to social conditions and the socialist, syndicalist and labour movements in France.

LEFRANÇAIS, Gustave

See under LEFRANÇOIS, Gustave.

LEFRANÇOIS, Gustave (1826–1901)*

French revolutionary socialist, anarchist and publicist. Leading Communard. First President of the Council of the Commune and member of its Executive Commission. Exiled in Geneva, 1871–9. Helped form the Fédération Jurassienne.

The unpublished manuscript of Lefrançois's *Dix années de proscription en Suisse, 1871–1880* is in the IISH, Amsterdam. This is a continuation of his *Souvenirs d'un Révolutionnaire* (Brussels, n.d.).

* Correct name, but known under the name Gustave Lefrançais.

LEGIEN, Karl (1861–1920)

German social democratic trade unionist. Chairman of the ADGB. President of the International Trade Union Federation. Member of the Reichstag and of the National Assembly.

Legien's papers covering the years 1872–1919 are in the Deutsches Zentralarchiv, Potsdam. (See Mommsen, *op. cit.*)

LE GUERN, Ernest (1870–1926)

French trade unionist. Secretary of the *Union départmentale des syndicats des Côtes-du-Nord*, 1911. Member of the CGTU, 1922.

Letters from Le Guern are to be found in the archives of Pierre Monatte (q.v.) and Alfred Rosmer (q.v.).

LEICHTER, Käthe (1895–1942)

Austrian social democrat arrested after the Anschluss and murdered at Ravensbruck.

The DÖW, Vienna, has a collection of correspondence from 1938 and 1939, press cuttings, correspondence with Otto Leichter (q.v.) in Zürich, and a manuscript of her memoirs entitled 'Kinderheitserinnerungen'.

LEICHTER, Otto (1897–1973)

Austrian social democrat.

The IISH, Amsterdam, has a small collection of Leichter's material which includes manuscripts and interviews. Other papers are at the DÖW, Vienna.

LEINERT, Robert (1873–1937)

German social democratic politician. Lord Mayor of Hannover. Chairman of the Central Council of German Workers' and Soldiers' Councils. President of the Prussian Land Assembly and then of the Landtag (SPD).

Mommsen, *op. cit.*, reports that Leinert's papers were in private hands and destroyed during the Second World War.

LEIPART, Theodor (1867–1947)

German social democratic trade unionist. From 1893 Chairman of the Holzarbeiterverband (Association of Woodworkers). Minister of Labour in Württemberg 1919–20. Chairman of the ADGB 1921–33. President of the Vorläufiger Reichswirtschaftsrat (Provisional Reich Economic Council).

The DGB Archive at Düsseldorf has a very small collection of Leipart's papers for the years 1910–47. This comprises mainly personal correspondence. (See Mommsen, *op. cit.*)

LEIVO-LARSSON, Tyyne (1902–77)

Finnish social democratic politician. Official in the Finnish Labour Organisation 1919–29.

Executive member of the Finnish Social Democratic Party (SDP). Chairwoman of the League of Social Democratic Women. Executive member of the Social Democratic League of Workers and Small Farmers (TPSL). Chairwoman of its parliamentary group. Member of Parliament 1948–57 (SDP) and 1966–9 (TPSL). Second Minister of Social Affairs 1948–50, 1954–7 and 1958. Minister of Social Affairs 1954 and 1957. Ambassador to Oslo 1958–65.

A large collection of Leivo-Larsson's papers for the years 1940–77 is in the Finnish Labour Archives, Helsinki. This is an important source for a wide range of organisations and issues: it is particularly useful for material concerned with her work on women's issues and social policy in Finland and internationally, as well as for a large number of letters from ordinary people describing their own situation. In addition, these papers include extensive private and political correspondence, manuscripts (writings and speeches), a large quantity of printed material, and collections of documents from the League of Social Democratic Women, the TPSL (1961–8), the UNO and International Postal Union, Finnish and international women's organisations, and on Finnish foreign policy (1958–69). An inventory is available, and all the papers except for those on foreign policy are open.

LÉO, André*

* Pseudonym of CHAMPSEIX, Léodile.

LEONETTI, Alfonso

Italian socialist.

There is some of Leonetti's correspondence and other manuscript material in the Feltrinelli Institute, Milan.

LEROUX, Pierre (1797–1871)

French journalist, philosopher and politician. Initially, supported Saint-Simon in *Le Globe*. Deputy for the Seine, 1848, in the Constituent Assembly. Defended June Insurrection.

The IISH, Amsterdam, has a small collection of Leroux's manuscript material (n.d.).

LESSEN, Ludwig (1872–1943)

German social democratic editor and writer. Contributor to social democratic newspapers. Editor of an SPD paper in Halle in 1900. Features Editor of *Vorwärts* in 1904 and Editorial Director of the illustrated Sunday supplement of *Vorwärts-Neue Welt* 1905–19 (which, in 1919, became *Volk und Zeit*, and continued to be edited by Lessen until 1933). Published poetry and prose popular amongst socialist youth.

The AdsD at the Friedrich-Ebert-Stiftung, Bonn, has a small collection of Lessen's editorial correspondence. (See Mommsen, *op. cit.*)

LEUSCHNER, Wilhelm (1890–1944)

German social democratic politician and trade unionist. Member of the Hessian Landtag (SPD) in 1924. Hessian Minister of the Interior 1928–33. Vice-Chairman of the ADGB in 1933.

The main part of Leuschner's papers were confiscated by the Gestapo and almost certainly destroyed. However, a substantial collection survives at the Staatsarchiv, Darmstadt. This comprises personal papers, notes and speeches, remnants of files concerning the Hessian Land-Theatre, the reform of the Reich, separatism and trade unions (1933); drawings and letters from the concentration camp Lichtenberg 1933–4 and 1939; newspapers and printed material; remnants of his political correspondence 1919–33. In addition, there are a small number of Leuschner's papers incorporated in the papers of Jakob Kaiser at the Bundesarchiv, Koblenz. These include items concerning administrative reforms in Hesse 1927–8 and a legal action involving Leuschner 1932–3. (See Mommsen, *op. cit.*)

LEVAL, Gaston (1894–1978)

French libertarian socialist and publicist. Printer. War resister 1914–18. Exile in Spain. In 1921 delegate of the Spanish CNT to the Third World Congress of the Comintern. From 1923 renewed exile in Argentina during the dictatorship of Primo de Rivera. In 1936 returned to Spain and participated in the Revolution. Dedicated to recording the revolutionary achievements of ordinary people (author of *Collectives in the Spanish Revolution* (London: 1975), the most complete account of the life of the collectives).

Leval's papers were given to the IISH, Amsterdam, in 1978, by his widow, Marguérite Liégeois. The papers include the manuscript of his memoirs, together with files and documents on the collectivist movement in Spain.

LEVI, Paul (1883–1930)

German communist and then social democratic politician. Lawyer. Defended Rosa Luxemburg (q.v.) against a charge of incitement to mutiny in 1914. Leading member of the Spartakus League during the First World War. Founding member of the KPD, December 1918. Chairman, from March 1919, of the KPD after the murder of Rosa Luxemburg and Karl Liebknecht in January 1919. Early 1921 resigned the Chairmanship and in the same year expelled from the Party. Formed the KAG. Joined the USPD and, upon reunification, the SPD. Member of the Reichstag (SPD) from 1924. Prominent leader of the SPD left. Editor of *Sozialistische Politik und Wirtschaft* (known as the 'Levi-Korrespondenz'). An important influence on the origin and development of the SAP after his death.

A collection of Levi's papers for the years 1909–30 are in the AdsD, Bonn. These comprise correspondence, notes and extensive collections of material (above all newspaper cuttings and leaflets) concerning the November Revolution, the founding and early years of the KPD, the Comintern, the foreign labour movement generally, the USPD, trade unions (the right to strike and factory councils), the SPD (especially its defence programme), political offences, trials and draft laws in the Reichstag. In addition, thanks to the Levi papers the AdsD has the only complete file of *Sozialistische Politik und Wirtschaft* (which it has made available on microfilm), together with numerous manuscripts of Levi's articles for this journal. Finally, there are also some documents collected after his death relating to Levi and his papers. In addition, the Hoover Institute, Stanford University, California, has a copy of a funeral oration delivered by Levi in memory of Karl Liebknecht and Rosa Luxemburg, and a catalogue of the books in his private library.

LEVIN, Harry (b. 1907)

Swedish. Director of the Labour Publicity Organisation.

One box of Levin's papers is in the ARAB, Stockholm. This collection is particularly interesting for its material concerning the Communist Youth International in the 1930s.

LEVINÉ, Eugen (1883–1919)

Communist leader. Born in Russia. Joined the Social Revolutionaries in 1903 (twice imprisoned). Settled in Germany *c.* 1908 and later became a German citizen. At first member of the SPD. Propagandist. Worked with the 'Left Radicals'. Opposed the war. Member of the USPD and Spartakus League in 1917. Founding member of the KPD 1918. KPD representative in Munich 1919. Chairman of the Executive Committee of the Bavarian Council Republic. Executed in the subsequent counter-revolution.

See also his wife, Rosa Meyer-Leviné.

LEVINÉ, Rosa

See under MEYER-LEVINÉ, Rosa.

LEVY, Leo (b. 1877)

German communist.

The IISH, Amsterdam, has a small collection containing correspondence, personal documents, files, and printed material. Most of the collection covers the period 1921–2, but there are a few items from 1894 and from the years 1924–32.

L'HERMINIER, Edmond (b. 1850)

French Communard.

See Appendix I.

LICHTENSTEIN, Kurt (1911–61)

German communist politician. Trade unionist. Exile in the Saar 1933, then France. From 1945 Executive member of the KPD in the British zone. From 1946 Chief Editor of *Die Freiheit* and the *Neue Volkszeitung* in Herne, Westphalia. Member of the North Rhine-Westphalia Landtag (KPD), 1947–50.

The Hauptstaatsarchiv, Düsseldorf, has a small collection of Lichtenstein's papers concerning the KPD and SPD 1950–55 and the Ruhr mining industry. (See Mommsen, *op. cit.*)

LIEB, Fritz (1892–1902)

Swiss protestant theologian. Pacifist and social democratic member of the Grand Council.

The IISH, Amsterdam, has photocopies of Lieb's manuscripts, notes, reports, circulars, and printed material. Most of the small collection dates from the period 1917–21, but there are a few items from 1914.

LIEBKNECHT, Karl

See under LIEBKNECHT, Theodor and LIEBKNECHT, Wilhelm.

LIEBKNECHT, Theodor (1870–1948)

German left-wing socialist. Prominent in the USPD. Opponent of both Comintern affiliation and reunification with the SPD. Leader with Ledebour (q.v.) of the rump USPD after the majority had reunited with the SPD (1922), and main leader after the departure of Ledebour and until its entry into the SAP in 1931. Son of Wilhelm Liebknecht (q.v.) and brother of Karl Liebknecht.

Theodor Liebknecht's papers are in the IISH, Amsterdam. However, these are mainly from the years of his exile in Switzerland (1933–48). They comprise political and personal correspondence with friends and fellow exiles, manuscripts (including memoirs), research notes on the history of the international labour movement in the nineteenth century, and a small collection of memorabilia concerning Wilhelm and Karl Liebknecht.

LIEBKNECHT, Wilhelm (1826–1900)

Pioneer German socialist and leader of the SPD. Active as a student in the 1848 Revolution. Became a friend and supporter of Marx (q.v.) and Friedrich Engels (q.v.) in exile. After his return to Germany the most important early representative of Marx and his ideas in the newly-emergent German labour movement (although he did not always have the full political confidence of Marx). Crucial breakthrough with the winning over of August Bebel (q.v.) to Marxism. Founding member of the SDAP. Voted against war credits in the Reichstag with Bebel in 1870. On trial for High Treason in 1872 and sentenced to two years' imprisonment. Editor-in-Chief of *Vorwärts*. Member of the Saxon Landtag, and of the Reichstag (from 1874).

The main part of Wilhelm Liebknecht's papers is in the IISH, Amsterdam. This comprises personal documents of Liebknecht and his family, printed material (including leaflets and newspaper cuttings) and, in particular, his family and political correspondence. The former includes letters to and from Karl Liebknecht, while the latter contains letters from, amongst others, A. Bebel (q.v.), J. Guesde (q.v.) and P. Lafargue (q.v.). There are also some letters from third parties to third parties. In addition, there are also a few of Liebknecht's manuscripts as well as a greater number of manuscripts from others. The main body of Liebknecht's academic papers, however, is in the Institut für Marxismus-Leninismus, Berlin. (There are copies of some of these papers, for the years 1864–1901, at the Deutsches Zentralarchiv, Potsdam.)

LILJENCRANTZ, Jaquette (1845–1920)

Baroness and socialist pioneer of the Danish Labour movement. Close to Louis Pio (q.v.).

Two boxes of Liljencrantz's papers from the 1870s to 1920 are in the ABA, Copenhagen. These contain letters and manuscripts (including the typescript of her memoirs published in Swedish).

LIMASSET, Joseph (b. 1843)

French Communard.

See Appendix I.

LIND, Albin (fl. 1930s)

Swedish trade union official. Official in the LO. Editor of the LO paper from the 1930s onwards.

Nine boxes of Lind's papers are in the ARAB, Stockholm.

LINDBERG, August (1885–1966)

Swedish trade union leader. Chairman of the LO (post-1945).

Five boxes of Lindberg's papers are in the ARAB, Stockholm. An inventory is available.

LINDLEY, Charles (1885–1957)

Swedish trade union leader and social democratic politician. Seaman. Organiser of dockers and seamen in Sweden and internationally. Chairman of the Transport Workers' Union 1897–1941. Founding member 1898, and Executive member of the LO 1900–12 and 1922–6. SAP Member of Parliament 1906–41. Vice-President 1898, Executive member from 1919, and Chairman of the International Transport Federation 1933–46.

A large collection of Charles Lindley's papers, containing material from 1830–1955, is in the ARAB, Stockholm. As well as notebooks, correspondence and manuscripts, this collection also comprises material arising from his trade union and political activity such as pamphlets, leaflets, photographs, newspaper cuttings and other printed material. An inventory is available, but access to this collection is restricted.

LINDLEY, Elin (1873–1946)

Swedish social democratic women's leader. One of the initiators of the Domestic Servants Union in 1904. Co-founder of the social democratic women's movement. Participant in the first social democratic women's conference in 1907. Member of the SAP Committee on women's questions 1907–11. Extensive activity in the field of municipal social policy. Wife of Charles Lindley (q.v.).

Four boxes of Elin Lindley's papers for the years 1915–46 are in the ARAB, Stockholm. These include personal documents as well as correspondence, manuscripts and photographs. An inventory is available, but access to this collection is restricted.

LINDQVIST, Herman August (1863–1932)

Swedish trade union leader and social democratic politician. Carpenter. Chairman of the LO during the period of the 1909 General Strike. Cabinet Minister.

Three boxes of Lindqvist's papers are in the ARAB, Stockholm.

LINDSTRÖM, Rickard (1894–1950)

Swedish social democratic politician. Sawmill worker. Publicist. Chairman of the Social Democratic Youth Movement 1922–8, and Editor of its paper *Frihet* 1920–29. Assistant Party Secretary 1920–26 and 1930–33. From 1936 member of the SAP Executive. Editor-in-Chief, 1933–9, of the SAP paper in Göteberg *Ny-Tid*, and of the SAP central organ *Social Demokraten* 1940–44. Member of Parliament 1930–50. Executive member of the Labour and Socialist International 1932–9. Active in workers' education.

Two boxes of Lindström's papers for the years 1920–48 are in the ARAB, Stockholm. These contain correspondence, manuscripts and notes. An inventory is available.

LISBONNE, Maxime (1839–1905)

French Communard.

The manuscript of Lisbonne's *Mémoires* survives, and has been used by E. Lepelletier in *Histoire de la Commune de 1871* (3 vols, 1911–13) and Marcel Cerf, *Le D'Artagnan de la Commune (le colonel Maxime Lisbonne)*. (See Maitron, *op. cit.*)

LÖBE, Paul (1875–1967)

German social democratic politician. Editor of the Breslau *Volkswacht* and then of *Vorwärts, Das Volk* and *Telegraf* in Berlin. City Councillor in Breslau 1904. Vice-President of the National Assembly (SPD). Member of the Reichstag and its President 1920–32. After 1945 Editor of the socialist paper *Das Volk* in Berlin. From 1948 member of the Parliamentary Council and of the first Bundestag. President of the German Council of the European Movement in 1949.

Löbe's papers have been much divided over the years, while at least part of those from the period before 1945 were destroyed during the Second World War. However, at least part of Löbe's papers from the period before 1932 survives in the Deutsches Zentralarchiv, Potsdam. The AdsD at the Friedrich-Ebert-Stiftung, Bonn, also has a large collection of Löbe's papers from the period since 1945. This comprises mainly correspondence with, amongst others, SPD colleagues and organisations. Although far from complete for the early years, the content of this correspondence mainly concerns reparations proceedings, Party membership and anti-fascist views, congratulations, scientific inquiries, invitations and conference documents. (See Mommsen, *op. cit.*)

LOCQUIN, Jean (1879–1949)

French socialist politician. Deputy from Nevers, 1914–32. Mayor of Balleray (Nièvre) 1908–34. Especially interested in agricultural, educational and financial matters.

There are two holdings of Locquin's papers. The first comprises 46 boxes containing personal papers, files arising from his legal work, and many documents of economic, social and political interest. These, together with papers concerning his official function in the 1937 Exhibition, are in the Archives Nationales, Paris. Secondly, 51 files of letters received by him in the years 1916–34 have been deposited by his family in the Departmental Archive of Nièvre.

LONE, R.*

* Pseudonym of DE ANDRES, Jesus Louzara.

LOUIS, Nestor*

* Pseudonym of ROUSSEAU, Nestor.

LOUZON, Robert (b. 1882)

French communist. Joined POSR 1900. Joined SFIO 1905. Collaborated on *Vie Ouvrière* 1909–13. Secretary, Tunisian Communist Federation, 1921. Returned to France. Co-founder of *Révolution Proletarienne*. Fought for Republican Spain.

Louzon's papers are in the Musée Social (CEDIAS), Paris.

LÖWENSTEIN, Kurt (1885–1939)

German social democratic politician. Joined the USPD in 1918. Member of a soldiers' council. Went over to the SPD in 1922. City Councillor for the school system in Berlin-Neukölln 1921–33. Member of the Reichstag 1920–33. Extensive journalistic and literary activity for socialist papers and journals as well as specialist educational journals. Author of a number of pamphlets and books. Pioneer of educational reform as a component of social transformation. After an attempt on his life by the SA, exiled in France (1933). President and Secretary of the Socialist Educational International while in exile.

Löwenstein's papers for the years 1910–39 are in the AdsD, Bonn. These comprise a small quantity of correspondence (with, amongst others, Mara and Dino Löwenstein), but is mainly made up of material from his activity as a publicist and concerning the Kinderfreunde movement.

LÜBBE, Erich (1891–1977)

German social democratic trade unionist and politician. At first electrician/electrical engineer. SED member and City Councillor in Berlin 1946–8. SPD member in the FRG 1948. Until 1969 Director of the Co-Determination Departments of the DGB Centre in Düsseldorf. Manager of the Mitbestimmung in Düsseldorf.

There are two holdings of Lübbe's papers. The first and largest, covering the years 1932–65, is in the AdsD at the Friedrich-Ebert-Stiftung, Bonn. This comprises personal papers and material concerning the unification of the KPD and SPD into the SED 1946–8, municipal politics in Berlin 1946–8, and the Stiftung Mitbestimmung. The second collection is in the DGB Archive, Düsseldorf. This comprises correspondence and other documents mainly from his early years as Factory Council Chairman at Siemens (1920–26) and his time as a City Councillor and SPD and SED functionary in Berlin 1945–50. (See Mommsen, *op. cit.*)

LUCE, Maximilien (1858–1941)

French neo-impressionist artist and militant libertarian. Follower of Jean Grave (q.v.) and collaborator on *Les Temps Nouveaux*.

See under GRAVE, Jean.

LUND, Karl (1874–1953)

Swedish trade union leader. Chairman and Secretary of various local branches of the Engineering Workers' Union (including Malmö 1905–9 and Nyköping 1910–13). Executive member of both the union and of the LO and Editor of the Engineering Workers' Union journal *Järnarbetaren* (later *Metallarbetaren*) 1913–35.

Some 23 boxes of Lund's papers covering the years 1885–1953 are in the ARAB, Stockholm. These include personal documents, correspondence and manuscripts, as well as other material arising out of his trade union and journalistic activity such as pamphlets and other printed matter. A provisional inventory is available.

LUTERAAN, Barend (1878–1970)

Dutch trade unionist and member of social democratic, socialist and communist parties.

The IISH, Amsterdam, has Luteraan's correspondence, 1918–60. A list is available. (See M. Campfens, *op. cit.*)

LUXEMBURG, Rosa (1871–1919)

Social democratic and then communist leader and theorist. Born in Poland. University of Zürich 1890–98. Founding member of the Social Democracy of the Kingdom of Poland (SDKP). Moved to Germany in 1898. Active in the SPD (made her reputation as a theorist and polemicist with an early attack on Bernstein's (q.v.) revisionism). Continued in the leadership of the SDKP. In Warsaw 1905 but returned to Germany after arrest and subsequent release. Worked to change the SPD's tactics in the light of the 1905 Revolution. Consequently forced into a political break with the social democratic mainstream, and a personal break with her former mentor, Karl Kautsky (q.v.) (*c.* 1910). Leader of the SPD's 'Left Radical' tendency. Member of staff at the SPD Central School in Berlin 1908–14. Active as both publicist and theoretician (published her controversial theory of imperialism *The Accumulation of Capital* in 1913). Uncompromising opposition to the war. Imprisoned, but was still a major influence on the anti-war left and the formation of the Spartakus League. Enthusiastic – but not uncritical – supporter of the Bolshevik revolution. Founding member and leader of the KPD. Murdered in January 1919 by army officers in the reaction against the so-called Spartakus Uprising.

Although Rosa Luxemburg was an indifferent keeper of letters, and although her own papers were ransacked by troops immediately after her final arrest on 15 January 1919, a remarkable amount of material has survived. The biggest collection of Luxemburg's letters is in the Institute for Marxism-Leninism, Moscow (ref. Fund 209). This collection contains over a thousand items. Other letters from and to Rosa Luxemburg are to be found in other related funds such as Franz Mehring (Fund 201). Further archival collections are in the Institute for Marxism-Leninism, East Berlin, and Archiwum Zakladu Historii Partii, Warsaw. Individual items from these collections have been printed. A collection of letters is also in the Archive of the SPD, Bonn. The letters to Alfred Henke (q.v.) and Wilhelm Dittmann (q.v.) form the most interesting part of this collection. The bulk of the collection of the letters at the IISH, Amsterdam, has now been published but there are still a few unpublished letters in various collections (for example, the Guesde Archives). In addition, two boxes of her papers (*c.* 125 letters, 1913–18) are in the Hoover Institution, Stanford University, California. This collection consists of letters and postcards to her secretary, Mathilde Jacob (q.v.), a diary (1915, 1917–18) and letters from Mathilde Jacob to Karl Liebknecht, Franz Mehring (q.v.) and Klara Zetkin (q.v.).

MACCHI, Mauro (fl. 1840s–70s)

Italian democrat. Organiser of workers' society.

A large archive of Macchi's papers covering the period 1846–80, is in the Feltrinelli Institute, Milan.

MACHNO, Nestor Ivanovič (1884–1934)

Russian anarchist. In the years before 1917 built up an anarchist movement among the Ukrainian peasantry. Head of the anarchist insurgent movement in the Ukraine, 1918–21; defeated by the Red Army. Escaped into exile. Died in poverty in Paris.

The IISH, Amsterdam, has a very small collection of correspondence, manifestos and printed material, partly photocopies, from 1920.

MAGNUSSON, Gustav Gerhard (1872–1940)

Swedish social democrat. Printer. Editor of *Social Demokraten*. Chairman of Stockholm Council.

Nineteen boxes of Magnusson's papers are in the ARAB, Stockholm.

MAISEL, Karl (b. 1890)

Austrian social democrat. Minister for Social Affairs 1945–56.

The VGA, Vienna, has a small collection, consisting mainly of personal memorabilia and photograph albums.

MAITRON, Jean

Historian of the French labour movement. Editor of the *Dictionnaire biographique du mouvement ouvrier français*.

In 1980 Maitron began to deposit his extensive private archive in the CRHMSS, Paris. This is a rich collection of historical sources, and is particularly significant for material on Blanqui (q.v.), Hasfeld, Marty (q.v.) and Nassart.

MALATESTA, Errico (1853–1932)

Italian anarchist.

Some correspondence and papers 1913–32 appertaining to Malatesta are in the IISH, Amsterdam.

MALATO DE CORNET, Charles (1857–1938)

French militant libertarian.

There is some of Malato de Cornet's correspondence in the Grave (q.v.) papers.

MALMBERG, Aino Emma (1865–1933)

Finnish author and journalist. Member of the Independent Labour Party. Contributor to the *Manchester Guardian*.

Malmberg's papers are in the National Archives of Finland, Helsinki. Special permission from the Director is necessary to consult these papers.

MALON, Benoît (1841–93)

Pioneer French socialist, journalist and writer. Leader of the Co-operative Movement. A founder and organiser of the International in France, 1865. Member of the Paris Commune. Exiled in Switzerland. Founded, 1880, *La Revue Socialiste*.

Malon's correspondence and papers are reported to be found both in the Feltrinelli Institute, Milan, and the IISH, Amsterdam. His important correspondence with A. Richard is in Lyons Municipal Library. Two letters (15 March 1871, 12 December 1874) are in the IFHS, Paris. See also Léodile Champseix and Jules Guesde.

MAN, Henri de (1885–1953)

Belgian socialist theoretician and leader. Member 1902, and then leader, of the socialist Young Guard. Anti-militarist. Studied in Leipzig and worked on the left-radical SPD paper the *Leipziger Volkszeitung*. Collaborated with Karl Liebknecht in founding the Socialist Youth International. Head of the *Comité de l'Education Ouvrière* for the training of cadres. Active in attempting to win over the Belgian Workers' Party to a radical Marxist position (especially opposing electoral co-operation with the Liberals against the Catholic Party). Supported the war in 1914 and became an officer in the Belgian army. Accompanied Emile Vandervelde (q.v.) in 1917 on an official mission to persuade the Kerensky (q.v.) Government to stay in the war. Hostile to the Bolsheviks. Taught at the Frankfurt Labour College. Published his critique of Marxism, the *Psychology of Socialism* in 1926. Professor of Social Psychology at the University of Frankfurt 1929. Author, in 1933, of the *Plan du Travail* adopted by the Belgian Workers' Party as a programme of 'structural' economic reforms to overcome the depression. Entered the tripartite Government of National Renovation as Minister of Public Works and Employment 1935. Minister of Finance in succeeding governments 1935–8. Late 1930s titular head of the Belgian Workers' Party. Proponent of a corporatist economic council. Supporter of appeasement – the only important Belgian political leader to support Leopold II in his decision to surrender to the invading German army. Left Belgium in 1941 and eventually settled in Switzerland. After the war convicted *in absentia* for treason by a Belgian military court.

The most important collection of de Man's papers is in the IISH, Amsterdam. These are mainly from the period 1914–39, and include a large quantity of published and unpublished documentation concerning his activity in the Belgian Workers' Party and his theoretical innovations. It should be noted that apart from drafts of speeches, the unpublished material comprises largely routine letters. Karl Kautsky's (q.v.) papers, however, contain correspondence with de Man. Secondly, the AMSAB in Ghent has a collection including material on the *Comité de l'Education Ouvrière*, the promotion of the Plan du Travail and other political questions, as well as correspondence with foreign politicians. In addition, other primary material is to be found in the Archives Générales du Royaume in Brussels, in the Archief en Museum voor het Vlaamse Cultuurleven in Antwerp and in the hands of his family. Finally, the Hoover Institution, Stanford University, California has acquired a collection of miscellaneous papers from the years after 1923. This includes letters, writings and cuttings relating to Marxism, Belgian politics, European socialism, the German occupation of Belgium during the Second World War, and de Man's conviction for collaboration.

MANDL, Hans (b. 1899)

Austrian social democrat. Joined SDAP in 1922. Deputy Mayor of Vienna, 1959–64.

The WSLA, Vienna, has one box of papers, mainly speeches.

MANNOURY, Gerrit (1867–1956)

Dutch SDAP activist. Later communist.

A small collection of Mannoury's correspondence covering the period 1904–53 is in the

IISH, Amsterdam. A list is available. Other non-political correspondence is in the Universiteitsbibliotheek, Amsterdam. (See M. Campfens, *op. cit.*)

MÅNSSON, Fabian (fl. 1900s)

Swedish social democratic leader. Writer. Member of Parliament (early twentieth century).

Five boxes of Månsson's papers are in the ARAB, Stockholm. An inventory is available.

MARAT, Jean-Paul (1743–93)

French revolutionary. Publicist and leading Jacobin.

There are letters of Marat in the Bibliothèque Nationale, Paris.

MARCHAND, Louis (1842–1901)

French Communard. Member of a Blanquist cell from 1864. Official representative of the Commune in Bordeaux. Secretary of the *Société des proscrits* in Geneva. Collaborated on *Révolution Sociale* (Organ of the Fédération Jurassienne).

A number of letters written by Marchand are in the Fonds Fazy at the Bibliothèque Publique et Universitaire, Geneva. (See Maitron, *op. cit.*)

MARKSCHEFFEL, Günther (b. 1908)

German social democratic politician. Journalist. Member of the SPD 1927. Exile in the Saar and then France. Active in the Resistance (link-man with the SPD Executive in London). Secretary of the German social democrats in France 1945. Chief Editor of *Freiheit* (Mainz) 1947–57 and of the Social Democratic Press Service 1957–70. Chairman of the SPD District Rhein-Hessen 1948–57. Member of the Rhineland-Palatinate Landtag 1950–57.

Markscheffel's papers covering the years 1945–70 are in the AdsD, Bonn. These comprise material concerning the organisation of the press, parties, trade unions and universities in the French Occupation Zone, the SPD (including youth work, cultural policy and the SPD in Rhineland-Palatinate), and the Social Democratic Press Service.

MARTEAU, Joseph (b. 1841)

French Communard.

See Appendix I.

MÄRTEN, Lu (1879–1970)

German socialist, afterwards communist writer and theorist of art.

The IISH, Amsterdam, has a substantial collection of papers mainly from 1902–69, containing correspondence, manuscripts, notes and printed material. Other papers are to be found in the Akademie der Künste in the GDR.

MARTENS, Gerrard (b. 1916)

Dutch conscientious objector and pacifist.

The IISH, Amsterdam, has a small collection of Martens's correspondence covering the years 1936–9. (See M. Campfens, *op. cit.*)

MARTIN, Pierre (1856–1916)*

French anarchist. Militant propagandist and strike organiser in Lyons and Vienne. Collaborated on *Le Libertaire*. Active at national anarchist congress, 1913.

Martin's correspondence whilst imprisoned in 1894 was confiscated by the police. It now survives in the Drôme Departmental Archive (See also GRAVE, Jean).

   * Known by the pseudonym Le Bossu.

MARTINI, Ferdinando (1841–1928)

Italian left liberal politician. Minister of Education 1892–3. Colonies Minister, 1914–16. Civil commissioner, Eritrea 1897–1907.

The Archivio Centrale dello Stato, Rome, has 21 boxes and one volume of Martini's documentary material from the period 1874–1925. The collection includes material on education questions and documents relating to Eritrea (for source see *Guida generale degli Archivi di Stato*, Rome).

MARTINSSON, Moa (1890–1964)

Swedish authoress of working-class origins writing about working-class life. Collaborated with the syndicalist movement.

Two boxes of Martinsson's papers are in the ARAB, Stockholm.

MARTOV, L.*

   * Pseudonym of TSEDERBAUM, Yulii Osipovič.

MARTY, André Pierre (1886–1956)

French communist leader. Joined PCF 1923. Collaborated on *L'Humanité* (Deputy Director 1934–5). Deputy for Seine-et-Oise 1924–8. Deputy for the Seine 1929–32 and 1936–40. Representative of the Spanish Republic and organiser of the International Brigade 1936–9. Went to Russia 1939.

Marty's papers are reported in the IFHS, Paris. A microfilm (4 reels) of papers relating to communism in France, 1917–39, is in the Hoover Institution, Stanford University, California.

MARX, Karl (1818–83)

German co-founder of scientific socialism.

Marx's personal and political documents, correspondence, manuscripts and notes, etc. are inseparable from those of Friedrich Engels (q.v.), with which they form a single collection in the IISH, Amsterdam. Ostensibly the largest part of the Marx-Engels papers, however, together with photocopies of the Amsterdam collection, is in the Institute for Marxism-Leninism, Moscow. Nearly all original Marx letters have, of course, been published.

MATTHIASEN, Niels (1924–80)

Danish social democratic politician. Secretary of the SDP. Several times Minister of Culture after 1971.

Twelve boxes of Matthiasen's manuscripts and articles covering the years 1971–80 are in the ABA, Copenhagen.

MAUGER, Hippolyte (1857–1946)

French socialist militant and politician. Co-operator and trade unionist in Cher. Proponent of agricultural unionism. Municipal Councillor in Dun-sur-Auron 1892–8. Deputy for Cher 1910–19. During the First World War held an official post. Expelled from the SFIO in 1919 for voting for the Treaty of Versailles. Senator for Cher 1920–39. Became Vice-President of the Democratic-Radical and Radical Socialist Group in the Senate.

Mauger's papers are in the Departmental Archives of Cher. These are particularly relevant to the *syndicat de bûcherons*, and trade unionism generally, in Cher in the years 1879–1913.

MAURIN, Joaquin (1896–1973)

Spanish communist leader and then oppositionist. Journalist and author. Leader of the Spanish Communist Party. Resigned and formed the Catalan-Balearic Communist Federation – later known as the Workers' and Peasants' Bloc of which he was General Secretary, and which merged with the former Spanish Left Opposition to create the POUM. General Secretary of the POUM in 1935. Member of Parliament 1936. Arrested by Franco's troops when the civil war broke out. Not recognised and so escaped execution. Upon release went into exile and ceased all political activity.

An extensive collection of Maurin's papers covering the years 1920–73 is in the Hoover Institution, Stanford University, California. These comprise correspondence, writings, newspaper and magazine clippings, other printed material, and photographs relating to communism and socialism in Spain, the Spanish Civil War, and the American Literary Agency.

MAXIMOV, Grigorij P. (1893–1950)

Russian anarcho-syndicalist. After the October Revolution, Editor of the anarcho-syndicalist papers *Golos Truda* (*Labour Voice*) and *Novy Golos Truda* (*New Labour Voice*). Arrested in March 1921 at the time of the Kronstadt uprising. Exile in Berlin and, finally, Chicago. Writer on the Russian terror and anarchism.

There is a collection of Maximov's papers – including correspondence, manuscripts, excerpts and documents – in the IISH, Amsterdam.

MAYER, Bernhard (1866–1946)

German anarchist.

The IISH, Amsterdam, has a very small collection of Mayer's correspondence and a manuscript.

MAYER, Gustav (1871–1948)

German historian of the labour movement. Biographer of Friedrich Engels (q.v.).

There is a collection of Gustav Mayer's correspondence in the Feltrinelli Institute, Milan. Another part of his papers, together with his collection of material from and on Lassalle, and the General German Workers' Union, is in the IISH, Amsterdam. The British Library of Political and Economic Science, London, has manuscripts on the English labour movement. (See Mommsen, *op. cit.*)

MAYWALD, Karel (1902–79)

Czech social democratic politician. Academic. Researcher for the State Statistical Office in Prague 1931–45. During the Nazi occupation member of the underground group 'PVVZ'. President of the newly-constituted State Planning Office in Prague 1945 and of the State Planning Board. Social Democratic member of the provisional Parliament and Vice-Chairman of the Parliamentary Budget Committee. Exile in 1949 following the Communist takeover. From 1950 in Britain. Active in the Czechoslovak exile. Critical of the Council of Free Czechoslovakia based in the United States.

Maywald's papers are in Churchill College, Cambridge.

MAZON, Albin (fl. 1860s)

French democratic socialist in Largentière (Ardèche).

Mazon's papers are in the Departmental Archive of Ardèche. These include his *Mémoires d'un songeur*, as well as many documents concerning Paul Mathieu Laurent (Laurent de l'Ardèche).

MAZZINI, Giuseppe (1805–72)

Italian patriot, writer and political philosopher. Architect of Italian *Risorgimento*.

Mazzini's papers are in the Museo del Risorgimento, Milan.

MEHRING, Franz (1846–1919)

German social democratic and finally communist publicist, historian and theorist. At first a radical democrat. Influenced by Lassalle (q.v.) in the 1870s but maintained a liberal opposition to socialism until *c.* 1882. Took up the defence of social democrats against Bismarck's anti-socialist laws and moved away from liberalism. Began to study Marxism. Joined the SPD in 1891. Contributed articles on history, philosophy and literature, as well as current political issues to *Die Neue Zeit*. Published (at the request of the SPD) his history of German social democracy in 1897–8. Published early works of Marx (q.v.) and Friedrich Engels (q.v.). Prominent opponent of revisionism. One of the leaders of the SPD left.

Opposed the First World War. Forced to resign from *Die Neue Zeit*. Helped found *Die Internationale* in 1915 as the organ of the anti-war left. Helped found the Spartakus League. Imprisoned in 1916. Elected to the Prussian Parliament in 1917. Supported the Bolshevik Revolution. Helped found the KPD but too ill to attend its founding conference. Died shortly after the murder of his friends Rosa Luxemburg (q.v.) and Karl Liebknecht. Biographer of Marx.

The main part of Mehring's papers was plundered and destroyed by the SA in 1933. However, a small collection of his papers covering the years 1914–18 survives at the Hoover Institution, Stanford University, California. This comprises writings and correspondence relating to political conditions in Germany and to the peace movement during the 1914–18 war. There is other substantial material in the Institute for Marxism-Leninism, Moscow. Details are not available.

MEIDNER, Rudolf (b. 1914)

Swedish trade union economist. Researcher for the LO (post-war).

Ten boxes of Meidner's papers, containing – in particular – material on LO economic policy, are in the ARAB, Stockholm.

MEIJER, Willem H. (1877–1951)

Dutch SDAP member.

The IISH, Amsterdam, has a small collection of Meijer's manuscripts covering the period 1901–11. (See M. Campfens, *op. cit.*)

MEIROP, Lodewijk van (1876–1930)

Dutch Christian anarchist.

The IISH, Amsterdam, has some of Meirop's correspondence and also some organisation archives (1915–37). (See M. Campfens, *op. cit.*)

MEL'GUNOV, Sergei Petrovič (1879–1956)

Russian populist. Historian and political writer. Opposed to the October Revolution. Went into exile 1923.

There are two collections of Mel'gunov's papers. The first is in the Hoover Institution, Stanford University, California, and comprises correspondence, reminiscences, memoranda of political prisoners and newspaper cuttings relating to the activities of the Cheka 1918–37 and the Russian Terror campaigns. The second is in the British Library of Political and Economic Science, London.

MÉLIN, Jeanne (1877–1964)

Militant French socialist and pacifist. Campaigned for female suffrage.

The unpublished manuscript of her *Lettres au jour le jour ou tranches de vie d'une Parisienne* is in the Bibliothèque Bouglé.

MELTTI, Väinö (1898–1964)

Finnish socialist. Principal of the Kotka Labour College 1932–41 and 1945. Member of the Finnish Social Democratic Party and later of the Finnish People's Democratic League (SKDL). Member of Parliament 1941 and 1944.

Meltti's papers are in the National Archives of Finland, Helsinki. Special permission from the Director is necessary to consult these papers.

MENDE, Fritz (d. 1879)

Pioneer German social democrat. Writer. Member of the Reichstag.

Before 1937 Mende's papers were in the Reichsarchiv, Potsdam. Their whereabouts is now uncertain. (See Mommsen, *op. cit.*)

MENDELS, Maurits (1868–1944)

Dutch SDAP member in the States Council.

The IISH, Amsterdam, has Mendels's personal archives and correspondence. (See M. Campfens, *op. cit.*)

MENNE, Bernhard*

* Pseudonym of RUDERT, Max.

MENŠČIKOV, Leonid Petrovič (b. 1871)

Ochrana agent-provocateur in the Russian revolutionary movement.

A large collection of Menščikov's papers covering the years 1886–1912 is in the IISH, Amsterdam. This includes correspondence and manuscripts relating to his activities as an agent-provocateur. A provisional inventory is available.

MENZEL, Walter (1901–63)

German social democratic politician. District President in Weilburg/Lahn 1931–3. After 1934 lawyer in Berlin. Adviser to the American Control Commission in Berlin 1945. Executive member of the SPD. Minister of the Interior 1946–50 in North Rhine-Westphalia and member of the Landtag 1947. Member of the Parliamentary Council 1948–9 and of the Bundestag 1949–62 (leader of the SPD group).

Most of Menzel's papers are in the AdsD at the Friedrich-Ebert-Stiftung, Bonn. Although a large collection, it is limited to files of his time as a Land Minister and in the Bundestag. These concern in particular, constitutional and suffrage questions, emergency legislation and the protection of the constitution, border protection and the working group *Kampf dem Atomtod* (1958–62). In addition, the Hauptarchiv Düsseldorf has a small collection of Menzel's papers concerning administrative reform (1947), the Evangelical Church and the SPD 1946–50. (See Mommsen, *op. cit.*)

MERA, Cipriano (1897–1975)

Spanish anarchist. In 1933, organiser of insurrection in Aragon. Arrested. After the assassination of Durruti in November 1936 the most important military leader of the anarchist militias.

There is a small collection of Mera's papers in the IISH, Amsterdam. This includes a letter from Mera to the IISH in 1960, as well as photocopies of correspondence between P. Alfareche, I. Prieto, S. Subero and M. Yoldi, a typewritten manuscript of his unpublished *De Nuestra Guerra: Diario de Campana* (1939–70), and a photocopy of an article by I. Prieto ('Francisco Largo Caballero y Federica Montseny'). Access to this collection is still restricted.

MERCIER VEGA, Louis (1914–77)

French anarchist.

The IISH, Amsterdam, has a small collection of Mercier Vega's correspondence for the years 1958–63, and a manuscript from the same period.

MÉRIC, Victor (1876–1933)*

French socialist. Contributor to *La Guerre Sociale*. Joined the SFIO 1906. Member of the CAP 1920. Entered the PCF. Resigned 1923.

A collection of letters received by Méric is in the Bibliothèque Nationale, Paris.

* Known as Henri Coudon, and by the pseudonym Flax.

MERING, Berta Borisovna (1885–1970)

Russian Menshevik and Bundist.

The IISH, Amsterdam, has a small collection of correspondence from the years 1923–59.

MESCHI, Alberto (1879–1959)

Italian anarchist.

Meschi's papers were acquired by the IISH, Amsterdam, in 1967. They include unpublished manuscripts, memoirs, correspondence, and documents concerning Meschi's trial at Carrara, 1952. There is correspondence with Erasmo Abate (Hugo Rolland) (q.v.) and letters to Meschi from Borghi, Marzocchi, Treai (Fedeli) (q.v.), Tresca, etc. There are also newspaper cuttings and his articles published in *La Révolution Prolétarienne*. The collection is open and a provisional list available.

METZ, Franz (1878–1945)

German social democratic trade unionist and politician. Secretary of the Deutscher Metallarbeiterverband (Association of German Engineering Workers) in Frankfurt and then in Stuttgart. Member of the Reichstag (SPD). Concentration camp victim.

Metz's papers are in private hands. However, the Stadtarchiv, Frankfurt, has copies including extracts from his diaries 1933–45, papers concerning the Reichstag (1933) and his letters from Dachau (1944). (See Mommsen, *op. cit.*)

METZKOW, Max (1854–1944)

German–American anarchist. Comrade of Emma Goldman (q.v.).

There is a small collection of Metzkow's papers from *c.* 1880–1944 in the IISH, Amsterdam. This includes both letters to Metzkow (from, amongst others, Richard Baginski and Max Baginski, E. Keppel and A. Prinz) and letters from Metzkow to A. Sanftleben (*c.* 1925–44), as well as several handwritten manuscripts (some of an autobiographical nature).

MEULEN, Jacob (1884–1962)

Dutch pacifist and librarian at the Peace Palace, The Hague.

The IISH, Amsterdam, has various documents and correspondence appertaining to Jacob Meulen (1908–60). A list is available. (See M. Campfens, *op. cit.*)

MEULEN, Lodolf A. van der (1893–1979)

Dutch SDAP member and later Independent Socialist.

The IISH, Amsterdam, has a small collection of Lodolf Meulen's dossiers on the SDAP from the period 1931–70. (See M. Campfens, *op. cit.*)

MEUNIER, Régis (1864–1936)

French militant anarchist in the Trélazé area (Maine-et-Loire). Several times imprisoned.

See under GRAVE, Jean.

MEUNIER, Théodule (1860–1907)

French militant anarchist. Cabinet maker. In 1894 sentenced to forced labour for life for a bomb attack.

See under GRAVE, Jean.

MEY, Henriette van der (1850–1945)

Editor and member of Dutch SDAP.

The IISH, Amsterdam, has some of Mey's correspondence and various other documents (1894–1919).

MEYER, A. C. (1858–1938)

Pioneer Danish socialist and SD politician. Author and song writer.

Two boxes of A. C. Meyer's papers for the 1880s to 1938, including manuscripts, and a large collection of letters to Meyer are in the ABA, Copenhagen.

MEYER, Ernst (1887–1930)

German communist leader. Founding and Executive member of the KPD. Member of the

Prussian Landtag 1921–4 (Leader of the KPD group). Chairman of the KPD Politburo 1921–3 (proponent of the united front). Removed from office in 1923. Again in the leadership 1926–8.

There are photocopies of a collection of Ernst Meyer's papers covering the years 1921–9 in the British Library of Political and Economic Science. This comprises reports to the Politburo and the Central Committee of the KPD, and to the Comintern, as well as correspondence with August Thalheimer, Walter Ulbricht and Zinoviev. In addition, see Rosa Meyer-Leviné.

MEYER, Håkon (b. 1896)

Norwegian labour leader. Collaborator. Publicist. Executive member of the Norwegian Labour Party 1924–6. Leading figure in the Party's left opposition and youth organisation in the 1930s. Editor of the Party's theoretical journal *Det tyvende aarhundrede* 1929–34. Co-founder of a trade union opposition which collaborated with Quisling's *Nasjonal Samling* and the Nazi occupation authorities in 1940. Condemned in 1945.

A small collection of Håkon Meyer's papers for the years 1936–61 is in the ARAB, Stockholm. These include correspondence, articles, newspaper cuttings and other printed material. An inventory is available.

MEYER-LEVINÉ, Rosa (b. 1890)

Communist. Born in Russia. Came to Germany *c*. 1910 and there married the future KPD leader Eugen Leviné (1915) and, after his death, the KPD leader Ernst Meyer. Lived in England from 1934. Biographer of her first husband and author of a history of the Munich Soviet Republic and a volume of memoirs of the KPD.

The Bundesarchiv, Koblenz, has a small collection of Meyer-Leviné's correspondence with her husbands, Eugen Leviné (q.v.) and Ernst Meyer (q.v.).

MEYER-WICHMANN, Clara G. (1885–1922)

Dutch anti-militarist and anarchist.

There are two collections of Meyer-Wichmann's papers. The IISH, Amsterdam, has a collection of correspondence and personal archives. Access is restricted. Other papers are held by her family.

MICHEL, Louise (1830–1905)

French Communard. Militant anarchist, writer and educator. Member of the International.

Michel's surviving papers are widely dispersed. There is material in the Bibliothèque Marguerite Durand at the Town Hall, 5th Arrondissement, Paris, as well as various files in the archives of the Prefecture of Police, Paris. There is also material in the Lucien Descaves collection on the Paris Commune (in the IISH, Amsterdam) and also at the Feltrinelli Institute, Milan.

MIDDENDORP, Wilhelm (1886–1976)

Dutch SDAP member.

The IISH, Amsterdam, has one of Middendorp's manuscripts. (See M. Campfens, *op. cit.*)

MIERENDORFF, Carlo (1897–1943)

German social democratic politician. Trade unionist, journalist and writer. Member of the Reichstag (SPD) 1930–33. Active in the resistance. Concentration camp victim.

A very few of Mierendorff's papers are in the Stadtarchiv, Darmstadt.

MIGSCH, Alfred (b. 1919)

Austrian socialist. Resister. Minister of Transport, 1947–9.

The Institute of Contemporary History, Vienna, has three bundles of papers covering the period 1945–65, including material on nationalisation and on the Austrian state treaty of 1955.

MILIUKOV, Paul N. (fl. 1900–30)

Russian liberal. Leader of the Kadet party. Historian.

Eight boxes of his papers are at the Bakhmeteff Archive, Columbia University, New York. The collection contains documents and correspondence, 1918–37; documents and correspondence of the Kadet Party, 1900–30s, including draft programmes, constitutions, reports and publications; his *Vospominaniia F. I. Rodicheva o 1917*; his memoirs; and a notebook relating to the congress of the Constituent Assembly members in Paris. There are restrictions on the use of the material.

MILLERAND, Alexandre (1859–1943)

French socialist and politician. Deputy for the Seine, 1885–1920. A founder of the Republican-Socialist Federation of the Seine 1893. Minister of Commerce in the Waldeck-Rousseau cabinet 1899–1902. Expelled from the PSF 1904. Frequent ministerial office, including Minister of War, 1912–13, 1914–15, Foreign Affairs, 1920, and Prime Minister, 1920. President of the Republic, 1920–24.

There are two holdings of Millerand's papers. The first is contained in 102 boxes deposited by his son in the Manuscript Department of the Bibliothèque Nationale, Paris. Apart from personal papers, this holding comprises files on elections, the Ministries of Commerce, Public Works, Posts and Telegraph, and War (including military operations, armaments, war production and stocks), the General Commissariat at Strasbourg (1919), the Presidency of the Council and Ministry of Foreign Affairs (domestic and foreign policy), the Presidency of the Republic, as well as speeches and conferences. An inventory has been prepared. The second is in 95 volumes of papers deposited by his son in the Archives du Ministère des Affaires Étrangères. These are files examined by Millerand as the President of the Republic (1920–24), and concern German reparations, disarmament, inter-allied war debts, the Balkan question, the Eastern question, Russia and the Genoa Conference. An inventory is available.

MISEFARI, Bruno (1892–1936)

Italian anarchist.

The IISH, Amsterdam, has a small collection of Bruno Misefari's papers for the period after 1918, containing correspondence, personal documents, manuscripts, notes, files, and printed material. Other papers are in the Basso-Issoco Foundation, Rome.

MISEFARI, Enzo

Italian socialist.

Enzo Misefari's correspondence and papers are to be found in the Feltrinelli Institute, Milan. The collection includes early documentation of the embryonic forms of workers' associations, c. 1700 to 1843. For 1843 to 1900 there is documentation on the birth of the 'Self-Help' Societies. For 1900–24 there is material on the peasant movement.

MODIGLIANI, Giuseppe Emanuele (1872–1947)

Italian socialist. Opponent of Italian intervention in the First World War. Co-founder with Treves (q.v.) and Turati (q.v.), of the Italian Unitary Socialist Party in 1922. President of the PSU.

The Archivio Centrale dello Stato, Rome, has 15 boxes of Modigliani's papers covering the period 1900–45. The collection comprises material relating to his political, parliamentary and party activity.

MOLKENBUHR, Hermann (1851–1927)

Early social democratic politician. From 1890 Editor of the Hamburg *Echo*. Member of the Reichstag (and of the National Assembly) until 1924. Co-Chairman of the SPD group and its expert on social policy. Executive member of the SPD from 1904 until his death.

Molkenbuhr's papers are in the AdsD at the Friedrich-Ebert-Stiftung, Bonn. These comprise four handwritten volumes of his diary from 1904 as well as four volumes of memoirs covering the years 1864–80, personal documents, manuscripts etc. In addition, there are letters from – amongst others – Ignaz Auer, August Bebel (q.v.), Wilhelm Liebknecht (q.v.) and Edouard Vaillant (q.v.) as well as Molkenbuhr's own letters to his son Arthur. (See Mommsen, *op. cit.*)

MOLL, Frédéric (b. 1853)

French Communard.

See Appendix I.

MÖLLER, Gustav (1884–1970)

Swedish social democratic politician (sometimes known as the 'father of the welfare state'). Journalist. Chairman of the Social Democratic Youth organisation 1907–12 and Editor of its paper *Fram* 1911–12. Director of the publishing company Tiden 1913–17. Secretary of the SAP 1916–40 (with certain interruptions) and Editor of its central organ *Social Demokraten* 1921–40. Member of Parliament 1918–54. Member or Chairman of the Socialisation Commission 1920–33. Social Minister (responsible for the setting up of the welfare state) 1924–6, 1932–8 and 1939–51. Executive member of the Labour and Socialist International 1922–4 and 1926–32.

A large collection of Möller's papers covering the years 1916–69 is in the ARAB, Stockholm. This comprises personal documents, correspondence, manuscripts, printed matter and other material concerning his political activity. In particular, this collection includes a large quantity of material concerning the work of the Socialisation Commission, and agrarian policy. An inventory is available.

MOLLET, Guy (fl. 1940s–60s)

French socialist leader. Secretary-General, SFIO, 1946–69.

Mollet's entire archive has been placed in the Office Universitaire de Recherche Socialiste (OURS), Paris (which he founded in 1969).

MOLTKE, Kai (1902–79)

Danish communist. Later in the People's Socialist Party (PSP). Writer and editor. Member of Parliament.

One box of Moltke's papers for the years 1922–75 is in the ABA, Copenhagen. This includes correspondence, manuscripts and interviews concerning both the DKP and the PSP.

MOMMER, Karl (b. 1910)

German KPD member and then social democratic politician. Imprisoned in 1934 for illegal activity for the KPD. Exile 1935. Joined the SPD 1937. SPD representative in the Frankfurt Economic Council 1947–9. Member of the Bundestag from 1949 (on the SPD group Executive). Expert on the Saar. Member of the Advisory Assembly of the Council of Europe 1950–58.

Mommer's papers covering the years 1945–56 are in the AdsD at the Friedrich-Ebert-Stiftung, Bonn. These comprise documents concerning the Saar, foreign policy, the Council of Europe, all-German questions, draft laws in the Bundestag (tax, finance and family law) and Bundestag elections. (See Mommsen, *op. cit.*)

MONATTE, Pierre (1881–1960)

French revolutionary syndicalist. Editor, *Action syndicale*, 1905. Founded *La Vie ouvrière* 1909. Opposed CGT's attitude to First World War. Resigned, December 1914, from CGT Confederal Committee. Joined PCF 1923. Expelled November 1924, because of support for Trotsky (q.v.). Co-founder, 1925, of *La Révolution prolétarienne*. Denounced Stalinism.

Monatte's papers are in the IFHS, Paris. The most important have been published in C. Chamberland and J. Maitron, *Syndicalisme révolutionnaire et Communisme. Les Archives P. Monatte* (Paris: Maspéro 1968). They are particularly important for the history of revolutionary syndicalism, and of the journals *La Vie ouvrière* and *La Révolution prolétarienne*.

MONIN, Jean-Baptiste (b. 1823)

French Communard.

See Appendix I.

MONTELS, Jules (1843–1916)

French revolutionary socialist. Member of the International. Active in the Fédération Jurassienne. Settled in Tunis. Editor of the *Tunis Journal*. Joined, 1907, the SFIO.

One important manuscript (*Qu'est-ce que la Commune?*) survives in the IISH, Amsterdam. In addition, a number of Montels's letters are in the Jean-Louis Pindy (q.v.) papers in the IFHS, Paris.

MORGARI, Oddino (1865–1929)

Italian socialist. Journalist and deputy.

The Archivio Centrale dello Stato, Rome, has 20 boxes of Morgari's papers covering the period 1897–1925. The collection comprises correspondence and miscellaneous papers relating to his journalistic, parliamentary and party political activity, and on his contacts with leading socialists in other countries, above all in Germany, Hungary and Russia.

MORIZET, André (1876–1942)

French socialist politician. Elected, 1917, to the CAP of the SFIO. Resigned, and rejoined SFIO 1928. Mayor of Boulogne-Billancourt 1919. Senator for the Seine 1927–42.

The *Journal d'André Morizet*, from 3 June 1940 to 30 November 1941, is in the IFHS, Paris.

MOTTELER, Julius (1838–1907)

Pioneer German socialist. Co-founder of the SDAP. Member of the Reichstag 1874–8. During the years of Bismarck's anti-socialist laws, responsible for publishing and organising the illegal distribution of *Der Socialdemokrat* (at first from Zürich and then from London) and became known as the 'rote Feldpostmeister'. Organised the Party's defence against police agents. Undertook special missions for the Party. Member of the Kommunistischer Arbeiterbildungsverein (Communist Workers Educational Association) in London 1888–1901. Returned to Germany in 1901 and became a member of the Reichstag (SPD). Gathered material for the basis of a Party achive.

Motteler's extensive papers are in the IISH, Amsterdam. This collection is virtually the archive of German social democracy during the years of the anti-socialist laws (1878–90). The material relating to *Der Socialdemokrat* concerns not only the production and distribution of the newspaper but also, for example, the distribution of other Party literature, the support of exiled social democrats, obtaining and evaluating political reports, aid for strikes, the Party 'security service' and archive. There is also considerable correspondence in this connection as well as material concerning Party conferences in this period. There is also correspondence and other material arising from his activity as a member of the Reichstag, manuscripts of articles, notes, printed matter and collections of material for the Party archive. A very detailed inventory and guide is available.

MÜHSAM, Erich (1878–1934)

German anarchist writer and revolutionary. Edited and collaborated on revolutionary and satirical journals. In Munich from 1909. Associated with an anti-war group around Kurt Eisner (q.v.), but broke with him over support for Bolshevism. Member of the Central Council of the Munich Soviet Republic 1919. Sentenced to 15 years' imprisonment under the subsequent reaction (released 1924). Active in *Rote Hilfe* (Red Aid). Murdered in concentration camp.

Mühsam's papers arising from his activity in *Rote Hilfe* were confiscated and destroyed in 1933. There are two collections of his surviving papers. First, there are his papers mixed together with those of his wife, Krezentia Mühsam (born Elfinger): these include manuscripts and diaries (1910–33), as well as family and political correspondence (including letters to his wife and parents as well as to, amongst others, Gustav Landauer (q.v.)). The originals of these are in the Institute for World Literature (Gorki Institute), Moscow: microfilm copies are held at the Archiv der Deutschen Akademie der Künste, East Berlin.

Finally, another such mixed collection of papers – including personal and family correspondence as well as literary manuscripts – is in the Leo Baeck Institute, New York. (See Mommsen, *op. cit.*)

MÜLLER, Fritz (b. 1900)

German social democrat. Before 1933 Manager of the Consumer Cooperative in Kaiserslautern, and Secretary of the SPD in the Palatinate. Concentration camp victim 1933 and 1944. District Secretary of the SPD in Rhein-Hessen 1946–66. Member of the Working Group of Persecuted Social Democrats.

Fritz Müller's papers covering the years 1890–1976 are in the AdsD, Bonn. These comprise personal documents, memoirs and correspondence concerning Landtag and Bundestag elections, the SPD District Rhein-Hessen and Sub-District Mainz-Bingen, resistance against the Nazi regime, the Working Group of Persecuted Social Democrats, reparations, *Die Freiheit* (Mainz) and relations between the SPD, KPD and SED.

MÜLLER, Hermann (1876–1931)*

German social democratic politician. From 1919 Chairman of the SPD. Member of the Reichstag 1916–31 (of the National Assembly in 1919). From 1920 Chairman of the SPD group. Member of the Executive Council 1918 and then the Central Council of the German Republic. Reich Foreign Minister 1919. Reichskanzler (Chancellor) March–June 1920 and June 1928–March 1930.

Part of Hermann Müller's papers were confiscated by the Gestapo in France (1940) and have not subsequently been located. Those that survive are in two collections. The first, comprising four box-files from the years 1910–31, is in the Deutsches Zentralarchiv, Potsdam. The second is in the AdsD at the Friedrich-Ebert-Stiftung, Bonn. This comprises mainly files from his time as Reich Chancellor (including the process of forming governments) together with correspondence concerning his book on the November Revolution. (See Mommsen, *op. cit.*)

* Also known as Müller-Franken.

MÜLLER, Willy (1903–77)*

German social democratic politician. White-collar trade unionist. Member of the SPD 1946. Member of the Bundestag for Worms 1949–69. Committee for Nutrition, Agriculture and Forestry.

Willy Müller's extensive papers are in the AdsD at the Friedrich-Ebert-Stiftung, Bonn. These comprise manuscripts of lectures 1950–75, material relating to his trade union activity before 1933, private correspondence from the Nazi period, his correspondence as a Bundestag deputy and supplementary press cuttings from 1949, printed material concerning trade unions before 1945 and other material concerning the SPD and the politics of the BRD. (See Mommsen, *op. cit.*)

* Also known as Müller-Worms.

MÜLLER-FRANKEN, Hermann

See under MÜLLER, Hermann.

MÜLLER-WORMS, Willy

See under MÜLLER, Willy.

MUSINI, Luigi (d. 1903)

Italian socialist. Elected to Parliament 1884.

A large collection of Musini's papers, covering the years 1860–1903 (with gaps for 1872–6 when Musini was in Uruguay) is in the Feltrinelli Institute, Milan. The collection relates mainly to the workers' movement in Emilia.

MUSSOLINI, Benito (1883–1945)

Italian dictator.

Mussolini's papers are in the Archivio Centrale dello Stato, Rome.

MYRDAL, Alva (b. 1902)

Swedish social scientist, social democratic politician and diplomat. Director of the Institute for Social Policy 1936–48. Head of the UNO Department for Social Questions 1949–50, and of the Social Science Department of UNESCO 1951–5. Swedish ambassador to several countries (including India 1955–9). Member of Parliament 1962–70. Minister for Disarmament 1967–73. Head of the Swedish disarmament delegation in Geneva 1962–73. Prolific author. Wife of Gunnar Myrdal (q.v.).

An enormous and continuously supplemented collection of both Alva and Gunnar Myrdal's papers from 1919 onwards is in the ARAB, Stockholm. This comprises correspondence, manuscripts, notes, drafts, transcripts and photographs, as well as other material arising out of their political and scientific activity such as pamphlets, newspaper cuttings and other printed material, and tape recordings. A two-volume inventory is available, but access to the collection is restricted.

MYRDAL, Gunnar (b. 1898)

Swedish economist and social democratic politician. Member of Parliament 1935–8 and 1944–7. Minister of Trade 1945–7. Internationally politically active. Head of the UNO Economic Commission for Europe 1947–57. Prolific social scientist. Husband of Alva Myrdal (q.v.).

See Alva Myrdal.

NABRINK, Gé (b. 1903)

Dutch anti-militarist and pacifist.

The IISH, Amsterdam, has an extensive collection of Nabrink's organisational archives and correspondence covering the years 1945–75. (See M. Campfens, *op. cit.*)

NACHT, Max (1881–1973)*

Anarchist. Born in Eastern Galicia and lived in the USA. Writer on the anarchist movement, notably on Johann Most, with whom he had been personally acquainted.

There is a large collection of Max Nacht's papers in the IISH, Amsterdam. This comprises correspondence, articles and printed documentary material on various anarchists, Marxists, political groups, and ideologies, and also files with material from his brother Siegfried Nacht (q.v.), files with material on Waclaw Machajski, and single issues of various magazines. The manuscripts include an unabridged version of the chapter on Nechayev from Nacht's *Apostles of the Revolution, Reflections at Ninety* (1972), *Reflections of a Pessimist* (1969–70) and an autobiographical sketch. Finally, the files on Machajski contain articles by Machajski (often translated by Nacht), articles on Machajski (collected and sometimes written by Nacht), notes and documentary material. Access to this collection is restricted.

* Known by the pseudonym Max Nomad.

NACHT, Siegfried (1878–1956)*

Anarchist. Born in Eastern Galicia. Delegate from the London Kommunistischer Arbeiter-bildungsverein (Communist Workers' Educational Association) to the 1907 international anarchist congress in Amsterdam. Friend and comrade of Rudolf Rocker (q.v.). Later lived in the USA. Adviser to the FBI on communism.

There are several files of Nacht's papers amongst the papers of his brother, Max Nacht (q.v.), in the IISH, Amsterdam. These include correspondence, manuscripts, articles on Latin America, and his curriculum vitae. (The files also contain obituaries of Nacht.) The manuscripts and works by Nacht include *Aus der Odyssee eines Rebellen, Reminiscences* (1925), *Die theoretischen Voraussetzungen des syndikalistischen Anarchismus* and *Literatur-Anarchismus oder revolutionärer Anarchismus*.

* Known by the pseudonyms Stephan Naft and Andrew Roller.

NADAR, Félix (1820–1910)

French supporter of persecuted communards. Life-long revolutionary sympathiser and friend of Jean Grave (q.v.). Famous as a photographer and aeronaut.

Nadar's papers were deposited in 1943 and 1950 in the Bibliothèque Nationale, Paris. The latter holding comprises 80 letters from Jean Grave (q.v.) to Nadar.

* Known by the pseudonym, Félix Tournachon.

NAFT, Stephan*

* Pseudonym of NACHT, Siegfried.

NAUMANN, Friedrich (1860–1919)

German theologian and social reformer. Founder of the Nationalsozialer Verein. Editor of *Hilfe*. Member of the Reichstag.

A small collection of letters from Friedrich Naumann and Helmuth von Gerlach to P. Haag in the years 1898–1906 is in the AdsD, Bonn.

NAVEAU, Eugène (b. 1828)

French Communard.

See Appendix I.

NELLEN, Peter (1912-69)

German Christian democrat and then social democratic politician. At first teacher. Joined CDU 1946. Member of the Bundestag (CDU) 1949-60. Resigned from the CDU over foreign and defence policy disagreements. Joined the SPD Bundestag group and represented the SPD until his death.

The AdsD at the Friedrich-Ebert-Stiftung, Bonn, has a large collection of Nellen's papers from the years 1960-9. These concern Federal matters (laws), Church questions (especially the relations between the SPD and Catholics), conscription and atomic weapons.

NELSON, Leonard (fl. 1882-1927)

German socialist theoretician and philosopher. Leading intellectual influence on the ISK.

Nelson's papers for the years 1882-1927 are in the AdsD, Bonn. These include personal documents and memoirs, personal and academic correspondence (but very little for the years after 1913) and manuscripts. In addition, this collection is supplemented by a large collection of books and pamphlets (some published by Nelson himself).

NĚMEC, Antonín (fl. 1897-1932)

President of the Czech Social Democratic Party.

The *Ústav Marxismu-Leninismu úv KSČ*, Prague, has two boxes (209 archive units) containing his papers from the period 1897 to 1932. The collection contains correspondence with leading figures of the international socialist movement.

NERMAN, Ture (1886-1969)

Swedish communist leader. Writer and publicist. Active in the temperance movement, and from 1906 in the Social Democratic Youth organisation. Participant in the Zimmerwald Conference 1915. Founding member of the Left-Socialist Party 1917. Member of the SKP, and from 1929 of the Independent Communist Party (Socialist Party). Editor and writer 1916-37 for the paper of the SAP opposition, and then of the SKP, *Politiken* (becoming *Folkets Dagblad Politiken*). Rejoined the SAP in 1939. Editor of the anti-fascist *Trots allt!* 1939-45. Extensive activity in workers' education.

A large collection of Nerman's papers covering the years 1902-61 is in the ARAB, Stockholm. These comprise correspondence, manuscripts, transcripts, leaflets, photographs, newspaper cuttings and other material arising from his political and journalistic activity. An inventory is available.

NETTLAU, Max (1865-1944)

Austrian born historian of anarchism. In London 1885. Member of the Socialist League. Under the influence of Kropotkin (q.v.), turned towards anarchism. Studied the history of anarchism in London, Paris, Geneva, Barcelona and Vienna, and finally settled in Amsterdam. Numerous publications about anarchism.

Nettlau's papers are in the IISH, Amsterdam. In the main, these comprise his enormous collection of material concerning the history of anarchism. This includes correspondence with anarchists and socialists from all over the world, as well as material on anarchist, socialist and radical movements in various countries.

NEUBERGER, Josef (1902–77)

German social democratic politician. Lawyer. Exile in Holland 1938 and then Palestine. Town Councillor in Düsseldorf 1956–9. Member of the North Rhine-Westphalian Landtag 1959–75. Minister of Justice in North Rhine-Westphalia 1966–72.

Neuberger's papers for the years 1922–76 are in the AdsD, Bonn. These comprise personal papers and large quantities of material concerning his legal, political and ministerial career.

NEUMANN, Franz (1904–74)

German social democratic politician. From 1949 representative of Berlin in the Bundestag.

Neumann's papers are in the Franz-Neumann-Archiv, Berlin-Charlottenburg. (See Mommsen, *op. cit.*)

NEUTEBOOM, Hendrik (1884–1976)

Dutch SDAP member and associated with publishers and booksellers' organisation. Later PvdA member.

The IISH, Amsterdam has an extensive collection of Neuteboom's papers, including manuscript memoirs, correspondence and other documents. (See M. Campfens, *op. cit.*)

NICOLAEVSKY, Boris Ivanovič (1887–1966)

Russian Menshevik. Historian and archivist. Organised a radical student circle while still at school. Arrested in 1904. Emerged from prison a Marxist. Member of an RSDLP committee to organise the strike movement in Samara 1905. Head of a socialist organised self-defence force against the Black Hundreds. Worked to establish an RSDLP military-revolutionary organisation. Arrested in 1906. Finally split with the Bolsheviks and joined the Mensheviks in 1907. Clandestine and legal work for the Mensheviks 1907 (including membership of the Baku RSDLP Committee, work for the Menshevik Duma Deputy, M. I. Skobelev, and work for the Menshevik paper *Luch* (*Ray*)). Exiled to Siberia in 1914. A Menshevik Internationalist in 1917. On the editorial board of the Menshevik paper *Rabochaia gazeta* (*Workers' Gazette*). Member of the All-Russian Soviet of Workers' and Soldiers' Deputies. Increasingly disillusioned with Menshevik policies, turned to historical and archival work. Played an important part in the early organisation of Soviet archives. Exiled in 1921, but continued to assist the Marx-Engels Institute in gathering material throughout Europe. Instrumental in saving the archives of the German SPD – including the Marx (q.v.) – Friedrich Engels (q.v.) Nachlass – from the Nazis. Settled in New York in 1940.

Nicolaevsky was not only an activist, historian and political analyst of the Russian revolutionary movement and Soviet society, but also a tireless collector and conserver of historical material. The fruits of his efforts now form the B. I. Nicolaevsky collection in the

Hoover Institution, Stanford University, California. This extensive acquisition includes letters, memoranda, writings, speeches, memoirs, minutes of meetings, underground leaflets, photographs, clippings and other miscellaneous historical documents relating primarily to the Russian revolutionary movements (radicals, populists, anarchists, and, more specifically and extensively, the Russian Social Democratic Party, as well as the Socialist Revolutionary Party); the Tsarist government; the 1906 revolution; the Imperial Duma; the February and October Revolutions; the Civil War; Russian émigré politics; the Vlassov movement during the Second World War; Russian displaced persons after the Second World War; history and activities of the First, Second, and Third Internationals; and the labour and socialist movements in Europe and the United States. Consists of approximately 300 units of collected materials, including records of organisations, such as the Social Democratic and Socialist Revolutionary Parties, and personal papers of such political figures as P. Aksel'rod (q.v.), M. Bakunin (q.v.), V. Chernov (q.v.), A. Herzen (q.v.), P. Lavrov (q.v.), G. Plekhanov (q.v.), L. Trotsky (q.v.), Tsederbaum (Martov) (q.v.), and I. Tseretelli (q.v.) among others.

NIELSEN, Marie (1875–1951)

Danish revolutionary. At first teacher. Member of the SD until 1916. Attempted to form a new Socialist Workers' Party. Active in the syndicalist movement. Joined the DKP. Prominent in the Women Workers' Educational League in the inter-war period.

Four boxes of Nielsen's papers for the years 1910–47 are in the ABA, Copenhagen. As well as containing personal documents, they constitute an important collection of material on the Danish and international revolutionary movement (especially in the years 1910–36). In particular, it contains much material on the attempt to organise a new Socialist Workers' Party, as well as letters from, amongst others, Balabanoff (q.v.), Höglund (q.v.), Kollontai (q.v.), Münzenberg and Trier (q.v.). A printed inventory is available.

NIEUWENHUIS, Roelof (1896–1980)

Dutch trade unionist associated with NAS.

The IISH, Amsterdam, has a one-file dossier of Nieuwenhuis's activities (1922–7). (See M. Campfens, *op. cit.*)

NIKOLAEV, N. N. (fl. 1914–18)

Russian liberal. Kadet member of the fourth duma.

His papers are at the Bakhmeteff Archive, Columbia University, New York. The collection contains items relating to his work in the duma; material on the Kadet party; poems, essays on Russian liberalism; material on the Civil War in the Kuban area; correspondence; typed notes on the Provisional Government, the Civil War, émigré politics, and the emigration in the United States.

NILSSON, Torsten (b. 1905)

Swedish social democratic politician. Secretary of the SSU (Swedish Young Socialists) in the 1930s. Secretary of the SAP. Minister of Defence. Foreign Minister (1960s). Social Minister (up to 1974).

Nilsson's papers are in the ARAB, Stockholm. Apart from a large collection of press cuttings, however, these remain closed.

NOBS, Ernst (1886–1957)

Swiss social democratic politician. Member of the SPS left during the First World War. Editor of the Zürich *Volksrecht* (SPS daily). First socialist elected to the Federal Council 1943. Later the first socialist Executive member.

Many of Nobs's papers are to be found among the SPS archive deposited at the Schweizerisches Sozialarchiv, Zürich. In addition, there are collections of his papers in the City Archive of Zürich, as well as a few in the IISH, Amsterdam (which includes papers concerning Lang's (q.v.) wartime activities and the Stockholm Conference).

NOËL, Ernest (b. 1846)

French Communard.

See Appendix I.

NÖLL, Heinrich (1900–76)

German social democrat. Bookkeeper. Employee of the SPD in Frankfurt 1930–33. After 1945 active as a City Councillor in Frankfurt, Federal Chairman of the Arbeiterrat und Kraftfahrerbund, and the Workers' Samaritan League.

Nöll's papers for the years 1946–70 are in the AdsD, Bonn. These include material on the SPD in Frankfurt, and sport.

NOMAD, Max*

* Pseudonym of NACHT, Max.

NOSKE, Gustav (1868–1946)

German social democratic politician. Editor-in-Chief of the Chemnitz *Volksstimme* 1903. Member of the Reichstag (SPD) 1906–20. Specialist in military colonial questions. Represented the far right (pro-imperialist) wing of the SPD. Member of the Reich Government December 1918 and Minister for the Reichswehr 1919–20 (in this capacity he directed the bloody suppression of the revolutionary left in the first half of 1919). Forced to resign by pressure from the left. Temporarily strengthened by the defeat of the Kapp Putsch. Oberpräsident of Hannover 1920–32. Arrested by the Gestapo 1944.

The main part of Noske's papers is lost. Those that survive are in three small collections. The first is in the Deutsches Zentralarchiv, Potsdam. The second is in the Bundesarchiv, Koblenz, and comprises personal documents as well as correspondence, speeches and articles arising out of his activity as Reichswehr Minister. The third is in the AdsD, Bonn. This comprises personal papers and memoirs (especially concerning his period as Oberpräsident of Hannover, as well as manuscripts of his war diary (1914) and of his book *Von Kiel bis Kapp*. In addition, the manuscript of his memoirs (published in 1947 as *Erlebtes aus Aufstieg und Niedergang einer Demokratie*) is in the Hoover Institution, Stanford University, California. (See Mommsen, *op. cit.*)

OHLIG, Fritz (1902–71)

German social democratic politician. Secretary of the Socialist 'Arbeiterjugend' (Young

Socialist Workers, SAJ) in Silesia, 1924. Director of the SAJ publishing company and national treasurer of the SAJ, 1930. Full-time worker for the SPD executive, 1964–6. Deputy Chairman of the Federal Compensation Office, 1967.

Ohlig's papers – mainly printed material – are in the AdsD, Bonn. (See Mommsen, *op. cit.*)

OITTINEN, Reino (1912–78)

Finnish social democratic politician. Cabinet Minister 1957–68. Director of the National Board of General Education.

Oittinen's papers are in the National Archives of Finland, Helsinki. Special permission from the Director is necessary to consult these papers.

OLAYA, Francisco (b. 1923)

Spanish anarchist.

The IISH, Amsterdam, has a small collection of Olaya's correspondence, official documents, minutes, files, and reports.

OLJELUND, Ivan (b. 1892)

Swedish writer and anarchist. Prominent author of working-class origins writing about working-class life. Anarchist in Stockholm. Editor of the anarchist paper, *Brand*. Involved in 1916 treason trial. Turned to religion in the 1920s.

One box of Oljelund's papers is in the ARAB, Stockholm.

OLLENHAUER, Erich (1901–63)

German social democratic politician. From 1928 Chairman of the SAJ. From 1923 Secretary of the Socialist Youth International. After 1933, in exile. Member of the SOPADE in Prague (Otto Wels' (q.v.) 'right hand man'). From 1946 Deputy Chairman of the SPD. Schumacher's successor as Party Chairman and Leader of the Opposition in the Bundestag.

Ollenhauer's papers are in the AdsD at the Friedrich-Ebert-Stiftung, Bonn. The main part of this collection consists of his reference files with their associated correspondence from the years 1948–63 (concerning, *inter alia*, European integration and the labour and youth movement in Germany), subject files on foreign and security policy as well as drafts and plans of speeches. This holding also contains a collection of Ollenhauer's speeches and articles, biographical material and messages of condolence upon his death. (Additional correspondence of Ollenhauer is to be found in the holding Büro der Westzonen for 1946).

OLSEN, Christian Martin (1853–1926)

Danish trade union leader and social democratic politician. Chairman of the Joiners' Trade Union. Chairman of the Danish Federation of Trade Unions 1903. SD Member of Parliament (later in the Upper Chamber).

A large collection of Olsen's papers for the years 1873–1926 (*c.* 28 boxes) is in the ABA, Copenhagen. This is an important collection for the history of Danish trade unionism from the 1880s to *c.* 1920.

OLSSON, Oscar (b. 1877)

Swedish educator and social democratic politician. Known as the 'father' of the 'Study Circle' method of workers' self-education. Member of Parliament.

Six boxes of Olsson's papers are in the ARAB, Stockholm.

ORGERS, Petrus C. (1869–1946)

Dutch railway workers' trade unionist.

The IISH, Amsterdam, has a dossier of Orgers's on union affairs (1903–13). (See M. Campfens, *op. cit.*)

ORTLOFF, Siegfried (b. 1915)

German social democrat. Member of the SAJ 1930. Clandestine work for the SAJ and SPD. Imprisoned 1935. After 1937 exile in Czechoslovakia and then Sweden. Official in 1946–60 with the SPD Executive in Hannover and Bonn.

Ortloff's papers for the years 1943–6 are in the AdsD, Bonn. These concern his exile in Sweden (the 'Kleine Internationale' and SPD groups in particular) and include letters received from Kurt Heinig (q.v.).

OSSIETZKY, Carl von (1889–1938)

German social democrat. Writer and publicist. Editor, *Die Weltbühne*. Nobel Peace Prize.

Relevant papers of the 'Freundeskreis Ossietzky' are in the IISH, Amsterdam.

OSTERROTH, Franz (b. 1900)

German social democrat. Son of Nikolaus Osterroth (q.v.). Publicist. Co-founder of the 'Hofgeismarer Kreis' of the Young Socialists (non-Marxists) 1923. On the editorial staff of *Das Reichsbanner* 1928–33, and other functions in the Reichsbanner. In exile in 1934 in Czechoslovakia (working on SPD publications) and Sweden (member of the 'Kleine Internationale'). Secretary of the SPD in Kiel 1948–53. Member of the Cultural Policy Commission and of the Programme Commission of the SPD Executive.

Two manuscripts of Franz Osterroth's memoirs are in the AdsD, Bonn.

OSTERROTH, Nikolaus (1875–1933)

German social democratic politician and trade unionist. Member of the National Assembly and Prussian Landtag 1919–33. Departmental chief in the Reich Ministry of Economics, 1928.

There are two collections of Nikolaus Osterroth's papers. The first, covering the years 1900 to 1932 is in the AdsD, Bonn, and contains *inter alia*, material on the Saar, Lower Silesia and the mining and steel industries. The second is in the Geheimes Staatsarchiv Preuss, Kulturbesitz, Berlin. This also contains material on the Saar and Lower Silesia, along with material on Westphalia, mining and parliamentary politics. (See Mommsen, *op. cit.*)

OSTROWSKI, Otto (1883–1963)

German social democratic politician. Mayor of Lankwitz, Finsterwalde and Prenzlauer Berg (Berlin) 1918–33. District Mayor of Berlin-Wilmersdorf and Mayor of Berlin 1946 (resigned in 1947 after negotiations with the SED lost him the confidence of his own Party).

Ostrowski's papers for the immediate post-war years are in the AdsD, Bonn. These are particularly relevant to the politics of the administration of Berlin and questions such as reparations.

OSWALD, Eugen (1826–1912)

German journalist and writer.

The IISH, Amsterdam, has a small collection of Oswald's correspondence.

OTTESEN-JENSEN, Elise (1886–1973)

Syndicalist and campaigner for sexual emancipation in Sweden. Norwegian, who married Albert Jensen (q.v.). Founder and main agitator of the RFSU (a movement for sexual emancipation embracing birth control, sex education and childrens' health).

Five boxes of Ottesen-Jensen's papers are in the ARAB, Stockholm.

PABLO-LARSEN, Hans (1871–1953)

Danish social democrat. Prominent in the SDP youth movement. Editor of one of its papers, *Socialist*.

Six boxes of Pablo-Larsen's papers covering the years 1897–1947 are in the ABA, Copenhagen. These contain material of international relevance (especially before 1930), including letters from Karl Kautsky (q.v.) and Louise Kautsky (q.v.). A summary inventory is available.

PAEPE, César de (1842–90)

Pioneer and leader of Belgian socialism in the nineteenth century. At first printer, later doctor. Influenced by Proudhon (q.v.). Prominent member of the IWMA – both in Belgium, and from 1868 in its international congresses. Founding member of the Belgian Socialist Party, 1879, the suffrage movement 1881, and the Belgian Workers Party 1885.

There is a small collection of de Paepe's papers for the years 1876–86 in the IISH, Amsterdam. This includes letters from Belgian and foreign socialists, as well as a manuscript entitled *Cours de Religion*. Finally, it should be noted, the collection also includes photocopies of letters from the papers of Louis Bertrand (q.v.). The whole collection is open and an inventory is available.

PALM, August Theodor (1849–1922)

Pioneer of the Swedish labour movement. As an apprentice tailor journeyed in Schleswig and Denmark. Imported socialist ideas from Germany and Denmark to Sweden. Most important agitator and initiator of both trade union and party organisation in the 1880s, but eclipsed from the 1890s. Several times imprisoned.

Eleven boxes of Palm's papers for the years 1869–1922 are in the ARAB, Stockholm. These comprise personal documents, correspondence, work and notebooks, manuscripts (including one of the first socialist speeches in Sweden) and newspaper cuttings. An inventory is available.

PALMSTIERNAS, Hans (fl. 1950s–60s)

Swedish social democratic politician. One of the first ecology activists.

Some 95 boxes of Palmstiernas's papers are in the ARAB, Stockholm. An inventory is available, but special permission must be obtained before consulting this collection.

PANELLIER, Constant (b. 1842)

French Communard.

See Appendix I.

PANNEKOEK, Anton (1873–1960)

Dutch SDAP member and later communist. Contacts with SPD in Germany 1906–14.

The IISH, Amsterdam has Pannekoek's manuscripts and other documentation, 1908–14. His diaries are in the Institute A. Pannekoek, Amsterdam. (See M. Campfens, *op. cit.*)

PARFAIT, Noël (1813–98)

French political journalist. Participated in the 'July Days' of 1830 as a republican. Imprisoned for condoning insurrection 1833–5. Elected to the Legislative Assembly from Eure-et-Loire in 1849. Resisted the *coup d'état* 1852. Exile. Returned to France in 1859. Collaborated on *L'Association* (organ of the co-operative movement) in 1864. Republican Deputy for Eure-et-Loire 1871–98.

A collection of letters addressed to Parfait is in the Archives Nationales, Paris. An inventory is available. (See Maitron *op. cit.*)

PARTOS, Paul (1911–64)

Hungarian anarcho-syndicalist.

The IISH, Amsterdam, has a collection of correspondence and manuscripts from 1939–64.

PARVUS*

  * Pseudonym of HELPHAND, Alexander Israel.

PASS, Rudolf (b. 1905)

German social democrat. Member of the SPD 1925. Active in the Reichsbanner. Exile in the Netherlands 1934, in France 1935 and in Sweden 1938. Member of the 'Kleine Internationale'. Official responsible for economic policy to the SPD Executive 1948–70. Also journalist.

A small collection of Pass's papers covering the years 1943–64 is in the AdsD, Bonn. In the main this concerns the SOPADE Group in Stockholm (1943 and 1945), trade unions and economic policy.

PAULIN, Albert (b. 1881)

French socialist politician. Tailor. Regional Secretary of the Union des syndicats ouvriers of Puy-de-Dôme and Haute Loire. Secretary of the Socialist Federation of Puy-de-Dôme 1908–20. Administrator-Secretary of *L'Ami du Peuple* 1905. Co-founder of the regional daily *La Montagne* 1919. Deputy for Puy-de-Dôme 1924–42.

An important collection of Paulin's papers, together with numerous works and pamphlets, has been deposited by his daughter in the CHS, Paris.

PAVLOV, Iv. (fl. 1920s)

Russian member of a Trotskyist opposition group (1924–8).

The Hoover Institution, Stanford University, California, has a typescript memoir of Pavlov's (in Russian) entitled *Notes of an oppositionist: Reminiscences, Impressions and Encounters* and relating to the Trotskyist opposition in Russia.

PAWLOWITSCH, Paul (1864–1930)

German anarchist. Later trade unionist and social democrat.

Pawlowitsch's papers from *c.* 1875 are in the AdsD, Bonn. These include correspondence with, amongst others, Victor Dave, Paul Eltzbacher (q.v.), Gustav Landauer (q.v.), and Max Nettlau (q.v.). In addition, this collection also comprises pamphlets, single texts, leaflets, calendars and papers from Hans and Peter Pawlowitsch (his sons).

PECQUEUR, Constantin (1801–87)

French socialist. Economist and writer. Influenced first by Saint-Simon and then Fourier (q.v.). Collaborated on *Phalanstère*. Member of the Luxemburg Commission 1848.

The major part of Pecqueur's papers is in the Library of the Assemblée Nationale, Paris. The minor part, comprising some correspondence and manuscripts, is in the IISH, Amsterdam.

PEDERSEN, P. J. (1870–1962)

Danish social democratic politician. Minister of Education.

Two boxes of Pedersen's papers for the years 1909–40 including, in particular, manuscripts on social democratic education policy, are in the ABA, Copenhagen.

PÉGUY, Charles (1873–1914)

French writer and poet. Militant socialist in his youth. Came to socialism under the influence of Lucien Herr (q.v.) at the École Normale Supérieure. Delegate to the first general congresses of French socialist organisations 1899 and 1900. From *c.* 1900 moved away from socialism.

A large number of letters received by Péguy at the *Cahiers de la Quinzaine* (which he founded in 1900) are to be found in the Centre Charles Péguy at Orleans. These are particularly interesting in connection with the penetration of socialism amongst intellectuals. (See Maitron, *op. cit.*)

PELLIGRIN, Antoine (1837–78)

French Communard.

See Appendix I.

PELLOUTIER, Fernand (1867–1901)

French revolutionary-syndicalist organiser and theorist. At first radical-republican journalist. Evolved from republicanism towards socialism. Joined the POF *c.* 1892 and became Secretary of the Saint Nazaire section. At the same time helped found the Bourse du Travail of Saint Nazaire. Came into conflict with Guesde over the question of the general strike. Resigned from the POF and moved towards anarchism in the form of revolutionary-syndicalism. General Secretary of the Fédération National des Bourses du Travail 1895. Proponent of the political independence of trade unions.

Pelloutier's papers are in the IFHS, Paris. These are particularly relevant to the Fédération des Bourses du Travail in the years 1895–1901.

PÉRICAT, Raymond (1873–1957)

French revolutionary syndicalist. At first plasterer. Secretary of the Fédération du Bâtiment 1908–12. Ordinary member of the Confederal Committee 1912. Leader of the 24-hour general strike and demonstration leading to violent crashes with troops. Fled to Belgium to avoid arrest. Alone on the Confederal Committee in urging action against the First World War. Founding member of the *Comité pour la reprise des relations internationales*. Responsible in February 1919 for the appearance of *l'Internationale*. Agitated for the formation of a communist party. Member of the Provisional Committee of the revolutionary 'minority' of the CGT September 1919. Attended the Second Congress of the Third International. Deputy Secretary of the Fédération du Bâtiment 1939.

Péricat's papers are in the IFHS, Paris. These are particularly relevant to the Fédération du Bâtiment (*c.* 1914–36).

PÉRILLAT, Francis (1875–1954)*

French socialist militant. Jewellery worker. Joined the POSR in 1893. One of the pioneers of socialism in the Savoy *c.* 1898–1905. Lifelong member of the SFIO in Paris.

From 21 July 1895 to 21 March 1911, Périllat preserved all the letters he received, together with copies of his own letters. The former have been collected in two volumes and the latter in six volumes now in the possession of his son M. Louis Périllat-Mandry. This inventorised and indexed correspondence not only informs about the life and ideas of Périllat, but constitutes a unique document from a socialist militant on working-class life in Paris and the provinces as well as on the socialist movement. (See Maitron, *op. cit.*)

* Known as Périllat-Mandry.

PÉRILLAT-MANDRY, Francis

See under PÉRILLAT, Francis.

PERNERSTORFER, Engelbert (1850–1918)

Austrian social democrat.

The VGA, Vienna, has two files containing manuscripts, notes, poems, press cuttings, speeches, lectures and contributions to the Austrian press. There is also correspondence with Schönerer, one of the founders of the German Nationalist movement in Austria. The Vienna City Library (WSLB) has a collection of thirty-five letters written by Pernerstorfer.

PERRIER, Léon (1873–1948)

French politician. Colonies Minister 1925–6, 1926–8.

The departmental archives of Isère have thirteen boxes of Perrier material, including lecture notes, political notes, and personal documents. The collection is of particular relevance to the history of the Radical Socialist Party. (See Archives Nationales, *Guide des papiers*.)

PERRIN, Henri (1870–c. 1940)

French socialist militant. Joined the POSR in Besançon 1893. Federal Secretary of the SFIO in the Department Doubs 1907. After the Tours Congress (1920) went into the PCF from which he was expelled some years later.

Towards 1940 Perrin wrote memoirs on militants of all ranks who had been known to him personally in the course of his activity. These documents, comprising a manuscript of 40 pages (without title), have been deposited in the Bourse du Travail at Besançon. (See Maitron, *op. cit.*)

PERSSON, Edvin E. (1896–1954)

Swedish communist leader. From 1910 active in the Social Democratic youth organisation. Member of the SAP-opposition of the Left-Socialist Party from 1917, and of the SKP from 1921. From 1924 Central Committee member. Leading functionary of the Stockholm District 1929–33. From 1929 Director of the Party publishing company Ny Dag, and since the 1930s Director of the publishing company Arbetarkultur.

Four boxes of Persson's papers for the years 1915–40 are in the ARAB, Stockholm. These include personal documents, correspondence, manuscripts, reports, transcripts, leaflets and other material concerning his political activity. An inventory is available.

PETERSEN, Alfred (b. 1895)

Danish trade union leader. Chairman of a union for unskilled workers.

One box of Alfred Petersen's papers, including speeches from the years 1956–9 and newspaper cuttings, is in the ABA, Copenhagen.

PETERSEN, Gerd (b. 1927)

Founder, with Aksel Larssen (q.v.), and subsequently Chairman, of the Danish Peoples' Socialist Party (SF).

Twelve boxes of Gerd Petersen's papers for the years 1958–74 are in the ABA, Copenhagen. These contain documents concerning the SF, notes on SF meetings and letters of international relevance. An inventory is available.

PETERSEN, Sophus (b. 1868)

Pioneer Danish socialist.

Two boxes of Sophus Petersen's papers for the years 1888–1943, containing letters and manuscripts, are in the ABA, Copenhagen.

PETIT, Gabrielle (1860–1930)

French militant feminist and socialist. Published, 1904–8, *La Femme affranchie*. Six months imprisonment in 1907 for an appeal to soldiers during a strike. Independent of all parties but collaborated, in particular, with syndicalists and libertarians.

A collection of Petit's correspondence, as well as material about her, is reported to be found in the Bibliothèque Marguerite Durand at the Town Hall of the 5th Arrondissement, Paris.

PETITJEAN, Claude (b. 1845)

French Communard.

See Appendix I.

PEUKERT, Josef (1855–1910)

Bohemian anarchist. Early 1880s Editor of the Vienna *Zukunft* (*Future*), organ of the radical anarchist wing of Austrian social democracy. Exile in London 1884 to escape state repression. Follower of Kropotkin. Theorist of anarcho-communism. Member of the Kommunistischer Arbeiterbildungsverein (Communist Workers' Educational Association). Bitter dispute with Johann Most for the leadership of the German-anarchist Erste Sektion (First Section). Led the split of the Autonomie group in 1886 (the New York branch of which attracted Emma Goldman (q.v.) and Alexander Berkman (q.v.)).

Peukert's papers from the 1880s and 1890s (with some later material) are in the IISH, Amsterdam. These comprise correspondence with anarchists (including Berkman (q.v.), Grossmann (q.v.), Issak, Kelly, Landauer (q.v.), Most, Neve and Rinke), and various anarchist papers, letters to his sister and brother-in-law, pocket diaries, pocket notebooks, manuscripts (including *Anarchie und die soziale Bewegung des 19. Jahrhunderts* and *Meine Erinnerungen/Erfahrungen aus der Arbeiterbewegung*), and collections of material, including correspondence, manuscripts, testimonials, notes – some by Max Nettlau (q.v.) – and newspaper cuttings on the Neve-Peukert-Dave-Most case, as well as reports on the 1888 Reichstag debates (on the prolongation of the 'Socialist Laws'). A provisional inventory is available.

PICART, Achille (1878–1962)

French interwar trade union leader.

There are two collections of Picart's papers. The first, concerning building workers' trade unionism in the years 1913–19, is in the CRHMSS, Paris. This includes correspondence with overseas correspondents and the Internationale du Bois (based in Germany). The second is in the IFHS, Paris and concerns building workers' trade unionism c. 1910–60.

PIERRET, Désiré (b. 1852)

French Communard.

See Appendix I.

PINDY, Jean-Louis (1840–1917)

French revolutionary socialist. Communard. Anti-authoritarian. Founding member of the International in Brest 1867. Represented the Chambre Syndicale of Parisian joiners at the Basle Congress in 1868. Active in the Federal Council. Imprisoned April 1870. Member of the Provisional Executive Commission of the Central Committee of the National Guard in March 1871. Elected member of the Council of the Commune (member of the Military Commission). Opposed the Committee of Public Safety and gave the order to burn the Town Hall. Went into hiding. Exile in Switzerland 1872. Prominent militant in the Fédération Jurassienne and supporter of the Bakuninist International. Co-founder with Brousse (q.v.) of the French Federation of the International.

Pindy's papers are in the IFHS, Paris. In addition, there are a number of letters written by Pindy to Guillaume (q.v.) in the Archive d'Etat, Neuchâtel, as well as 17 letters from Guillaume to Pindy (1903–16) in the Library of La Chaux de Fonds (Switzerland).

PIO, Louis (1841–94)

Pioneer Danish socialist. Member of the IWMA. Marxist social democrat. Founder of the SD and of the social democratic press (Editor of *Socialisten* from 1871). Died in the USA.

Eight boxes of Louis Pio's papers for the years 1860–94 are in the ABA, Copenhagen. These, however, are mainly organisational papers about Pio and his activity. An inventory is available.

PIO, Sylvia (1878–1932)

Prominent in the Danish Women's Movement (1920s). Daughter of Louis Pio (q.v.).

One box of Sylvia Pio's papers for the years 1920–32 is in the ABA, Copenhagen. This includes correspondence with Friedrich Adler (q.v.) on the problems of organising women.

PISSARRO, Camille (1830–1903)

French artist and anarchist. Illustrator for *Les Temps Nouveaux*.

Pissarro's papers were reported sold in a sale in the Hôtel Drouot (21 November 1975). (See Maitron, *op. cit.*) There is some correspondence in the Grave papers (q.v.).

PITTERMANN, Bruno (b. 1905)

Austrian social democrat. President of Socialist International, 1964. SPÖ President, 1957–67.

The Vienna City Library (WSLB) has a collection of correspondence from the years 1963–74.

PIVERT, Marceau (1895–1958)

French revolutionary socialist. Delegate to the Internationale ouvrière 1934–7. Secretary of the Parti Socialiste ouvrière et paysan (PSOP) 1938.

Pivert's correspondence with various figures on the socialist left is in the Archives Nationales, Paris. Special permission is needed to consult these papers.

PLATIEL, Nora (1896–1979)

German social democratic politician. Member of the ISK. After 1933, exile in France and then Switzerland. Member of the Hessian Landtag 1954–66.

Platiel's papers are in the AdsD, Bonn. These include general correspondence as well as manuscripts, articles, speeches and other material concerning the Political-Philosophical Academy (associated with the ISK) and the exile.

PLEKHANOV, Georgii (1856–1918)

'Father' of Russian Marxism. By 1877 a leading populist. Leader of the minority favouring the continuation of mass agitation and opposed to the new terrorist orientation of the majority of the Land and Liberty organisation. In exile 1880–1917. Embraced Marxism 1880–82. Co-founder of the Emancipation of Labour Group. Began a devastating critique of populism and created the theoretical foundations of Russian Marxism both politically (the 'two-stages' perspective on the revolution in Russia) and intellectually (contributing major works on the theory and history of Marxism, philosophy, sociology and political economy, the history of Russian and world socialist ideas, literary criticism, aesthetics, etc.). Worked in 1890s to link up disparate circles of social democratic intellectuals with contacts among factory workers so as to lay the basis for the formation, in 1898, of the RSDLP. Harsh critic of deviations from orthodox Marxism – one of the earliest critics of Bernstein (q.v.). At first supported Lenin in 1903, but shortly after the Second Congress of the RSDLP supported the Mensheviks. Unable to develop his 'two-stages' theory in the light of the 1905 Revolution, he became dogmatic in his political ideas and suffered a loss of influence (although intellectually his contributions on theoretical questions were still held in high regard). Dismayed many social democrats by his 'defencist' and class collaborationist position during the First World War. Returned to Russia after the February Revolution. Supported the Provisional Government and urged moderation. Bitterly anti-Bolshevik.

There is an important collection of Plekhanov's correspondence (with his wife and others), together with some photographs, in the IISH, Amsterdam. Access is restricted, and a provisional inventory is available.

PLOEG, Hendrikus (1894–1976)

Dutch SDAP and PvdA member.

See Anna Ploeg-Ploeg.

PLOEG-PLOEG, Anna C. (1894–1969)

Dutch SDAP and PvdA member. Wife of Hendrikus Ploeg.

The IISH, Amsterdam, has a collection of the Ploegs's personal papers and some organisational documents covering the period 1912–68. Access is restricted.

POESCHKE, Michael (1901–59)

German social democrat. Lord Mayor of Erlangen. President of the District Assembly of Mittelfranken. Editor of the *Volksblatt* (Erlangen).

Poeschke's papers are in the Stadtarchiv, Erlangen. (See Mommsen, *op. cit.*)

PÖHLER, Heinz (b. 1919)

German social democratic politician.

Pöhler's papers for the years 1953–72 are in the Stadtarchiv, Mönchengladbach. (See Mommsen, *op. cit.*)

POLAK, Eduard (1880–1962)

Dutch journalist and SDAP member.

The IISH, Amsterdam, has a very little of Eduard Polak's correspondence (1927–31). (See M. Campfens, *op. cit.*)

POLAK, Henri (1868–1943)

Dutch diamond workers' union member. Founder member of the SDAP.

The IISH, Amsterdam, has some of Henri Polak's manuscripts and personal papers, 1905–42. (See M. Campfens, *op. cit.*)

POLAK EMZ, Wim (fl. 1950s)

Dutch PvdA member.

The IISH, Amsterdam, has a small collection of Polak Emz's documents covering the years 1959–69.

POLLAK, Marianne (1891–1963)

Austrian social democrat and feminist. Deputy and journalist (see below).

POLLAK, Oskar (1893–1963)

Austrian social democrat. Editor-in-Chief, *Arbeiterzeitung*, 1931–4, 1945–63.

The VGA, Vienna has twenty-five files containing their papers. The collection includes personal documents, letters and contributions to the AZ, correspondence, 1945–62, articles for Oskar Pollak's time in London, press cuttings, notes, unpublished material, and AZ articles from 1945–63. The Vienna City Library (WSLB) has a collection of Marianne Pollak's correspondence, and a letter and a poem by Oskar Pollak.

PONTUS, Hubert Henri (1903–68)

Belgian socialist politician. Mechanic on the SNCB (Belgian Railways). Councillor in Montzen 1953–64. Regional Senator in Liège 1950–65. Senator for Verviers 1965–6.

Pontus's correspondence for the years 1950–58 is in the archive of the Verviers Federation of the Belgian Socialist Party.

PORTAL, Étienne (b. 1850)

French Communard.

See Appendix I.

PORTUGEJS, Semen Osipovič (1880–1944)

Russian right-wing social democrat.

A small collection of Purtugejs's papers for the years 1918–22 is in the IISH, Amsterdam. These include correspondence, manuscripts and leaflets relating to social democratic groups in Moscow, Petrograd and London. An inventory is available.

POTIER, Ernest (fl. 1870s)

French Communard.

See Appendix I.

POTRESOV, Aleksandr Nikolaevič (1869–1934)

Prominent Russian Menshevik. Active in the workers' movement from the 1890s. Member of the St Petersburg Union for the Emancipation of the Working Class. Emigrated in 1900. Took part in the foundation of the *Iskra* organisation and the journal *Zaria* (*Dawn*). After the schism in the RSDLP became a leading Menshevik in 1903. Prominent in the production of Menshevik publications. After 1905 member of the Liquidationist faction. During the First World War supported the Tsarist war effort. Co-director in 1917 of the paper *Den* (*Day*) which bitterly opposed the Bolsheviks. After the October Revolution emigrated. Assisted in the production of Kerensky's weekly journal *Dni* (Days).

There is a collection of Potresov's papers for the years 1889–1905 in the IISH, Amsterdam. These include correspondence (with, amongst others, Akselrod (q.v.), F. I. Dan (q.v.), Kautsky (q.v.) and Struve) and manuscripts, relating to Russian social democracy (in particular, to Menshevism). An inventory is available.

POUGET, Emile (1860–1931)

French revolutionary syndicalist. At first shopworker. Anarchist. Imprisoned in 1883 after a violent demonstration of the unemployed and anti-militarist activity. Amnestied in 1886. Founded *Le Père Peinard* in 1889. Sought refuge in England against repression of anarchists in 1894–5. Founded *La Sociale* in 1895. Saw in trade unions the new means for anarchists to spread their ideas. Hostile to political organisations. Editor of the CGT's *La Voix du Peuple* in 1900. Secretary of the Section for the Federations of the CGT in 1902. Leading organiser/ spokesman for revolutionary syndicalism. Signatory of the Amiens Charter in 1906.

Imprisoned with other CGT leaders in 1908. After his release, founded *La Révolution* as a revolutionary syndicalist daily. Retired from activity after its early failure.

Pouget's papers are in the IFHS, Paris. These are particularly relevant to the history of anarcho-syndicalism, and the journal *Le Père Peinard* (*c.* 1880–1930).

POULAIN, Louis (b. 1835)

French Communard.

See Appendix I.

POUTSMA, Hessel J. (1866–1933)

Dutch SDAP member.

The IISH, Amsterdam, has a few of Poutsma's letters after 1893. (See M. Campfens, *op. cit.*)

PRAGER, Theodor (fl. 1960s)

Austrian communist.

The Institute of Contemporary History, Vienna, has fourteen files containing his papers. The collection includes press cuttings; material on Czechoslovakia in 1968; and manuscript material relating to missing Austrian communists and members of the *Schutzbund* in the Soviet Union.

PRÉAU DE VEDEL, Edmond (b. 1837)

French Communard.

See Appendix I.

PRELLER, Ludwig (1897–1974)

German social democratic politician. At first civil servant, but in 1933 sacked for political reasons. Director of the Social and Cultural Policy Department of the South German Land Council in Stuttgart in 1946. Minister in Schleswig-Holstein 1948–50. Member of the Bundestag (SPD) 1951–7. Expert on social policy and health care.

Preller's extensive papers for the years 1946–68 are in the AdsD at the Friedrich-Ebert-Stiftung, Bonn. These comprise correspondence, notes, material from his journalistic activity and collections of material on social, economic and education policy, refugees, the SPD's work amongst women, foundations, atomic physics and philosophy.

PRINCE, Yvonne (fl. 1950s–60s)

Belgian socialist politician. Secretary of the Thuin Federation of the Belgian Socialist Party. From 1959 Member of Parliament.

Prince's correspondence for the years 1950–60 is in the archive of the Thuin Federation of the Belgian Socialist Party.

PRIPP, Anna-Stina (fl. 1920s–40s)

Prominent Swedish communist.

Eight boxes of Pripp's papers are in the ARAB, Stockholm.

PROFT, Gabriele (1879–1971)

Austrian social democratic women's leader. Deputy.

The VGA, Vienna, has twelve files containing manuscript notes, typescript notes and documents, notebooks, and correspondence. Her correspondents included Bruno Kreisky.

PROLE, Jean*

* Pseudonym of DOMMANGET, Maurice.

PROUDHON, Pierre-Joseph (1809–65)

French theorist of the 'mutualist' and federalist strand of anarchism. Writer and journalist. Deputy for the Seine, June 1848.

Some of Proudhon's correspondence and manuscripts are to be found in the Feltrinelli Institute, Milan.

PRUDHOMMEAUX, Jules (1833–1915)

French socialist.

The IISH, Amsterdam, has a collection of correspondence, manuscripts, files and printed material.

PUSA, Eeno (1888–1975)

Finnish social democratic politician. Agrarian specialist. Farmer. Member of the Council of Social Democratic Small Farmers. Executive member of the Social Democratic Party (SDP). Active in municipal politics (Viipurin maalaiskunta – now in the USSR). Member of Parliament 1945–50 and 1955–7 (SDP) and 1961 (Social Democratic League of Workers and Small Farmers – TPSL). Served on many state committees on agriculture, settling and forestry etc.

A large collection of Pusa's papers for the 1920s–60s is in the Finnish Labour Archives, Helsinki. These include correspondence, manuscripts, press-cuttings and a few photographs, but is especially important for the collections of organisational papers it contains from, for example, the SDP's Negotiation Council for Small Farmers, the Negotiation Committee of the Ministry of Agriculture, the Committee of Workers and Small Farmers of Karelia, the SDP's Department of Evacuees, the TPSL (see above), and the paper *Kansan Työ*. An inventory is available.

PUTZRATH, Heinz (b. 1916)

German social democrat. Member of the KPDO. Arrested 1933–4. Exile in the Netherlands, Czechoslovakia and Britain 1937. Member of the *Neu Beginnen* Group. Chairman of the

Young Socialists 1947–51. Director of the SPD's International Department 1949–60. Departmental Director of the Friedrich-Ebert-Stiftung, Bonn, 1969–81.

Putzrath's papers for the years 1940–45 and 1947–82 are in the AdsD, Bonn. These comprise a small quantity of correspondence together with notes, articles, journals, pamphlets and newspaper cuttings concerning resistance activities, exile groups (especially in England), his relations with overseas socialist organisations and individuals in the post-war period, SPD conferences, the Socialist International and International Union of Socialist Youth.

PY, Emile (1870–1957)

French reformist trade unionist. From the early 1890s Secretary, and then President of the Typographers' Union. Leading trade unionist in Belfort. Editor of the radical *La Frontière*. After the war a municipal councillor for the radicals.

Py's papers are in the possession of his family in Belfort.

QUARCK, Max (1860–1930)

German social democratic lawyer. Editor of various social democratic newspapers 1886–1917. From 1901 City Councillor in Frankfurt (SPD). From 1912 member of the Reichstag (and from 1919 of the National Assembly).

The bulk of Quarck's extensive papers is in the Stadtarchiv, Frankfurt. As well as his correspondence as a political journalist, these comprise reference files arising from his work as journalist and editor, as well as newspaper articles and small written items. The most significant of two smaller collections is at the Archiv der Sozialen Demokratie at the Friedrich-Ebert-Stiftung, Bonn. Amongst the correspondence are 110 letters from Wilhelm Liebknecht (q.v.) as well as letters from leading figures concerning the politics of the SPD, press matters, agrarian and labour questions. In addition, there is material concerning the Robertus-Gemeinde 1883–1907. Finally, a collection of printed material on the 1848 movement is in the Frankfurt branch of the Bundesarchiv (where it has been divided amongst various holdings. (See Mommsen, *op. cit.*)

QUETSCH, Wilhelm (fl. 1904–28)

German democratic and trade union activist. Trade union secretary in the German Engineering Workers' Union.

The DGB Archive in Düsseldorf has a small collection of Quetsch's papers for the years 1904–28. These comprise personal documents, as well as material concerning his work as a trade union secretary and as SPD Chairman and local councillor in Bretzenheim. (See Mommsen, *op. cit.*)

QUIDDE, Ludwig (fl. 1920s)

German pacifist.

Quidde's private papers are in the Bundesarchiv, Koblenz. In addition, reference should be made to the United Nations Library in Geneva. Part of Quidde's own library was given to the United Nations Library, which also houses the records of the *Deutsches Friedenskartell* (Fonds Quidde). This organisation, which served as liaison between several German pacifist organisations, was founded in 1922. Its activities seem to have ceased in 1929. The records of the *Friedenskartell* comprise ten boxes of material, 1919–28.

QUILICI, Paul (b. 1882)

French postal worker and trade union militant. Several times victimised for his activity.

Quilici's papers are in the CRHMSS, Paris. These comprise diverse material on the trade union movement generally, and on postal workers' unionism in particular, from the time of the postal workers' strike in 1909, to 1931.

QUILLARD, Pierre (1864–1912)

French intellectual and anarchist sympathiser. Poet and publicist. Secretary of the League for the Rights of Man. Collaborated with anarchist and anarcho-syndicalist journals (including *Les Temps Nouveaux* and *La Bataille Syndicaliste*).

See under GRAVE, Jean.

RADBRUCH, Gustav (1878–1949)

German social democratic politician. At first professor of law. Reich Minister of Justice. Member of the Reichstag.

The largest collection of Radbruch's papers is in Heidelberg University Library. This includes some political material but mainly comprises personal correspondence and large amounts of material arising from his academic work and position. There are also two smaller collections. The first is a copy of his notes on events during the Kapp Putsch in Kiel and the surrounding area in the Landesarchiv, Schleswig. The second is a copy of the manuscript of *Die reitende Bürgergarde der Stadt Kiel* in the Stadtarchiv Kiel. (See Mommsen, *op. cit.*)

RADTKE, Leo (1897–1969)

German trade unionist and social democrat. Trade union official in 1920s. Imprisoned 1933 and 1936–42, concentration camp victim 1944. Active in trade union and SPD reconstruction. From 1948 member of the District Administration in Arnsberg. Many positions in the Dortmund SPD and municipal politics.

Radtke's papers for the years 1933–6 and 1945–68 are in the AdsD, Bonn. These comprise correspondence, notes, documents, newspaper cuttings and pamphlets concerning, in particular, Nazi persecution, reparations, de-nazification and relations between the trade unions and the SPD.

RALOFF, Karl (1899–1976)

German social democratic politician. Member of the Reichstag 1932–3. Exile in Scandinavia 1933.

Raloff's papers for the years 1933–76 are in the AdsD at the Friedrich-Ebert-Stiftung, Bonn. Material from the period of exile includes correspondence with, amongst others, Fritz Tarnow (q.v.). In addition, there is also material concerned with his journalistic activity in Scandinavia in the post-war period. (See Mommsen, *op. cit.*)

RAMUS, Pierre*

* Pseudonym of GROSSMANN, Rudolf.

RAPPOPORT, Charles (1865–1941)*

Russian-born thinker and publicist. Militant in the French socialist and communist movements. Founded *Contre la guerre* (1912) and opposed the union sacrée (1914). Executive member, PCF, 1920. Editor *Revue communiste*. Paris correspondent of *Izvestia*. Resigned from PCF (over Moscow trials) and rejoined SFIO. Author of numerous books.

The papers in the IISH, Amsterdam, include Rappoport's correspondence, notes, personal documentation and printed material for the period 1900–36. The collection is not listed and access is restricted. The unpublished manuscript of his autobiography is in the Bibliothèque Nationale, Paris.

* Known by the pseudonym Felix Arnold.

RAUSCHENPLAT, Helmut von (b. 1896)*

Leading member of the ISK in Germany 1933–7. After 1945, social democratic politician. Executive member of the German Trade Union. Member of the Baden-Württemberg Landtag and Secretary of State in the Ministry of State 1947. Head of the German Office for Questions of Peace. Member of the Parliamentary Council 1948–9. Director of the Süddeutsche Rundfunk, Stuttgart 1949. Since 1961 Head of the Institute for Journalism at the Free University, Berlin.

The Institut für Zeitgeschichte, Munich, has a large collection of Rauschenplat's papers and collections of material. This comprises notes, outlines, articles and printed manuscripts; correspondence with, amongst others, Erich Mende and Erich Ollenhauer (q.v.); material arising from work in exile (including material on the activity of German and foreign exile-groups) on the German Office for Questions of Peace, broadcasting matters, the trade union movement, domestic politics in Baden-Württemberg and the Second World War. (See Mommsen, *op. cit.*)

* Known by the pseudonym Fritz Eberhard.

RAVATÉ, Jules (1875–1916)*

French militant trade unionist and co-operator. Late 1890s leader of textile workers in Roanne (Loire). From 1901 dedicated himself to a popular university and library in Roanne. Active anti-militarist.

Ravaté's private papers and correspondence were left by his widow to the Municipal Library of Roanne. (See Maitron, *op. cit.*)

* Known by the pseudonym Sauvert.

RAVESTEYN, Willem van (1876–1970)

Dutch SDAP activist and later communist.

The IISH, Amsterdam has a large collection of Ravesteyn's correspondence, notes and manuscripts. A list is available. Other papers are with the Gemeentearchief, Rotterdam. (See M. Campfens, *op. cit.*)

RAYET (fl. 1945–60)

French trade unionist.

Rayet's papers, concerning trade unionism in an electrical company, 1945–60, are in the Departmental Archives of Aveyron.

RECLUS, Elisée (1830–1905)

French anarchist.

The IISH, Amsterdam, has a small collection of Reclus's correspondence and manuscripts covering the period 1868–1904.

REESE, Maria (b. 1889)*

German social democrat then communist politician and writer. Member of the Reichstag (SPD then KPD).

There is a small collection of Reese's papers in the Bundesarchiv, Koblenz. This comprises personal items, memoirs (c. 1920–45) and copies of her diary 1944–5 and 1954, as well as material arising from her activity for the KPD, and defence of her friend Torgler (q.v.) in 1933. (See Mommsen, *op. cit.*)

* Née Meyer

REIJNDORP, D. G. C. (1870–1950)

Dutch social democrat and later SDAP member.

The IISH, Amsterdam, has a few of Reijndorp's notes and manuscripts. (See M. Campfens, *op. cit.*)

REIMERS, Otto (1902–84)

German anarchist.

The IISH, Amsterdam, has a collection containing correspondence, manuscripts and notes from the period 1940–84.

REINOWSKI, Hans (b. 1900)

German social democratic exile. Socialist publicist in Scandinavia after 1933.

A large collection of Reinowski's papers is in the Institut für Zeitgeschichte, Munich. As well as correspondence and manuscripts, this collection contains material on the circumstances of exiles in Denmark and Sweden, social democratic politics in exile, arrangements with the KPD and trade union activity. (See Mommsen, *op. cit.*)

RELGIS, Eugen (b. 1895)

Romanian-born anarchist. Lived in Italy.

There is a collection of Relgis's papers in the IISH, Amsterdam. These comprise letters from various anarchists, from Italians both in and outside Italy (including about 130 from Gaspare Marcuso, 1962–72) and from Henri-Léon Follin (c.1938–49), manuscripts (including *L'Homme libre face à la Barbarie Totalitaire, Un Cas de Conscience: Romain Rolland*), printed matter (including articles by and about Relgis, interviews with Relgis, and copies of the *Quaderni degli Amici di Eugen Relgis*), and files on Han Ryner, Henri-Léon Follin and G. F. Nicolai. In addition, this collection contains biographies of Relgis and bibliographies of his works, as well as material from an international inquiry in 1947 by Pavel Dascalescu,

Bucharest, 'Les Voies qui mènent a la démolition des barrières entre les Nations'. Access to this collection is restricted.

RÉMY, Paul (1879–1948)

French trade unionist. Friend of Albert Thomas (q.v.).

Three boxes of Rémy's papers are with the Albert Thomas papers in the Archives Nationales, Paris.

RENNER, Karl (1870–1950)

Austrian social democratic politician. Austro-Marxist legal specialist. Adopted a patriotic standpoint and came to be regarded as the leader of the right wing of the Austrian Social Democratic Party (SDAP), 1914–18. First Chancellor of the Austrian Republic 1918. Leader of the reformist minority in the SDAP. President of the Second Austrian Republic 1945.

Renner's papers are split between various locations. The AVA, Vienna, has 34 boxes of papers, including material on the labour movement and diplomacy. The Haus-, Hof- und Staatsarchiv, Vienna has 4 boxes of material. There is other correspondence 1908–50 in the VGA, Vienna and also in Vienna City Library (WSLB).

REUMANN, Jakob (1853–1925)

Austrian social democrat. First social democratic Mayor of Vienna, 1919–24.

The WSLA, Vienna has thirteen boxes of his papers, dating from the time when he was Mayor of Vienna. The Vienna City Library (WSLB) has a collection of correspondence from the years 1920–30.

REUTER, Ernst (1889–1953)*

German communist, then social democratic politician. Pacifist then prisoner of war in Russia 1915–18. Commissar of the Soviet Republic of Volga 1918. Member of the KPD 1919–21 and temporarily General Secretary, 1921. Expelled from the KPD because of his position on the 'March Action'. Joined the KAG then, as part of this group, the USPD, and finally the SPD upon reunification 1922. Editor of *Vorwärts*. Member of the Berlin City Council 1926. Lord Mayor of Magdeburg 1931. Member of the Reichstag (SPD) 1932. Exile in Turkey (worked as Government advisor and academic). From 1947 Mayor of Berlin (and in this capacity became a statesman of European renown).

Ernst Reuter's papers for the period before 1945 have been largely destroyed. However, a collection of his papers, as well as a large documentation concerning Reuter, is in the Landesarchiv, Berlin. There are also microfilm copies of this holding in the Hoover Institution, Stanford University, California. These include personal papers and family correspondence, radio broadcasts and interviews, as well as material concerning his years as a prisoner of war, his membership of the KPD, his activity with *Freiheit* and *Vorwärts* and as Mayor of Berlin (especially the blockade and the 1953 uprising). (See Mommsen, *op. cit.*)

* Known also as Reuter-Friesland.

REUTER, Georg (1902–69)

German trade unionist. After 1945 General Secretary of the trade unions in Bavaria. Vice-Chairman of the DGB in 1949.

The DGB Archive in Düsseldorf has a small collection of Georg Reuter's correspondence for the years 1946–59. This concerns mainly the reconstruction of the trade union movement in Bavaria and the Akademie der Arbeit. (See Mommsen, *op. cit.*)

REUTER-FRIESLAND*

* See under REUTER, Ernst.

REVENTLOW, Rolf (1897–1981)

German social democratic journalist and official collaborator on the social democratic *Münchner Post* and various trade union publications. After 1933 in exile. Republican volunteer in Spain 1936–9. Interned in North Africa 1939–43. Later active in the SPD in Munich.

Reventlow's papers for the years 1939–80 are in the AdsD, Bonn. Apart from personal documents, these comprise extensive correspondence (1943–80), articles and autobiographical manuscripts concerning the exile, the Spanish Civil War, and political and journalistic activity in Germany (notably the SPD Sub-District Munich).

REY, Joseph (1779–1855)

French supporter of Robert Owen. Propagated Owenite ideas in the Saint-Simonist *Le Producteur*.

Rey's papers are in the Municipal Library of Grenoble. His correspondence with Bentham was published in 1890 in the *Journal des économistes*. (See Maitron, *op. cit.*)

REYNIER, Joseph François (1811–92)

French Fourierist (q.v.). Participated in the 1831 insurrection at Lyons. Founded, in 1845, *L'Écho de l'Industrie* and in 1846, *L'Avenir*.

According to Maitron, *op. cit.*, the manuscript of Reynier's *Mémoires* survives in the possession of his family.

RICHTER, Gustav*

* Pseudonym of BUTTINGER, Josef.

RICHTER, Willi (1894–1972)

German social democratic trade unionist. Leading participant in the post-war reconstruction of the trade union movement. Chairman of the DGB 1956–62. Member of the Constitutional Land Assembly in Hesse 1946. Member of the Bundestag (SPD) 1949–57.

There are three holdings of Richter's papers. The largest, at the Bundesarchiv, Koblenz, comprises papers for the years 1933 and 1945–72. These concern trade union reconstruction after 1945, his activity in the Bundestag and DGB as well as, amongst other matters, pension reform and the setting up of a Training Centre in Brazil. Secondly, the DGB Archive in Düsseldorf has a collection of speeches and some correspondence arising from his capacity as Federal Chairman of the DGB. Finally, the AdsD at the Friedrich-Ebert-Stiftung, Bonn, has a small collection for the years 1950–52. In addition, there is material concerning the Bundestag election campaign of 1961 and the SPD's government team. (See Mommsen, *op. cit.*)

RIGOLA, Rinaldo

Italian socialist.

An important collection of papers is in the Feltrinelli Institute, Milan. It includes not only Rigola's papers but the archive of the *Associazione Nazionale Studi – Problemi del Lavoro*. The collection is a rich source on the Italian trade union movement. Between 1896 and 1945 there is correspondence from nearly all the major figures in the workers' movements, including Andrea Costa (q.v.), Kuliscioff, Turati (q.v.) Lazzari, Prampolini, Treves (q.v.), Cabrini, Bissolati, D'Aragona, Calda, Buozzi, Bacci, Serrati, Mussolini (q.v.), Schiavi, Pagliari, Badaloni, Agnini, Graziadei, Modigliani (q.v.), Bertesi, Bertini, Berenini, Sacerdote, Riguzzi, Pareto, Mondolfo, Campolonghi (q.v.), Baldesi, Labriola, Zibordi, Ciccotti, Bombacci, Reina, Mazzoni, Canepa, Podrecca, Maffi, Zerboglio, Massarenti, Gobetti and Tremelloni.

RIMBAULT, Louis (1877–1944)

French libertarian. Active proponent of veganism. Founded, 1923, *Terre libérée*. Earlier involved in a libertarian communist experiment.

The 508-page manuscript of Rimbault's *La Vie tragique des guides d'humanité*, together with other pamphlets and songs published by *Terre libérée* are in the CHS, Paris.

RITZEL, Heinrich (1893–1971)

German social democratic politician. Member of the Reichstag 1930–33. Worked in the League of Nations administration of the Saar 1933–5. Exile in Switzerland 1933–47. General Secretary of the European Union in Basle. Delegate to the Council of Europe 1950–57. Member of the Bundestag (expert on budgetary policy) 1949–64. Numerous political and literary publications.

An enormous collection of Ritzel's papers is to be found in the AdsD at the Friedrich-Ebert-Stiftung, Bonn. This includes his journalistic work and correspondence for the period of exile (with, amongst others, Otto Braun (q.v.)). Yet while containing only a few scattered items from the Weimar period, this collection comprises an extraordinarily detailed documentation of Ritzel's public life since 1947. (See Mommsen, *op. cit.*)

ROBIN, Paul (1837–1912)*

French educational reformer. A founder of the International in Belgium. Collaborator on *Bulletin de la Fédération Jurassienne*.

There is some correspondence with Robin in the Grave (q.v.) papers.

* Also known as Bripon and Vindex.

ROCHETTE, Paul (fl. 1830s)

French journalist.

The IISH, Amsterdam, has a small collection of correspondence and manuscripts.

ROCKER, Rudolf (1873–1958)

German anarchist. At first social democrat. Turned to anarchism in protest against the 'authoritarianism' of the SPD. Political exile in Paris 1893–5. In England 1895–1917. Worked amongst the Jewish workers of London's East End. Editor of the Yiddish-language *Arbeterfraint* and *Germinal*. Leader of the Jewish anarchist movement. Returned to Germany in 1919. Secretary (with Augustin Souchy and Alexander Schapiro) of the Syndicalist International (IAA) in Berlin. From 1933 lived in the USA.

Rocker's extensive papers (mainly from the period after 1933) are in the IISH, Amsterdam. These include correspondence, manuscripts and personal documents and constitute one of the most important collections on the history of anarchism.

RODIČEV, Fedor Izmailovič

Russian liberal. Member of the Kadet party and zemstvo leader.

The Bakhmeteff Archive, Columbia University, New York, has twenty-eight boxes of his papers. The collection contains personal and political correspondence, copies of letters relating to the family of A. I. Herzen, account books, essays on subjects such as refugees in the Crimea in 1920, correspondence from the 1920s and 1930s, memoirs of his youth and duma career, and handwritten copies in French of letters between Natalie and Alexander Herzen before their marriage. There are restrictions on the use of the material.

RODRIGUEZ, Léon (1878–1969)

French activist. Implicated with the *Bandits tragiques*. Arrested but acquitted.

Rodriguez's autobiographical account is in the CHS, Paris.

ROGER, Émile (b. 1842)

French Communard.

See Appendix I.

ROGER, Pierre (b. 1826)

French Communard.

See Appendix I.

ROLAND, Jules (fl. 1930s–50s)

Belgian socialist politician. Councillor and then Deputy Mayor of La Louvière. Senator 1936, 1939 and 1958.

There is a file of Jules Roland's correspondence and notes for the years 1944–7 in the archive of the Soignies Federation of the Belgian Socialist Party.

ROLAND, Lucien (1862–1948)

French socialist leader and song-writer. Printer. Represented the Bourse du Travail of Lille on the Confederal Committee of the CGT. Member of the Federal Council of the Paris Region in 1899, and of the National Council of the POF. Member of the CAP of the SFIO from 1905. Full-time propagandist for the SFIO 1914–29.

Lucien Roland's personal papers passed into the hands of Maurice Dommanget (q.v.), and now constitute part of the archive of the latter in the IFHS, Paris. These comprise, in particular, letters received by Roland after 1905. His correspondents before 1905 included Paul Lafargue (q.v.) as well as various militants from Gard.

ROLAND, Pauline (1805–52)

Pioneer French socialist. Educator and propagandist. Fighter for women's emancipation.

See under Lucien Descaves.

ROLAND HOLST, Henriette (1869–1952)

Founder member of the Dutch SDAP. Later revolutionary socialist and communist. Close friend of Rosa Luxemburg (q.v.).

The IISH, Amsterdam, has a small collection of Roland Holst's correspondence. (See M. Campfens, *op. cit.*)

ROLLAND, Hugo*

* Pseudonym of ABATE, Erasmo.

ROLLAND, Romain (1866–1944)

French communist and intellectual.

One volume of Romain Rolland's miscellaneous papers was given to the Hoover Institution, Stanford University, California, in 1963 by Branko Lazitch. The papers, covering the years 1932–5, comprise correspondence and printed matter relating to the communist and pacifist movements in France, especially the *Association Républicaine des Anciens Combattants*. It includes correspondence of Henri Barbusse (q.v.), Guy Jerram and other pro-communist French intellectuals. A preliminary list is available.

ROLLER, Arnold*

* Pseudonym of NACHT, Siegfried.

ROMEIN, Jan M. (1893–1962)

Dutch academic, newspaper editor and communist.

The IISH, Amsterdam, has a substantial collection of Romein's manuscripts, correspondence and publications. (See M. Campfens, *op. cit.*)

ROMERS, Michiel A. (1893–1955)

Dutch anarchist and Christian Socialist.

The IISH, Amsterdam, has a small collection of Romer's correspondence from 1918. (See M. Campfens, *op. cit.*)

RONDA, Andries (1875–1962)

Dutch SDAP member.

The IISH, Amsterdam, has a very small collection of Ronda's personal papers and pamphlets dating from the years 1936 to 1946. (See M. Campfens, *op. cit.*)

ROODE, Justus Jan de (1866–1945)

Dutch journalist.

See under ROODE-HEIJERMANS

ROODE-HEIJERMANS, Catherine Marie de (1859–1937)

Dutch SDAP member. Wife of Roode (q.v.).

The IISH, Amsterdam, has a very small collection of Roode's and Roode-Heijermans's papers and personal correspondence covering the period 1899–1941.

ROPSHIN, V.*

  * Pseudonym of SAVINKOV, Boris Viktorovič.

ROSCHAR, Bastiaan A. (b. 1909)

Dutch pacifist.

The IISH, Amsterdam, has a very small collection of Roschar's correspondence covering the period 1918–35. (See M. Campfens, *op. cit.*)

ROSDOLSKY, Roman (1898–1967)

Ukrainian-born Trotskyist. Historian and Marxist theoretician. During the First World War co-founder of the International Revolutionary Socialist Youth of Galicia – an underground organisation devoted to the struggle against the war, and after the outbreak of the Russian Revolution providing the leadership of the Communist Party of West Ukraine (which later became a section of the Communist Party of Poland). After the war emigrated. Worked in Vienna for the Marx-Engels Institute (Moscow) on historical sources, and began researching the nationalities problem and the history of the peasantry. Early 1930s joined the Trotskyist movement and until the end of his life identified with the ideas of Trotsky. Forced by the seizure of power by Austro-Fascism to return to his native land in 1934 (by then part of Poland). Worked as a historian at Lemberg University. Arrested in 1942 by the Gestapo in Cracow and spent the following years in German concentration camps (Auschwitz, Ravensbruck and Oranienburg). Emigrated to the USA in 1947. Prevented by his political past from obtaining an academic post. Now best known for his posthumously published commentary on Marx's *Grundrisse* and interpretation of Marx's method (in English as *The Making of Marx's Capital*, London: 1977).

Rosdolsky's papers for the years 1945–67 (but mainly after 1950) are in the IISH, Amsterdam. This extensive collection comprises political and scholarly correspondence (with, amongst others, Isaac Deutscher (q.v.), Paul Fröhlich (q.v.), Karl Korsch (q.v.), Paul Mattick and Tatjana Moszkowska), manuscripts of books and articles, a lexicographical subject index of *c*.12 000 cards to the works of Marx (q.v.), as well as research notes and collections of printed sources (originals and copies) relating to his main fields of research (including the social history of Galicia under Austrian rule, the revolution of 1848, and the history and theory of Marxism). A provisional inventory is available.

ROSE, Cornelis (1886–1976)

Dutch communist.

The IISH, Amsterdam has a collection of Rose's papers and organisational pamphlets covering the period 1926–59. (See M. Campfens, *op. cit.*)

ROSENBERG, Ludwig (1903–77)

German social democratic trade unionist. Member of the DGB Executive from 1949, Vice-Chairman 1959–62, then Chairman, 1962–9.

The AdsD at the Friedrich-Ebert-Stiftung, Bonn, has a large collection of Rosenberg's papers for the years 1947–77. This comprises manuscripts of his speeches, articles and reports, as well as documents and manuscripts concerning trade unions, social and economic questions, SPD trade unionists, international trade union affairs. (It also includes his appointments diary.) A substantial quantity of Rosenberg's papers from the years 1951–69 are also held at the DGB Archive in Düsseldorf. As well as manuscripts of speeches and lectures, these comprise odd correspondence as well as newspaper articles by and about Rosenberg. (See Mommsen, *op. cit.*)

ROSETTE, Jean-Baptiste (b. 1832)*

French Communard.

See Appendix I.

  * Known as Rozette-Guinot.

ROSMER, Alfred (1877–1964)

American-born French revolutionary and anarchist. Friend of Monatte (q.v.). Collaborated on *La Vie ouvrière* and *Bataille syndicaliste*. Worked to reform the International along revolutionary syndicalist lines.

Of the collections of papers divided by Rosmer when he left for Mexico in 1939 the only surviving collection is that divided between Pierre Godeau (family documents and papers) and Colette Chambelland. It is this latter collection which is believed to be the one now deposited in the Musée Social (CEDIAS), Paris. This deposit includes letters from such revolutionary socialists as Monatte (q.v.), Boris Souvarine (q.v.), Pierre Naville, Pierre Frank, Livio Maitan, Max Schachtmann, Albert Camus, etc. – as well as files on Isaac Deutscher (q.v.) and Sarah and Louis Jacobs, personal papers (notably memories of

Trotsky (q.v.) and correspondence with Olga Nin and her daughters (from 1939). In addition there is a large collection of papers from Natalia Trotsky (including documents concerning her breach with the Fourth International). The collection has been enriched by post-war material.

ROSSEL, Louis (1844–71)

French military leader during the Paris Commune.

One box of Rossel's papers is in the Archives Nationales, Paris. These comprise letters, notes and manuscripts from the whole of his life and in particular, from the time of the war of 1870 and the Commune.

In addition, there are family papers as well as various documents concerning his official military role under the Commune. Written permission from the depositor is needed to consult these papers. An inventory is available. (See also Appendix I.)

ROSSI, Giovanni (1856–1943)

Italian anarchist.

A small amount of Rossi's printed and manuscript material (1897) is in the IISH, Amsterdam.

ROSSMANN, Erich (1884–1953)

German social democratic politician. From 1924 member of the Württemberg Landtag and of the Reichstag. General Secretary of the Land Council of the American Zone 1945–8. General Secretary of the European Union 1948.

The first part of Rossmann's papers for the period before 1943 was destroyed by bomb damage. The second part, covering the years 1946–53 is in the Bundesarchiv, Koblenz. This comprises personal papers and memoirs (1884–1945) relating to the reforming of the SPD in Thuringia after 1945, as well as his activity in the Land Council, and as General Secretary of the European Union and on behalf of war casualties, refugees and pensioners. (See Mommsen, *op. cit.*)

ROT, Thomas S. (1909–82)

Dutch journalist and International Red Help member.

The IISH, Amsterdam, has a small collection of Rot's papers relating to various organisations from the period 1934–65. Access is restricted.

ROTH, Wolfgang (b. 1943)

German social democratic politician. Vice-Chairman and then Chairman of the Jusos (Young Socialists) 1969–75. Member of the SPD Executive 1973–9. From 1976 member of the Bundestag.

Roth's papers are in the AdsD, Bonn. These include material on youth policy, the SPD Executive and various SPD working groups.

ROUSSEAU, Nestor (1819–c.1879)*

Militant French republican. Delegate, 1871, to the Central Committee of the National Guard. Exiled, 1851–9, 1872–9.

There is a manuscript (without title or date) in the collection Comité Central de la Garde National at the Archive of the War Ministry in which Rousseau talks about his patriotic motives and republican opinions.

* Known by the pseudonym Nestor Louis.

ROUSSEL

* Pseudonym of CLÉMENCE, Adolphe.

ROZETTE-GUINOT, Jean-Baptiste

See under ROSETTE, Jean-Baptiste.

ROŽDESTVENSKIJ, Aleksandr N. (fl. 1916–24)

Russian lawyer and public prosecutor.

The IISH, Amsterdam, has his memoirs from the period 1916–24 (0.10 m).

RÜCK, Friedrich (Fritz) (b. 1895)

German émigré in Sweden. Writer and journalist. Worked on *Sia* and *Arbetartidningen*.

Some 19 boxes of Rück's papers – containing, in particular, material on German organisations and individuals – are in the ARAB, Stockholm. An outline inventory is available.

RUDERT, Max (1901–68)*

German journalist. Editor of *Welt am Sonntag* 1948–68. Member of the KPD until 1930, when he joined the SPD.

The Bundesarchiv, Koblenz, has a small collection of correspondence covering the period 1925–55, but mainly from his time in exile, when he edited the *Prager Mittag* (until 1938), and was secretary of the Thomas-Mann-Gesellschaft in London (from 1939).

* Known by the pseudonym Bernhard Menne.

RÜDIGER, Helmut (1903–66)

Anarchist. Journalist, editor and writer.

Some 18 boxes of Rüdiger's papers, with a provisional inventory, are in the ARAB, Stockholm.

RÜHLE, Otto (1874–1943)

German social democratic politician and later left-communist. Teacher and educationalist.

SPD Deputy in the Diet of Saxony 1911 and member of the Reichstag 1912. Supporter of the SPD-left. Second Deputy (after Karl Liebknecht) to refuse to vote for war credits in the Reichstag 1912. Founder member of the Spartakus League. Leading role (as a leader of the IKD-German International Communists) during the Revolution in Saxony. Spokesman for the left at the founding conference of the KPD. Founding member of the Communist Workers' Party (KAPD), and of the General Workers' Union of Germany – United Organisation (AAUD-E) in October 1921. Left active politics in 1925 to concentrate on literary and cultural work. Exile in Prague 1933, and in Mexico 1936. Member of the Dewey Committee. Contributor to *International Council Correspondence* (later *Living Marxism*).

Rühle's papers are in the IISH, Amsterdam. However, these are exclusively from his exile period (1933–43), comprising mainly correspondence and manuscripts. Rühle's correspondence was mainly with friends and political contacts abroad (including Erich Fromm, Henry Jacoby, Paul Mattick, A. O. Mendel and Leon Trotsky (q.v.)), or concerned with his work as a professional advisor to the Mexican Ministry of Education (copies of letters sent out, 1936–9). His manuscripts include *Brauner und roter Faschismus* and *Weltkrieg-Weltfaschismus-Weltrevolution*, as well as various articles (1933–41). A provisional card index is available.

RUTGERS, Sebald J. (1879-1961)

Dutch SDAP member. Later member of the CPSU.

There are two collections of Rutgers's papers. The first, a very small collection of correspondence for the period 1918–27, is in the IISH, Amsterdam. The second is in the Institute for Marxism-Leninism, Moscow, and consists of personal papers.

SABROE, Peter Rasmus (1867–1913)

Danish social democratic politician. Orator and trade union organiser. Well known as an organiser and agitator among domestic servants. SD Member of Parliament.

Six boxes of Sabroe's papers covering the years 1905–13 are in the ABA, Copenhagen. These include manuscripts concerned with *Sabroes Blad*, as well as a large number of letters from the many people in whose cases he became involved. A summary inventory is available.

SACKE, Georg (1902–45)

German communist historian. Resistance fighter.

Sacke's papers for the years 1911–45 are in the Staatsarchiv, Leipzig. These comprise correspondence and manuscripts as well as letters written from prison.

SADOUL, Jacques (1881–1956)

French socialist.

One folder of Sadoul's correspondence, given by Theodor Draper in 1966, is in the Hoover Institution, Stanford University, California. The correspondence relates to political conditions in France and Europe at the beginning of the Second World War. Correspondents include Léon Blum (q.v.), Pierre Laval and Paul Reynaud.

SAINT-JUST, Louis Antoine de (1767–94)

French revolutionary democrat. Friend of Robespierre. Member of the Convention and of the Committee for Public Safety. Reorganised the Rhine Army 1793–4. Executed under the 'Thermidor'.

Saint-Just's letters and main manuscripts are in the Bibliothèque Nationale, Paris.

SALEMBIER

French anarcho-syndicalist and trade unionist.

A large collection of Salembier's papers for the years 1916–65 is in the CRHMSS, Paris. This is particularly rich on the post-war history of anarcho-syndicalism, as well as the metal workers' federation of the CGTU in the interwar period.

SALMELA-JÄRVINEN, Martta (b. 1892)

Finnish social democratic politician and women's leader. Writer. Leader of the Association of Female Workers. Leading member of the Finnish Social Democratic Party (SDP) and then of the Social Democratic League of Workers and Small Farmers (faction of the SDP in the late 1950s and 1960s).

Salmela-Järvinen's papers for the years 1904 and 1918–80 are in the Finnish Labour Archives, Helsinki. These comprise correspondence (1940–80 – mainly private), manuscripts (including speeches and an unpublished history of the SDP District Uusimaa), a collection of plays and books, and a few photographs.

SALOMON, Adolphe (b. 1844)

French Communard.

See Appendix I.

SALOMON, Friedrich (b. 1890)

German social democrat. Private Secretary to Wolfgang Heine (q.v.) 1924–8. After 1933 in exile. Active in the SOPADE.

Friedrich Salomon's correspondence for the years 1933–40 is in the AdsD at the Friedrich-Ebert-Stiftung, Bonn. This, however, mainly concerns his work for the IISH, Amsterdam. The IISH has a small collection covering the period 1909–30.

SALOMON, Gottfried (1892–1964)

German sociologist.

A collection of papers is in the IISH, Amsterdam.

SALOVAARA, Väinö (1888–1964)

Finnish trade union leader and social democratic politician. Executive member, Secretary and Treasurer of the Metal Workers' Union 1919–24. Executive member of the Union of

Finland's Workers. Executive member of the SAK. Chairman of the Uusimaa District Organisation of the Social Democratic Party (SDP). Chairman of the SDP 1942–4. Member of Parliament 1939–44. Second Minister of Transport and General Works (Relief Work) 1937–8. Minister of Transport and General Works 1938–44.

Salovaara's papers are in the Finnish Labour Archives, Helsinki. These contain mainly cuttings and photographs concerning his work in the Transport Ministry (including a large collection of cuttings from the Wages Department) and the SAK after 1945.

SAND, George (1804–76)*

French writer. Known as the 'Red Baroness'. Republican. Sympathetic to the working class. Author of novels of working class life. Active in defence of republicans under the Second Empire.

The George Sand Museum at La Châtre contains her letters (in particular to Alphonse Fleury), manuscripts, documents and portraits.

* Known by the pseudonym Baroness Dudevant.

SANDER, Wilhelm (1895–1978)

German social democratic politician. After 1933 exile in Czechoslovakia and then in England (where he was a leader of the SPD in exile). Secretary of the SPD-Group in the Bundestag 1950–62.

Sander's papers covering the years 1917–78 are in the AdsD at the Friedrich-Ebert-Stiftung, Bonn. Apart from a collection of pamphlets from the labour movement in Dresden (1917–58), however, this collection contains material mainly arising from the social democratic exile. (See Mommsen, *op. cit.*)

SANDLER, Richard (1884–1964)

Swedish social democratic politician. Academic. Founder of the Workers' Educational Movement 1912. Prominent leader of the SAP. Member of Parliament. Minister in several governments, including Foreign Minister immediately prior to the Second World War.

Sixteen boxes of Sandler's papers, with an inventory, are in the ARAB, Stockholm.

SÄNGER, Fritz (b. 1901)

German social democratic politician. Member of the Bundestag 1961–9.

There are three collections of Sänger's papers. The first, in the Bundesarchiv, Koblenz, is a collection of material arising from his editorial work in the years 1933–43. The second, also concerning his editorial work, is in the Institut für Zeitgeschichte, Munich. The third concerns press affairs generally as well as wider political issues in the years 1960–69, and is in the AdsD at the Friedrich-Ebert-Stiftung, Bonn. (See Mommsen, *op. cit.*)

SANTILLÀN, Diego Abad de*

* Pseudonym of HERNANDEZ, Sinesio Garcia.

SARRAUT, Albert (b. 1872)

French radical-socialist politician. Senator for Aude 1902–24 and 1926–45. Many times Minister 1909–40 – including Minister of State for African Affairs. Voted full powers to Marshal Pétain in July 1940.

Sarraut's papers are in the Departmental Archives of Aude. An inventory is available in manuscript.

SASSENBACH, Johannes (1866–1940)

German and international trade unionist. Executive member of the ADGB. General Secretary of the International Federation of Trade Unions.

Sassenbach's papers are in the DGB Archive, Düsseldorf.

SAUMONEAU, Louise (1875–1950)

French socialist and feminist. Co-founder, 1914, of the Socialist Women's Group of the SFIO. Militant pacifist. Elected to the CAP of the SFIO 1918. Secretary again of the SFIO's Socialist Women's Group 1924–31. Left the SFIO 1939. Leader of Paul Faure's (q.v.) Parti Socialiste Démocratique.

There is a letter written by Saumoneau to J. R. Bloch, together with some conference notes, in the Bibliothèque Nationale, Paris. In addition, there is a file concerning Saumoneau in the Bibliothèque Marguerite Durand in the Town Hall, 5th Arrondissement, Paris.

SAUVERT*

* Pseudonym of RAVATÉ, Jules.

SAVINKOV, Boris Viktorovič (1870–1926)*

One of the leaders of the Russian Socialist Revolutionary Party. Terrorist. Member of Sotsialist (a St Petersburg group with a programme based on the ideas of Plekhanov (q.v.)). Arrested 1901 and exiled to Vologda. Under the influence of Breshko-Breshkovskaîa (q.v.) abandoned Marxism for Populism. Escaped from Vologda 1903. In Geneva became a member of the Socialist Revolutionary (SR) Battle Organisation (involved in the assassination of the Interior Minister and the Governor-General of Moscow). Became a Central Committee member of the SR Party. Unsuccessfully tried to rehabilitate the Battle Organisation after its leader Evno Azef was exposed as an Okhrana agent. Returned to exile 1911 and turned to literary activity. Volunteer in the French army 1914. Assistant War Minister under Kerensky (q.v.) July 1917. Expelled from the SR Party for complicity in Kornilov's attempted coup. After the October Revolution devoted himself to promoting the military overthrow of Bolshevik rule. Formed the National Union for the Defence of Freedom and the Fatherland in 1921 to promote the internal subversion of the Soviet regime (but unable to do so with the arrest and execution of many of Savinkov's agents after 1922). Returned to Russia in August 1924 and arrested. Sentenced to 10 years' imprisonment.

There is a collection of Savinkov's papers for the years 1919–21 in the IISH, Amsterdam. This includes correspondence, reports and manuscripts relating to his role in the Civil War. An inventory is available, but the collection is still closed. In addition, in the Hoover Institution, Stanford University, California, there is a typewritten letter written by Savinkov in 1920 to the White Russian military commander, General Wrangel, concerning White Russian military activities, as well as a typewritten translation of his trial in 1924 for counter-revolutionary activities. In addition, the Bakhmeteff Archive, Columbia University, New York, has about five and a half boxes of his papers. The collection contains documents, correspondence, minutes of meetings, proclamations, reminiscences and newspapers relating to the history and activity of the Socialist Revolutionary Party in Russia and in exile from the 1890s to the 1920s. There are restrictions on the use of the material.

* Known by the pseudonym V. Ropshin.

SCHAEFER, Anton (1868–1945)

Czech social democratic politician. Member of the Czech Parliament c.1930.

Schaefer's papers for the years 1912–36 are in the Library of Congress, Washington. They concern domestic politics in Czechoslovakia in the years 1912–36. In addition, two boxes of papers were returned from the Bundesarchiv, Koblenz, to the AVA, Vienna, in 1986. They contain material relating to provisioning during the First World War, a district conference in Reichenberg, 1926, elections, 1920, and correspondence 1918–1921 and 1925–1931.

SCHAPER, Johan H. A. (1868–1934)

Dutch social democrat. Founder member, SDAP.

The IISH, Amsterdam, has Schaper's memoirs and correspondence. An inventory is available. Other papers are reported still with the family. (See M. Campfens, *op. cit.*)

SCHAPPE, Josef

German communist. Founder of the *Unabhängige Arbeiterpartei* (UAP). Editor of *Freies Volk*.

Schappe's papers are in the Hauptstadtarchiv, Düsseldorf. (See Mommsen, *op. cit.*)

SCHEIDEMANN, Philipp (1865–1939)

German social democratic politician. Member of the Reichstag 1903–33. Secretary of State in the cabinet of Prince Max von Baden 1918. Proclaimed the Republic on 9 November 1918. Member of the Council of People's Commissars. First Chancellor of the Weimar Republic 1919. Lord Mayor of Kassel 1920–25. Died as an exile in Denmark.

According to Mommsen, the main part of Scheidemann's papers was lost in 1933, while another part remained in private hands. In addition, the whereabouts of his diaries remains unknown. The remainder is divided between three collections. The first comprises written material (notes and other records), articles written by Scheidemann and minutes of SPD-Group meetings in the National Assembly and the Reichstag. This is in the Institut für Marxismus-Leninismus, Berlin. Secondly, there are manuscripts and private letters from the exile period in the AdsD, Bonn. Finally, a small quantity of correspondence and other material was placed in the Labour Movement Library and Archive, Copenhagen, by his widow in 1952. (See Mommsen, *op. cit.*)

SCHEPS, Johannes H. (b. 1900)

Dutch SDAP and PvdA member.

The IISH, Amsterdam, has a large collection of documents relating to Scheps's career covering the period 1935–6. Access is restricted. Other papers are in the possession of Scheps himself.

SCHEU, Adolf (1907–78)

German social democratic politician. Member of the Christlich-Sozialer-Volksdienst 1929–33. Imprisoned 1941. One of the founders of the Gesamtdeutsche Volkspartie 1953. Went over to the SPD with Gustav Heinemann (q.v.) and others in 1957. City Councillor in Wuppertal 1961–70. Member of the Bundestag 1969–78.

Adolf Scheu's papers are in the AdsD, Bonn. These comprise an extensive general correspondence arising from his activity as a Bundestag Deputy and at various levels in the SPD.

SCHEU, Andreas (1844–1927)

Pioneer Austrian socialist. Furniture designer. Member of the IWMA. Attracted to Marxism. One of the pioneers of Austrian social democracy and a leading 'radical'. Arrested 1870 with other leaders of the young workers' movement. Exile 1874 in Britain. Correspondent for *Gleichheit* and then for the *Arbeiterzeitung*. Active in émigré groups. Founding member and on the Executive of the Social Democratic Federation (SDF). Helped form the Scottish Land and Labour League in Edinburgh and affiliate it to the SDF. Opponent of Hyndman's jingoism. Close colleague of William Morris whom he helped push into opposition to Hyndman. Took the Scottish Land and Labour League over to the Socialist League of which he was a Council member. Participated in the early Congresses of the Second International. Participated in the Zimmerwald Movement.

Andreas Scheu's papers for the years 1877–1914 are in the IISH, Amsterdam. These are especially interesting for political and personal correspondence from his British period (including William Morris and G. B. Shaw) and French colleagues (including Edouard Vaillant (q.v.)) The correspondence includes copy-books of letters sent out in the years October 1885–December 1887, May–July 1888, January 1889, and July 1910–December 1914. In addition, this collection also contains notebooks and manuscripts of poetry, as well as a small biographical file by and about his brother Heinrich (q.v.). A provisional inventory is available.

SCHEU, Heinrich (1845–1926)

Pioneer Austrian socialist. Brother of Andreas Scheu (q.v.). Engraver. Secretary of a workers' educational club in Leipzig in 1869 of which August Bebel (q.v.) was President. Took over the leadership of Austrian social democracy March 1870–February 1871 while its leading members were on trial for high treason. Editor of the *Volkswille*. Organised support for the victims of persecution. Relinquished the editorship of *Volkswille* after the amnesty of the workers' leaders in February 1871, and left Austria. Represented Austria at the Fifth Congress of the IWMA. Continued to write for the workers' press. Settled in Switzerland 1893. Represented Swiss workers at the Zürich Congress of the Second International. Supporter of the Zimmerwald Movement.

See under Andreas Scheu.

SCHEU, Josef (1841–1904)

Austrian social democrat.

The Vienna City Library (WSLB) has a collection of correspondence.

SCHEU, Robert (1873–1964)

Austrian social democrat.

The Vienna City Library (WSLB) has a collection of correspondence from the period 1900–49.

SCHEUER, Georges (b. 1915)

French socialist.

The IISH, Amsterdam has a collection of correspondence, manuscripts, files, circulars and printed material. The collection covers the period 1937–52, but most of the material dates from the years 1940–49. Access is closed.

SCHEVENELS, Walter (1894–1966)

Belgian international trade union official. General Secretary of the International Federation of Trade Unions 1930–45, (at first in Berlin but from 1933 in Paris). General Secretary of the European Regional Organisation of the International Confederation of Free Trade Unions 1951–66.

Schevenels's papers for the years 1930–66 are in the Hoover Institution, Stanford University, California. These comprise correspondence, writings, speeches, interviews, reports, pamphlets, bulletins, cuttings and other printed material concerning European trade unions, as well as the European and wider international working-class and workers' movements.

SCHILP, Dirk (1893–1969)

Dutch trade unionist. Chairman, local government workers' union (PCOD) 1923–5.

The IISH, Amsterdam, has Schilp's diary, together with some correspondence, manuscript articles etc. 1925–56. An inventory is available. (See, M. Campfens, *op. cit.*)

SCHIMMEL, Kurt (1879–1967)

German social democratic politician and trade unionist. Member of the Bavarian Ministerialrat.

Schimmel's papers are in the Hauptstaatsarchiv, Stuttgart. These concern his political activity and include socialist publications at the time of the 1914–18 war – SPD conferences, labour movement, women's questions, workers' education etc. – as well as collections of newspapers and cuttings, posters and leaflets etc. (See Mommsen, *op. cit.*)

SCHLESINGER, Rudolf (b. 1901)*

German communist. KPD official and economic theorist.

Schlesinger's papers, including the manuscript of his memoirs, are in the Bundesarchiv, Koblenz. (See Mommsen, *op. cit.*)

* Known by the pseudonym Rudolf Gerber.

SCHLÜTER, Hermann (1851–1919)

German socialist. Collaborated on the *Socialdemocrat* (Zürich) and on the New York *Volkszeitung*.

One part of Schlüter's papers is in the IISH, Amsterdam. This comprises correspondence, manuscripts, and documents, arising partly from his activity (alongside Julius Motteler (q.v.)) on the *Socialdemocrat*, and partly from his activity on the New York *Volkszeitung*. In addition this collection includes papers of Joseph Weydemeyer (q.v.) (including about 100 letters from Marx (q.v.) – and Friedrich Engels (q.v.) and Friedrich Albert Sorge (q.v.)). The second part of Schlüter's papers is at Madison University, Wisconsin. (See Mommsen, *op. cit.*)

SCHMID, Carlo (1896–1979)

German social democratic politician. Lawyer. Member of a Soldiers' Council at the end of the First World War. Land Chairman of the SPD in Südwürttemberg-Hohenzollern. Vice-President and Minister of Justice in Südwürttemberg-Hohenzollern 1947–50. Member of the SPD Executive 1947–73. Member of the Parliamentary Council 1948–9 and of the Bundestag 1949–72. Vice-President of the European Union 1950–52, and Member of the Consultative Assembly of the Council of Europe 1950–66 and 1969–73. Executive member of the German Council of the European Movement 1970–74. Influence on the Godesberg Programme. Minister for Bundesrat and Land affairs 1966–9.

Schmid's extensive papers for the years 1945–79 are in the AdsD, Bonn. This enormous collection comprises correspondence, publications, manuscripts and autobiographical material concerning all aspects of his political career.

SCHMIDT, Frieda (fl. 1930s–40s)

German pacifist.

Frieda Schmidt's diary, 1932–45, is in the Hoover Institution, Stanford University, California.

SCHMIDT, Helmut (b. 1918)

German social democratic politician. Member of the Bundestag 1953–62 and from 1965. Defence expert. Vice-Chairman 1965 and Chairman 1967 of SPD Group. From 1958 member of the SPD Executive. Minister of Defence 1969–72 and Minister of Finance 1972–4. Federal Chancellor 1974–82.

Helmut Schmidt's papers from 1947 onwards have been deposited in the AdsD, Bonn. These document his entire political career but are not yet catalogued or available.

SCHMIDT, Karl (b. 1878)

German trade unionist.

A small collection of Karl Schmidt's papers for 1918–20 is in the AdsD at the Friedrich-Ebert-Stiftung, Bonn. These comprise notes and other material on the revolution in Bavaria. (See Mommsen, *op. cit.*)

SCHMIDT, Robert (1864–1943)

German social democratic politician. Member of the Reichstag. Reich Minister for Food Supply, Economy and Reconstruction.

Mommsen (*op. cit.*) reported that no papers could be located.

SCHMIDT-KÜSTER, Gustav (b. 1902)

German social democrat. Bookbinder. Before 1933 member of the SPD. Persecuted under the Nazis. Participated in reforming the SPD in Magdeburg after 1945 and in Hannover from 1947.

Schmidt-Küster's papers are in the AdsD, Bonn. These concern the concentration of socialist enterprises, the Socialist Publishers and Book Sellers' Group, press matters, Ernst Thape (q.v.) and Fritz Heine (q.v.).

SCHMITT-VOCKENHAUSEN, Hermann (1923–79)

German social democratic politician. Member of the Bundestag 1953–79. For 20 years (until 1971) SPD Sub-District Chairman in Main-Taunus. From 1971 member of the Central Committee of German Catholics. From 1973 President of the German Cities and Communities League. Co-founder of the Scientific Freedom League.

Schmitt-Vockenhausen's papers from the years 1953–79 are in the AdsD, Bonn. This large collection comprises private and general correspondence as well as material concerning nearly all aspects of his political and public life.

SCHNEIDER, Eugène (b. 1846)

French Communard.

See Appendix I.

SCHOENLAND, Bruno (1859–1901)

German social democratic politician. Writer and journalist. From 1892 editor on *Vorwärts* and then Chief Editor of the Leipzig *Volkszeitung*. Reformer of the social democratic press. Member of the Reichstag.

A few of Schoenland's papers are in the AdsD, Bonn. These comprise his diary (1897–8) and correspondence.

SCHOETTLE, Erwin (1899–1976)

German social democratic politician. Printer and journalist. Member of the *Neu Beginnen* Group. In England 1939. Member of the Baden-Württemberg Landtag 1946. Member of the Economic Council 1947–9 and of the Bundestag 1949–69. Until 1962 Chairman of the SPD in Baden-Württemberg.

A large collection of Schoettle's papers is in the AdsD at the Friedrich-Ebert-Stiftung, Bonn. This comprises correspondence, as well as material relating to the Economic Council, the Bundestag and the SPD. (See Mommsen, *op.cit.*)

SCHOLZ, Arno (1904–71)

German social democrat. Before 1924 Secretary to Alexander Helphand (q.v.). Editorial work 1925–33 on *Vorwärts* and the *Volkswillen* (Hannover). Victimised 1933. After 1945 leading figure in the West Berlin press and West German television.

Scholz's enormous collection of papers from 1946–71 is in the AdsD at the Friedrich-Ebert-Stiftung, Bonn. It comprises correspondence and various material on the press in these years.

SCHOUTEN, Anton J. S. (b. 1908)

Dutch revolutionary socialist.

The IISH, Amsterdam, has some of Schouten's documents and also publications of various organisations 1934–51. There are restrictions on access. (See M. Campfens, *op. cit.*)

SCHRAMM, Carl August (1830–1905)

Prominent German theorist and spokesman of the 'state socialist' tendency within social democracy.

Some of Schramm's papers are in the IISH, Amsterdam. This collection includes a few letters from August Bebel (q.v.), Wilhelm Liebknecht (q.v.), Johann Most and Karl Rodbertus.

SCHREIBER, Adele (1872–1957)

German social democrat and feminist. Member of the Reichstag.

Schreiber's papers are in the Bundesarchiv, Koblenz. These relate to the women's movement as well as to legal questions concerning mothers and children. (See Mommsen, *op. cit.*)

SCHRÖDER, Karl (1884–1950)

German social democrat. Novelist. Travelling teacher for the SPD. Expert on cultural policy.

Schröder's papers comprise a collection of letters – mainly from Franz Mehring (q.v.) to Karl Korn in the years 1902–19 – which are in the AdsD, Bonn. (See Mommsen, *op. cit.*)

SCHROEDER, Max (1900–58)

German communist. Writer. After 1933 exile in France and then the USA. Editor of German language papers. From 1947 Chief Editor of the *Aufbauverlag*, Berlin.

A large part of Schroeder's papers are reported lost. However, there are 4600 pages of correspondence, diary-notes and manuscripts for the years 1931 and 1947–58 in the Archiv der Deutschen Akademie der Künste, Berlin. (See Mommsen, *op. cit.*)

SCHRUB (fl. 1870s)

French socialist. Leading member of the International in Rouen after 1867.

Copies of a number of letters addressed by Schrub to the Editor of the *Courrier Français* are in the Archives de la Préfecture de Police, Paris. These are particularly relevant to the membership and situation of the International in Rouen. (See Maitron, *op. cit.*)

SCHUMACHER, Kurt (1859–1952)

German social democratic politician. Member of the Württemberg Landtag 1924 and, after 1930 of the Reichstag. Ten years in concentration camp. Pioneer in 1945 of the reconstruction of the SPD through the 'Büro Dr. Schumacher' that constituted itself as the 'Büro der Westzonen'. Chairman of the SPD 1946–52.

Schumacher's papers are in the AdsD at the Friedrich-Ebert-Stiftung, Bonn. These include the correspondence of the 'Büro der Westzonen' and as Chairman of the SPD. In addition, there is also a collection of articles, speeches, press releases, interviews and manuscripts. (See Mommsen, *op. cit.*)

SCHÜTTE, Ernst (1904–72)

German social democrat. Hessian Minister of Education 1959–69. Member of the Cultural Policy Group of the SPD Executive.

Schütte's papers for the years 1947–72 are in the AdsD, Bonn. These comprise personal documents and memoirs (1928–69), general correspondence, manuscripts, and a large quantity of material concerning educational and cultural matters, the SPD, and the Hesse Land Government.

SCHWARZ, Max (1904–79)

German social democratic politician. Left the SAJ 1930 for the Union of Social Youth (SJV). Publisher of the SJV monthly *Roter Pionier*. Active in the anti-Nazi resistance. From 1945 member of the SPD and 1947–59 member of the Landtag in Lower Saxony. Assistant Director in the Lower Saxony Ministry of the Interior 1959–69.

Schwarz's papers are in the AdsD, Bonn. These include correspondence and other material concerning his activity as a Landtag member and in the Ministry of the Interior of Lower Saxony.

SCHWIMMER, Rosika (1877–1948)

Hungarian pacifist and feminist. Minister to Switzerland 1918–19.

Schwimmer's papers, in part typewritten transcripts, and covering the period 1914-33, are in the Hoover Institution, Stanford University, California. The collection includes correspondence, monographs and petitions, as well as newspaper cuttings and photographs, relating to such matters as the pacifist movement during the 1914–18 war, her affiliation with the Henry Ford Peace Expedition (1915–16), her participation in the Neutral Conference for Continuous Mediation (1916), the International Congress of Women, and her subsequent career both in Hungary and the United States. A preliminary inventory is available.

ŠČUPAK, Samuil Davidovič (1880–c.1943)

Russian Bundist and social democrat.

The IISH, Amsterdam has a collection of correspondence and memoirs.

SECCHIA, Pietro (fl. 1930s–40s)

Italian communist.

An important and extensive archive of Secchia's papers is in the Feltrinelli Institute, Milan. The archive is of particular value for the advent of fascism, the resistance period and material on the PCI and anti-fascism after 1945. The collection is in six major parts – correspondence, notes, documentation on his travels abroad, the administration of the PCI, publications, and photographs.

SEGALL, Fritz (1901–73)

German social democrat. From 1939 exiled in England. After 1945 the SPD's link-man with the Labour Party. Chairman of the Association of German Social Democrats in Great Britain 1950.

Segall's papers are in the AdsD at the Friedrich-Ebert-Stiftung, Bonn. These comprise printed materials, minutes of meetings, etc. from the organisations of German socialists and trade unionists in exile in England, together with correspondence on Anglo-German relations (1953–6). (See Mommsen, *op. cit.*)

SEGITZ, Martin (b. 1853)

German social democratic politician. Bavarian State Commissar for demobilisation. Minister of State for the Interior and then for Social Welfare. Member of the Bavarian Landtag and of the Reichstag.

Segitz's papers, concerning the municipal election programme in Bavaria, are in the Institut für Sozialforschung, Frankfurt. (See Mommsen, *op. cit.*)

SEIDEL, Robert (1850–1933)

Swiss ethical socialist. Social scientist. Close connections with German social democracy until the end of the 1870s.

There are two collections of Seidel's papers. The first is in Zürich Central Library, and comprises correspondence and manuscripts (including drafts of scientific works and memoirs). Access is restricted. The second is in the Schweizerisches Sozialarchiv, Zürich.

SEITZ, Karl (1869–1950)

Austrian social democrat. President of the National Assembly, 1918–20.

Most of his papers are at the AVA, Vienna. Eighteen boxes are described as *Nachlass* and six more have the title 'National Assembly, 1918–20, Office of the President, Karl Seitz'. The collection comprises those papers that were seized in 1934. The *Nachlass* contains five boxes of correspondence from the years 1907–34, material relating to the SDAP, and papers relating to industry during the First World War. There is also material on the period after 1920, and a collection of printed material and speeches from the years 1924–30 (ref. 27/24). The WSLA, Vienna, has eight boxes (73 files) of his papers, with a detailed inventory, and the Vienna City Library (WSLB) has twenty-five letters. In addition, the VGA, Vienna, has seven files containing personal documents, press cuttings, a cartoon collection, photographs, and condolences on his death.

SELLIER, Henri (1883–1943)

French socialist politician. Collaborated with Jaurès (q.v.) and Albert Thomas (q.v.). Followed the majority at 1920 Tours Congress, but expelled from PCF in October 1921. Active at municipal and cantonal level. Senator for the Seine, 1935–43. Minister of Public Health, June 1936–June 1937.

A large collection (70 boxes) of his papers has been deposited by his daughter at the Communal Archives in the Town Hall, Suresnes. These relate to his activity as Mayor of Suresnes (1919–40), as a General Councillor for the Canton of Puteaux (1910–25) and at the Canton of Suresnes et Nanterre-Sud (from 1925), as Senator, and as Minister of Public Health. In addition, there are personal papers, and others concerning his work as an urbanist and sociologist. An inventory has been prepared.

SEMBAT, Marcel (1862–1922)

French socialist politician and lawyer. Deputy for Paris 1893–1922. Joined the CRC 1895. Opponent of 'Ministerialism'. Member of the National Council of the SFIO 1905. Minister of Public Works October 1915–December 1916. Opponent of Comintern affiliation. Member of the CAP of the SFIO. Involved with *Populaire*.

The whole of Sembat's papers have been deposited in the OURS, Paris. These comprise correspondence (with amongst others, Jaurès (q.v.) and Vaillant (q.v.)) as well as his private diary, files and other materials. (See Maitron, *op. cit.*)

SENDER, Tony (1888–1964)

German social democratic politician. From 1919 Editor of the USPD *Volksrecht*. Member of the Reichstag 1920–33 (USPD – SPD 1922). International work for the German engineering workers' union and for the ADGB. Exile in Belgium 1933 and the USA 1935. From 1949 with the ICFTU.

Sender's papers for the period before 1933 are reported lost. His papers from the years 1933–64, however, are held by the State Historical Society of Wisconsin in Madison, Wisconsin. These comprise documentation arising from his various activities – especially with the ICFTU – as well as extensive correspondence concerned with emigration, resistance, the political situation since 1945, and the ICFTU. (See Mommsen, *op. cit.*)

SERGE, Victor (1890–1947)

French anarchist then communist. Collaborated on *L'Anarchie*. Held official posts in Russia after the Revolution. Member of the Left Opposition. Expelled from the Communist Party in 1927. Returned to France 1936 and left for Mexico 1940.

Serge's papers are in the Musée Social (CEDIAS), Paris.

SERGENT, Victor (b. 1854)

French Communard.

See Appendix I.

SERRA MORET, Manuel (fl. 1930s)

Spanish socialist politician. Founder of the Unió Socialistade Catalunya (socialist party in Catalonia 1920–39). Minister in the Catalonian Government. Finally a member of the Partit Socialista Unificat de Catalunya. Died in exile.

Serra Moret's papers are in the Centre D'Estudis Historics Internacionals at the University of Barcelona.

SERRET, Gilbert (fl. 1920s–30s)

French educational trade unionist.

The papers are in the IFHS, Paris. They concern, in particular, the Fédération de l'Enseignement in the interwar period.

SEUFFERT, Walter (b. 1907)

German social democratic politician. Member of the Bundestag 1949–67.

Seuffert's papers are in the AdsD at the Friedrich-Ebert-Stiftung, Bonn. They concern his activity in the SPD and the Bundestag in the period 1949–64.

SEVERING, Carl (1875–1952)

German socialist. Reich Minister of the Interior, 1928–30.

The papers, 1892–1952, are in the AdsD, Bonn.

SEVERINS, Frans (b. 1889)

Swedish social democratic politician. Syndicalist in his early days. Editor of the social democratic *Tidningen-Arbetaren*. Member of Parliament. Under Secretary of State.

One box of Severins's papers, with a provisional inventory, is in the ARAB, Stockholm.

SHNEYEROFF, M. M. (b. 1880)

Member of the Russian Socialist Revolutionary Party.

Shneyeroff's papers (in Russian and English) for the years 1918–57 are in the Hoover Institution, Stanford University, California. These comprise memoirs, writings, and photographs relating to the Russian revolutionary movement in the early 20th century. A preliminary inventory is available.

SIEMSEN, Anna (1882–1951)

German social democratic politician. Professor at the University of Jena. Member of the Reichstag.

Siemsen's unpublished manuscripts and correspondence were reported in private hands by Mommsen (*op. cit.*)

SIGNAC, Paul (1863–1935)

French neo-impressionist artist and libertarian. From 1896 collaborated on *Les Temps Nouveaux*. Deeply disagreed with the support of Jean Grave (q.v.) and others for the union sacrée.

See under GRAVE, Jean.

SILLANPÄÄ, Miina (1866–1952)

Finnish social democratic politician and leader of the co-operative movement. Executive member of the Social Democratic Party. Chairwoman of the League of Social Democratic Women. Chairwoman of the League of First Homes (organisation for helping unmarried mothers). Member of Helsinki City Council. Member of Parliament 1907–10, 1917, 1919–32 and 1936–47. Second Minister of Social Affairs (first woman minister in Finland) 1926–7.

A large collection of Sillanpää's papers covering the years 1904–52 is in the Finnish Labour Archives, Helsinki. These papers are especially notable for Sillanpää's social work and material on the life of the working class in the first years of the 20th century. The collection comprises, in particular, correspondence (1904–52 – mainly private but some political – including some from her time as a minister), diaries (1939, 1943–6 and 1949–52), collection of material on the question of abortion, housemaids, the Committee for Helping Children (1918) and the League of First Homes, extensive printed material (including newspaper cuttings), and an excellent photograph collection. An inventory is available.

SILLEN, Hugo (b. 1892)

Prominent Swedish communist. Editor of the communist *Ny-Dag*. Member of Stockholm City Council.

One box of Sillen's papers, with a provisional inventory, is in the ARAB, Stockholm.

SILONE, Ignazio*

* Pseudonym of TRANQUILLI, Secondo.

SIMON, Gustave (b. 1829)

French Communard.

See Appendix I.

SIMON, Josef (1865–1949)

German social democratic politician. Member of the Bavarian Chamber of Deputies 1907–18 and of the Reichstag 1912–33 (SPD; USPD).

The manuscript of Josef Simon's memoirs is in the DGB Archive, Düsseldorf.

SIP, Everhard (b. 1897)

Dutch communist.

The IISH, Amsterdam, has a little of Sip's material, mainly cuttings and pamphlets 1945–59. There are restrictions on access. (See M. Campfens, *op. cit.*)

SIROLA, Yrjö (1876–1966)

Finnish social democratic, and then communist leader. Teacher. Editorial Secretary of *Työmies* 1906–9 and 1913–17. Head Teacher of the Finnish Workers' College in Deluth (USA) 1910–13. Executive member 1905–9 and 1917–18, Secretary 1905–6 and Chairman 1909–11 of the Finnish Social Democratic Party. On the left of the Party. Member of Parliament 1907–9 and 1916–17. Executive member 1918 in charge of foreign affairs of the Revolutionary Government (Suomen Kansanvaltuukunta). Escaped to Soviet Russia. Teacher 1922–4 and Head Teacher 1925–6 at the University of the Western Minority Nationalities. In the service of the Comintern 1926–8, and member of the Control Commission 1931–6. Commissar for Education in the Karelian Autonomous Soviet Republic 1928–31. Central Committee member of the Finnish Communist Party 1918–36.

Sirola's papers for the years 1899–1917 are in the Finnish Labour Archives, Helsinki. These include writings, aphorisms, etc. on literature, theoretical writings on different subjects (especially socialist theory), letters from his period in the USA (1910–11), together with writings concerning social order and structure in the USA (1912), and a press-cutting collection of Sirola's writings (1905–16). An inventory is available.

SIXTE-QUENIN, Anatole (1870–1957)

French socialist politician. A Guesdist socialist. Deputy for Arles 1910–19, 1928–36. Remained with SFIO after Tours Congress 1920. Anti-communist. Member, CAP of SFIO, 1929. Collaborated on such journals as *L'Humanité*.

Twelve boxes of Sixte-Quenin's papers for the period 1892–1945 are in the CRHMSS, Paris. These contain correspondence, notes, documents, collections of material, etc. of particular importance for the history of socialism in Bouches-du-Rhône.

SJÖKVIST, Karl Wilhelm (1863–1925)

Early Swedish trade unionist. Tailor. President of the Tailors' Union in Stockholm.

One box of Sjökvist's papers, with a provisional inventory, is in the ARAB, Stockholm.

SMÅLAN, Albert Johansson (fl. 1900s)

Prominent agitator on the Swedish left (early 20th century).

One box of Smålan's papers is in the ARAB, Stockholm.

ŠMERAL, Bohumír (fl. 1914–1918)

Czech social democrat.

The *Ústav marxismu-Leninismu úv KSČ*, Prague, has a collection of papers relating to his activity in the Czech Social Democratic party. The material covers the period 1914 to 1917, with some documents from 1906 (ref. 105–8).

SMIRNOV, Valerian Nikolaevič (1849–1900)

Russian Narodnik, collaborator of P. L. Lavrov.

The IISH, Amsterdam, has a collection of correspondence, manuscripts and files from the years 1870–1900 (4 m).

SNEEVLIET, Hendricus J. F. M. (Henk) (1883–1942)

Dutch member of revolutionary socialist groups, related trade unions, communist and Trotskyist groups. Executed by the Germans in 1942.

The IISH, Amsterdam, has a collection covering the period 1907–42.

SOCIAL, Jean*

* Pseudonym of DOMMANGET, Maurice.

SOEP, Abraham B. (1874–1958)

Dutch socialist publisher.

The IISH, Amsterdam, has some of Soep's notes and manuscripts. (See M. Campfens, *op. cit.*)

SOLLMANN, Wilhelm (1881–1951)

German social democratic politician. Journalist. Member of the National Assembly 1919–20 and of the Reichstag 1920–33. Reichsminister of the Interior 1923. Emigrated to the USA in 1933.

Sollmann's papers are held by Swarthmore College, Swarthmore, Pennsylvania. These include correspondence for 1901 and 1909–50 with, amongst others, Konrad Adenauer,

Heinrich Brüning, Max Sievers and Otto Strasser. Copies are to be found in various libraries, including the Stadtarchiv, Cologne. His family papers remain in private hands. (See Mommsen, *op. cit.*)

SØRENSEN, Hans Peter (1886–1962)

Danish social democratic editor and local politician.

Nineteen boxes of Sørensen's papers for the years 1900–60 are in the ABA, Copenhagen. As well as manuscripts, these include extensive correspondence with Danish and international socialists (especially Germans).

SORGE, Friedrich Albert (1828–1906)

German revolutionary of 1848. Emigrated to the USA. Member of the General Council and organiser of the International in the USA. Comrade, friend and correspondent of Marx (q.v.) and Friedrich Engels (q.v.).

The main part of Sorge's papers is in the New York Public Library. Copies of this collection are in the IISH, Amsterdam. In addition, some of Sorge's papers are in the Swiss Labour History Archive, Zurich. See also Hermann Schlüter.

SOUCHY BAUER, Augustin (1892–1984)

German anarchist.

The IISH, Amsterdam, has a substantial collection of Souchy Bauer's correspondence, manuscripts, notes, minutes, reports, files, circulars and printed material for the years 1942–83. Access is restricted.

SOUVARINE, Boris Konstantinovič (1895–1984)

Russian-born French journalist and author. Leader of French communism.

Two boxes of Souvarine's papers, in French and Russian, covering the period 1925–71, are in the Hoover Institution, Stanford University, California. One part was purchased from Souvarine in 1977, the other was a gift from Stanley Plastrik in 1978. A preliminary list is available. The collections include correspondence, writings, clippings, and printed matter and other material, relating to the French Communist Party, the Communist International, Marxism, Soviet agricultural and economic policies and political events in Russia. It includes correspondence with Ekaterina Kuskova, Sergei Prokopovič, Nikolai V. Vol'skii (q.v.) and the Marx-Engels Institute, Moscow. A small amount of material is also available in the IISH, Amsterdam.

SOYER, Thomas (b. 1818)

French activist. Involved in riots incited by La Marianne secret society, August 1855. Deported. Subsequently pardoned 1859.

Some of Soyer's letters to his wife are in the Departmental Archive of Maine-et-Loire. (See Maitron, *op. cit.*)

SPÅNGBERG, August (b. 1893)

Swedish trade union leader and social democratic politician. Prominent in the Railway Workers' Union. Member of Parliament.

Three boxes of Spångberg's papers, with a provisional inventory, are in the ARAB, Stockholm.

SPEYER, Hélène

See under VANDERVELDE, Lala.

SPIEKER, Wolfgang (b. 1931)

German trade union official. Director of the Economic and Social Science Institute of the DGB.

Spieker's papers for the years 1960–75 are in the AdsD, Bonn. These include material concerning the SPD Executive for the Sub-District Düsseldorf, the Young Socialists, and the City Council and SPD Group in Düsseldorf.

SPIEKMAN, Hendrik (1874–1917)

Dutch trade unionist. Founder member of the SDAP.

The IISH, Amsterdam, has some of Spiekman's personal letters for 1917. (See M. Campfens, *op. cit.*)

SPITS, M. (fl. 1890s)

Dutch socialist.

The IISH, Amsterdam, has one file of Spits's correspondence for 1891. (See M. Campfens, *op. cit.*)

STAMPFER, Friedrich (1874–1957)

Austrian social democratic journalist and editor in Germany. Editor of the Leipzig *Volkszeitung*. From 1916 to 1933 Chief Editor of *Vorwärts* and of the *Neuer Vorwärts* in exile in Prague and Paris.

Stampfer's papers for the period before 1933 were destroyed during the Second World War. His papers for the years 1933–57, however, are in the AdsD at the Friedrich-Ebert-Stiftung, Bonn. These are notable for the complete correspondence of Stampfer with the SOPADE leadership as well as numerous social democratic leaders. In addition, these papers include personal papers, manuscripts and articles. (See Mommsen, *op. cit.*)

STANKEVIČ, Vladimir Benediktovič (1834–1968)

Lithuanian jurist.

The IISH, Amsterdam has a collection of correspondence from the period 1945–8. Access is restricted.

STAPEL, Harry (b. 1911)

Member of the Dutch PvdA.

The IISH, Amsterdam, has a few of Stapel's documents relating to organisations and covering the period 1926–55. Access is restricted.

STARKENBERG, Ivar (1886–1947)

Swedish cartoonist. Member of the Left-Socialist Party and then the SKP. Eventually rejoined the SAP.

Many of Starkenberg's cartoons are preserved in the Picture Archive of the ARAB, Stockholm.

STAUNING, Thorvald (1873–1942)

Danish social democratic politician. Chairman of the SD 1910–42. First social democratic Prime Minister (1924–6 and from 1929).

Some 66 boxes of Stauning's papers from c.1900–42 are in the ABA, Copenhagen. These contain speeches, manuscripts and correspondence (including many letters from rank and file members). A printed inventory is available. In addition, it should be noted that most of Stauning's political papers form part of the SDP archive in the ABA.

STECHERT, Kurt (1906–58)

German socialist and writer.

Some 41 boxes of Stechert's papers are in the ARAB, Stockholm. An inventory is available, but special permission is needed before consulting this collection.

STECK, Albert (fl. 1880s)

Founder of Swiss social democracy. President of the SPS in its early years.

The largest part of Steck's papers is in the Landesbibliothek, Berne.

STEGERWALD, Adam (1874–1945)

German Christian trade union leader and Centre Party politician.

Many of Stegerwald's papers, including the greater part of his correspondence, was destroyed after 1933. However, there remains a sizeable collection of his papers covering the years 1908–45 in the Archiv für Christlich-Demokratische Politik at the Konrad-Adenauer-Stiftung, St Augustin bei Bonn. (See Mommsen, *op. cit.*)

STEIMER, Mollie (1879–1980)

Russian-American anarchist. Born in the Ukraine. Emigrated with her family to New York in 1912. Factory worker. Joined the anarchist group 'Freedom' in 1917. Supported the Bolshevik Revolution and campaigned against Allied Intervention. Sentenced to 15 years' imprisonment for violation of the 1917 Espionage Act. Deported to the Soviet Union in

1921. Became lover of Senya Flechine (q.v.). Continued anarchist activities and deported from the USSR. During 1920s exile in France and Germany and after 1933 in France. Arrested in 1940 and sent to concentration camp, but escaped and left for Mexico with Flechine.

Steimer's papers, including correspondence with, amongst others, Emma Goldman (q.v.), constitute part of the Flechine archive in the IISH, Amsterdam.

STEIN, Alexander (1881–1948)

German socialist and historian of the labour movement.

Alexander Stein's papers are in the IISH, Amsterdam. These comprise correspondence, articles, lectures, printed matter and other material. Of particular interest are sizeable collections of material from and about Rosa Luxemburg (q.v.) and Rudolf Hilferding (q.v.). (This latter includes manuscripts and other material, as well as original letters and extracts of letters from Hilferding to Paul Lazarsfeld and Oscar Meyer.)

STEIN, Hans (1894–1941)

German socialist.

Hans Stein's papers, covering the period 1911–40, have been placed in the IISH, Amsterdam. A preliminary list has been prepared.

STEINBERG, Isaac Nachman (1888–1957)

Russian socialist. Lawyer in Moscow. From 1906 member of the Social Revolutionary (SR) Party. Left-SR People's Commissar of Justice December 1917–March 1918. Opposed to the Treaty of Brest Litovsk and resigned from the Council of Ministers. From 1923 in Berlin. In London 1933–9. From 1943 in New York. Several publications concerned with the Russian Revolution and the Bolshevik Left-SR Coalition Government.

Steinberg's papers, in part transcripts, covering the period 1916–57, are in the Yivo Institute for Jewish Research, New York. The collection includes correspondence, documents of the early Soviet era in Russia, and manuscripts of Steinberg's published and unpublished works. It includes the correspondence files (1937–52) of the Freeland League, important letters of Russian revolutionaries such as Maria Spiridonova and others, introductory letters and correspondence by a number of important personalities in connection with Steinberg's Kimberley project to settle Jews in Australia. A list is available at the Yivo Institute.

STEINHOFF, Fritz (1897–1969)

German social democratic politician. Miner. Secretary of the SPD in Hagen 1928–33. Clandestine activity. Three years' imprisonment in 1938 and concentration camp victim 1944–5. Lord Mayor of Hagen 1945–56. From 1946 member of the North Rhine-Westphalian Landtag. SPD Group Chairman 1954. Minister of Reconstruction 1949–50 and Prime Minister of North Rhine-Westphalia 1956–8. Member of the Bundestag 1961–9. Positions in SPD Executive and the North Rhine-Westphalian Land Executive.

A part of Steinhoff's papers from the years 1933–69 is in the AdsD, Bonn. Apart from material concerning the SPD District of Western Westphalia, however, this collection does not contain his political papers.

STEINKE, Karl (1881–1962)

Danish social democratic politician. Author and social reformer. Active in the SD youth movement in the interwar period. Later Minister for Social Affairs and Minister of Justice.

A large collection of Steinke's papers is in the Royal Danish Library, Copenhagen.

STEINKOPF, Willy (b. 1884)

German social democratic politician. Journalist and writer. Member of the Governing Board of the *Deutscher Reichspost*. Member of the National Assembly and of the Reichstag.

Steinkopf's papers for the years 1900–44 are in the Deutsches Zentralarchiv, Potsdam. As well as personal documents, these include correspondence arising from both his professional and political careers. (See Mommsen, *op. cit.*)

STEPNIAK, S.*

* Pseudonym of KRAVCHINSKY, Sergei Mikhailovič.

STERKY, Anna (1856–1939)

Leading woman activist in the Swedish trade union and social democratic movements. Originally from Denmark. Wife of Fredrik Sterky (q.v.) Official in the LO. Active in the SAP. Active in the women's movements of both the LO and SAP. First Chairwoman of the Social Democratic Women's Organisation 1907. Editor of *Tidningen Morgonbris*. First woman in the leadership of both the LO and SAP.

Although Anna Sterky destroyed many of her papers, ten boxes of them survive in the ARAB, Stockholm.

STERKY, Fredrik (1860–1900)

Early Swedish trade union leader and social democrat. Wealthy origins but devoted himself to trade union organisation. First Chairman of the LO. Editor of *Ny-Tid*. Prominent in the SAP.

One box of Fredrik Sterky's papers is in the ARAB, Stockholm.

STOCK, Christian (1884–1967)

German social democratic politician. From 1910 Secretary of the Tobacco Workers' Union. After 1919 member of the National Assembly. Under Secretary of State at the Ministry of Defence 1920. Member of the Constituent Assembly for Grosshesse 1946 and Prime Minister of Hesse 1947–50.

Christian Stock's papers are in the Staatsarchiv, Darmstadt. Apart from personal items and a small quantity of correspondence, these comprise files and speeches from mainly the post-war period relating to the aspects of his political career mentioned above, and, in particular, questions of social policy. (See Mommsen, *op. cit.*)

STOCK, Jean (1893–1965)

German social democratic politician. Member of the USPD 1917 and of the Workers' and Soldiers' Council in Aschaffenburg (Bavaria) 1918–19. Imprisoned in Dachau Concentration Camp for several months in 1944. Lord Mayor of Aschaffenburg 1945 and then District President in Lower Franconia. Member, Bavarian Landtag 1946–62 (Chairman of the SPD Group until 1960).

Jean Stock's papers for the years 1918–64 are in the AdsD at the Friedrich-Ebert-Stiftung, Bonn. These relate to the different aspects of his political career mentioned above, together with de-nazification and reparations, and the organisation of the SPD in Bavaria. (See Mommsen, *op. cit.*)

STÖCKER, Helene (1869–1943)

German pacifist, reformer and feminist. Founder, *Deutscher Bund für Mutterschutz und Sexualreform*. Vice-President of the *Friedenskartell*.

Stöcker's papers, covering the period 1896–1943, are in the Friends Historical Library, Swarthmore College (Peace Collection), Swarthmore, Pennsylvania. The collection includes correspondence, diaries, autobiographical notes, address books, lectures, literary manuscripts, published writings, press-cuttings, etc. Although there is material on her pacifist and feminist work in Germany, the bulk of the material concerns her travels from country to country in exile after 1933. Correspondents include Gertrude Baer, Fenner Brockway, H. Runham Brown, William Henry Chamberlin, Dorothy Detzer, Emma Goldman (q.v.), George Gretor, Margarete Jaraczewsky, Benjamin de Jong van Beek en Donk, Anna T. Nilsson, the Nobel Peace Prize Committee, Ludwig Quidde (q.v.) and Rosika Schwimmer (q.v.).

STOKVIS, Jozef E. (1875–1951)

Dutch SDAP member and journalist.

The IISH, Amsterdam, has a collection of Stokvis's letters, reports and other documentation 1920–40. A partial inventory is available. (See M. Campfens, *op. cit.*)

STRÖBEL, Heinrich (1869–1964)

Social democratic politician and oppositionist. Writer. Member of the Prussian Chamber of Deputies 1908–18 and of the Reichstag 1924–31. Co-founder of the SAP 1931–2. Exile in Zürich 1934.

There is a manuscript written by Ströbel in the AdsD at the Friedrich-Ebert-Stiftung, Bonn. (See Mommsen, *op. cit.*)

STRÖM, Fredrik (1880–1948)

Swedish left-wing social democratic leader. Academic and writer. One of the leaders of the SAP opposition and of the Left Socialist Party. Leading member of the SAP. Editor of social democratic papers. Member of Parliament (SAP). Close friend of Aleksandra Kollontai (q.v.). Russian consul for a time.

Ten boxes of Ström's papers are in the ARAB, Stockholm. In particular, these contain letters from Aleksandra Kollontai, as well as material about the Comintern, the Red Trade Union International and Red Labour Aid. An inventory is available.

STÜCKLEN, Daniel (1869–1945)

Leader of Hungarian social democracy. Later social democratic politician in Germany. Editor of the labour press in Budapest. Co-founder of the Deutscher Metallarbeiterverband. Member of the Reichstag.

Stücklen's papers were destroyed during the war. (See Mommsen, *op. cit.*)

STUDER, Fritz (1873–1945)

Swiss social democrat. Long standing President of the SPS Directorate. Justice of the Federal Supreme Court.

Studer's papers are in the Schweizerisches Sozialarchiv, Zürich.

SÜDEKUM, Albert (1871–1934)

German social democratic politician. Journalist. Prussian Minister of Finance and member of the Reichstag.

Südekum's papers covering the years 1905–33 are in the Bundesarchiv, Koblenz. These comprise diaries and manuscripts as well as notes for speeches and articles. Most of his correspondence, however, has been lost: only a small quantity survives in this collection. (See Mommsen, *op. cit.*)

SUHR, Otto (1894–1957)

German social democratic politician. Secretary of the ADGB. After 1945 General Secretary of the SPD in Berlin. Mayor of Berlin.

Suhr's papers for the years 1920–57 are in the Landesarchiv, Berlin. These comprise articles and speeches together with documentation on his political and academic activity. (See Mommsen, *op. cit.*)

SUNDIN, Albert (b. 1883)

Swedish social democrat. Editor of social democratic papers. Official in the Temperance and Peace Movements.

One box of Sundin's papers, with an inventory, is in the ARAB, Stockholm.

SUNDSTRÖM, Carl-Johan 'Cay' (1902–59)

Finnish socialist politician and diplomat. Member of the Academic Socialists' Association (ASS). Member of the Finnish Social Democratic Party 'Kuutoset' (an opposition of six Members of Parliament and SDP leaders in the late 1930s and early 1940s). From 1944 member of the Finnish People's Democratic League (SKDL). Ambassador to Moscow.

Sundström's papers are in the National Archives of Finland, Helsinki. Special permission of the Director is necessary to consult these papers.

SUONTAUSTA, Tauno (1907–74)

Social democratic politician. Diplomat 1934–47. Cabinet Minister 1948–50.

Suontausta's papers are in the National Archives of Finland, Helsinki. Special permission of the Director is needed to consult these papers.

SUSINI, Étienne (1837–1908)

French Blanquist. Active with Eudes (q.v.) in Paris 1880s. First revolutionary to be elected a municipal councillor in Corsica.

A letter written by Susini to Eudes (2 March 1888) is in the IFHS, Paris.

SUTTNER, Baroness Bertha von (fl. 1885–1914)

German pacifist.

Suttner's papers form part of the Suttner-Fried collection in the United Nations Library, Geneva. The Suttner papers consist of letters received by the Baroness, 1885–1914, as well as several literary manuscripts (one written by Baron Otto Guntrachar von Suttner) and her diary 1897–1914. A card index of correspondents provides a useful finding aid.

SVAHN, Birger (b. 1882)

Swedish social democrat and activist in the Peace Movement. Young Socialist. Editor of *Tidningen Arbetaren*.

Six boxes of Svahn's papers, with an inventory, are in the ARAB, Stockholm.

SVENSSON, Gösta A. (1910–62)

Swedish trade union official. Editor of various trade union papers, including *Tidningen Metallarbetaren* (of the Engineering Workers' Union). Press officer for the LO (post-war).

One box of Gösta Svensson's papers, with an inventory, is in the ARAB, Stockholm.

SVENSSON, Gustav (fl. 1890s)*

Early Swedish socialist agitator.

A small collection of Gustav Svensson's papers is in the ARAB, Stockholm.

* Known as 'Röde Gustav'.

SVOBODA, Jan

Czech social democrat. Personal secretary to Blazej Vilim (q.v.).

See under Blazej Vilim.

SZENDE, Pál (1879–1934)

Hungarian socialist.

The IISH, Amsterdam, has a collection of Szende's manuscripts from the period 1920–34.

TABARANT, Adolphe (1863–1950)

French artist and libertarian socialist.

See under GRAVE, Jean.

TABOR, Peder (1892–1974)

Danish social democrat. From 1941 Chief Editor of the *Social-Demokraten*.

Ten boxes of Tabor's papers for the years 1919–74, containing correspondence from the 1930s and 1940s, are in the ABA, Copenhagen.

TAK, Pieter Lodewijk (1848–1907)

Dutch SDAP member and newspaper editor.

The IISH, Amsterdam, has a collection of Tak's notes, articles and letters covering the period 1894 to 1907. (See M. Campfens, *op. cit.*)

TAKMAN, John (b. 1912)

Swedish communist. Member of a group of socialist doctors known as 'social doctors'. Prominent in the SKP, especially for his pro-Soviet position in the 1960s.

One box of Takman's papers, with an inventory, is in the ARAB, Stockholm.

TANDLER, Julius (1869–1936)

Austrian doctor and social democrat. Under Secretary for Public Health 1919–20. Responsible for the reform of public health in 'Red Vienna'.

The Institut für Geschichte der Medizin, Vienna, has twenty-three boxes of his papers, and the Vienna City Library has a collection of correspondence from 1902–36. There is also some material at the League of Nations Archive, Geneva.

TANNER, Väinö Alfred (1881–1966)*

Finnish social democratic politician and leader of the co-operative movement. Commercial School 1900–1. Editor of *Viipuri* 1905–6 and of *Sosialidemokraatti* 1907–9. Executive Member 1909–11, 1913–17, 1919–26 and 1955–7 and Chairman of the Finnish Social Democratic Party 1919–26 and 1957–63. Member of Parliament 1907–10, 1913–16, 1919–27, 1930–45, 1951–4 and 1958–62. Chairman of Social Democrats 1919–26, 1930–37, 1940–45 and 1951–4. Minister of Finance 1917. Prime Minister December 1926–December 1927. Minister of Finance 1937–9 and 1942–4. Foreign Minister December 1939–March 1940. Minister of National Nutrition (war economy and food supply) 1940. Minister of Commerce and Industry 1941–2. Central Committee member 1910–27 and President of the International Co-operative Alliance 1927–45.

There are three collections of Tanner's papers. The first, for the years 1918–63, is in the Finnish Labour Archives, Helsinki. This includes documents, minutes, memoirs and correspondence of the Committee of Co-operation of Social Democrats in the Nordic countries, material concerning the State Bank, documents and notes on Tanner's government, documents concerning negotiations on a non-aggression pact with the USSR, documents on legal proceedings, material from Tanner's period as Foreign Minister during the Winter War, speeches delivered in social democratic organisations, transcripts of trials of war criminals, and a 29-volume collection of press-cuttings concerning Tanner's activity in the years 1905–63. An inventory is available. In addition, the greater part of Tanner's papers concerning his ministerial activities is in the State Archive, Helsinki, while a further collection of his papers remains in the hands of his family.

* Known as Thomasson until 1895.

TARNOW, Fritz (1880–1951)

German social democratic trade unionist and politician. Member of the Reichstag and of the Reich Economic Council 1928–33.

Tarnow's papers for the years 1933–49 are in the DGB Archive, Düsseldorf. In the main, these comprise correspondence from exile and his activity with the UN Trade Union Council. (See Mommsen, *op. cit.*)

TASCA, Angelo

Italian socialist.

An important collection of papers is in the Feltrinelli Institute, Milan.

TAUSK, Martha (1881–1957)

Austrian social democrat. Secretary to Friedrich Adler (q.v.) in the Second International. Responsible for women's organisation in the Social Democratic Party of Austria and the Second International.

A small collection of Tausk's papers – comprising mostly letters to her – is in the IISH, Amsterdam. They mainly cover the period 1928–52. A list is available.

TAUTE, Wilhelm (1836–99)

Pioneer German socialist. Bookbinder. Member of the Leipzig Arbeiterbildungsverein (Workers' Educational Association). Instrumental in inviting Lassalle (q.v.) to voice his opinion on the labour movement (in the *Offenes Antwortschreiben*). Became a close friend and loyal supporter of Lassalle. Leader of the Leipzig social democrats. Expelled from Leipzig in 1882. Employed by the socialist publisher Dietz (q.v.). Organiser of bookbinders and executive member of their union.

Taute's papers are in the AdsD, Bonn. These include his diaries, his Wanderbuch, workbook and a pamphlet on the social democratic *Zukunftsstaat* (1883).

TEMPEL, Jan van den (1877–1955)

Dutch trade unionist and SDAP member. Later Minister of Social Affairs 1939.

The IISH, Amsterdam has a part-archive of Tempel's papers and documents. (See M. Campfens, *op. cit.*)

TENTHOFF, Johannes (1847–1916)

Dutch pastor and socialist.

The IISH, Amsterdam, has a small collection of Tenthoff's documents, manifestos and correspondence covering the period 1882–93. (See M. Campfens, *op. cit.*)

TERSON, Jean (b. 1803)

French propagandist for Saint-Simonism. A follower of Enfantin (q.v.). Published *L'Idéalie* in 1882. Committed suicide.

The manuscript of his *Mémoires* forms part of the Enfantin collection in the Bibliothèque de l'Arsenal, Paris.

TERVO, Penna (1901–56)

Finnish social democratic politician. Editor-in-Chief of *Suomen Sosiaalidemokraatti* (central organ of the Finnish Social Democratic Party – SDP). Member of Parliament (SDP) 1945–56. Cabinet Minister 1951–6.

Tervo's papers are in the National Archives of Finland, Helsinki. Special permission of the Director is necessary to consult these papers.

TESTE, Charles Antoine (fl. 1790s–1830s)

French republican. Egalitarian and publicist. Friend of Buonarrotti (q.v.) and Voyer d'Argenson. Joined *L'Association libre pour l'education du peuple*.

Teste's correspondence and other papers are in the Bibliothèque Nationale, Paris.

THAPE, Ernst (b. 1892)

German social democrat. Editor of the Magdeburg *Volksstimme* in the 1920s. Concentration camp victim 1939–45. Co-author of the 'Buchenwald Manifesto'. Minister of Economics and Culture in the Land Government of Sachsen-Anhalt. Resigned from the SED 1948. Settled in West Germany.

Thape's papers are in the AdsD, Bonn. These include his 'Buchenwald Diary' (1945), the manuscript of his memoirs, and tapes of conversations between Thape and Arthur Dietzsch (the 'German Dreyfus').

THIERRY, Aimé (b. 1844)

French Communard.

See Appendix I.

THIERRY, Eugène (b. 1852)

French Communard.

See Appendix I.

THOMAS, Albert (1878–1932)

French socialist politician and diplomat. Founded *La Revue Syndicaliste* 1905. Under Secretary of State for War (Artillery and Military Equipment) 1915. Under Secretary of State for War (Artillery and Munitions) 1915–16. Minister of Armaments and War Manufactures 1916–17. Extraordinary ambassador to Moscow 1917–18. Member of the Peace Conference, 1918–19. Director of the ILO, 1920–32.

The Archives Nationales, Paris, has a very large collection of material (484 boxes), relating to all aspects of Albert Thomas's career (Ref. 94 AP 1–484). The collection includes correspondence addressed to him as President of the *Bureau international du Travail* (94 AP 378–394), material on the colonial question and international economic relations (94 AP 338–343) and the papers of Paul Rémy (q.v.), founder of the Union of Blind Workers (94 AP 396–399). Other papers are reported in the ILO archive.

THOMAS, Theodor (1876–1955)

German trade unionist. Member of the SPD from 1898. Leader of building workers' unions from 1919. From 1946 Editor of one of the first trade union papers – *Stimme der Arbeit*. Until 1953 Executive member of the IG Bau-Steine-Erde and Editor of *Grundestein*.

Theodor Thomas's papers from 1895 are in the AdsD, Bonn. These include diary material, other notes, newspaper articles and minutes concerning his trade union activity. (See Mommsen, *op. cit*.)

THOMASSON, Väinö Alfred

See under TANNER, Väinö Alfred.

THORBERG, Avid (1887–1930)

Swedish trade union leader and social democratic politician. From 1920 to 1930, Chairman of LO. Active in the international trade union movement. Member of Stockholm City Council. Member of Parliament.

Four boxes of Thorberg's papers, with an inventory, are in the ARAB, Stockholm.

THORÉ, Théophile (1807–69)

French socialist journalist. Founded the independent socialist daily *La Vraie République* (suppressed after the events of June 1849). Proponent of the organisation of labour. Elected Deputy for the Seine September 1848. Exile after June 1849.

Thoré's papers are in the Bibliothèque de l'Arsenal, Paris. In addition a number of letters received by Thoré are in the Bibliothèque Nationale, Paris.

THOREZ, Maurice (1900–64)

French communist leader. Joined SFIO (1919) and PCF (1920). Elected to the Central Committee, then Politburo, and eventually General Secretaryship of the PCF, 1930–64. Member ECCI 1928–43. Deputy for the Seine 1932–40.

Thorez's papers have been deposited in the Institut Maurice Thorez, Paris. No further details are available. One folder of material (the gift of Guy Jerram in 1967, and Branko Lazitch in 1972) is in the Hoover Institution, Stanford University, California. It consists of letters (and photocopies) to Guy Jerram and Roger Garaudy *re* French communism.

THORSSON, F. W. (1865–1925)

Swedish social democratic politician. First working-class Cabinet Minister. Shoemaker. Second only to Hjalmar Branting (q.v.) in his importance in the early SAP. Briefly succeeded Branting as Chairman. Member of Parliament. From 1917, Minister of Finance in the Liberal/SAP coalition government. After 1920, Minister of Trade.

One box of F. W. Thorsson's papers, with an inventory, is in the ARAB, Stockholm.

THORSSON, Inga (b. 1915)

Swedish social democrat. One of the most prominent social democratic women. Chairwoman of the Social Democratic Women's Organisation. Member of Parliament. Especially well known for her work on peace and disarmament.

Some 41 boxes of Inga Thorsson's papers are in the ARAB, Stockholm. Special permission must be obtained before consulting this collection.

THUNBORG, Folke (1909–57)

Swedish trade union official and social democrat. Secretary of the Young Socialists (SSU) in the 1930s. Official in the Shop Workers' Union.

One box of Thunborg's papers is in the ARAB, Stockholm. In particular, this includes material concerning his visit to the USA in 1939. An inventory is available.

TILANUS, Liede (1871–1953)

Dutch SDAP member.

The IISH, Amsterdam, has a collection of Tilanus's notes, cuttings, manuscripts and correspondence covering the period 1915–43. (See M. Campfens, *op. cit.*)

TISSOT, Pierre François (1768–1854)

French liberal republican. Sympathiser with views of Babeuf. Publicist. Historian of the French Revolution.

Tissot's papers are in the Bibliothèque Cantonale, Corsica, and the University of Lausanne. A list is available.

TJADEN VAN DER VLIES, Anke (1873–1939)

Dutch SDAP member and Christian Socialist.

The IISH, Amsterdam has a collection of Tjaden's correspondence and a manuscript. The collection is for the period 1909–22. (See M. Campfens, *op. cit.*)

TOL, Dirk Jan van (b. 1916)

Dutch anarchist.

The IISH, Amsterdam, has a little of Tol's correspondence and documents on congresses, covering the years 1949–55. Access is restricted. (See M. Campfens, *op. cit.*)

TOLLER, Ernst (1893–1939)

German communist politician and writer. Member of the Munich Council Government 1919. From 1933 exile in the USA.

Part of Toller's papers were lost during the Second World War. Those that survive are divided between three collections. The first is in the Archive of Yale University Library, New Haven, Connecticut. This is almost exclusively made up of manuscripts and single copies of plays, film scripts and other prose writing. There are, however, a few letters both from and to Toller as well as material on Spanish Aid. A second collection containing literary manuscripts and letters from Max Hoelz is in the Bundesarchiv, Koblenz. The third, containing correspondence and newspaper cuttings retrieved from a police file, is in the Leo Baeck Institute, New York. (See Mommsen, *op. cit.*)

TOPALOVIČ, Živko (1886–1972)

Yugoslav socialist militant. Exiled in France.

Topalovič's correspondence for the years 1945–71, together with reports to the Socialist International and collections of periodicals, are in the OURS, Paris. The IISH, Amsterdam, has a small collection of his correspondence, and files, for the period 1944–55.

TÖPFER, Karl (b. 1888)

German social democrat in Danzig. Writer. Member of the social democratic group in the Volkstag of Danzig (from 1935).

Töpfer's papers for the years 1924–60 are in the AdsD at the Friedrich-Ebert-Stiftung, Bonn. These comprise material on the SPD in Danzig (short biographies of members), together with reports on the activity of the League of Nations in Danzig, and material on the prosecution of Gauleiter Albert Forster. (See Mommsen, *op. cit.*)

TOPINARD, Camille (b. 1835)

French Communard.

See Appendix I.

TORGLER, Ernst (1893–1963)

German communist. Chairman of the Workers' and Soldiers' Council in Neuruppin. Official in the ADGB. Member of the Reichstag. One of the accused in the Reichstag fire trial.

Torgler's papers were reported in private hands. (See Mommsen, *op. cit.*)

TOURNACHON, Félix*

* Pseudonym of NADAR.

TOUZERY (fl. 1926–40)

French Christian trade unionist.

Touzery's papers are in the Departmental Archives of Aveyron. These concern, in particular, the CFTC in the years 1926–40.

TRANQUILLI, Secondo (1900–78)*

Italian journalist. Communist and later socialist.

The IISH, Amsterdam, has a collection of Tranquilli's correspondence, notes, manuscripts, minutes, reports and printed material from the years 1942–4, with some papers dated up to 1954.

* Known by the pseudonym Ignazio Silone.

TREINT, Albert (1889–1971)

French communist leader.

The Hoover Institution, Stanford University, California has the photocopy of a typescript one-volume study (in French), *L'Infernal Paradis*. This relates to capitalism, social classes, international politics etc., especially in communist-dominated countries, 1900–57.

TRENI, Ugo (1898–1964)*

Italian anarchist.

Treni's papers (*c.*300 files) are in the IISH, Amsterdam. The collection includes correspondence and files of documentary material on anarchist movements, especially in Italy and Latin America. There is also material on Makhno's (q.v.) Insurgent Army of the Ukraine. A list of the extensive collection is available.

* Known by the pseudonym Ugo Fedeli.

TRESSO, Pietro (1893–1943)

Italian socialist.

The IISH, Amsterdam, has a small collection, mainly photocopies, of Tresso's correspondence and printed material. The collection covers the period 1922–44.

TREVES, Paolo (1908–58)

Italian socialist. Secretary of Filippo Turati (q.v.). Member of the PSDI. Under Secretary of State for Foreign Trade.

The IISH, Amsterdam, has a small collection of Treves's correspondence and manuscripts, largely from 1944–5.

TRIER, Gerson (1851–1916)

Pioneer Danish socialist. At first teacher. Marxist opponent of reformism within Danish social democracy. Translator of Friedrich Engels (q.v.).

A small collection of Trier's papers, including correspondence with Friedrich Engels (q.v.) is in the Rigsarkivet, Copenhagen.

TRISTAN, Flora (1803–44)

French socialist and feminist. Advocate of female emancipation, abolition of slavery and the international organisation of the working class.

A small amount of material (n.d.) is in the IISH, Amsterdam.

TROEGER, Heinrich (1901–75)

German social democratic politician. Finance Minister of Hesse 1951–6. Member of the Bundesrat. President of the Central Land Bank of Hesse and Vice-President of the Deutsche Bundesbank in Frankfurt.

There are two main collections of Troeger's papers. The first, comprising papers from the years 1910–75, is in the AdsD, Bonn. These include personal documents and family correspondence, together with diary notes, correspondence and other material concerning his political activity. With the exception of pages from his diary in the Staatsbibliothek der Stiftung Preuss, Kulturbestiz, Berlin, the second collection is in the Hauptstaatsarchiv, Wiesbaden. These papers comprise material concerning financial policy (especially fiscal reform), the Land Council and the economic policy committee of the SPD Executive. (See Mommsen, *op. cit.*)

TROELSTRA, Dirk (1870–1902)

Dutch SDAP member and propagandist.

The IISH, Amsterdam, has a small collection of Troelstra's personal papers and correspondence after 1888. A list is available. (See M. Campfens, *op. cit.*)

TROELSTRA, Pieter Jelles (1860–1930)

Founder member and Chairman of the Dutch SDAP.

The IISH, Amsterdam, has a large collection of manuscripts, notes and correspondence. An inventory is available. (See M. Campfens, *op. cit.*)

TROLLE, Børge (b. 1917)

Danish Trotskyist. Later a writer for the paper of the Peoples' Socialist Party.

One box of Trolle's papers for the years 1937–66 is in the ABA, Copenhagen. Especially rich in papers and letters concerning the Fourth International in the years 1940–52, this collection also contains manuscripts, material on revolutionary communists, left-wing socialists and the Left Socialist Youth (VSU), as well as correspondence with German revolutionary socialists (including Georg Jungclas).

TROTSKY, Leon (1879–1940)*

Russian revolutionary and foremost Bolshevik opponent of Stalin's regime. Co-founder and organiser of the Southern Russian Workers' Union 1897. Arrested and exiled to Siberia 1898. Exile in London 1902–5. Attended second RSDLP congress 1903, where he opposed Bolshevik faction, but remained independent of Mensheviks. Chairman of St. Petersburg Soviet of Workers' Deputies; arrested and exiled to Siberia 1905. Exile in Vienna 1908–12. Attended Zimmerwald Conference 1915. Return to Petrograd 1917, after February Revolution. Chairman of Petrograd Soviet and its Military Revolutionary Committee. Commissar of Foreign Affairs in first Soviet government. Commissar for Military Affairs 1918 (Military and Naval Affairs 1922). Chairman of Revolutionary Military Council. Organiser of Red Army. Organiser of Commissariat of Means of Communication 1920–21. Leader of the Left Opposition. Dismissed from Commissariat 1925. Expelled from Politburo 1926. Expelled from Central Committee and ECCI, 1927. Expelled from Communist Party 1927. Internal exile 1928. Exiled from USSR 1929. Organiser of the International Left Opposition. Founder of Fourth International 1938. Assassinated by a GPU agent in August 1940.

Trotsky is the only prominent Bolshevik to have left extensive and uncensored private papers. The most important collection is in the Houghton Library at Harvard University, and covers the period from January 1918 to August 1940. The archive is divided into four sections. Section A comprises mainly correspondence with other Soviet leaders; Section B contains, in 25 dossiers, Trotsky's manuscripts and correspondence up to 1929; Section C, also in 25 dossiers, contains letters and memoranda (most of this correspondence is from Trotsky's internal exile at Alma Ata, and contains documentary material on the work of the Trotskyist opposition in the Soviet Union); Section D contains correspondence with groups and members of the Fourth International.

A part of the Harvard collection is made up of carbon copies of c.800 letters from the years 1917–22. Most of the correspondence is with Lenin. There are a further 58 photocopies of handwritten documents. This collection has been published as *The Trotsky Papers, 1917–1922*, Jan M. Meijer (ed.) (The Hague: 2 vols 1964, 1971). The ABA, Copenhagen, has a collection on Trotsky and Trotskyism, mainly in Denmark, which contains copies, mainly from the Harvard collection, of letters to and from Trotsky.

* Pseudonym of BRONSTEIN, Lev Davidovič.

TROUSEVILLE, Eugène (b. 1834)

French Communard.

See Appendix I.

TSEDERBAUM, Yulii Osipovič (fl. 1900s-20s)

Russian Menshevik leader. One of the founders of the RSDLP. By 1900 working closely with Lenin as a contributing editor of *Iskra* and in the struggle against 'economism'. One of the most prominent Menshevik leaders 1903. Mainly in Paris 1905–14. Polemicised with Lenin on a wide range of issues. During the First World War, and the Revolution, leader of the Menshevik left. Opposed alliance with the Constitutional Democrats. Gained control of the Menshevik Party after the October Revolution. Critical of Bolshevik rule but opposed all actions aimed at overthrowing the Soviet Government. Went into exile 1920. Executive member of the International Union of the Socialist Parties (the 'Two-and-half' International). Helped found the Russian language *Sotsialisticheskii vestnik* (*Socialist Herald*).

A collection of Tsederbaum's papers is to be found among the Nicolaevsky (q.v.) collection in the Hoover Institution, Stanford University, California. In addition, the Hoover Institution also has a typescript (in Russian) of Tsederbaum's *Defence of the Revolution and Social Democracy: Collected Articles*, concerning the Russian Revolution and Civil War.

* Known by the pseudonym L. Martov.

TSERETELLI, Irakly Georgiyevič (1882–1959)

Georgian Menshevik leader and member of the Russian Provisional Government. Russian Menshevik leader from Georgia. Deputy to the Second Duma. Centrist position during the First World War. After the February Revolution 1917 entered the Provisional Government as Minister of Post and Telegraphs. Minister of the Interior following the July events. After the October Revolution leader of the anti-Bolshevik bloc in the Constituent Assembly. One of the leaders of the Menshevik Government in Georgia. After the establishment of Soviet power in Georgia went into exile (1921).

A collection of Tseretelli's papers is to be found among the Nicolaevsky collection (q.v.) in the Hoover Institution, Stanford University, California.

TURATI, Filippo (1857–1932)

Italian socialist. Founder of the Socialist Unitary Party, 1922.

An important collection of papers is deposited in the Feltrinelli Institute, Milan. The collection covers the period 1881–1926, but most of the material dates from two periods: 1881–1900 and 1917–26. Apart from a long correspondence with Kuliscioff, the collection includes correspondence not only with socialists but with representatives of the entire Italian political spectrum, including Leonida Bissolati, Ivanoe Bonomi, Andrea Costa (q.v.), Arturo Labriola, Constantine Lazzari, Achille Loria, Giacomo Matteotti, Giuseppe Emanuele Modigliani (q.v.), Benito Mussolini (q.v.) Pietro Nenni, Giacinto M. Serrati, Paulo Treves (q.v.), Giovanni Zibordi, etc.

There is also correspondence between Turati and foreign socialists such as Friedrich Adler (q.v.), Angelica Balabanoff (q.v.), August Bebel (q.v.), Jean Baptiste Godin, Jules Guesde (q.v.), Arthur Henderson, Karl Kautsky (q.v.), Vera Zasulič, etc. The collection also includes literary material, poetry, and printed material.

TURREL, Jean (b. 1827)

French Communard. Member of the National Guard under the Paris Commune. Deported 1872–9.

See Appendix I.

UHLEN, Axel (b. 1885)

Swedish social democrat. Writer about working-class song and poetry. Editor of social democrat and trade union papers. Member of Parliament.

Some 19 boxes of Uhlen's papers are in the ARAB, Stockholm. A large part of this collection, however, is made up of newspaper cuttings.

ULRICH, Fritz (1888–1969)

German social democratic politician. After 1945 Minister of the Interior and member of the Landtag in Baden-Württemburg. Member of the Bundesrat.

A photocopy of Ulrich's papers for the post–1945 period is in the Hauptstaatsarchiv, Stuttgart. (See Mommsen, *op. cit.*)

ULRICH, Karl (1853–1933)

German social democratic politician. Member of the Reichstag from 1907 and of the National Assembly from 1919. State President and Prime Minister of Hesse 1919–28.

Ulrich's memoirs and a small quantity of correspondence, together with reference files and cuttings, are in the Staatsarchiv, Darmstadt. (See Mommsen, *op. cit.*)

URBAIN, Raoul (1837–1902)

French. Elected member of the Paris Commune. Member in turn of the Education, External Relations and War Commission. Deported 1871–9. Active as a member of the Central Committee of the Co-operative Union 1889–1901.

The unpublished diary of Urbain passed into the possession of Lucien Descaves (q.v.), and may well be among the papers of the latter deposited in the IISH, Amsterdam.

URSIN, Nils Robert af (1854–1936)

Finnish social democratic pioneer and leader. Baron. Founder of the Workers' Association of Viipuri 1886. Chairman of the Workers' Association of Turku 1891–1900. First Chairman of the Finnish Labour Party (Social Democratic Party from 1903) 1899–1900. Editor-in-Chief of *Länsi-Suomen Tÿomies* 1900. Member of the City Council of Turku. Member of the nobles of the Finnish Diet 1881–1900 and 1905–6. Member and Vice-President of Parliament 1907–8. Exiled in Soviet Russia from 1918 to 1920, and, from 1920 to 1922 in Sweden. Leading figure in workers' education. Author of many books for the working class.

A small collection of Ursin's papers from the 1870s to the 1930s is in the Finnish Labour Archives, Helsinki. These comprise correspondence (1879–1936) and postcards (about 1880 to about 1920), a diary (1903), manuscripts, printed material (including press cuttings), and photographs.

VAGNER, Ekaterina Nikolaevna (fl. 1870s–1930s)

Russian social revolutionary.

Vagner's papers covering the period 1876–1936 are in the Hoover Institution, Stanford University, California. These comprise correspondence (including letters from Ekaterina Breshko-Breshkovskaîa (q.v.), diaries, writings (including the 'Reminiscences of N. N. Dzvonkevič, her father, and a study of the Strelnikovskii trial in Odessa) and printed matter relating to revolutionary movements and events in Russia. A preliminary inventory is available.

VAILLANT, Edouard (1840–1915)

Pioneer French socialist. Supporter of Blanqui. Member of the International. Member of the Executive Commission and prominent leader of the Paris Commune. Exile in London. Influenced by, and briefly co-operated with, Marx. Returned to agitate in Cher in 1880. Helped move the CRC from traditional Blanquism towards Marxism. Acknowledged leader of the PSR in 1898. Prominent leader of the USR/PSF. Member of the CAP of the SFIO. Supported the union sacrée in 1914. Deputy for Paris 1893–1915.

Vaillant's papers were destroyed during the Second World War. A large number of letters written by Vaillant, however, survive amongst the papers of other socialist leaders of his time. (See Maitron, *op. cit.*)

VAILLANT-COUTURIER, Paul (1892–1937)

French communist leader. Writer. At first lawyer. Joined SFIO in 1916. Wounded and decorated for bravery at the front. Helped found the Association Républicaine des Anciens Combattants. Arrested for his political activity. From 1919–28 and 1936–7 Deputy for the Seine. Mayor of Villejuif 1929. Member of the PCF after the Tours Congress (1920). Three times imprisoned for anti-militarist activities. Editor-in-Chief of *L'Humanité*. Co-founder of the Association des écrivains et artistes révolutionnaires.

Vaillant-Couturier's papers are in the Institut Maurice Thorez, Paris.

VALLOTTON, Félix (1865–1925)

Swiss-born artist and anarchist (naturalised French in 1900). Collaborated on *Les Temps Nouveaux*. Close to Jean Grave (q.v.). Later broke with anarchism.

See under GRAVE, Jean.

VALPAS, Edvard (1873–1937)*

Finnish social democratic leader. Editor 1899 and Editor-in-Chief 1901–18 of *Työmies*. Chairman of the Executive of the Finnish Social Democratic Party 1905–9. Member of Parliament 1907–17. Did not take part in the Civil War, but forced to escape to Soviet Russia. Returned in 1919. Imprisoned 1919–24. Education Secretary in the Finnish Labour Organisation (SAJ) 1924–30.

A large collection of Valpas's papers is in the Finnish Labour Archives, Helsinki. This contains some of his literary output, descriptions from his journeys to the USA and polemical writings, material concerning *Työmies*, manuscripts (including a survey on the history of Russia before 1905 and a four-part work on 'Class Justice in Finland'), material on the situation of Finnish industry, reports of the situation of the Party to the International Socialist Bureau (ISB) (1903-7) and material of the ISB 1905–9, reports to Party conferences and other organisations, material concerning his parliamentary work, material on the Russian Revolution (1917), letters from prison, material concerning the trade union movement in the 1920s, and international correspondence.

* Known also as Valpas-Hänninen.

VANCAUWENBERGHE, André (fl. 1950s)

Belgian socialist politician. Journalist. Secretary of the Charleroi Federation of the Belgian Socialist Party. From 1961 Senator.

Vancauwenberghe's correspondence for the years 1950–59 is in the archive of the Charleroi Federation of the Belgian Socialist Party.

VANDERVELDE, Emile (1866–1938)

Belgian socialist leader. Prominent figure in European socialism. Lawyer. Joined the Belgian Workers Party in 1889. Influenced by Hector Denis (q.v.). Member of Parliament 1894. Prominent in the suffrage movement. From 1900 played a leading role in the congresses of the Second International. Minister throughout the 1914–18 War. Secured the inclusion of clauses favouring labour 1919–20 (including one advocating the 8-hour day) at the Paris Peace Conference. Minister of Justice 1919. Minister of Foreign Affairs in the Socialist–Catholic coalition government 1925 (pursued an anti-militarist line). Helped negotiate the Locarno Pact. President of the Second International 1929–36. Minister without portfolio 1935–6 and Minister of Public Health 1936–7.

The extensive papers of Emile Vandervelde – together with those of Lala Vandervelde and Jeanne Emile Vandervelde – are in the Institut Emile Vandervelde, Brussels. These cover his range of activities as a national and international socialist leader and statesman. Particularly noteworthy, however, is the correspondence of the Vanderveldes with numerous leading figures in the Belgian and international labour movement, other national and international political leaders, academics and writers. The Vandervelde collections have been exhaustively itemised in three published inventories, by Robert Abs: *Catalogue* II (1969); *Catalogue* III (1972); and *Catalogue* IV (1974) of the Institut Emile Vandervelde.

VANDERVELDE, Jeanne Emile*

See Emile Vandervelde.

* Born Jeanne Beeckman.

VANDERVELDE, Lala*

See Emile Vandervelde.

* Also known as Hélène Speyer.

VÄSTBERG, Disa (1891–1966)

Swedish social democratic politician. Writer. Leading member and Chairwoman of the Social Democratic Women's Organisation. Member of Parliament (after 1935). Wife of Mauritz Västberg (q.v.).

Among Disa Västberg's material in the ARAB, Stockholm, are the books and periodicals belonging to herself and her husband.

VÄSTBERG, Mauritz (1886–1982)

Swedish social democratic politician. Editor of various social democratic papers. Member of Parliament. Husband of Disa Västberg (q.v.).

Two boxes of Mauritz Västberg's papers, with a provisional inventory, are in the ARAB, Stockholm.

VEENSTRA, Tinus (b. 1896)

Dutch anarchist.

The IISH, Amsterdam, has a small collection of material which comprises correspondence from anarchists, anti-militarists and others, drafts of letters, memoirs, speeches, printed material, including articles by and on Veenstra, circulars, minutes and leaflets of the Vrije Socialistische Beweging (Free Socialist Movement). Access is partly restricted.

VEIT, Hermann (1897–1973)

German social democratic politician. Lawyer. Lord Mayor of Karlsruhe. 1946–9. Deputy Prime Minister of Baden-Württemburg, 1951. Member of the Bundestag, 1949 onwards.

Veit's papers are in the Generallandesarchiv, Karlsruhe. They comprise correspondence, manuscripts and copies of his articles and speeches concerning his professional and political career. (See Mommsen, *op. cit.*)

VEITER, Theodor (fl. 1932–1946)

Austrian social democrat.

The Institute of Contemporary History, Vienna, has six files of papers, covering the period 1932–46, with a few later items.

VERDET, Désirée

See under GAY, Désirée.

VERDURE, Augustin Joseph (1825–73)

French Communard and co-operator. Member of the International.

Verdure's correspondence with his daughter Maria is in the Archive of the Ministry of War, Paris. (See also Appendix I.)

VEREEKEN, Georges (1897–1978)

Belgian communist and from the 1930s one of the leaders of the Belgian Trotskyist movement.

There is a large collection of Vereeken's papers for the years 1926–78 (1947–78 copies only) in the IISH, Amsterdam. This comprises letters (including a few personal letters), internal bulletins of the Trotskyist movement, the manuscript (later published) of *Le GPU dans le Mouvement Trotzkiste*, leaflets and other printed material. The collection is open and an inventory covering the years 1930–47 is available.

VERMERSCH, Eugène (1845–78)

French revolutionary journalist. Co-founder of *Père Duchêne* of 1871. Exile in London.

There are Vermersch papers among the Descaves (q.v.) collection in the IISH, Amsterdam.

VERMOREL, Auguste J. M. (1841–71)

French journalist, member of the Paris Commune.

The IISH, Amsterdam has a collection of correspondence, personal documents, manuscripts, a report, files and printed material from 1867–1911.

VERWEY, Cees (1866–1943)

Dutch liberal-socialist.

The IISH, Amsterdam, has a collection of Verwey's articles, notes and lectures dating from the years 1904 to 1942. (See M. Campfens, *op.cit.*)

VÉSINIER, Pierre (1824–1902)

French revolutionary journalist. One of the founders of the French section of the International in London, 1865. Elected member of the Paris Commune April 1871. Exile in London from 1871.

Vésinier's papers from *c*.1849 to *c*.1892 were acquired as part of the Nettlau (q.v.) collection by the IISH, Amsterdam. These comprise correspondence and unpublished manuscripts (including one on the history of the International), as well as printed material.

VIDALENC, Georges (fl. 1950s)

French trade unionist.

Vidalenc's papers are in the IFHS, Paris. They concern, in particular, the International Labour Organisation and workers' education in the post-war period.

VILIM, Blazej (1909–76)

Czech socialist, trade unionist and journalist. Secretary (1931), Czech Metal Workers Union. Instrumental in defeating the communist wing at the 1947 Brno Conference of the Social Democratic Party. Fled Czechoslovakia in 1948.

Part of Vilim's papers have been deposited in the British Library, the remainder in Churchill College, Cambridge. The collection in Churchill College comprises correspondence, personal papers of Blazej and Mirka Vilim, writings by Lausman and Panek, (with Vilim, prominent members of the exiled Czech Social Democratic Party) and various writings by Vilim himself. Certain of the files are closed until 1997.
 As a supplement to this Vilim collection, Churchill College also holds a small collection of the papers of Jan Svoboda (q.v.) who was his personal secretary for some years. The Svoboda papers, also in Czech, consist mainly of writings on politics and articles from the magazine *Perspektivy Socialismu*, founded by Vilim in 1971.

VINAVER, Maksim Moiseevič (fl. 1919–26)

Russian liberal. Kadet party leader.

His papers are at the Bakhmeteff Archive and include copies of his correspondence with I. Petrunkevič, another leading Kadet, 1919–26. The letters discuss the civil war, party politics, and foreign policy. The collection also contains a typed stenographic report of his speech to the first duma; a typed copy of reminiscences of the October manifesto and the first KD party congress, and an undated political article written in Paris.

VINDEX

See under ROBIN, Paul.

VIOLLETTE, Maurice (1870–1960)

French radical-socialist politician. Lawyer. Joined the FTSF while a student. From 1892 assisted Millerand in legal defence work. Municipal Councillor in Janville 1896 and in Tours 1898–1902. Mayor of Dreux 1908–59. Deputy for Eure-et-Loire 1902–19, 1924–30 and 1946–55. Joined the radical-socialist group. Minister for Revictualling and Maritime Transport March–July 1917. Governor-General of Algeria 1925–8. Senator for Eure-et-Loire 1930–39. Minister of State under Blum June 1936–June 1937, under Chautemps June 1937–January 1938, and under Blum, March–April 1938. Member of the two National Constituent Assemblies.

There are two holdings of Viollette's papers. In 1931 Viollette deposited 50 files of his papers in the Department Archives of Eure-et-Loire. Apart from the letters he received, these comprise documents which largely relate to French interests overseas in the years 1906–31.

A second holding is maintained at the Maison de Maurice Viollette, Dreux, Eure-et-Loire. This comprises personal papers, papers concerning his political career (in particular, from his time as Governor-General of Algeria), and the manuscript of his *Mémoires*. Access is restricted: requests should be directed to M.le Conservateur du musée d'art et d'histoire et des archives municipales de la ville de Dreux, Président de la Société des amis de Maurice Viollette.

VISHNIAK, Mark Veniiaminovič (1883–1976)

Leader of the Russian Socialist Revolutionary Party. Lawyer and historian.

Vishniak's papers (in Russian and English) from *c*.1910–68 are in the Hoover Institution, Stanford University, California. These include correspondence, writings and cuttings relating to Russian and Soviet history, Russian revolutionaries, Russian émigrés, and political conditions in the Soviet Union. A preliminary inventory is available.

VLEGGEERT, J. C. (1899–1970)

Dutch trade unionist.

The IISH, Amsterdam has a small collection of Vleggeert's manuscripts and documents. (See M. Campfens, *op.cit.*)

VLIEGEN, Willem H. (1862–1947)

Founder member of the Dutch SDAP.

The IISH, Amsterdam, has a few of Vliegen's manuscripts and other correspondence, 1886–1931. (See M. Campfens, *op.cit.*)

VOGEL, Hans (1881–1945)

German social democratic politician. Member of the Bavarian Landtag 1909–18, of the National Assembly 1919 and of the Reichstag 1920. Member of the SPD Executive 1927 and Co-chairman of the SPD 1931. Exile in Prague 1933. Co-director of the overseas centre of SOPADE.

Vogel's papers are in the AdsD at the Friedrich-Ebert-Stiftung, Bonn. These comprise letters and speeches by Vogel. In addition, there is material relating to discussions between representatives of the SPD Executive and the KPD Central Committee in Prague in 1934. (See Mommsen, *op. cit.*)

VOGT, Franz (1899–1940)

German social democrat and trade union leader.

The IISH, Amsterdam has a collection of correspondence, personal documents, and a manuscript. The collection dates largely from 1933–38, with some material from 1920–33.

VOGT, Heinrich (fl. 1930s)

German Christian trade unionist.

Vogt's papers for the years 1926–32 are in the DGB Archive, Düsseldorf. (See Mommsen, *op. cit.*)

VOIGT, Karsten (b. 1941)

German social democratic politician. Federal Chairman of the Young Socialists 1969–72. Vice-President of the International Union of Socialist Youth 1971–3. From 1976 member of the Bundestag.

Voigt's papers for the years 1966–77 are in the AdsD, Bonn. These comprise notes and collections of material concerning the Young Socialist Executive, the Young Socialists in Hesse and Frankfurt, and the SPD in Frankfurt.

VOIGT, Richard (1895–1970)

German social democratic politician in Braunschweig and Helmstedt (Lower Saxony). Member of the Lower Saxon Landtag 1951–63. Minister of Culture in Lower Saxony 1948–56 and 1959–63.

There are two collections of Voigt's papers from the post-war period. The first is in the AdsD at the Friedrich-Ebert-Stiftung, Bonn, and comprises manuscripts of speeches from his period as a Minister, as well as documents concerning the 'school struggle' after 1952. The second contains material relating to educational legislation in Lower Saxony and the Concordat between Lower Saxony and the Catholic Church, and is in the Hauptstaatsarchiv, Hannover. (See Mommsen, *op. cit.*)

VOIONMAA, Väinö (1869–1947)

Finnish social democratic politician. Academic. Member of Parliament 1919–47. Minister of Communications 1917. Foreign Minister 1926–7. Minister of Commerce and Industry 1937–9. Acting Foreign Minister 1938. Member of the Finnish delegation to general assemblies of the League of Nations. Member of the Tartto peace treaty delegation 1920. Member of the Moscow peace treaty delegation 1940 and 1944. Active in the temperance movement.

There are two collections of Voionmaa's papers. The first is a large collection from c.1910–c.1950 in the Finnish Labour Archives, Helsinki. This comprises correspondence (both personal and political), manuscripts, printed material (including some from the international temperance movement), and a few photographs. Perhaps the main content of this collection is concerned with his own academic work. A second collection, however, is to be found in the State Archive, Helsinki. This includes, in particular, much of his political and official correspondence, as well as material on foreign policy (including peace negotiations with the USSR), and material concerning the war-time social democratic parliamentary group.

VOJTINSKIJ, Vladimir Savel'evič (1885–1964)

Russian. Bolshevik at the time of the 1905 Revolution. In 1914 took a patriotic position on the war while still calling himself a Bolshevik. Took part in the All-Russian Conference of Bolsheviks in March 1917 and propounded an explicitly patriotic position. Shortly after joined the Mensheviks. Close to Kerensky (q.v.). Participated in military opposition to the Bolsheviks.

There is a collection of Vojtinskij's papers in the IISH, Amsterdam. The collection (1919–60) has been listed.

VOLKHOVSKY, Felix Vladimovič (1846–1914)

Russian Socialist Revolutionary Party Leader. Journalist. Editor of *Free Russia* (London).

There is a collection of Volkhovsky's papers for the years 1875–1914 in the Hoover Institution, Stanford University, California. This comprises correspondence, writings, journals, cuttings, and photographs, relating to revolutionary movements in Imperial Russia. A preliminary inventory is available.

VOLLMAR, Georg von (1850–1922)

German social democratic politician. Writer and journalist. Member of the Reichstag. Early proponent of reformism.

Von Vollmar's papers are in the IISH, Amsterdam. These comprise his extensive correspondence and manuscripts, and are particularly relevant to the history of Revisionism. (See Mommsen, *op. cit.*)

VOL'SKII, Nikolai Vladislavovič (1879–1964)

Russian revolutionary and author.

There is a collection of Vol'skii's papers (in Russian and English) for the years 1908–64 in the Hoover Institution, Stanford University, California. This comprises correspondence, writings, cuttings, reports and photographs, relating to Russian revolutionary movements and émigré life, Imperial Russia, Soviet agricultural and economic policies, labour movements, Menshevism, and political events in Russia. A preliminary inventory is available.

VOS, Hein (1903–72)

Dutch SDAP member and Minister for Commerce and Industry 1945–6. Minister for Transport and Waterways 1946–8.

The IISH, Amsterdam, has a small collection of Vos's documents relating to the 'Plan van de Arbeid' and post-war matters. (See M. Campfens, *op. cit.*)

VUOLIJOKI, Hella (1886–1954)

Finnish leftist intellectual and politician (originally from Estonia). Author. Member of Parliament. General Manager of the Finnish Broadcasting Company 1945–9.

Vuolijoki's papers are in the National Archives of Finland, Helsinki. Special permission from the Director is necessary to consult these papers.

WACHENHEIM, Hedwig (1891–1969)

German social democrat. Social worker. After 1933 exile in the USA. Employed as an American citizen by the US Occupation authorities in 1946.

Wachenheim's manuscripts, together with tapes of her memoirs, are in the AdsD at the Friedrich-Ebert-Stiftung, Bonn. (See Mommsen, *op. cit.*)

WACHT, Jan (1885–1967)

Dutch trade unionist and SDAP member.

The IISH, Amsterdam, has a small collection of Wacht's memoirs and correspondence. (See M. Campfens, *op. cit.*)

WAEGER, Hermann (1883–1942)

German social democratic politician. Secretary of the SPD Executive. Member of the Reichstag.

A small part of Waeger's papers concerning the murder of Karl Liebknecht and Rosa Luxemburg (q.v.) is in the Bundesarchiv, Koblenz. Other papers are reported in private hands. (See Mommsen, *op. cit.*)

WAGNSSON, Ruben (1891–1978)

Swedish social democratic politician and white-collar trade union leader. Teacher. From 1911 member, and 1932–6 Executive member, of the SAP. Member of Parliament 1922–47. Chairman of the White-Collar Employees' Union (TCO) 1937–47. Prominent in the Swedish and International Teetotaller movement.

Five boxes of Wagnsson's papers for the years 1912–65 are in the ARAB, Stockholm. These comprise correspondence, manuscripts, transcripts and newspaper cuttings. An inventory is available.

WALD, Eduard (1905–78)

German communist and later social democrat. Member of the KPD 1924. Removed from party office as a 'conciliator' in 1930. Clandestine work in the communist resistance. From 1938 concentration camp victim. Member of the KPD Land Executive for Lower Saxony 1950. Editor of the Lower Saxony *Volksstimme*. DGB press official. Went over to the SPD.

Wald's papers for the years 1937–77 are in the AdsD, Bonn. These include correspondence and other material concerning, in particular, the ISK and the trade union movement.

WALLE, J. G. (1871–1945)

Swedish social democrat politician. Member of Parliament.

One box of Walle's papers is in the ARAB, Stockholm.

WALLENTHEIM, Adolf (1898–1953)

Swedish social democratic politician. Leading member of the Young Socialists (SSU) 1919–34. Member of Parliament 1937.

Two boxes of Wallentheim's papers, with a provisional inventory, are in the ARAB, Stockholm.

WEBER, Max (1897–1974)

Swiss social democratic politician. Radical in his early years, but later moved to the right. Researcher for the trade union movement in the 1930s. Member of Parliament. Member of the Bundesrat.

A large collection of Weber's papers, covering both his academic and political activity, is in the Schweizerisches Sozialarchiv, Zürich. These comprise documents from his time at school and as a student, publications (newspaper articles, manuscripts of lectures, pamphlets, etc.), documents from his academic activity (seminar papers, dissertations, letters from students and doctoral candidates), documents from his parliamentary activity (reports and material concerning various parliamentary commissions), documents concerning his activity in the SPS and Trade Union Federation, and letters received (ordered alphabetically, according to sender).

WEERTH, Georg (1822–56)

German revolutionary and communist of 1848. Founder member of the Communist League. Worked on the editorial staff of the *Neue Rheinische Zeitung* (NRZ). Exile in England. Friend and comrade of Marx (q.v.) and Friedrich Engels (q.v.).

There are two collections of Weerth's papers. The first, in the IISH, Amsterdam, comprises correspondence with family and friends, together with manuscripts of his poems and essays, and documents on the history of the NRZ. The second is in the State Library of Detmold. (See Mommsen, *op. cit.*)

WEINBRENNER, Karl (1877–1946)

German Christian trade unionist.

Weinbrenner's papers are in the Stadtarchiv, Duisburg. Apart from his correspondence with Franz Wieber, these comprise transcripts of Congresses of the Workers' and Soldiers' Councils, as well as notes and collections of material on the Kapp Putsch. (See Mommsen, *op. cit.*)

WEINERT, Erich (1890–1953)

German communist. After 1933 exile in France and then the USSR. President of the Nationalkomitee Freies Deutschland. From 1945 Vice-President of the Central Directorate for Education in the DDR.

Weinert's papers from the period before 1933, together with some of his papers from the exile period, were destroyed by the Nazis or otherwise lost. Those that survive none the less constitute a large collection in the Archiv der Deutschen Akademie der Künste, Berlin. This comprises autobiographical notes (1890–1924), manuscripts, articles, speeches, poems and notes from the exile period and later, together with correspondence, diaries, printed material, photographs and papers concerning the Nationalkomitee Freies Deutschland. In addition, this collection contains letters written by Weinert to Wilhelm Pieck. (See Mommsen, *op. cit.*)

WEISKOPF, Franz Karl (1900–55)

Czech communist. Writer. Communist journalist in Prague. Foreign correspondent for *Tass*. Exile in the USA 1939. Czech diplomat 1947–52.

Weiskopf's papers are in the Archiv der Deutschen Akademie der Künste, Berlin. These comprise correspondence and manuscripts and printed material from both his literary and diplomatic activity. (See Mommsen, *op. cit.*)

WEISSER, Gerhard (b. 1898)

German social democratic politician. Mayor of Hagen and member of the Westphalian Provincial Landtag. General Secretary of the Zonal Advisory Council in the British Occupation Zone. Secretary of State in the Finance Ministry of North Rhine-Westphalia.

Weisser's papers are in the Bundesarchiv, Koblenz. These comprise minutes of meetings of the Zonal Advisory Council and its committees, together with material concerning inter-zonal matters in the years 1946–9. (See Mommsen, *op. cit.*)

WELS, Otto (1873–1939)

German social democratic politician. From 1907 Party Secretary in the SPD and then member of the SPD Executive. Member of the Reichstag 1912–33 (and of the National Assembly 1919–20). Town Mayor of Berlin during the November Revolution. From 1918 Chairman of the SPD and then of the SOPADE. Died in exile (Paris).

A small collection of Wels's personal papers and documents from his years of exile (first in Prague, and from 1938 in Paris) is in the AdsD at the Friedrich-Ebert-Stiftung, Bonn.

WERTZ, Hans (b. 1922)

German social democratic politician. Finance Minister of North-Rhine Westphalia 1966–76. Member of the North Rhine-Westphalian Landtag and of the Bundesrat 1954–76.

Wertz's speeches on financial policy, fiscal policy and social policy in the years 1967–75 are in the Hauptstaatsarchiv, Düsseldorf. (See Mommsen, *op. cit.*)

WESSEL, Helene (1898–1969)

German Zentrum (Centre Party) and then social democratic politician. Social worker. Member of the Parliamentary Council 1948–9 and of the Bundestag (Centre) 1949–53. Co-founder in 1952 of the Gesamtdeutsche Volkspartei (GVP) Member of SPD 1957. SPD Member of the Bundestag 1957–69.

Wessel's extensive papers are in the AdsD at the Friedrich-Ebert-Stiftung, Bonn. Apart from research on Catholic families before 1945, these are all from the post-war period. As well as correspondence, personal papers, speeches and manuscripts, there are political files concerning the history of the Centre Party (1945–52), the Notgemeinschaft für den Frieden Europas (1951), the GVP (1952–7), her entry into the SPD and political career up to 1969. In particular, there is a considerable quantity of material on social and economic policy, welfare, family and women's questions, and foreign policy. (See Mommsen, *op. cit.*)

WEYDEMEYER, Joseph (1818–66)

German revolutionary of 1848. Friend of Marx (q.v.) and Friedrich Engels (q.v.). Exile in the USA.

Weydemeyer's papers – comprising correspondence, manuscripts and documents – are in the IISH, Amsterdam. This collection also includes letters of Weydemeyer to members of his family.

WEYL, Gerda (1904–64)

German social democrat. Before 1933 USPD and later SPD member. Active in the peace movement. Daughter of Klara Weyl (q.v.).

A small collection of Gerda Weyl's papers for the years 1902–52 is in the AdsD, Bonn. These comprise letters, memoirs and articles of Klara Weyl, her mother, as well as her own personal documents and leaflets.

WEYL, Klara (1872–1941)*

German social democrat. Wife of the Berlin City politician Hermann Weyl. After 1918 City Councillor in Berlin.

See under Gerda Weyl.

   * Born Klara Haase.

WIARDI BEEKMAN, Herman B. (1904–45)

Dutch social democrat and newspaper editor.

The IISH, Amsterdam, has a small collection of Wiardi Beekman's lecture notes and documents covering the period 1933–40. (See M. Campfens, *op.cit.*)

WIBAUT, Florentinus M. (1859–1936)

Dutch SDAP member. Active in the Second International and the co-operative movement.

The IISH, Amsterdam, has a substantial collection of Wibaut's correspondence with individuals and organisations, including the SDAP and the Second International. The collection covers the period 1896–1935. (See M. Campfens, *op. cit.*)

WIBAUT-BERDENIS VAN BERLEKOM, Mathilde (1862–1952)

Dutch SDAP member. Active in the women's suffrage movement.

The IISH, Amsterdam, has a collection of Wibaut-Berdenis's lectures, articles, manuscripts and correspondence on various subjects, for 1895–1918.

WIECZOREK-ZEUL, Heidemarie (b. 1942)

German social democratic politician. Federal Chairman of the Young Socialists 1974–7. SPD member of the European Council.

Wieczorek-Zeul's papers for the years 1967–78 are in the AdsD, Bonn. These comprise general correspondence and other material concerning the Young Socialist Executive and Congresses (1973–6), and the SPD District Hessen-Süd.

WIEDIJK, Piet (1867–1938)

Dutch social democrat and SDAP member.

The IISH, Amsterdam, has a collection of Wiedijk's personal papers and manuscripts for the period 1882–1938. (See M. Campfens, *op. cit.*)

WIEGMINK, Ab (1896–1969)

Dutch trade unionist and member of the International Red Help.

The IISH, Amsterdam, has a small amount of Wiegmink's correspondence and memoirs, 1918–31. (See M. Campfens, *op. cit.*)

WIGFORSS, Ernst (1881–1977)

Swedish social democratic politician and leading theoretician of the SAP. Academic. Member of Parliament from 1919. Minister of Finance 1925, 1926 and from 1932.

Most of Wigforss's correspondence is in the University Library of Lund. However, there are also 21 boxes of his papers, including manuscripts and copies of the correspondence at Lund, in the ARAB, Stockholm. An inventory is available.

WIIK, Karl (1883–1946)

Finnish social democratic politician. Socialist theorist. Member of the Finnish Social Democratic Party (SDP) and of 'Kuutoset' (an opposition of six Members of Parliament and SDP leaders in the late 1930s and early 1940s). Director of the Archives of the Finnish Labour Movement.

Wiik's papers are in the National Archives of Finland, Helsinki. Special permission from the Director is necessary to consult these papers.

WIJK, Jan H. van (Hein) (1907–81)

Dutch lawyer and defender of conscientious objectors. Later active in the SDAP and independent socialist movement.

The IISH, Amsterdam, has an enormous collection of documents on Wijk's legal work and peace organisations, along with some correspondence. Access is restricted.

WILLEMSE, Hein (1902–58)

Dutch SDAP and PvdA member.

The IISH, Amsterdam, has a small collection of Willemse's manuscripts, notes and documents for the period 1925–58. (See M. Campfens, *op. cit.*)

WILLICH, August (1810–78)

German revolutionary of 1848 and communist. Professional soldier. Leader of the workers' uprising in Cologne March 1848. Military leader in the Baden uprising 1849. Member of the Executive of the Social Democratic Committee for the Assistance of German Refugees. Co-opted member of the Central Committee of the Communist League. Proponent of immediate revolutionary action. Leader of the opposition to Marx (q.v.). Unionist General in the American Civil War.

Willich's papers are in the IISH, Amsterdam. These fall into two groups. The first comprises his correspondence as Commander of the German refugees interned in Besançon. The second comprises documents (especially military) from the final phase of the Reich constitutional campaign (June–July 1849)

WIMMER, Thomas (1887–1964)

German social democratic politician. Lord Mayor of Munich and member of the Bavarian Landtag 1948–60.

Wimmer's papers are in the Stadtarchiv, Munich. These include his diary for the years 1908–63, and are particularly relevant to municipal politics and the SPD. (See Mommsen, *op. cit.*)

WINBERG, Carl (1867–1957)

Swedish trade unionist and left wing social democrat. Editor of the paper of the Railway Workers' Union. On the left of the SAP. One of the leaders of the Left-Socialist Party, but rejoined the SAP. Member of Parliament.

One box of Winberg's papers, with an inventory, is in the ARAB, Stockholm.

WINKELHEIDE, Bernhard (b. 1908)

German Christian trade unionist and politician. During 1948–9 member of the Frankfurt Economic Council and of the Bundestag (CDU) 1949–72. Until 1962 Chairman of the German Christian Trade Unions.

Winkelheide's papers are in the Archiv für Christlich-Demokratische Politik of the Konrad-Adenauer-Stiftung, St Augustin bei Bonn. These include material on the CDU and workers' questions. (See Mommsen, *op. cit.*)

WINNIG, August (1878–1956)

German social democratic trade unionist and politician. Chairman of the Building Workers' Union. Member of the Hamburg Bürgerschaft 1913–19. Member of the National Assembly 1919 and of the Reichstag 1919–20. German Ambassador to the Baltic States in 1918. First President of the Province of East Prussia 1919. Political writer.

Winnig's papers from the period before 1945 were destroyed during the Second World War. However, there are two collections for the years 1945–56. The first comprises mainly manuscripts and correspondence associated with his literary work, and is in the Staatsarchiv Preussischer Kulturebesitz, Berlin. The second is a small collection, comprising mainly correspondence, in the Bundesarchiv, Koblenz. (See Mommsen, *op. cit.*)

WINS, Alex (1896–1964)

Dutch diamond worker, conscientious objector, and later communist newspaper editor.

The IISH, Amsterdam, has Wins's memoirs and a little correspondence. The collection covers the period 1925–44. (See M. Campfens, *op. cit.*)

WINTER, Friedrich (b. 1896)

German social democratic politician. Mayor of Silixen bei Rinteln (North Rhine-Westphalia) 1925–33. Member of the Lippe Landtag 1928–33. Member of the North Rhine-Westphalian Landtag 1945–56.

Winter's papers for the years 1949–72 are in the Staatsarchiv, Detmold. These include minutes of meetings of the Lemgo Kreistag and its committees, as well as minutes of the assemblies of the Landesverband Lippe. (See Mommsen, *op. cit.*)

WINTER, Max (1870–1937)

Austrian social democrat.

His papers are at the Vienna Chamber of Labour.

WINTSCH, Jean (1880–1943)

French anarchist.

The IISH, Amsterdam, has a very small collection of Wintsch's correspondence for 1903–14.

WISSEL, Rudolf (1869–1962)

German social democratic politician. Secretary of the ADGB 1909–18. Member of the Council of Peoples' Commissars 1918. Reich Economics Minister and member of the ADGB executive 1919. Arbitrator for wage-rate conflicts, Berlin, 1924–30. Reichstag member 1920–33.

The Bundesarchiv, Koblenz, has a collection of Wissel's papers covering the years 1885 to 1962. The collection includes correspondence, memoirs and material relating to political and trade union matters.(See Mommsen, *op. cit.*)

WITKOWSKI, Felix Ernst

See under HARDEN, Maximilian.

WITTENBERG, Jean (fl. 1939–45)

Belgian socialist. Active in the anti-Nazi resistance.

The Hoover Institution, Stanford University, California, has acquired papers collected by Wittenberg relating to the Belgian resistance movement (1940–45). These include pamphlets and other clandestine material.

WODAK, Walter (fl. 1940s–50s)

Austrian social democrat and diplomat.

Nineteen boxes of his papers are at the Haus-, Hof- und Staatsarchiv, Vienna. The collection includes a variety of material relating to his emigration in London and the London Bureau of Austrian Socialists, a file entitled 'Allied Commission Papers/British Element', including memoranda to the British section of the Allied Council, papers relating to Renner's control commission and the Renner administration, political papers and memoranda from his diplomatic career after the Second World War, including memoranda on British foreign policy, the Austrian state treaty of 1955, Yugoslav–Soviet relations, 1959, foreign aid, economic co-operation with Hungary, Poland, India and Indonesia, embassy reports to the Foreign Ministry, copies of telegrams concerning the negotiations over the South Tyrol in the United Nations, and material on the EEC and its relations with Austria. There is a great deal of correspondence, and Wodak's correspondents included Friedrich Adler (q.v.), Karl Renner (q.v.), Adolf Schärf (q.v.), Figl, Kreisky, Oskar Pollak (q.v.), Waldheim, Raab, Gratz, (q.v.), Klenner, Androsch, Leichter (q.v.) and Kirchschläger. The DÖW, Vienna, has a collection of papers from Wodak's emigration, including correspondence, memoranda, protocols, resolutions, etc., relating to the London Bureau.

WOLF, Friedrich (1888–1953)

German communist. Doctor and writer. Co-founder of the National Committee of Free Germany, the Deutsche Film-AG (DEFA) and the Bund Deutscher Volksbühnen. Ambassador of the DDR to Poland.

Wolf's most important manuscripts were lost in exile. However, there is a large collection of his papers for the years 1888–1953 in the Archiv der Deutschen Akademie der Künste, Berlin. These comprise correspondence (1908–53), personal papers (1888–1953), diaries (1915–53), manuscripts (including medical manuscripts) (1907–53), printed documentation

(1919–53), and collections of material arising from the whole of his activity. In addition, this collection is supplemented by material about Wolf and letters written by him. (See Mommsen, *op. cit.*)

WOLFF, Sam de (1878–1960)

Dutch economist and SDAP member.

The IISH, Amsterdam, has a collection of Wolff's correspondence for the years 1945–58. (See M. Campfens, *op. cit.*)

WOLFF, Wilhelm (1809–64)

German member of the Communist League.

The IISH, has a collection of correspondence, personal documents, minutes, and printed material from the period 1848–64.

WOLLENBERG, Erich Julian (1892–1973)

German communist leader and journalist.

A typescript photocopy of his memoirs (in German) was purchased by the Hoover Institution, Stanford University, California, from Klaus Haetzel in 1978. The memoirs relate to the Bavarian Soviet Republic of 1919, the development of the German communist movement to 1933, activities within the Communist International and the development of communism in the Soviet Union to 1933. Not more than 500 words may be quoted from the memoirs.

WOUDENBERG, Cornelis (1883–1954)

Secretary – Treasurer of the Dutch SDAP and PvdA.

The IISH, Amsterdam, has a small collection of Woudenberg's memoir albums and some letters for the years 1947–53. (See M. Campfens, *op. cit.*)

WOYTINSKY, Vladimir (1885–1960)

Russian revolutionary. From March to July 1917 member of the Executive Committee of the Petrograd Soviet. In Berlin 1922–33. Anti-Bolshevik. Director of the Research Institute of the ADGB 1929. Co-author of the 'BTW-Plan' for job creation. Emigrated to the USA.

Woytinsky's manuscripts – on the world economic crisis and job creation – as well as other fragmentary material for the years 1926–32, are in the AdsD at the Friedrich-Ebert-Stiftung, Bonn.

WRIGHT, Viktor Julius von (1856–1934)

Pioneer of the Finnish Social Christian Labour Movement. Representative of the nobility in the Finnish Diet. Founder of the Helsinki Labour Association, 1882. Editor of the workers' paper *Työmies*.

Wright's papers are in the National Archives of Finland, Helsinki. Special permission from the Director is necessary to consult these papers.

WUORI, Eeero A. (1900–66)

Finnish trade union leader. Leader of the Central Organisation of Finnish Trade Unions (SAK) 1938–45.

An important collection of Wuori's papers is in the Finnish Trade Union Archive, Helsinki.

YELENSKI, Boris V. (d. 1974)

Russian anarchist. Key figure among the anarchists of the Novorossiisk factory-committee movement. Forced into exile in the USA in the early 1920s. Dedicated himself to relief work to aid imprisoned comrades.

There is a large collection of Yelenski's papers in the IISH, Amsterdam. This includes correspondence with a great number of people and organisations (mainly anarchists, but including files with correspondence on, and with, German refugees, letters from Spanish refugees, letters from Russian prisoners, and correspondence with the Cooperative American Remittances to Europe, as well as correspondence about the books *In the Struggle for Equality* (1958), and *In the Shadow of Death, Love and Life* (1969), the manuscript of his memoirs *In the Social Tempest (memories of the Russian Revolution)*, collections of materials from anarchist societies and refugee organisations (notably the Alexander Berkman Russian Aid Fund for Political Prisoners), and a file on Maximoff's book *The Guillotine at Work* (1940). This collection is particularly rich in relation to anarchism and aid work for refugees (especially from Soviet Russia). An initial provisional inventory is available.

ZACCARIA, C. Damiani Luigi (1876–1953)

Italian anarchist.

The IISH has a very small collection of Zaccaria's correspondence and manuscripts from the years 1864 to 1932.

ZEBISCH, Franz (b. 1920)

German social democratic politician. Member of the Bundestag, 1965–80.

Zebisch's extensive papers for the years 1950–79 are in the AdsD, Bonn. These comprise all kinds of written material concerning Bundestag and constituency work in the SPD District Nieder-Bayern/Oberpfalz, and the sub-district Weiden, and Bundestag and Landtag elections, and his activity in the Bundestag.

ZEIDLER, Wolfgang (b. 1924)

German social democratic jurist. SPD member from 1945. Federal Secretary of the SDS (social democratic students) 1946. Member of the Federal Constitutional Court in Karlsruhe 1975.

Zeidler's papers for the years 1946–9 are in the AdsD, Bonn. In the main, these concern the SDS Secretariat and the SDS group in Hamburg.

ZENNSTRÖM, Pet Olov (1920–77)

Prominent Swedish communist. Writer and art critic.

Five unsorted boxes of Zennström's papers are in the ARAB, Stockholm.

ZENZINOV, Vladimir Mikhailovič (fl. 1930s–50s)

Russian revolutionary.

The Bakhmeteff Archive has about fifty-two boxes of his papers. The collection includes thirteen boxes of correspondence from the 1940s, diaries, photographs of the SR Party, typed protocols of SR central committee sessions, September 1917–January 1918, a report on finances and statistics on elections to SR Party Congresses, 1917–18, information on the Petrograd collective, a typescript about the SR Party and the Revolution, and diaries from the 1940s to 1950s.

ZETKIN, Klara (1857–1933)

German communist leader.

Some of Zetkin's letters, relating to the communist and feminist movements in Germany, are in the Hoover Institution, Stanford University, California. They include five original and ten photocopies, 1916–32, addressed to 'Fanny'.

ZÉVAÈS, Alexandre (1873–1953)*

French socialist politician. Lawyer. Publicist and writer. Secretary and collaborator of Guesde (q.v.) 1890–1903. Organiser and propagandist for the PO (especially amongst students). Co-founder and representative of the Étudiants collectivistes at the POF Congress 1893. Member of the National Council of the POF. Deputy for Isère 1898–1902 and 1905–10. Attributed his election defeat in 1902 to intransigence. Resigned from the PSdeF and set up a dissident socialist federation. Re-elected with the support of the radicals (as a republican-socialist) 1905–10. His eventual defeat by the SFIO candidate marked the effective end of his political career.

The manuscript of Zévaès's unpublished autobiography is in the possession of his son, M. Bourson. Apart from his childhood, the four chapters of this work cover his years as a student and his agitation amongst students, as well as his period as a socialist militant (describing in details meetings he attended and speeches he gave). (See Maitron, *op. cit.*)

   * Known as Bourson.

ZHERBI, A. (fl. 1906)

Russian marxist.

The Bakhmeteff Archive has typescripts in German about his activities for the SD Party in the 1905 Revolution and meetings with Miliukov in 1906 and afterwards.

ŽHITLOWSKY, Chaim (1865–1943)

Russian socialist theoretician. Publicist and philosopher.

An extensive collection of Žhitlowsky's papers is in the Yivo Institute for Jewish Research,

New York. The collection of about 12 000 letters, covering the period 1893–1943 includes correspondence from well-known Russian socialist leaders, Yiddish writers and European personalities. There are also manuscripts of his writings, a large collection of circulars and other papers. An unpublished inventory is available.

ZHOOK, Vasilij Pavlovič

See under ŽUK, Vasilij Pavlovič

ZIELENZIGER, Kurt (1890–1944)

German economic journalist.

The IISH, Amsterdam, has a collection of correspondence, manuscripts, notes, files and printed material, including press cuttings.

ZINDEREN BAKKER, Rindert von (1845–1927)

Dutch social democrat and author.

The IISH, Amsterdam, has a small scrapbook of Zinderen Bakker's articles and letters compiled by his grandson. (See M. Campfens, *op. cit.*)

ZINN, Georg August (1901–76)

German social democratic politician. Justice Minister, Hesse, 1945–9. Land SPD Chairman, Hesse, 1947. Member of the Parliamentary Council, 1948–9. Member of the Bundestag, 1949–51. Member of the Hessian Landtag, 1954–70.

Zinn's papers are in the AdsD, Bonn. They concern the organisation of the SPD in Hesse. (See Mommsen, *op. cit.*)

ZIRARDINI, Claudio (fl. 1880s)

See under Zirardini, Gaetano.

ZIRARDINI, Gaetano (fl. 1880s–1920s)

Italian socialist.

The archive of the two brothers, Claudio and Gaetano Zirardini, is in the Feltrinelli Institute, Milan. The collection covers the period from the 1880s to the advent of Fascism.

ZO D'AXA (1864–1930)*

French nihilist. Writer. Director of the journal *En Dehors* 1891. Imprisoned for incitement to mutiny 1892–4.

According to his wishes, the numerous unpublished manuscripts of Zo d'Axa were burnt after his death by his daughter (See Maitron, *op. cit.*)

ZOEBELÉ, Gustave (fl. 1870)

French Communard.

See Appendix I.

ZOESTBERGEN, Johannes W. A. (1866–1935)

Dutch trade unionist and SDAP member.

The IISH, Amsterdam, has one file of correspondence, 1890–91. (See M. Campfens, *op. cit.*)

ŽUK, Vasilij Pavlovič

Russian anarchist.

There is a small collection of Žuk's papers in the IISH, Amsterdam. This includes about 30 letters and postcards written by Kropotkin (q.v.) to Žuk in Britain as well as manuscripts by Kropotkin (notably *Modern Science and Anarchism*).

ZUTPHEN, Jan A. van (1863–1958)

Dutch diamond worker and trade unionist active in the SDAP.

The IISH, Amsterdam, has a substantial collection of Zutphen's personal papers, notes, articles and discussions, along with dossiers on various organisations. The material dates from the years 1905 to 1953. (See M. Campfens, *op. cit.*)

ZYROMSKY, Jean (1890–   )

French socialist. Full-time official of the SFIO. Advocate of a merger between the SFIO and PCF in the mid-1930s. Joined the PCF after the Second World War.

Zyromsky's papers have been donated by his family to the CRHMSS, Paris.

APPENDIX I

A Note on Archives relating to the Paris Commune

In addition to the surviving personal archives described in this volume there are individual letters from many Communards written during their imprisonment. These letters, usually to members of their families, are often very revealing of the views of the Communards.

Much of this material is to be found in the files of the Ministry of Justice in the Archives Nationales, Paris. The following list gives an indication of the material available.

Jean Duclos (three letters to his parents, 1870–75); Louis Fouet (two letters from his wife, 1875); Stanislas Helgorski (one letter to his brother, 1876); Auguste Hocquard (one letter to his wife, 1873); Paul Houpillard (one letter, 1876); François Laloge (nine letters to his wife, 1873–76); Charles Lambert (one letter to his wife, 1875); Gustave Larroque (two letters to his wife, 1872); Edmond L'Herminier (one letter to his aunt, 1875); Joseph Limasset (several letters to his parents, 1875–76); Joseph Marteau (nine letters to his mother, 1872–76); Frédéric Moll (one letter to his parents, 1875); Jean-Baptiste Monin (five letters to his wife, 1874–76); Eugène Naveau (one letter to his sister, 1878); Ernest Noël (one letter to his father, 1876); Constant Panellier (one letter to his wife, 1877, and her reply); Antoine Pellegrin (two letters to his parents, 1874, 1876); Claude Petitjean (one letter to his parents, 1876); Désiré Pierret (one letter to his mother, 1875); Étienne Portal (one letter to his parents, 1876); Ernest Potier (one letter to his wife, 1876); Louis Poulain (two letters to his sister, 1875, 1876); Edmond Préau de Vedel (one letter to his parents, 1876); Émile Roger (one letter to his wife, 1876); Pierre Roger (one letter to his wife, 1876); Jean-Baptiste Rosette (known as Rozette-Guinot, two letters to his wife 1875, 1876); Adolphe Salomon (one letter to his wife, 1876) Eugène Schneider (one letter to his father, 1875); Victor Sergent (one letter to his father, 1878); Fernand Servat (two letters, setting out his defence, 1879); Gustave Simon (one letter to his wife, 1878); Daniel Tastet (one letter, 1872); Aimé Thierry (one letter to his wife, 1876); Eugène Thierry (one letter to his parents, 1876); Camille Topinard (four letters to his father, 1872–76); Eugène Trousseville (four letters, 1876); Gustave Zoebelé (five letters to his parents, 1872–75).

In addition, some similar material of active Communards can be found in the Archives de la Préfecture de Police, Paris. Examples are: Ambroise Lyaz (two letters, 1877, 1879); Antoine Malato (one letter, 1881); Jules François Miot (reports and other documents seized from his home, May 1871); Angèle Razoua (facsimiles of two letters, July and November 1870).

APPENDIX II

A Note on the Archives of the Norwegian Labour Movement

Resources did not permit the inclusion in this volume of full details of the many important personal papers held by the Norwegian Labour Movement Archive in Oslo (Arbeiderbevegelsens Arkiv, Youngsgatan 11 C, Oslo). However, the following list gives an indication of the richness of their holdings. All historians of the Norwegian labour movement should begin their research at this Institute. It is hoped to include fuller details of the holdings listed below in later volumes of this series.

The numbers in parentheses after each name give an approximate indication of the number of boxes of material.

Kjell Aabrek (13); Arne Paasche Aasen (2); Alf Andersen (2); Aake Anker-Ording (111); Hans Berntsen (1); Ole Colbjørnsen (8); Paul Engstad (1); Ivar Ertresvåg (1); Kaare Fostervoll (1); Jacob Friis (1); Anders Frihagen (29); Peder Furubotn (40); Omar Gjesteby (2); Gerda Grepp (2); Kyrre Grepp (1); Ragna Hagen (3); Sigurd Halvorsen (1); Arvid G. Hansen (7); Frank Hansen (1); Fredrik Haslund (4); Rolf Hofmo (138); Chr. Hornsrud (2); Carl Jeppesen (1); Chr. Holtermann Knudsen (1); Arne Kokkvoll (21); Olav Kringen (7); Per Kviberg (2); Nils Langhelle (11); Haavard Langseth (4); Einar Li (1); Just Lippe (1); Harald P. Lysaker (2); Einar Lysholm (2); Anton Malmedal (1); Sven Mattson (1); Håkon Meyer (8); Ludvig Meyer (3); Finn Moe (14); Magnus Nilssen (1); Konrad Nordahl (4); Johan Nygaardsvold (1); Olav Oksvik (10); Gunnar Ousland (10); Eivind Reiersen (3); Tom Rønnow (1); Arne Skaug (41); Sverre Støstad (1); Georg Svendsen (1); Mimi Sverdrup Lunden (7); Sigrid Syvertsen (2); Thorbjørn Thorsen (1); Reinert Torgeirsson (2); Oscar Torp (3); Martin Tranmael (7); Ellisif Wessel (1); Johan P. Ødegaard (1); Ole Øisang (14).

APPENDIX III

Select Bibliographical Note

Among the many reference works used in the compilation of this volume, particular use was made of the following:

Bittner, L. *Das Gesamtinventar des Haus-, Hof- und Staatsarchiv*, 5 vols. (Vienna, 1936–40).

Andreucci, F. and Detti, D. *Il movimento operaio italiano: dizzionario biografico, 1853–1943*, 5 vols. and index (Rome, 1975).

Faure, S. *Encyclopédie Anarchiste* (Paris, 1934).

Favier, J. (ed.) *Les Archives Nationales: État Général des Fonds*, vol. 2 (1789–1940) (Paris, 1978).

Grant, S. A. and Brown, J. H. *The Russian Empire and Soviet Union: A Guide to Manuscripts and Archival Materials in the United States* (Boston, Mass., 1981).

Maitron, J. *Dictionnaire biographique du mouvement ouvrier français, 1ᵉ Partie: 1789–1864*, 3 vols., (Paris, 1964–68) *2ᵉ Partie: 1864–71*, 6 vols. (Paris, 1967–71) *3ᵉ Partie: 1871–1914*, vols. 10–15 (Paris, 1971–) *4ᵉ Partie: 1914–1939, Introduction* (vol. 16), vols 17–25 (Paris, 1982–85).

Maitron J. and Haupt G. (eds) *Dictionnaire Biographique du Mouvement International: Autriche* (Paris, 1971).

Mommsen, W. A. *Die Nachlässe in den deutschen Archiven (mit Ergänzungen aus anderen Beständen) Teil I*, (Boppard am Rhein, 1971); *Teil II* (Boppard am Rhein, 1983).

Müssener, H. *Exil in Schweden* (Munich, 1974).

Palm, C. and Reed, D. *Guide to the Hoover Institution Archives* (Stanford, Calif., 1980).

Schmutz-Pfister, A-M. *Repertorium der handschriftlichen Nachlässe in den Bibliotheken und archiven der Schweiz/Répertoire des fonds manuscrits conservées dans les bibliothèques et archives de Suisse/Repertorio sommario dei fondi manoscritti nelle bibliotheche e negli archive della Svizzera* (Berne, 1967) (*Zuwachsliste/liste complémentaire/lista complementare 1968–78* (Berne, 1980).

Spalek, J. M. *Guide to the Archival Materials of the German-Speaking Emigration to the United States after 1933* (University of Virginia, Charlottesville, 1978).

de Tourtier-Bonazzi, C. and d'Huart, S. *Archives Nationales – Archives Privées: État des fonds de la série AP*, vol. 1 (1 to 315 AP) (Paris, 1973).

de Tourtier-Bonazzi, C. and Pourcelet, F. *Guide des papiers des ministres et secrétaires d'état de 1871 à 1974* (Paris, 1978).

Wieczynski, J. L. *The Modern Encyclopaedia of Russian and Soviet History*, vols. 1–31 (to Rudzutak) (Gulf Breeze 1976–83).

Who Was Who in the USSR. Compiled by the Institute for the Study of the USSR, Munich (Metuchen, New Jersey, 1972).